EURASIAN TRANSFORMATIONS,
TENTH TO THIRTEENTH CENTURIES

Eurasian Transformations, Tenth to Thirteenth Centuries

Crystallizations, Divergences, Renaissances

Edited by

Johann P. Arnason and Björn Wittrock

BRILL

LEIDEN · BOSTON

2011

This book is printed on acid-free paper.

This paperback was originally published in hardback under ISBN 978 90 04 14310 4 as volume 10 in the series *Medieval Encounters*.

ISBN 978 90 04 20577 2

Printed and bound in Great Britain by
CPI Antony Rowe, Chippenham and Eastbourne

CONTENTS

ACKNOWLEDGEMENTS

Thanks are due to the Swedish Collegium for Advanced Study in the Social Sciences (SCASSS), Uppsala, to the Bank of Sweden Tercentenary Foundation, and the European University Institute, Firenze, for the financial and organizational support that made the Uppsala workshop on June 26-27, 2003, held in the Organerie of the Linnean Garden. The editors would also like to thank the other organizers of the workshop, Bo Stråth and Peter Wagner, for their active and essential participation but also Shmuel Eisenstadt, who continues to play a crucial role in out joint long-term research programme; Åsa Klötzing, SCASSS, for flawless handling of organizational details and the copy-editors James Kaye and Karl Smith for their help in preparing the text.

Johann P. Arnason would like to thank the Alexander von Humboldt-Stiftung for supporting a three months' stay in Germany in 2003, during which his paper was drafted; the Institut für Sozialforschung, Frankfurt, for its hospitality during this period; and Monash University, Melbourne, for a research fellowship in 2004, during which much of the editorial work was done. Björn Wittrock similarly wants to express his gratitude to the Netherlands Institute for Advanced Study in the Humanities and Social Sciences (NIAS) at Wassenaar, where he spent the spring of 2004 as Guest of the Rector and also worked on the preparation of this issue.

LIST OF CONTRIBUTORS

MIKAEL S. ADOLPHSON is Associate Professor of Japanese history in the Department of East Asian Languages and Civilizations at Harvard University. His research focuses mainly on the interplay between social structures, politics and religion in pre-1600 Japan. His most recent publication is *Gates of Power: Monks, Courtiers and Warriors in Premodern Japan* (2002).

e-mail: adolphs@fas.harvard.edu

SAID AMIR ARJOMAND (Ph.D., University of Chicago, 1980) is Distinguished Service Professor of Sociology a the State University of New York at Stony Brook, and the inaugural Crane fellow and Visiting Professor of Public Affairs at the Woodrow Wilson School of Princeton University. He was Editor of *International Sociology* from 1998 to 2003, and the Founder and President of the Association for the Study of Persianate Societies (1996-2002). His most recent book, co-edited with Edward A. Tiryakian, is *Rethinking Civilizational Analysis* (London 2004).

e-mail: said.arjomand@stonybrook.edu.au

JOHANN P. ARNASON is Emeritus Professor of Sociology, La Trobe University, Melbourne, and currently Visiting Professor at the University of Leipzig. He was until recently editor of the journal *Thesis Eleven*. Recent publications: *Civilizations in Dispute—Historical Questions and Theoretical Traditions* (Leiden 2003); *Axial Civilizations and World History* (edited, with S. N. Eisenstadt and Björn Wittrock-Leiden 2004); *Elias Canetti's Counter-Image of Society* (with David Roberts-New York 2004). His current research focuses on comparative civilizational analysis.

e-mail: J.Arnason@latrobe.edu.au

SVERRE BAGGE, born 1942, is Professor of Medieval History at the University of Bergen and Director of the centre for Medieval Studies, devoted to comparative studies of centre and periphery in medieval Europe. His books include *The Political Thought of The King's Mirror* (1987); *Society and Politics in Snorri Sturluson's Heimskringla* (1991); *From Gang Leader to the Lord's Anointed: Kingship in Sverris Saga and Hákonar Saga* (1996); *Da boken kom til Norge. Norsk idéhistorie* (2001); *Kings, Politics and the Right Order of the World in German Historiography c. 950-1150* (2002).

e-mail: sverre.bagge@cms.uib.no

MICHAL BIRAN (Ph.D. in Middle Eastern Studies, Hebrew University, Jerusalem) is Lecturer at the Institute of Asian and African Studies at the Hebrew University. She has published on Inner Asian history in the Mongol and pre-Mongol periods, including *Qaidu and the Rise of the Independent Mongol State in Central Asia* (London 1997), *Mongols, Turks and Other: Eurasian Nomads and the Sedentary World* (edited, with Reuven Amitai-Leiden 2004); *The Qara Khitai Empire in Eurasian History: Between China and Islam* (forthcoming, Cambridge 2005). Her research interests include medieval and early modern Inner Asian history; cross-cultural contacts between China and the Muslim world; the Mongol Empire and its implications for world history. She is now working on a book about Chinggis Khan in the Muslim world.

e-mail: biranm@h2.hum.huji.ac.il

GÁBOR KLANICZAY is Permanent Fellow of Collegium Budapest, Professor of Medieval Studies at the Central European University, Budapest, and at Eötvös Loránd University, Budapest. Research interests: historical anthropology of medieval and early modern European popular religion (sainthood, miracle beliefs, healing, magic, withchcraft); comparative approaches to history, situating historical observations on Hungary and central Europe in a European context. Books in English: *The Uses of Supernatural Power. Transformations of Popular religion in Medieval and Early Modern Europe* (Cambridge and Princeton 1990);*Holy Rulers and Blessed Princesses. Dynastic Cults in Medieval Central Europe* (Cambridge 2002).

e-mail: Gabor.Klaniczay@colbud.hu

THOMAS LINDKVIST, born 1949, has been Professor of Medieval History at the University of Göteborg since 1999. Research fields include the social and agrarian history of medieval Scandinavia, Christianization and the formation of an early state in Sweden. His most recent book, co-authored with Maria Sjöberg, is *Det svenska samhället 800-1520. Klerkernas och adelns tid* (Lund 2003—a synthesis of Swedish history during the period).

e-mail:thomas.lindkvist@history.gu.se

R. I. MOORE was, until his retirement in 2003, Professor of Medieval History at the University of Newcastle upon Tyne, and before that taught at the University of Sheffield. He has also held visiting appointments at the University of Chicago and the University of California at Berkeley. He is the author of *The Origins of European Dissent* (London

1975), *The Formation of a Persecuting Society: Power and Deviance in Western Europe, 950-1250* (Oxford 1987) and *The First European Revolution* (Oxford 2001), and series editor of The Blackwell History of the World.

e-mail: therimoore@aol.com

SHELDON POLLOCK, born 1948, is Geo. V. Bobrinskoy Professor of Sanskrit and Indic Studies at the University of Chicago. He recently edited *Literary Cultures in History: Reconstructions from South Asia* (Berkeley 2003), and with Homi Bhabha et al., *Cosmopolitanism* (Durham 2002). His *Language of the Gods in the World of Men: Culture and Power in Premodern India* will be published in summer, 2005, by University of California Press. Currently he directs the international collaborative research project, "Indian Knowledge Systems on the Eve of Colonialism."

e-mail:s-pollock@uchicago.edu

PAUL JAKOV SMITH is Professor of History and East Asian Studies and the John R. Coleman Professor of Social Sciences at Haverford College. He specializes on China from the tenth to the sixteenth century and the impact of Sino-steppe relation on the Chinese state and society, and most recently is the co-editor of *The Song-Yuan-Ming Transition in Chinese History* (Cambridge/MA 2003).

e-mail:psmith@haverford.edu

PAUL STEPHENSON is John W. and Jeanne M. Rowe Professor of Byzantine History at the University of Madison, Wisconsin, which is a joint appointment with Dumbarton Oaks (Trustees for Harvard University). His research interests lie in the middle Byzantine period, and his publications include *Byzantium's Balkan Frontier* (Cambridge 2000) and *The Legend of Basil the Bulgar-Slayer* (Cambridge 2003).

e-mail:pstephenson@wisc.edu

BJÖRN WITTROCK (Ph.D. 1975), formerly Lars Hierta Professor of Government at Stockholm University, is now University Professor at Uppsala University and Principal of the Swedish Collegium for Advanced Study in the Social Sciences, Uppsala. He has published extensively in the fields of intellectual history, historical social science and social theory. His publications include fourteen books, among them: *Public Spheres and Collective Identities* (with S. N. Eisenstadt and Wolfgang Schluchter, 2001); *Participation and Democracy* (with Dietrich and Marilyn Rueschemeyer, 1998); *The Rise of the Social Sciences and the Formation of Modernity: Conceptual Change in Context* (with Johan Heilbron and Lars Magnusson, 1998 and

2001); *The European and American University Since 1800* (with Sheldon Rothblatt). In 2004 he was elected Vice-President of the International Institute of Sociology (founded in 1893).

e-mail: bjorn.wittrock@scasss.uu.se

INTRODUCTION

JOHANN P. ARNASON AND BJÖRN WITTROCK

Historians of otherwise different persuasions, and with different research interests (in geographical as well as substantive terms), now seem to have reached a near-consensus that the early second millennium CE constitutes a time of particularly momentous change—or, to use the terminology of several authors in this volume, a kind of cultural crystallization with long-term consequences for subsequent institutional developments across vast regions of the Old World. A precise chronological demarcation of the period in question is obviously impossible. But for most of the Eurasian macro-region, the thirteenth century Mongol invasions constitute a plausible *terminus ad quem* (even if their long-term impact on the destinies of various civilizations is still a matter of debate). As for the starting-point, tenth-century preludes or transitions in various parts of the Old World have been noted, but the most decisive developments are commonly attributed to the eleventh or the twelfth century. Although such perspectives have proved applicable to separate civilizational complexes, comparative analysis of trends, trajectories and outcomes has not progressed very far. To some extent, this situation reflects the inevitable tendency of historians to focus their research competence on relatively delimited periods and regions. However, it also reflects the inability—so far—of historical social scientists and historians proper alike to articulate a conceptual framework that would allow for comparative reflection across various regions of Eurasia in this period of profound transformations.

A more systematic comparative effort would have to focus on three sets of issues. Comparative historical study of the civilizations involved would deal with contrasts and parallels—as well as with the related question of contacts—between their patterns of transformation. For broader purposes, it would also be useful to compare the period in question with other formative phases of world history, especially the more clearly defined or more extensively studied ones. The Axial Age, mostly understood as a period of four or five centuries around the middle of the last millennium BCE, and the transition to modernity are the two outstanding cases in point; studies of their respective problematics are very unequally developed (much more is known and much more sustained arguments have been exchanged about the latter than the former), but in both cases, an ongoing debate can draw on a significant body of work. At this stage, it seems clear that the early centuries of the second millennium CE constitute a major formative phase within some parts of Eurasia. It is another matter whether developments in these different parts add up to a coherent pattern (such as, to use a term suggested by one author, an age of ecumenical renaissances). In any case, previous theorizing by social scientists has not provided a common analytical framework, while historical scholarship has exhibited an all too natural concern with detailed descriptive analysis. To the extent, however, that such descriptive analysis provides evidence of far-reaching and deep-seated transformations across Eurasia, the need for a comparative framework becomes all the more urgent.

Finally, there is comparative work to be done on the concepts used—but often in improvised and unreflective ways—in historical analyses of the period. Terms like "civilization", "transformation", "renaissance" and "revolution", to mention only some of the most obviously meaning-laden ones, call for closer examination of the contexts in which historians have introduced them, and of the overlapping as well as divergent meanings which they have acquired in this specific field.

Most of the papers included in this collection were first presented to a workshop in Uppsala in June 2003, organized under the auspices of the Swedish Collegium for Advanced Study in the Social Sciences (SCASSS) and the European University Institute (EUI). The contributors mostly analyze developments in specific regions and link them to comparative perspectives (primarily of the first kind mentioned above, but with some reference to the other two). Some questions are also raised about interconnections in the broader Eurasian context, and the last paper in the collection deals with the first Eurasian empire.

The first section contains two papers on theoretical and comparative perspectives. Johann P. Arnason begins with a brief discussion of formative phases and long-term processes, seen as complementary key categories of historical sociology. They have a direct bearing on the present debate; if formative changes took place in the early second millennium (in regional contexts, or even on a Eurasian scale), their significance can only be understood in light of prior and subsequent developments over much longer periods of time. As in other such cases, there is some room for disagreement on the relative importance of cultural patterns and power structures. This conceptual framework is then confronted with historical research and ongoing debates on the major civilizational complexes of the Eurasian macro-region. The strongest arguments for interpreting the period in question as a formative phase, and the most structured discussions about this issue, have emerged in fields of medieval European and Chinese history. In the European case, conflicting interpretations of the High Middle Ages are still very much in evidence; historians of China have perhaps moved closer to a shared frame of reference, with clear implications for the *longue durée* of imperial history. Historiographical perspectives on other regions and civilizations seem less clear-cut; but recent work on the formation of an Indo-Islamic world has thrown new light on both components of this synthesis. The separate cases of Byzantium and Japan pose specific problems. To sum up, it can be argued that all cases under consideration suggest some reasons to single out the centuries in question, but specific features vary widely; scholarship in the various fields is unequally developed, and recent work on connections and encounters in the Eurasian context is changing the received picture. Strong claims and ambitious theories about the period as a whole seem premature.

Björn Wittrock's paper begins with a general discussion of the comparative study of historical transformations, with particular reference to cultural crystallizations of the kind that lead to higher levels of reflexivity. This was, as Wittrock argues, the most momentous achievement of the Axial Age. Its innovations gave rise to epoch-making cosmological models, visions of history, and ways of imagining human agency. These cultural repatternings took different directions in the major civilizations of the Axial Age. Imperial formations that took shape during or in the aftermath of the period were particularly important for the long-term impact of the axial breakthroughs. But with the partial exceptions of Byzantium and China, continuities linked to imperial traditions were of limited significance in the early second millennium. If it is to be argued that breakthroughs to higher levels of reflexivity—"reconceptualisations along the same dimensions as during the Axial Age"—occurred during this period, they must be located in different contexts. Wittrock discusses some of the background changes taking place in various parts of Eurasia: from agricultural growth and urban developments to elite formation and contested models of political order. He then suggests that the intellectual movements responding to this changing environment tended to take the form of renaissances, "efforts to form a synthesis of the fundamental features of the tradition of a civilization with the emergent challenges to it." The eleventh- and twelfth-century renaissance in Western Christendom is discussed at some length; Wittrock argues that its socio-cultural meaning should be interpreted in terms of four revolutions (feudal, papal, urban and intellectual), and that this view has far-reaching implications for our understanding of the "rise of the West." The most comparable case outside Europe would seem to be Song China; these two civilizational areas seem to have been the only ones where "clerical elites become subject to a demanding formal training yet enjoy a high degree of autonomy from political power during their formation."

The second section deals with transformations inside Western Christendom, on its northern and eastern peripheries, and in the neighbouring Byzantine world, where history took a very different course. R. I. Moore's analysis of "the transformation of Europe as a Eurasian phenomenon" builds on his earlier writings and proposes an agenda for more wide-ranging discussion. Most of the following papers relate to it in direct or indirect ways. According to Moore, the transformation of Europe during the eleventh and twelfth centuries can also be described as "the first European revolution": it resulted in comprehensive changes to the structures of social power, and it consolidated Western Christendom—the historical matrix of Europe—as a distinctive civilizational complex. The key infrastructural precondition for this process was a shift from the early medieval economy of plunder to an economy of exploitation; the institutional changes associated with or made possible by it reached a mature stage in the twelfth century. As Moore sees it, a reorganization of power elites and their mutual relations is central to the whole transformation. In particular, he stresses the growing importance and changing position of clerical elites—in the double sense of trained administrators and ecclesiastical personnel. Their ascendancy was reflected in the dual power structure of papacy and monarchy (backed up by a "dual structure of landholding, by right of blood on the one hand and of profession and ordination on the other"); but the joint effect of developments on both sides was a major advance in state formation, "an aggrandisement of the state at the expense of the kin". This innovative turn had momentous consequences for the later history of Europe and its relations with the rest of the world. Moore concludes with reflections on comparable developments in other parts of Eurasia and suggests that roughly simultaneous crises of governing elites may have been addressed in different ways which enhanced the contrasts between different civilizations.

Gábor Klaniczay's paper focuses on the "new Europe" created by the eastward expansion of Western Christendom from the ninth century onwards, and taking a more autonomous shape after the turn of the millennium. Klaniczay surveys earlier work on the boundaries and divisions of Europe, with particular emphasis on the question of central Europe—as a transitional region between West and East—and its internal divisions. Historians from the "borderlands"—especially Oscar Halecki and Jenö Szücs—have made a strong case for seeing East Central Europe as a distinctive region. In Klaniczay's words, this is "a conflict-ridden intermediary zone between West and East, an '*antemurale*', a buffer region with recurrent existential insecurities and frequently resurgent split consciousness." Its historical core was made up of the Polish, Bohemian, and Hungarian kingdoms, whose relations with the more advanced West and with each other—including attempts to bring them into some kind of union—underwent significant changes in the course of a turbulent history. Klaniczay discusses the transfer of Western Christian cultural and institutional models to this region, especially with regard to the successive phases of Christianization (conversion, building of ecclesiastical institutions, and the fusion of religion and royal power exemplified by dynastic cults). He concludes with comments on the slower transformation of social structures. Even for those who accept the concept of feudalism in the Western context, it has proved difficult to apply in the East Central European one. Social patterns of nobility and peasantry differed markedly from the West, and Westernization on this level came later than at the summits of ecclesiastical and political power.

Sverre Bagge discusses the Scandinavian region, another European periphery transformed through closer contact with the centre, with direct reference to Moore's model. Here the transition from an economy of plunder to an economy of exploitation had a particularly dramatic character: for the Vikings, the economy of plunder seems to have been more profitable. The turn to accelerated state formation occurred in this context, and it went hand in hand with integration into Western Christendom. The long-term outcome was the consolidation of three kingdoms—Denmark, Norway and Sweden. But this was the result of historical processes, rather than of any natural division, and counter-trends were at work until early modern times. The Danish kingdom was closest to the centres of Western Christendom and best placed to aspire to control the rest of the region. Within this context, imported and adapted models of ecclesiastical and political power had a transformative impact. Their specific patterns differ from both the Western European centre and the East Central European periphery; there were also significant differences between the three emerging states. With regard to the region as a whole, the line of division between monarchy and aristocracy seems to have been less clearly defined than in Moore's account of Western Europe, and bureaucratic administration was much less developed. On the ecclesiastical side, there was no inquisition (a crucial part of the pattern that was—according to Moore—established in Western Europe during the High Middle Ages), and very little heresy before the rapid success of the Reformation in the sixteenth century. In the last section of the paper, Bagge suggests that the inclusion of Scandinavia in a more complex picture of Europe might bring some new perspectives to bear on comparison with other civilizations.

Thomas Lindkvist analyzes the "making of a European society" in Sweden as a specific case of a more general pattern. In contrast to societies on the east coast of the Baltic, "the Swedes Europeanized themselves" in the sense that indigenous elites imported European institutions and ideas and used them as frameworks for far-reaching social transformations. Compared to developments in East Central Europe as well as in other parts of the Scandinavian region, the Europeanizing turn in Sweden came relatively late, and some specific features of the process are related to this delay. In the Swedish case, the pre-feudal economy of plunder had been linked to uncoordinated colonization across the Baltic, and this continued under the new socio-economic order: a large part of the later Finland was integral to the Swedish state from an early phase of its formation. As for the movement towards statehood, Lindkvist distinguishes between the making of a kingdom, based on "more or less permanent territorial lordship", and the creation of a state, with "permanent and settled political institutions", and more specifically with relatively stable rules for the relationship between king and aristocracy. In Sweden, the first process was completed by the end of the twelfth century. Both phases were very closely linked to the building of ecclesiastical institution; but one characteristic feature of the Swedish case was a prolonged conflict between two dynasties that seem—to some extent—to have represented different policies towards the Church.

Paul Stephenson's paper on Byzantium stresses a recent and fundamental change to perceptions of the period: contrary to earlier assumptions, it is now generally accepted that for the Byzantine Empire, the centuries in question were a time of sustained demographic and economic growth. The merits and demerits of the most influential interpretations must be reassessed in light of this basic fact. It can still be argued that an aristocratic takeover undermined the imperial order and paved the way for the disaster that came from outside in 1204. But the whole process must be analyzed in terms adequate to more advanced scholarship. It seems clear that the Byzantine state was structurally incapable of harnessing economic expansion to its strategies (more so than the states of neighbouring civilizations), and this weakness was aggravated by power struggles at the top. On the other hand, a rising aristocracy succeeded in amassing wealth and power, and it could aspire to direct control of the political centre. The distinction between civil and military aristocracy seems to have been much less important than earlier historians assumed; the main issue was the relationship between the state and the most powerful magnate families. Seen in this perspective, the rule of the Komnenos dynasty was not simply a case of private interest capturing the state; rather, the Komnenos project aimed at a thoroughgoing fusion of state power with a dominant and privileged aristocratic family. But the result was, after some temporary successes in the twelfth century, a disintegrative process that left the state more incapacitated than ever. Stephenson concludes with comments on Moore's analytical model; as he sees it, the state-elite relationship is also central to Byzantine history during the same period, but the social character of both sides differed from the Western pattern.

The third part of the collection deals with major non-European civilizations. Said Amir Arjomand's analysis of transformations in the Islamicate world (this term, coined by Marshall Hodgson, serves to avoid a conflation of religious and civilizational identities) begins with general reflections on comparative approaches. As Arjomand observes, there has been a marked paradigm shift in this field: arguments about the presence or absence of certain preconditions are giving way to more complex models of common elements combined in different ways, with different relative weighting of the factors involved, and thus resulting in divergent developmental paths. Hodgson's work is one of the sources of this new approach, but his way of constructing ideal-typical contrasts between Islam and Christianity is open to some criticism. It calls for further historicization, which would be in line with some of his own arguments. The question of the "Islamic city" and its failure to match Occidental models of urban life serves to illustrate this point. There was more urban autonomy and civic agency in the Islamicate context than Western comparative historians have mostly wanted to admit, but the legal framework and the political impact differed from the West in significant ways. To tackle this issue in more concrete historical terms, Arjomand analyzes at some length the policies of the late Abbasid Caliph al-Nāsir at the turn of the twelfth and thirteenth centuries. His attempt to overcome the bifurcation of supreme authority, and thus to restore a powerful Caliphate, relied—among other things on extensive mobilization of urban forces, and his failure throws light on cultural and structural obstacles to such projects.

Sheldon Pollock's paper begins on a note of skepticism about grand strategies and sweeping conclusions. In his view, the debate on the Axial Age has not led to satisfactory conclusions, and it seems even more premature to construct a global pattern of "cultural crystallization" in the early second millennium CE. He suggests a more cautious strategy that might help to link up with better understanding of contacts and integrative processes on a macro-regional scale. This approach would focus on similar developments in separate civilizational settings that are known but not well understood (without any assumptions about parallels of global or Eurasian dimensions), and explore connections to the trans-civilizational dynamics that shaped the period in question. The vernacularizing process (vernacular languages replacing cosmopolitan ones, for both cultural and political purposes), extensively discussed in Pollock's earlier writings, fits into this framework. Vernacularization, accompanied by a shift from imperial to regional forms of statehood, did occur in the obviously separate and markedly different contexts of Indian and Western European history. Pollock goes on to discuss possible links to forces that might have affected the course of events on both sides. The development of Eurasian trade networks, described as a "world system" by some over-enthusiastic historians, does not explain the vernacular turn: there are no plausible historical correlations. Nomadic empires, however important for the long-term dynamic of globalization, did not directly affect the regions where vernacularization was most successful. Pollock suggests that Islamic expansion, although certainly not directly conducive to vernacularization, may have created a context that was of some importance. More specific connections have yet to be examined.

Paul Jakov Smith discusses the experience of Song China, a key theme for all comparative interpretations of the early second millennium. The governmental activism that gathered momentum in eleventh century China can be seen as a continuation of the new cycle of state formation, initiated by the tenth century successor states that disputed the heritage of the Tang Empire (their policies were more constructive than earlier accounts of the period tended to assume). Governmental activism built on structural foundations laid by the early Song rulers, as well as on intellectual orientations of a new administrative elite. But as Smith argues, it must also be analyzed in a broader context: its culminating

moments coincided with ambitious attempts to reconquer lost territories
on the northern border, and the defeat of activist policies was due to
a combination of military reversal and economic failure. The political
trajectory of Song China thus reflects the geopolitical dynamics of Sino-
steppe relations. When the Jurchen invasion drove the Song out of
North China in 1126, the balance of power shifted decisively in favour
of the "dual administration empires", using Chinese techniques of governance to complement Inner Asian power structures. But the second
phase of Song rule, now limited to South China, was also a time of
transformations. Against the background of a definitive setback to irredentist ambitions, the gentry—now based on a more flexible combination of office-holding with property and status—consolidated its social
power at the expense of central authority. Neo-Confucianism, the most
distinctive ideological product of the period, took shape in this context.
The twelfth century constellation was, however, in turn transformed by
the last great wave of Inner Asian expansion: the Mongol invasion.

Mikael S. Adolphson's analysis of Japan from the eleventh to the
thirteenth centuries reveals a pattern very different from all others discussed in this collection. Adolphson does not reject all comparisons with
other parts of Eurasia, but he argues that sweeping constructs of that
kind (especially those based on the highly problematic notion of feudalism) have done more harm than good, and that a more limited focus
on specific phenomena is needed. As for the changes occurring in Japan
during these three centuries, they are best described as "contained transformations". The terms refers to several forms of containment within
established geopolitical and socio-cultural structures: an island polity
whose contacts with the mainland were strictly limited; an exceptionally
durable pattern of authority, centred on the imperial institution and
capable of accommodating extensive changes to the social basis; an
adaptable and resilient power structure, centred on a court elite; and a
syncretic religious culture, embodying an "ideology of mutual dependence
between religious and secular authority". The transformations that took
place in this context had to do with the privatization of governmental
power at all levels. But they were also channelled into a more specific
tripartite division of power between courtiers, warriors and elite temples.
Changing relations and mutual arrangements between these "gates of
power" were central to Japanese history during the three centuries in
question. As Adolphson argues, there was no straight or obvious path
from warrior activism within the tripartite regime to the warrior domination
that began in the fourteenth century. But there was also a long-term

dynamic of commercial growth, more external to the tripartite regime yet crucial to its historical destinies. Adolphson concludes with the suggestion that students of Japanese history should take a closer look at the interaction between mercantilism and social containment.

Michal Biran's paper on the Mongol conquests—seen as a new phase in the history of Eurasian transformations—rounds off the discussion. For contemporaries, the Mongol invasions were a unique and unprecedentedly explosive event, upsetting the established geopolitical order and bringing an alien force to centre stage. But historians have contextualized the Mongol phenomenon in multiple ways. Biran analyzes several aspects of these broader interconnections. The Mongol Empire was the last chapter in a long history of Inner Asian imperial expansion; the successive protagonists active in that field had developed distinctive strategies of state building, learnt from the experience of sedentary civilizations and constructed ideological frameworks that reflect both rivalry with and dependence on agrarian empires. The Mongols drew on this vast historical experience and made major additions to it. At their most powerful, they presided over a Eurasian empire that represented a massive step towards hemispheric integration. Ecological, economic and cultural implications of this last and most global phase of Inner Asian expansion are still debated by scholars. And although the empire as such was short-lived, its impact on successor states in various regions—and linked to the Mongol past in various ways—was highly significant. Mongol statecraft obviously counted for something in the rise of the "gunpowder empires" (Marshall Hodgson) that dominated the last phase of Islamic history before European hegemony, even if the question of continuities across the Mongol interlude is far from settled (see also Arjomand's contribution to this volume). Through the Timurids and the Mughals, Mongol traditions were of some importance for the last pre-colonial version of the Indo-Islamic world. Recent work on Chinese history, in particular the debate on the Song-Yuan-Ming transition, has underlined the lasting significance of Mongol rule. The question of the Mongol-Russian relationship is perhaps the most controversial and ideology-laden one, but even the more cautious historians would find it difficult to overlook the element of mimetic rivalry in Muscovite strategies vis-à-vis the Mongols. All these historical affiliations are crucial to the question of early modernities in Eurasian regional contexts.

I. THEORETICAL AND
COMPARATIVE REFLECTIONS

PARALLELS AND DIVERGENCES: PERSPECTIVES ON THE EARLY SECOND MILLENNIUM

JOHANN P. ARNASON

ABSTRACT

This paper argues that more conceptual clarification and a more equal development of comparative history are needed before we can attempt a synthetic interpretation of the early second millennium CE. In conceptual terms, the debate centres on the idea of formative historical phases, characterized by major and lasting innovations on the levels of cultural patterns and/or power structures; but the dynamics of such phases can only be analyzed in relation to long-term processes of two kinds: those that precede the episodes of accelerated change and those through which their consequences unfold. This problematic is briefly explored with reference to classical as well as contemporary sources. As for historical analyses and controversies, there are good reasons to regard the period in question as a phase of formative changes in various fields and in different parts of the Eurasian macro-region, but there is also a broad spectrum of conflicting interpretations, more structured in some cases than others. The two most thoroughly analyzed cases—and the clearest examples of transformative dynamics—are Western Christendom and Song China.

Preliminary Reflections: Long-term Processes and Formative Phases

Let us start with some reflections on the categories and perspectives of historical sociology. The latter (whether understood as a new branch or a comprehensive reorientation of sociological inquiry) is frequently defined in terms of a focus on long-term processes—or, in other words, a processual approach to the *longue durée*. This interpretation, most closely associated with Norbert Elias and his disciples, is one-sided in that it bypasses a problematic which goes back to classical sociology and becomes more explicit in the works of later authors, even if a selective emphasis on separate aspects tends to obscure the connections: the question of the relationship between long-term processes and formative phases. The latter term is, in brief and without touching upon issues to be discussed later, used to refer to relatively short periods of comprehensive, condensed and decisive change.

The sociological classics did not pose the question in general terms, but evidence of sensitivity to both aspects can be found in some of their most seminal texts. The *Communist Manifesto* combines an account of the rise of the bourgeoisie as a long-term process with a particular emphasis on the more recent, abrupt and revolutionary transformations that have— as the authors see it—completed the story and created preconditions for a new beginning. In a very different vein, Max Weber analyzed the long-term rationalizing process involved in the "rise of the West", while at the same time stressing the importance of the more revolutionary innovations embodied in the medieval city; the second theme was neglected by some of the most influential interpreters of his work, but a brief reference to a whole sequence of revolutionary episodes—in the context of comparing China with the West—shows that he intended to tackle this question in a more systematic way. As these two examples suggest, revolutions are particularly revealing keys to the interrelations between different dimensions of history. Sociological reflections on revolutionary change go beyond the commonsensical view in two respects: through a broader idea of historical upheavals as formative phases rather than events or sequences of events, and through the reconstructive perspective that highlights a longer prehistory. Although it would be absurd to posit a precise chronological criterion, the distinction is not wholly arbitrary. Revolutionary phases may be defined in terms of centuries (see R. I. Moore's contribution to this volume, as well as his book on "the first European revolution"),[1] but nobody would describe the millennial dynamic of the long Middle Ages—as analyzed by Norbert Elias—as a revolution. Both categories are contextual, and chronological dimensions vary from one specific context to another.

The history of theoretical debates on revolutions shows that it is not easy to balance the two perspectives. With regard to the paradigmatic political revolution of modern times, Tocqueville's analysis of the *ancien regime* and its unintended achievements was rediscovered as an antidote to the dominant images of rupture. This became the starting-point for a new (still unfinished) round of controversy about the relative importance of long- and short-term frames of reference. Similarly, interpretations of the American revolution entered a new phase with the now widely accepted argument that the eighteenth century represents a turning-point in English state formation, with different ramifications and

---

[1] R. I. Moore, *The First European Revolution, c. 975-1215* (Oxford: Blackwell, 2000).

consequences on the two sides of the Atlantic. As for the industrial revolution, recent work by economic historians has reformulated the question
of its continuity or discontinuity with pre-existing patterns of growth,
but certainly not settled it in favour of any particular model.[2]

Here we are—as noted above—only concerned with the implications
of revolutionary change for the more general question of phases and
processes. One particular aspect of revolutionary episodes is crucial to
the broader perspective: the interplay of culture and power. There is
an obvious *prima facie* case for analyzing revolutions with reference to
these two components and their mutually formative dynamics. But when
it comes to concrete analyses and explanatory claims, one side is often
stressed at the expense of the other. Some of the most influential work
on revolutions during the last two or three decades focused on the transformations of power structures, in contrast to the earlier emphasis on
ideological projects and their cultural sources. If the field of inquiry is
broadened to include "revolutions from above", often triggered by the
imperatives of interstate competition and unfolding in ways which leave
no doubt about the secondary role of ideological factors, it seems advisable
to allow for variations in the relative weight of cultural currents and
the dynamics of power structures.

Such considerations may prove useful when we confront the more
general question of formative historical phases. This problematic will be
the main frame of reference for the following discussion (although the
complementary long-term perspectives will be of some relevance to the
argument). So far, the most seminal arguments have centred on "periods
of cultural crystallization".[3] The prime example is the idea of the Axial
Age, inherited from the philosophy of history and translated into the
language of historical sociology by S. N. Eisenstadt. The debate on its
strengths and weaknesses is in progress, but the main points at issue
are not in doubt: if the conception of the Axial Age makes any sense,
it is about cultural mutations generating a surplus of meaning and opening up new horizons for long-term developments. It also exemplifies the
relativity of distinctions between the *longue durée* and the short-term
dynamics of condensed change. The Axial Age is invariably defined as
a period of several centuries; but some interpretations relate it to a

---

[2] See especially Kenneth Pomeranz, *The Great Divergence. China, Europe, and the Emergence
of a World Economy* (Princeton: Princeton University Press, 2000).

[3] See Björn Wittrock, "Social theory and global history. The periods of cultural crystallization", *Thesis Eleven* no. 65 (2001), pp. 27-50.

much longer prehistory. The latter can, of course, be demarcated in different ways: the emphasis may be on developments beginning in the late Bronze Age (with a general crisis of state structures around the Eastern Mediterranean), or on the much older and more general trends that began with the separation of state and society (Marcel Gauchet's analysis of the Axial Age is the most representative example of the latter view).[4] On the other hand, some analysts of the Axial Age have identified a culminating phase—usually seen as more or less coextensive with the sixth century BCE—within the multi-secular period.

It remains to be seen whether this attempt to theorize the primacy of culture while avoiding the fallacies of cultural determinism can cope with objections from historians; but in any case, it may be suggested that Eisenstadt's account of the Axial Age is to the problematic of formative phases what Elias's analysis of European state formation is to that of long-term processes: a paradigmatic example that can serve as an illustration of more general problems and as a starting-point for more differentiated models. One question to be tackled in that context is whether there are formative phases primarily characterized by major shifts of power structures, political or economic, without corresponding or underlying changes of cultural orientations. One such case might be the emergence of imperial power in ancient Mesopotamia. The "imperial moment", i.e. the formation of a power centre through absorption of a pre-existing state system and with an inbuilt push for further expansion, was undoubtedly a turning-point in world history; but although Akkad can in a certain sense be described as the first world empire, it was only later that empires acquired the cultural dimensions which allow us to describe them as "ecumenic".[5] To add another example of a very different kind (and much more controversial), Kenneth Pomeranz's account of the "great divergence" suggests that the transition to advanced modernity and European domination at the end of the eighteenth century was due to a global redistribution of economic power, and that structural factors of the most material kind (fortuitous availability of key resources and access to vast spaces across the Atlantic) played a decisive role.

It may also be possible to contrast cases of power-centred transformation with others where the dynamics of culture and power seem to

---

[4] See Marcel Gauchet, *The Disenchantment of the World: A Political History of Religion* (Princeton: Princeton University Press, 1997).

[5] On Akkad, see Mario Liverani (ed.), *Akkad: The First World Empire. Structure, Ideology, Traditions* (Padova: Sargon, 1993).

be more closely interconnected. Here a comparison of the two great imperial formations at opposite ends of the Eurasian macro-region would seem particularly instructive. The consolidation of the Han Empire during the last two centuries BCE was accompanied and supported by a process of cultural crystallization (a selective codification of the legacy of the Chinese Axial Age). There was no comparable cultural side to the simultaneous transformation of the Roman city-state into a Mediterranean empire. Even when a major reorganization was undertaken (with the transition from republic to empire in a more specific sense), the scope of cultural innovation was limited, and this was reflected in a strikingly self-limiting logic of the institutional framework put in place by Augustus and left—in all essentials—unchanged until the third century CE. Another restructuring of the empire, including a radical redefinition of its cultural premises, was triggered by an acute crisis which marked the transition from classical to late antiquity; the latter is now increasingly recognized as a formative phase of the first order.

Finally, we may note a case where it seems particularly important to account for the combined dynamics of cultural patterns and power structures. "The seventh to eleventh centuries should be treated as the period of the economic supremacy of Islam",[6] but this period was also marked by continuing Islamic expansion through a proliferation of political centres (after a short-lived imperial phase), and by the ascendancy of the then world religion par excellence. It does not seem far-fetched to describe this formative phase as the beginning of an Afro-Eurasian age, to be dated from the seventh to the late fifteenth century CE—beginning with a shift to more intensive interaction across the macro-region and coming to an end with the beginning of globalization in a more literal sense, i.e. the conquest of the Americas. This last point has more far-reaching implications: there may be formative phases characterized by a broadening and intensification of intercivilizational encounters.

Eurasian Transformations, 1: Western Christendom

The above reflections should help to clarify the background to our proper topic: the question of transformations in the major civilizational complexes of the Old World during—very roughly speaking, give or take a few decades at both ends—the first quarter of the second millennium

---

[6] André Wink, *Al-Hind. The Making of the Indo-Islamic World*, v. 1 (Leiden: Brill, 1996), p. 225.

CE. Is there a case for describing this period as a formative phase, in terms of cultural crystallization or some of the other criteria suggested above? It seems advisable to allow for multiple defining features: a first glance at the literature on the period will show that it has very frequently (more so in some regions than others) been identified as a distinctive and decisive phase, but for a wide range of reasons, which taken together would add up to a kaleidoscope rather than a coherent overall picture. In this section, I will briefly survey some of the arguments and interpretations that have been put forward (there is, of course, no pretension to an exhaustive list).

For historians of medieval Europe, it is a commonplace that the early centuries of the second millennium—the "High Middle Ages"—should be regarded as a particularly important period, with long-term consequences for subsequent European and global history, but the variety of proposed explanations and definitions is astonishing. Europe—or more precisely Western Christendom—is the region/civilization where we find the broadest agreement on the formative character of the period in question, and the most complex debate on its specific features. There is a fairly general consensus on a rough chronological outline: some kind of new beginning in the late tenth and into the eleventh century, accelerated growth and innovation in the twelfth and mature flowering in the thirteenth century, followed by the onset of a crisis at its end.

At the most elementary geopolitical level, the High Middle Ages have been described as a shift to more autonomous and undisturbed development after the last wave of barbarian invasions (this latter factor figures less prominently in contemporary scholarship than in some earlier accounts). With regard to internal power structures, some historians have identified the period with a "feudal revolution" which was then channelled into a more stable institutional framework and took a more mature shape during the twelfth and thirteenth centuries. This is the most specific version of the otherwise often diffuse conception of "feudalism" as a historical formation with a more or less clearly demarcated path from early beginnings to terminal crisis. But it is not uncontested: the most obvious reason to relativize the idea of feudalism as a system is the linkage between feudal institutions and the process of state formation; some historians stress the primacy of the latter to such an extent that the notion of feudalism boils down to a retrospective misconception of the power structures in question.[7] Even when the idea of feudal insti-

---

[7] See Susan Reynolds, *Fiefs and Vassals: The Medieval Evidence Reinterpreted* (Oxford: Oxford University Press, 1994).

tutions (as a component of a more complex figuration, not as a self-contained system) is retained, there seems to be growing agreement on the importance of state formation—as a process with divergent trajectories and far-reaching socio-cultural ramifications—to the history of medieval Western Christendom. Various historians and historical sociologists—from Norbert Elias and Joseph Strayer to more recent authors— have singled out the-twelfth century as a time of decisive innovations. Such developments must, in turn, be seen in the context of the rivalry between papacy and empire, unique to Western Christendom. It would now seem to be generally accepted that it is misleading to talk about a conflict between sacred and secular power: the rivals represented different combinations of the sacred and the secular. The concept of a "papal monarchy" (consolidated in the twelfth century, after more revolutionary beginnings in the eleventh) sums up four aspects of the phenomenon in question: the strengthening of papal power within the Church; the separate quasi-statehood of the Church that enabled it to pioneer administrative techniques later borrowed by emerging territorial states; the attempts of the papacy to function as an overlord of territorial rulers with more limited jurisdictions; and, most controversially, the claim to represent a supreme authority set above imperial centres.

The conflict between empire and papacy can also be analyzed in the context of medieval European variants of monarchy. But there is another side to this historical field: the development of non-monarchic polities. Michael Borgolte compares the Icelandic and Italian versions of "free states among monarchies"; for our purposes, the innovations of the Italian communes are obviously more important, and they have figured prominently in arguments about the historical significance of the whole period.[8] The rise of more or less autonomous urban communities has been interpreted in various ways: the Weberian view, which stresses the creation of new forms of the social bond, lends a more radical revolutionary meaning to the whole process than the Marxian accounts of proto-bourgeois beginnings. Weber's analysis has been questioned and relativized by later historical research, and it seems clear that his ideal type of the medieval occidental city over-emphasized the revolutionary break with traditional authority. The discussion about the scope and impact of the "urban revolution" raises further questions about its relationship to the whole framework of ecclesiastical, royal and feudal power.

---

[8] Michael Borgolte, *Europa entdeckt seine Vielfalt* (Stuttgart: Ulmer, 2002), pp. 211-20.

But the urban component will, in any case, remain central to all interpretations of the High Middle Ages as a formative phase.

It is a matter of debate how closely it should be linked to another
epoch-making development: the intellectual innovations that gathered
momentum in the twelfth century. They had institutional as well as cultural implications. Jacques Le Goff's seminal work on medieval intellectuals stressed the emergence of a new social force and category (*studium*
alongside *regnum* and *sacerdotium*), and linked this phenomenon very directly
to the rise of towns. Others have questioned this argument and placed
a stronger emphasis on the ambiguous role of the intellectuals within
the field of tensions between ecclesiastical and royal power.[9] As for cultural innovations and their long-term consequences, some of the most
ambitious interpretations have singled out the twelfth century as a turning-point on the road to Western modernity; such claims may focus on
the rise of the individual or on the foundation of a scientific tradition.[10]
Johannes Fried has noted the links between apocalyptic beliefs and cognitive progress, and even suggested the term "apocalyptic enlightenment".[11] Benjamin Nelson developed a particularly complex version of
this argument: as he put it, the twelfth century saw the crystallization
of a whole set of structures of consciousness (he grouped them around
the notions of *eros, logos, nomos,* and *polis*), together with their inbuilt and
permanent conflicts, that became central to the whole subsequent trajectory of the West. Others have described these cultural transformations as a "renaissance", and seen them either as the most important
prelude to the more familiar Renaissance that began in the fourteenth
century, or as an—all things considered—more fundamental and far-
reaching transformation of the same type.

The recent experience (and problematic) of European integration has
opened up new perspectives on the past, and in that context, the High
Middle Ages are often invested with special significance: as a decisive
step towards the "Europeanization of Europe", the "first European rev-

---

⁹ See Alain Boureau, "Intellectuals in the Middle Ages", in Miri Rubin (ed.), *The
Work of Jacques Le Goff and the Challenges of Medieval History* (Woodbridge: Boydell, 1997),
pp. 45-56, and Jean Dubabin, "Jacques Le Goff and the intellectuals", ibid., pp.
157-67.

¹⁰ Colin Morris, *The Discovery of the Individual* (London: SPCK, 1972); Horst Bredekamp,
"Das Mittelalter als Epoche der Individualität", *Brandenburgische Akademie der Wissenschaften:
Berichte und Abhandlungen* (Berlin, 2000), pp. 191-240; Toby Huff, *The Rise of Early Modern
Science* (Cambridge: Cambridge University Press, 1999).

¹¹ Johannes Fried, *Aufstieg aus dem Untergang: Apokalyptisches Denken und die Entstehung der
modernen Naturwissenschaft* (München: Beck, 2001).

olution", synonymous with the "birth of Europe itself" as a separate civilizational sphere (Moore); or as the moment when Europe discovered its diversity (Borgolte). Here I cannot pursue the question further. But to sum up, let us note the variety of concepts that have been used to describe the period: discovery, reform, renaissance, revolution, as well as the less easily translatable German notions of *Aufbruch* and *Wende*; the self-invention of Europe and the beginning of European expansion can be added to the list. The recently proposed model of "four revolutions" (feudal, papal, urban and intellectual, the last one centred on the universities) underlines the pluralism of the period. But it seems to draw on different uses and interpretations of the term "revolution", without clarifying the relationship between them. Moore's analysis of the "first revolution" may be read as an attempt to impose a unified concept of revolution, re-centred on the process of state formation.

The above discussion applies, in the first instance, to the Western core of Latin Christendom; a few remarks on the particular case of East Central Europe should be added. As to boundaries and divisions, I follow Halecki's classic analysis: we can define Central Europe, roughly speaking, as the region that had not been part of the Roman Empire but was incorporated into the successor civilization of Latin Christendom; within this region, we can then draw an internal dividing line roughly corresponding to the frontier of the Carolingian Empire, and distinguishing the German part from another one best described as East Central Europe; the core of the latter consists of the historic states of Poland, Bohemia and Hungary. Here the period from the tenth to the thirteenth century represents the formative phase par excellence: the crystallization of East Central Europe as a distinctive region, separate from the Western and the Byzantine/Orthodox sphere. A crucial geopolitical and geocultural division thus emerges together with the civilizational unity and identity of Western Christendom. The East Central European trajectory during the period in question seems even more distinctive when linked to the "flowering" of several states in the region during the fourteenth century (this is now a major subject of debate among historians).[12]

Eurasian Transformations, 2: China

In short, a survey of the European historical experience during the early second millennium leaves us with an "embarrassment of riches": the

---

[12] See Marc Löwener, *Die Blüte der osteuropäischen Staaten im 14 Jahrhundert*, forthcoming.

problem is how to fit the multiple aspects and trends into a coherent model. The other obvious case of formative developments during this period is the Chinese one. In fact, it seems to have generated a more focused and structured debate than its Western counterpart. Developments at the beginning of the second millennium CE, especially under the Northern Song (960-1126) are universally recognized as crucial to the long-term course of Chinese history; more recently, they have been studied in connection with several other themes and lines of inquiry. The result is a complex problematic that links structural transformations to cultural crystallizations, formative turns to long-term dynamics, and internal trends to broader geopolitical contexts. The best starting-point for a survey of this field is a thesis which is also interesting as an episode in intellectual history: it represents one of the most significant contributions of East Asian scholarship to European understanding of the region. In the first and second decades of the twentieth century, the Japanese historian Naitō Konan (also known as Naitō Torajiro) developed an interpretation of Song China which seems to have had a significant influence on Western scholars in the field. He saw the Song period as the beginning of Chinese modernity (in that respect, he was perhaps the most important precursor of the current debate on "early modernities"; he used the term *kinsei*, which had been coined by Japanese scholars working on the Tokugawa period who were interested in its significance for the transition to modernity).Technological progress, economic growth and a new wave of urbanization—closely linked to growing commercialization of the economy—were the most obvious indicators of a transition to modernity; at the same time, aristocratic elites were replaced by a new—or newly consolidated—stratum of scholar-officials who represented a more bureaucratic conception of statehood; but Naitō also insisted on a more autocratic model of imperial rule (the analogy with early modern European absolutism was clearly of some importance to his argument). This last point is highly controversial: it is clearly not the case that Song emperors were uniformly or typically autocratic rulers, but some historians have argued that structurally autocratic power was exercised by chief councillors or small groups of court favourites.[13]

For historians responding to the Naitō thesis, theoretical conclusions about "early modernity" have obviously been less important than sub-

---

[13] On Naitō's work, see Joshua A. Fogel, *Politics and Sinology: The Case of Naitō Konan, 1866-1934* (Cambridge/MA: Harvard University Press, 1984). See also the discussion in Richard von Glahn, "Imagining Premodern China", in Paul Jakov Smith and Richard

stantive issues concerning the period, and details of the picture have been widely debated, but it seems safe to say that Naitō's interpretation of the Song period as a major breakthrough and a turning-point in Chinese history—prepared by trends at work under the late Tang and during the tenth-century phase of decomposition—remains central to a shared frame of reference. But questions related to socio-economic and political change during the period have been linked to other sets of issues with wide-ranging ramifications. The first of them has to do with intellectual developments under the Song. On this level, the dominant trend was the rise of a new interpretive synthesis of traditions going back to the Axial Age (Neo-Confucianism is the accepted Western sub-stitute for the Chinese terms *daoxue* [Learning of the Way] and *lixue* [Learning of Principle]). This movement is commonly taken to signify a return to stronger emphasis on the cultural identity of the Chinese world, after the Tang phase of cosmopolitan pluralism, but the new commitment to "this culture of ours" (Peter Bol's translation of a key phrase used by protagonists of the movement) was accompanied by intellectual elaboration of themes which had at first been marginal to Chinese thought and then brought to prominence by traditions with a different civilizational background (the emergence of Confucian meta-physics as a response to the Buddhist challenge).[14] These developments, long familiar to Western scholars, have often been seen as signs of a twelfth-century "renaissance" in China, and as inviting comparison with the roughly contemporaneous changes in the West. More distinctive approaches have taken shape in recent scholarship. In particular, Peter Bol's work on Neo-Confucianism suggests new perspectives with far-reaching implications. He stresses the significance of Neo-Confucian claims to re-establish the meaning and supremacy of a tradition (the properly understood teaching of the Way) that had been articulated by the classics, but then marginalized or misconceived for a very long time. Even more importantly, the reinstatement of the classical canon—the writings of Confucius and Mencius—was backed up by philosophical assumptions which could at the same time serve to relativize the author-ity of texts and sages: "Indeed, by asserting that the unity of principle was present in human nature and thus accessible to human cognition, the Neo-Confucians could posit that humans had a natural tendency to

---

von Glahn, *The Song-Yuan-Ming Transition in Chinese History* (Cambridge/MA: Harvard University Press, 2003), pp. 35-70.

[14] Peter K. Bol, *This Culture of Ours. Intellectual Transitions in T'ang and Sung China* (Stanford: Stanford University Press, 1992).

find unifying and integrating ideas"; by stressing "the autonomous ability of the individual to become conscious of principle", they "shifted Heaven-and Earth, the ultimate grounds for the 'system', to the individual will and subordinated the authority of the cultural and political traditions of history to that vision".[15] As Bol argues, this basic conceptual shift also entailed a denial of political authority over values, and a strong emphasis on unity as an overarching cosmic, moral and social value. In short, Neo-Confucianism represented a very major turning-point in Chinese intellectual history. But persistent ambiguities—with regard to the relation between cosmic and social order, innate insight and trans-mitted teaching, moral and political authority—kept the movement open to different interpretations (resulting in one of the most pluralistic configurations of Chinese intellectual history) and blunted its challenge to the traditional order.

The divergent potentialities of Neo-Confucianism were spelt out in changing socio-political contexts. Under the Southern Song dynasty (1126-1279), the gentry—an elite stratum which drew its strength from the combination of access to office, landed property and local power—made major gains at the expense of a state which became markedly less activistic. As Paul Jakov Smith argues in his contribution to this volume, class formation trumped state building, with lasting consequences for the following centuries of Chinese history, and Neo-Confucianism eventually emerged as the distinctive ideology of the ascendant elite. Naitō had noted this massive shift in the balance of social power, but later research has raised further questions (which may be seen as the second of the problem areas mentioned above), and various aspects of the long-term pattern are still controversial. It seems clear that on the whole and in the long run, the shift of power from imperial centre to local elites was irreversible, but attempts to reverse the trend through bursts of governmental activism, terror and indoctrination (as under the founding Ming emperor) were anything but insignificant, and the bal-ance could be readjusted within flexible limits (under the Qing dynasty). The local elites did not break the framework of the "stretched empire" (*l'empire distendu*), as one French historian has called it.[16] Moreover, the interplay of elites and state continued to reflect the ambiguities of Neo-Confucianism: it may have been most widely accepted and most solidly

---

[15] Peter K. Bol, "Neoconfucianism and local society, 12th-16th century: a case study", in Smith and von Glahn, *The Song-Yuan Ming Transition*, pp. 241-83, here pp. 251-52.
[16] Yves Chevrier, "L'empire distendu: esquisse du politique en Chine, des Qing à

entrenched as an ideology of local elites, but the emphasis on the ideal of "great unity" could, again and again, lend itself to use as a legitimizing framework for imperial projects of reform and rectification.

The third set of problems has to do with the geopolitical context. In this regard, Naitō's approach has been revised in more significant ways. It is now widely accepted that a long-term perspective on Chinese history must do justice to changing but increasingly essential connections with Inner Asian developments, especially the evolving patterns of state formation (up to and including the final synthesis of the two regional dynamics under the Qing dynasty), and that the Song era was also a formative phase on this enlarged scale. To quote Smith again, "the multi-state system that had prevailed in continental East Asia" after the downfall of the Tang Empire gave rise to a new "cycle of Sino-steppe relations that shaped Chinese society during this period".[17] Governmental activism under the Northern Song was inseparable from irredentist plans to reconquer territories lost to the new "dual administration empires" beyond the northern border; conversely, the disastrous loss of North China to the Jurchen in 1126 weakened the imperial centre beyond repair and enabled the gentry to stage a political and ideological counteroffensive.

Finally, interpretations of the Song era must, in one way or another, relate it to later Chinese imperial history. Naitō had drawn a sharp contrast between the precocious modernity of the Northern Song and the failure of later dynasties to continue on the same level of dynamism. Historians who did not follow him on specific points were nevertheless often inclined to take a similar view of the later imperial centuries: apart from the disruptive Mongol interlude, the Ming and Qing dynasties appeared as phases of stagnation or at best contained development. A very distinctive and influential account of the contrast was developed by Mark Elvin, who argued that a "medieval economic revolution", culminating in the twelfth century, had been followed by a very durable pattern of "quantitative growth and qualitative standstill", that only came to an end with the breakdown of the whole imperial order.[18] In the meantime, scholars studying the later imperial centuries have become much more inclined to stress economic dynamism, while questions of

Deng Xiaoping", in Jean-François Bayart (ed.), *La greffe de l'Etat* (Paris: Karthala, 1996), pp. 263-396.

[17] Paul Jakov Smith, "Introduction: Problematizing the Song-Yuan-Ming transition", in Smith and von Glahn, *Song-Yuan-Ming Transition*, pp, 1-34, here p. 7.

[18] Mark Elvin, *The Pattern of he Chinese Past* (London: Eyre Methuen, 1973).

social change and intellectual innovation remain more controversial. Most recently, new perspectives on Mongol rule—the Yuan dynasty— have prompted some scholars to construct a long "Song-Yuan-Ming transition", from the thirteenth to the sixteenth century.[19] In their view, this new periodization helps to put the Song breakthrough in proper perspective. The debate is still unfolding, with impressive results, and more can be expected; it is, in any case, a particularly instructive example of historical analysis in terms of formative phases and long-term processes.

Analogies between European and Chinese developments have not gone unnoticed. These two cases (together with the more puzzling Japanese one—see below) are the *prima facie* most convincing cases of early modernity, with a genealogy that includes crucial innovations during the period in question. Moreover, it seems justified—with due allowance for a very different context—to draw a parallel between the twelfth-century renaissance in Western Europe (which was, if we follow Richard Southern's analysis, in a sense superior to the fourteenth and fifteenth century one: more successful in linking the reappropriation of a cultural legacy to cognitive progress)[20] and the roughly simultaneous Confucian renaissance in China. But some basic contrasts are equally obvious: In China, the transformations took place within an enduring (if somewhat shrunken) imperial framework, whereas the Western Christian trajectory was characterized by the rivalry and ultimate failure of two attempts to translate civilizational unity into an integrative power structure (the papal monarchy and the Holy Roman Empire). The Chinese world entered a phase of more intensive interaction (and an increasingly unfavourable power balance) with Inner Asia, whereas Western Christendom was successfully insulated against pressures from that direction, and capable of expansion into a region (Eastern Europe) which to some extent functioned as a rampart against them.

Eurasian Transformations, 3: Islam and India

The picture is less clear-cut when it comes to the two most far-flung civilizational complexes of the Eurasian macro-region: the Islamic and the Indian one (the latter is to be understood in the broad sense which

---

[19] See Smith and von Glahn, *Song-Yüan-Ming Transition*.
[20] Richard W. Southern, *Scholastic Humanism and the Unification of Europe* (Oxford: Blackwell, 1995).

includes Indianized Southeast Asia). It is perhaps best to start with a basic fact which is central to some recent re-interpretations of the period in question: the (largely unilateral) development of closer contacts between the two civilizations and the formation of an Indo-Islamic world. André Wink refers to the first three centuries of the second millennium as a phase "in which the Middle East declines relatively in importance while Europe and China become ascendant, Central Asia is unified under the Mongols, and Islam expands far into the Indian subcontinent which then assumes its core position in the Indian Ocean".[21] With more specific reference to the pre-Mongol part of the period, we can thus speak of a new phase of Islamic expansion which to some extent counterbalances the setback to the Islamic heartland (loss of the absolute economic supremacy which it had enjoyed from the seventh to the eleventh century), and marks a major step towards Afro-Eurasian integration. Wink suggests a parallel with an earlier phase: if it makes sense to analyze the formation and early history of Islam in the context of interaction between three successor civilizations dividing the world of late antiquity, "another tripartite structure can be identified on the eastern frontier, one which is primarily determined by the interaction between the Islamic Middle East, Central Asia and India".[22] As he notes, the Islamic component of the latter tripartite structure had already been modified by the absorption and resurgence of another civilization, external to the original triangle: "Indo-Islamic civilization developed as an offshoot of eastern Persian Islam".[23] But another analogy may also be noted: the formation of an Indo-Islamic world was part of a differentiating process which replaced a "Pan-Indic civilization" (including Southeast Asia) with three successor civilizations: Hindu, Theravada Buddhist (much of continental Southeast Asia) and Indo-Islamic.[24] It is a matter of debate whether Indonesian Islam should be seen as an offshoot of the Indo-Islamic world or as a residual case outside the tripartite constellation.

These considerations raise an issue which will be discussed later: the global significance of the period in question may have more to do with intercivilizational encounters or constellations than with intra-civilizational changes. But at this point, a few words must be said about internal

---

[21] Wink, *Al -Hind*, p. 3.
[22] Ibid., p. 2.
[23] Ibid., p. 20.
[24] For a discussion of this configuration, see Jaroslav Krejčí, *The Civilizations of Asia and the Middle East: Before the European Challenge* (London: Macmillan, 1990).

transformations on the Islamic as well as the Indian side. As for the
Islamic world, there is a time-honoured and still influential interpretive
model which presents the first centuries of the second millennium as
the onset of a multi-secular decline. On this view, the fragmentation of
the Abbasid caliphate (completed during the tenth century) was accompanied by rapid failure of the counter-caliphates (the Fatimids and the
Andalusian Umayyads) and followed by the Seljuk takeover of the Islamic
heartland (the first case of frontier converts moving in rather than
enhancing the expansionist dynamic of Islam). The Seljuk—and more
generally Turkish—migration was seen as a case of nomads encroach-
ing on settled and cited civilization, and the much-debated Beduin invasion of the Maghreb was thought to have had the same effect in the
West. At the same time, the progressive militarization of political power,
combined with the spread of the Mamluk institution led to growing
alienation of power elites from society and a long-term breakdown of
linkages between state formation and socio-economic development.[25]
These structural causes of decline were connected to intellectual block-
age or regression. It should be noted that this last part of the argument
does not depend on assumptions about an invariant and supra-historical
anti-rationalist stance of Islam as a religion: one version of the thesis
centres on eleventh-century Islamic rationalism taking a self-destructive
turn (represented by Juwayni, d. 1085, and Ghazali, d. 1111) and re-
affirming the absolute primacy of revelation.[26] Finally, in the global context, the relative economic decline of Islam (in contrast to the new
dynamism of China and Western Christendom) is traced to internal and
absolute stagnation or regression.

It seems clear that this picture of the eleventh to thirteenth centuries
as a time of transition to long-term decline is being questioned and
revised from various angles.[27] The historical evidence does not support
the idea of general economic decline after the turn of the millennium,
and the view that nomadic incursions or migrations damaged the very
foundations of Islamic civilization seems untenable. Political fragmentation was to some extent accompanied by the development of more
effective techniques of state formation on a local scale; it is not obvi-

---

[25] See Patricia Crone, *Slaves on Horses: The Evolution of the Islamic Polity* (Cambridge:
Cambridge University Press, 1980).

[26] See Tilman Nagel, *Die Festung des Glaubens* (München: Beck, 1996).

[27] For a very informative survey, see Peter Feldbauer, *Die islamische Welt 600-11250.
Ein Frühfall von Unterentwicklung?* (Wien: Promedia, 1995). This account suggests that it is
too early for balanced conclusions.

ous that the Mamluk institution was invariably detrimental to relations between state and society, and the Seljuks can perhaps be credited with partial secularization of statehood.[28] The prospects for a revisionist history of Islamic thought are less clear; the most challenging anti-mainstream interpretation in that field, the work of Henry Corbin, centres on the flowering of esoteric philosophy in Iranian Islam and seems difficult to relate to our present agenda.

In the Indian case, it is perhaps more important than anywhere else to link the discussion of the eleventh to thirteenth centuries to the preceding phase, i.e. the last centuries of the first millennium CE. A traditional Western view of this period—the aftermath of the imperial phase that came to an end in the seventh century—stressed dissolution and fragmentation without any positive counter-trends. From this perspective, the "Brahmin restoration" could only be understood in negative terms: as a result of Brahmin authority and religiosity being more entrenched at the elementary levels of social organization, whereas Buddhism was more vulnerable because of its links to the decomposing larger-scale structures. Against this background, the formation of an Indo-Islamic world could then be seen as a matter of conquest and next to nothing else. It does not seem far-fetched to suggest that this picture has something to do with Western sources: a projection of an exaggerated image of the post-imperial "Dark Ages" in Western Europe. The Islamic conquest then becomes a mirror of the final disaster that might have struck Western Europe in the eighth century. Following Hermann Kulke, the shift to a more structured view of Indian history in the late first millennium involves four aspects: the rise of regional kingdoms, including those of South India which now came to play a much more central role than before; the transformation of classical "Brahmanism" into popular Hinduism; the formation of regional-vernacular languages; and, as a result of these three trends, the development of regional cultures, which greatly enhanced the internal diversity of Indian civilization.[29] All these trends continued to operate after the turn of the millennium and interacted with the dynamics of Islamization. It might be added that the rise of regional kingdoms did not put an end to all imperial projects: there was, as indicated in the title of a work by

---

[28] Ibid., pp. 335-36.
[29] Hermann Kulke and Dietmar Rothermund, *Geschichte Indiens* (München: Beck, 1998), p. 179.

Indian historians, a "struggle for empire"[30] and some of the players in the field made significant progress in that direction. On the other hand, it may be necessary to add a more concrete historical dimension to Kulke's model. Sheldon Pollock has analyzed the cultural and political implications of "vernacularization" in much greater detail, and with more specific reference to the first centuries of the second millennium (see his contribution to this volume). In any case, the changing perspective highlights connections between new patterns of state formation and cultural-religious transformations, as well as interaction between endogenous Indian trends and Islamic expansion; it thus gives a more concrete content to the tripartite model mentioned above.

A brief comparison of historical research on the Islamic-Indian complex and on the two other civilizations discussed above may be useful. For Western Europe and China, we have well-established interpretive frameworks which stress new beginnings and formative developments; different perspectives have given rise to ongoing debate, and new approaches can link up with existing problematics. But when it comes to the Islamic and Indian worlds, the debate seems to be at a different stage: historians are questioning and revising models which portrayed the period in question—in an overly streamlined fashion—as a transition to decline (which could, in both cases, be explained in terms of varying mixtures of internal and external factors). Alternative accounts are taking shape, but far from complete.

Eurasian Transformations, 4: Byzantium and Japan

In two other cases, we can also speak of revision(s) in progress, and to some extent of paradigms of decline being replaced with analyses of more complex developments.

An influential view of Byzantine history stressed the eleventh century turn towards more civilian aims and forms of rule, after the military successes of the late tenth and eleventh century (the first significant rollback of Islamic power in the Near East, followed by the conquest of Bulgaria); but after the defeat at Manzikert (which brought the Seljuks into Anatolia) and the Comnenian takeover in 1081, this promising development was cut short and the hegemony of a military aristocracy restored—spearheaded by the Comnenian dynasty. At its most adventurous, this analysis could develop into speculation about a proto-bour-

---

[30] R. C. Majumdar (ed.), *Struggle for Empire* (Bombay: Bharatiya Vidya Bhavan, 1957).

geois episode followed by feudal reaction. Some recent major works on eleventh- and twelfth-century Byzantium have questioned the basic assumptions of this model and put forward alternative views. Serious doubts have been raised about the very distinction between civil and military aristocracy: conflicts between regional actions and alliances may have been more significant.[31] Paul Magdalino argues that the Comnenian Empire, especially during its twelfth century heyday under Manuel I, may be seen as a synthesis of the civilian achievements of the eleventh century with new policies responding to Byzantium's geopolitical situation.[32] It also marked a return to more active involvement in Western affairs. In that context, it may be possible to draw some limited parallels with twelfth-century Western developments—especially with regard to urban growth and intellectual trends. At any rate, it can be said that the Byzantine trajectory during the period in question now looks less like an inversion of the Western Christian one than it did to some earlier historians.

This period also saw significant changes to the structure of the "Byzantine Commonwealth", i.e. the broader civilizational complex surrounding the imperial centre. Reinterpretations of the relationship between the Byzantine Empire and the rest of the "commonwealth" complement the revised account of internal history.[33] To begin with, the Bulgarian state should—in contrast to earlier accounts of the commonwealth—be seen as a rival empire with aspirations to equality or supremacy, rather than a polity with an ethnic identity. The second millennium begins with the definitive elimination of this rival centre, which enabled the Byzantine Empire to reclaim a civilizational monopoly; at the same time, a more marginal formation with imperial potential (Kievan Russia) appeared on the periphery of the commonwealth, but it was too distant and proved too vulnerable to fragmentation to become a serious rival to the centre.

Finally, it should be noted that the Byzantine trajectory during this period ends in a double disaster—more catastrophic than anything happening elsewhere during the same phase of world history. The sack of Constantinople by Western crusaders in 1204, "one of the great barbarities

---

[31] See especially Jean-Claude Cheynet, *Pouvoir et contestations à Byzance (963-1210)* (Paris: PUF, 1990).

[32] Paul Magdalino, *The Empire of Manuel Komnenos I* (Cambridge: Cambridge University Press, 1993).

[33] Paul Stephenson, *Byzantium's Balkan Frontier: A Political Study of the Northern Balkans, 900-1204* (Cambridge: Cambridge University Press, 2000).

of world history",[34] destroyed the Byzantine Empire—the restoration
that lasted from 1261 to 1453 was only a postscript. The Mongol conquest of the northeastern part of the commonwealth derailed Russian
history. But this latter event can perhaps be seen as a decisive shift
within a geopolitical and geocultural constellation that had always been
unstable: the region that later became Russia was an interface between
the Byzantine world (with significant Western contacts in the eleventh
century) and the Inner Eurasian one; the Inner Eurasian forces included
state-builders capable of different cultural-religious options (the Khazars
and the Volga Tatars) as well as groupings which retained more nomadic
structures (the Pechenegs and the Kumans); in a sense, the Mongols
combined the mobility of the latter with the consolidating capacity of
the former, and took both to a much higher level.

Taken together, the two disasters are a powerful corrective against
one-sidedly internalist historiography: geopolitical contexts and currents
can determine the destinies of states, empires and civilizations.

Japan is, as always, the odd case out. Among the regions and sub-
regions discussed here, it was by far the least integrated into Eurasian
contexts: during the period in question, its relations with China (from
which it was never completely isolated) were less intensive than at other
times, and the question of important contacts with other regions does
not even arise. Paradoxically, it is this marginal and self-contained part
of the macro-region that has been singled out as the prime case of parallels with developments at the other geographical extreme. The idea
of a Japanese feudalism, unfolding from the eleventh to the fourteenth
century and resembling its Western European contemporary in essential respects, goes beyond all other claims about similarities between
different parts of Afro-Eurasia in the early second millennium. It has
proved rather more resistant to criticism than other attempts to gener-
alize the concept of feudalism beyond the European case.

This model has, of course, been most extensively applied and developed
by Marxist historians. But in this case, the Marxist approach has some
fundamental points of contact with an older tradition. An earlier interpretation of the Heian period in Japanese history (late eighth to late
twelfth century) stressed the long-drawn-out disintegration of institutions
that had been modelled on Chinese patterns but proved—in the long
run—incompatible with indigenous realities (a classic version of this
argument can be found in the work of Kan'ichi Asakawa). As a result,

---

[34] Moore, *First European Revolution*, p. 183.

power structures were rebuilt on more local foundations. In the Marxist account, the rising local power elites (to all intents and purposes identical with the samurai) appear as a new dominant class. Both traditional and Marxist variations on this theme have been called into question by historians who emphasize a complex and long-term transformation of the Heian power structure.[35] This process, far from being reducible to mere decomposition, involved multiple shifts and recentrings (including a separation of authority and power at the apex of the regime, and competing strategies of privatization from above and below), and the emergence of military elites in a more autonomous role is best understood as part of the overall transformation. Moreover, it has been shown that the well-known rivalry between the imperial court and the military counterstate was not the whole story. A tripartite division of power—court, monasteries and military houses—emerged during the eleventh and twelfth centuries, and its dynamics shaped the course of Japanese history.[36] It is tempting to compare this pluralism with the internal divisions of Western Christendom (without equating particular actors in the two contexts with each other). And it is worth noting in the margin that the early fourteenth century saw a short-lived but exceptionally ambitious attempt to reunify the power structure under the aegis of the imperial institution (the Kenmu restoration, 1333-36—not, as has often been assumed, a short-sighted and reactionary bid to restore the court aristocracy to power, but an innovative project, to some extent inspired by the experience of Song China).

Another aspect of the Japanese trajectory during this period should be briefly mentioned. The doctrinal and organizational innovations of Kamakura Buddhism have sometimes been taken to represent a watershed in the history of Japanese religion, and some Western scholars (including Max Weber) have been tempted to compare them with the Reformation in early modern Europe. It has never been easy to reconcile this view with the more widely shared understanding of the period as a formative phase of Japanese feudalism. More recent work, especially by Kuroda Toshio and his disciples, has relativized the novelty of Kamakura Buddhism and drawn attention to the complexity of an older religious tradition, combining indigenous elements with esoteric

---

[35] See *The Cambridge History of Japan*, v. 2: *Heian Japan* (Cambridge: Cambridge University Press, 1999); also Eiko Ikegami, *The Taming of the Samurai: Honorific Individualism and the Making of Modern Japan* (Cambridge/MA: Harvard University Press, 1995).

[36] See Mikael Adolphson, *The Gates of Power. Monks, Courtiers and Warriors in Premodern Japan* (Honolulu: Hawaii University Press, 2000); also his contribution to this volume.

and exoteric Buddhism. The mixture could be adjusted to local and historical conjunctures, and developments during the Kamakura period can now more plausibly be seen as variations within this enduring framework. This new view of medieval Japanese religion links up with analyses of the tripartite power structure mentioned above.

Contrasts and Parallels

Can we—in light of this highly variegated background—speak of parallel developments or innovations across the Eurasian (or Afro-Eurasian) macro-region? It may be useful to begin with some general reflections. There are such things as contingent macro-historical parallels: to mention only one particularly striking and uncontestable case, the two most important imperial formations in Eurasian history—the Han and the Roman Empire—took shape at opposite ends of the Eurasian continuum during the two last centuries BCE. When noted by historians or historical sociologists, such parallels can facilitate comparison, but they can also easily tempt us to exaggerate, and to construct spurious uniformities. To take an example that illustrates both risks and rewards: the idea of the Axial Age, mentioned above, has given rise to a research programme which needs more work before any conclusive judgment can be attempted. A closer look at its complex history suggests that there has been an inbuilt bias towards homogenization of different historical experiences; but then it seems equally clear that the most constructive response is a more detailed examination of contrasts and affinities. Nothing can be gained by an a priori decision to write the whole idea off as an illusion.

Contingent parallels, then, do seem to be a fact of history—they need not be explained as a result of interconnections or interpreted as indicators of a latent unity. With regard to our period (late tenth to thirteenth centuries), there is of course a strong case for saying that it culminates in higher levels of connectivity across the macro-region (in part, but not only, "thanks" to the Mongols). But did it begin with more contingent parallels that might have paved the way for unification? As far as I can see, no case has been made for anything comparable to the axial model. The suggestion that this period might be analyzed in terms of an "ecumenical renaissance"[37] links together two valid points (there were renaissance-type developments in some regions, most obvi-

---

[37] See Björn Wittrock, "Social theory and global history".

ously China and Western Christendom, and the end result was—at least in some ways—a more ecumenical world), but to be convincing, it would have to be backed up by two further steps: it would have to be shown that the "renaissance" pattern applies to all major regions, and that the regional renaissances somehow converged in an ecumenical one. The term "ecumenical" seems to imply more than uniformity—it postulates some kind of unification. The sceptical view would, in short, be that there were renaissances, but not everywhere, and there was unification in important respects, but not primarily as a result of the renaissances.

R. I. Moore's view of the period, set out in his contribution to this volume as well as in other works, is very different.[38] The emphasis is on divergence rather than unity: "the differences between the civilizations themselves, and hence their identities, were greatly sharpened", as a result of divergent responses to crises which affected "clerical elites" and their respective "relations with society, the state, and the mass of the population". The broader context of this interpretation is important. Moore suggests that "a common economic, social and cultural intensification was accelerating in virtually all the cultivable regions of Eurasia in the second half of the Millennium; to this process the interaction of learned elites with people previously outside the structures of civilization, or poorly integrated with them, was crucial"; he adds that "the rural populations were now intimately involved in creating the new structures which replaced those [ancient] civilizations, and therefore in the processes of change themselves".[39] Around or after the turn of the millennium, this dynamic gives rise to a new divergence of large-scale and long-term cultural patterns and identities. To use a terminology which I have found useful in another context, an intensification of civilizing processes translates into a diversification of civilizational patterns.[40] On this view, a "great divergence" within the Eurasian macro-region took place much earlier than suggested by those (Pomeranz et al.) who are now using this term to describe the late eighteenth century change in the economic fortunes of East and West (and, by the same token, rejecting earlier datings of the beginning of Western hegemony).

This would seem to be the most challenging interpretation so far

---

[38] See especially R. I. Moore, "The eleventh century in Eurasian history: A comparative approach to the convergence and divergence of the medieval civilizations", *Journal of Medieval and Early Modern Studies* 33:1 (2003), pp. 1-21.

[39] Ibid., p. 5.

[40] See Johann P. Arnason, "Civilizational patterns and civilizing processes", *International Sociology* 16:3 (2001), pp. 389-407.

proposed for the period in question, and it opens up vast perspectives for comparative analysis. Here I can only adumbrate a few suggestions for further discussion. To begin with the notion of the clerical elite (central to the process described by Moore): The defining feature of a clerical elite is that it combines—or strives to combine—ideological and political power (the reference is to "les clercs" rather than to the Church); its relationship to the centre which comes to embody this combination may vary from case to case, as does the relationship to other elites based on or in pursuit of other combinations of social power. Finally, clerical elites stand at the intersection of power and meaning, and their modes of thought as well as their strategic projects are therefore affected by traditional patternings of the relationship between these two aspects of the social-historical world.

Moore's analysis of Latin Christendom places particular emphasis on the changing power balance between clerical and warrior elites; in China, the focus is on the relationship to (and the ultimate fusion with) a landholding gentry; the comments on the Islamic world suggest—more obliquely—a clerical elite on the defensive against warriors more alien to the broader social environment than in the West. In more general terms, the ambitions and destinies of clerical elites must be situated within a broader field of elite distinctions, rivalries and coalitions, with due allowance for changing historical constellations. In that connection, questions could be raised about some details of the argument. It might be premature to speak of a "marginalization of the warrior aristocracy" in twelfth century Western Europe, even if it is admitted that the process was neither complete nor irreversible. It seems clear that the twelfth century was a turning-point in the long-term process of state formation, and that the involvement of the clerical elites (including Le Goff's "intellectuals") was crucial, but from a broader perspective, that process might be better understood in terms of changing relations between political centres and multiple elites, with notable ups and downs for the warrior aristocracy. If the high medieval military expansion was essential to the "making of Europe",[41] it is part and parcel of the "first revolution", rather than a way of exporting it after the first success in the most central region; and this means that the warrior elite had a very central role to play.

There is also a case for comparing the structural and institutional

---

[41] Robert Bartlett, *The Making of Europe: Conquest, Colonization and Cultural Change, 950-1350* (Princeton: Princeton University Press, 1999).

preconditions of elite strategies—more particularly the unifying and frag-
menting dynamics of social power, with special emphasis on the different
divisions and combinations of religious and political power. Moore's reference to "titular fragmentation of power" suggests that such considerations are less important than the unity of the "effective ruling elite"[42]
and the logic of its long-term strategies. But wasn't the conflict between
imperial and papal centres, with their rival pretensions to authority on
a civilizational scale, crucial to the formation of multiple centres on
another level (the monarchic states), and thus to the fortunes of the
"clerical elites" associated with them? And if we pursue this line of comparison further, it will lead to reflections on the cultural patterns that
enter into the construction, concentration and fragmentation of power
structures. On this level, contrasts between Western Christian, Byzantine,
Islamic, Indian and Chinese traditions are obvious, but comparative
analyses of their implications are still in a very early stage.

From Intercivilizational Encounters to Hemispheric Integration?

To return to a question briefly considered at the beginning: the most
salient feature of the period in question may be a general intensification
of intercivilizational contacts across the Eurasian macro-region (accompanied by a consolidation—and perhaps a growing divergence—of civilizational identities). Jerry Bentley describes the overall result as a shift
towards "hemispheric integration".[43] But his account of that process
treats the whole period between 500 and 1500 CE as a relatively self-
contained phase, and does not single out the shorter period that concerns us here. When it comes to details on that level, it seems easier
to describe different regional constellations in specific terms than to
extract any kind of common denominator. The crystallization of Latin
Christendom as a separate civilization was inseparable from interaction
with its "significant others". The reappropriation of the classical legacy,
crucial to the intellectual renaissance of the twelfth century, was facilitated by closer contacts with the Byzantine and Islamic worlds—here
we have a case of two interconnected types of intercivilizational encounters, with rediscovered past sources and with more advanced present
rivals. At the same time, the period (which includes the crusades as well

---

[42] Moore, *First European Revolution*, p. 173, 178.
[43] Jerry Bentley, "Hemispheric integration, 500-1500 C.E.", *Journal of World History*
9:2 (1998), pp. 237-54.

as the most important phase of the *reconquista*) was characterized by an intensified military confrontation with Islam, which must be seen as essential to the "making of Europe". Attempts to coordinate this confrontation were an important part of the strategy of the "papal monarchy". As for the other (and less clear-cut) intercivilizational frontier, the same period saw a decisive and destructive turn towards antagonistic relations with the Byzantine world—although there is no direct connection between the religious estrangement that came to a head in 1054, and the conquest of Constantinople in 1204; and it is somewhat misleading to describe the former event as a final schism—it was neither the beginning nor the end of the long-drawn-out process that led to the separation of Latin and Orthodox Christendom. Finally, the "Europeanization" of the Nordic world was achieved during the period in question; even if we do not accept Toynbee's idea of an abortive Far Northern civilization, it can hardly be denied that the absorption into Latin Christendom set the region on a new course.

As for the Chinese world, three trends changed its situation within the broader Eurasian context: the shift in the power balance between China and Inner Eurasia, the development of closer economic contacts with the civilizations bordering the Indian Ocean, and the reaffirmation of a more particular cultural identity that made Chinese civilization much less receptive to inputs from elsewhere. And as for the Indian and Islamic worlds, it is enough to recall the points made above.

For our present purposes, it is convenient to see the Mongol conquests as the end of the period. This was the closest thing to an Eurasian empire that the world has ever seen, and it was created by conquerors from the margins—not by one of the power centres that had dominated the scene during the twelfth century. The Mongol episode affected the history of all major civilizational complexes in the macro-region, but in very different ways. In China, successful conquest was followed by failure to achieve a lasting synthesis of Chinese and Inner Asian patterns, and then by the re-emergence of an indigenous empire whose project and self-image reflected the Mongol experience in various ways. The most formative effects can be traced in the Islamic world, where the Mongol conquest gave a new twist to processes of state formation, thus initiating developments which culminated in the three early "gunpowder empires" (Ottoman, Safavid and Mughal). The impact on India was delayed: it materialized through the last phase of Muslim expansion into the subcontinent and the construction of the Mughal Empire. As for Western Christendom, the Mongol onslaught affected only its eastern margins, and it can perhaps be argued that this allowed the region to follow a more unbroken line of internal development than the other Eurasian civilizations did—thus changing its relative position in the macro-regional context.[44]

Joseph Fletcher's seminal essay on the Mongols, first published in 1986, began with a list of questions which still seem relevant.[45] But in light of more recent research and debate, it may be useful to add a few others. How to situate the Mongol empire within the much longer tradition of the Inner Asian "shadow empires", analyzed by Barfield?[46] In some respects, it represents the culmination of that tradition; but in other ways, it seems quite anomalous. How does the structure of Mongol imperialism at the height of its power compare with other ecumenical empires, and how well founded are the parallels that have been drawn with modern totalitarian regimes? And how to account for the very different patterns of interaction with other civilizations that emerged in the Chinese, Islamic and Russian domains of the Mongol Empire?

Note on "Early Modernities"

The debate on "early modernities" has so far not been characterized by clear agreement on the historical boundaries. If we compare the two programmatic essays at the beginning of the most representative collection,[47] the first (by S. N. Eisenstadt and W. Schluchter) stresses the sixteenth and seventeenth centuries, i.e. a period when the Western European nation-state came to play a key role in the mobilization of resources and the construction of collective identity, and raises questions about parallels in other regions. The second (by Björn Wittrock) goes back to the twelfth century and describes it as a turning-point, marked by several interconnected revolutionary transformations. Most of the other contributions would seem to be in line with one or the other of these two approaches: the papers on East Asia tend to take the first line, whereas Sheldon Pollock's essay on India is much closer to the second. It may even be possible to identify a third perspective: the

---

[44] See Archibald R. Lewis, *Nomads and Crusaders, A.D. 1000-1368* (Bloomington: Indiana University Press, 1988).

[45] Joseph Fletcher, "The Mongols: Ecological and Social Perspectives", in id., *Studies on Chinese and Inner Asia*, ed. Beatrice F. Manz (Brookfield,VT: Variorum, 1995), ix, 11-49.

[46] Thomas Barfield, *The Perilous Frontier: Nomadic Empires and China* (New York: Blackwell, 1989).

[47] *Daedalus* 1998/3, special issue on early modernities.

discussion initiated by Victor Lieberman seems (uncharacteristically) to have taken off from Southeast Asia, more precisely the phase of transition from the last Indianized empires to smaller and in some sense more "modern" polities, exemplified by the Theravada monarchies of continental Southeast Asia. Here we would, then, be looking at the fourteenth and fifteenth centuries.[48] And if we add Naitō Konan's pioneering work, mentioned above, we get an East Asia-centred approach, going back to eleventh-century China. Moreover, there is a wide variety of thematic foci: processes of state formation, public spheres, collective identities, commercial development, intellectual revolutions, etc. Finally, it should not be forgotten that some of the same issues have been raised from the opposite perspective: in the context of the "long Middle Ages", lasting until the end of the eighteenth century. Norbert Elias's work is a case in point.

In view of all this, it might be best to treat the notion of "early modernities" as a keyword for multiple lines of inquiry. It reflects the need for a long-term genealogy of modernity, but it has yet to be translated into more diversified comparison of phases and processes. More comparative study of Eurasian transformations in the early second millennium would be an important step in that direction.

---

[48] See the papers in *Modern Asian Studies* 31:3 (1997), later published in book form as Victor Lieberman (ed.), *Beyond Binary Histories: Re-Imagining Eurasia to 1830* (Ann Arbor: University of Michigan Press, 1999). See also Victor Lieberman, *Strange Parallels: Southeast Asia in Global Context, c. 800-1830* (New York: Cambridge University Press, 2003).

CULTURAL CRYSTALLIZATIONS AND WORLD HISTORY: THE AGE OF ECUMENICAL RENAISSANCES

Björn Wittrock

ABSTRACT

In the following I shall propose a way of conceptualising the nature of major societal transformations in the tenth to thirteenth centuries. Historians now largely agree that this is a period of deep-seated change with long-term consequences, a profound cultural crystallization, which affected vast regions of the Old World. At the same time, historians and historically orientated social scientists have hardly begun to articulate a conceptual framework that would open this period for comparative interpretations. It is in this period of still relatively small but growing global interactions that the trajectories of different civilizations become clearly discernible and solidify into institutional premises that come to characterize the histories of societies in the Old World for most of the rest of the second millennium CE. These processes, however, invariably involved a reinterpretation and rearticulation of a real or imagined cosmological and cultural heritage and tradition. It is in this sense that it is possible to speak of an age when there is a renaissance of trans-regional cultural ecumenes. It is for this reason that it is also necessary to indicate the contours of some of the major cosmological and civilizational legacies of relevance to these processes of ecumenical renaissance.

Introduction

In the following I shall propose a way of conceptualising the nature of major societal transformations in the tenth to thirteenth centuries. Historians now largely agree that this is a period of deep-seated change with long-term consequences, a profound cultural crystallization, which affected vast regions of the Old World. At the same time, historians and historically orientated social scientists have hardly begun to articulate a conceptual framework that would open up for comparative interpretations. In fact, it seems to be the case, as argued e.g. by Adolphson, Stephenson and Arjomand (in this volume), that even some of the most important among those few categories that have long been used for such purposes—with the comparative analysis of 'feudalism' in Western

Europe and Japan as perhaps the most obvious case in point—do not stand up to findings of contemporary scholarship.

Maybe the most famous example in the history of social science of a learned and wide-ranging comparative inquiry of the trajectories of different civilizations is that of Max Weber in his three massive volumes on the sociology of the great world religions first published in 1920-21.[1] In these volumes, full of empirical synthesis and comparative reflections, Weber's declared purpose is however not to engage in a broad comparative analysis *per se* but rather to discover, in the study of non-European contexts, points of comparison to 'our occidental cultural religions'.[2] In fact, the whole introduction, *Vorbemerkung*, starts with a passage highlighting the specificity and unique character of Western science and then asserts the unique nature of the major societal institutions in the Occident that are ultimately constituted by a specifically Western notion of rationality. Thus it is also only natural that Weber begins the collection with his famous analysis of the Protestant ethic and the spirit of capitalism. The achievements of the West implicitly serve as self-evident points of departure for comparative reflection. This entails, as noted by Arjomand (in this volume), that comparative interpretations tend to be cast 'in terms of the *absence* of certain preconditions'.

The very first question formulated by Weber in the introduction to the three volumes is: 'which chain of conditions has entailed that precisely on the terrain of the Occident, and only here, cultural manifestations appeared, which however—as we like to imagine—were placed in a direction of development of *universal* importance and validity?'[3] The immediately following sentence then reads: 'Only in the Occident is there '*science*' at the stage of development that we today recognize as 'valid'.' It is then not surprising that Weber later on ventures a number of statements about the unique nature of Western cultural, economic, political and administrative institutions as in the assertion that 'the legally trained civil servant as carrier of the most important functions of everyday life, has not been known in any country as in the modern Occident'.[4] Against the background of our current knowledge

---

[1] Max Weber, *Gesammelte Aufsätze zur Religionssoziologie*. I (Tübingen: J. C. B. Mohr (Paul Siebeck), 1920; II. *Hinduismus und Budhismus* (1921); III. *Das antike Judentum* (1920).

[2] Ibid., p. 15.

[3] Ibid., p. 3. The translations of this and the following quotations are mine.

[4] Ibid.

of the history of e.g. China, a statement of this type no longer looks like a bold conjecture but rather as an untenable claim.

If so, it is an urgent but difficult challenge to start to try to grasp these transformations both in empirical and conceptual terms. I shall argue that it is possible to view these transformations as processes of deep-seated cultural crystallization. One element in this type of analysis is the effort to link conceptual change to processes of socio-political transformations and upheavals. Another one is to explore different varieties of social formations both in ancient times and in the contemporary period. In this context, several colleagues and I have for instance argued that it is more fruitful and reasonable to discern different varieties of both modernity and of axiality, 'multiple modernities' and 'multiple axialities', rather than to subsume significant variations under all-embracing and historically blind categories.[5] Here the focus is on a third equally momentous period, namely that of the tenth to thirteenth centuries, when major civilizational trajectories became rearticulated and institutionally entrenched in a way that is still with us in many respects. In some contexts, I have labelled this period an age of ecumenical renaissances.

In these centuries there occurred processes of agricultural growth, urban expansion, elite contestation and state-formation across the Eurasian hemisphere that should not only been seen in terms of processes of institutional change. Rather they were intimately related to cultural processes that involved a questioning but more often a re-articulation of earlier forms of cultural attachment. Indeed, it has been argued that it is only in these centuries in the beginning of the second millennium CE—rather than during the Axial Age and the emergence of the great world religions—that the major civilizations of a world of agro-literate societies are distinctly formed and become clearly demarcated from each other, both in their self-image and that of members of other societies. They are also the centuries when cultural and institutional patterns emerge that we may characterize as seminal for shaping the later characteristically modern societies. It is in this context that some authors have used the expression 'early modernities'.[6]

---

[5] See e.g. the Winter issue 2000 of *Daedalus*, Vol. 129, No. 1; reprinted as S. N. Eisenstadt (ed.), *Multiple Modernities* (New Brunswick, N.J.: Transaction, 2002).

[6] 'Early Modernities', *Daedalus* 127:3 (Summer 1998); reprinted as S. N. Eisenstadt, Wolfgang Schluchter and Björn Wittrock (eds), *Public Spheres and Collective Identities* (New Brunswick, N.J.: Transaction Press, 2001).

It is in this period of still relatively small but growing global inter-actions, that the trajectories of different civilizations become clearly dis-cernible and solidify into institutional premises that come to characterize the histories of societies in the Old World for most of the rest of the second millennium CE. These processes, however, invariably involved a reinterpretation and rearticulation of a real or imagined cosmologi-cal and cultural heritage and tradition. It is in this sense that it is pos-sible to speak of an age when there is a renaissance of trans-regional cultural ecumenes. It is for this reason that it is also necessary in a first section briefly to indicate the contours of some of the major cosmo-logical and civilizational legacies of relevance to these processes of ecu-menical renaissance. The alternative would be to stay with a purely structural and institutional account. However such an account would either tie the analysis to precisely those conceptual categories that should be transcended—or else remain on a descriptive, rather than a con-ceptually articulated, level. I will then proceed as follows.

Firstly, I shall outline a conceptual framework for the analysis of cul-tural crystallisations and articulate an understanding of the nature of the civilizational trajectories that emerged in the Axial Age, i.e. in the centuries around the middle of the first millennium BCE. *Secondly* I shall describe in empirical terms what I take to be key elements in the changes occurring in high cultures across Eurasia in the early second millen-nium CE. I will outline some of the main paths of development that emerged during this period in different parts of the Old World. *Thirdly*, I shall suggest how these transformations may be interpreted with the help of basic conceptual categories that I take to be crucial in shed-ding light on changes occurring in this, as in other, periods of cultural crystallization.

The Idea of the Axial Age

One step in the elaboration of the research programme, indicated above, is to examine some lineages in scholarship that seem exceptionally promising in such a wide perspective. One important tradition of rele-vance to a reconstructive research programme in social theory and world history is the one that is associated with the works of Max and Alfred Weber, Karl Jaspers, Eric Voegelin, and S. N. Eisenstadt, who have all highlighted the cultural constitution of some of the most enduring social practices and institutions. Jaspers, to take jut one of these names, argued in his book, *Vom Urspung und Ziel der Geschichte*,[7] that our understanding of history is related to the emergence and institutionalisation of forms of critical reflexivity. Needless to say, it is, to some extent, an arbitrary decision whether that moment is associated by the most basic human activities in the form of the emergence of language itself or with some other form of human articulation. Jaspers argued that the emergence and institutionalisation of critical reflexivity is associated with the emergence of forms of thought that clearly transcend activities associated with the daily lives and needs of human beings. Thus it has to be possible to identify the expression of forms of thinking that involve an explicit formulation of ideas about human life beyond the constraints of existence as it looks at a specific time and place.

In other words, Jaspers believed that the distinctive feature in the emergence of human history, as opposed to the evolution of the human species, is the manifestation of a specific capacity. This was the capacity of human beings to reflect upon and to give expression to an image of the world as having the potential of being different from what it was perceived to be here and now. The emergence of such images of the world, based on critical reflection, marked, in Jaspers' classical formulation, the transition from *Mythos* to *Logos*, a breakthrough in critical reflexivity and, indeed, the emergence of history in the sense of the epoch in human existence characterised by a reflexive, historical consciousness.[8] He termed this period the Axial Age. In temporal terms he located it in the centuries around the middle of the first millennium BCE.

The idea of the Axial Age, as outlined by Jaspers, had the character of a bold idea briefly sketched. The same is true of analogous formulations by Alfred Weber and Eric Voegelin. In the 1970's this idea was taken up the Harvard sinologist Benjamin Schwartz and a group of prominent scholars, including Peter Brown, Louis Dumont, Eric Weil and Robert Darnton, in a special issue of the journal *Daedalus*, devoted to the theme 'Wisdom, Revelation, and Doubt: Perspectives on the first Millennium BCE'.[9] The idea was explored later and elaborated by S. N.

---

[7] Jaspers, 1949; English translation, *The Origin and Goal of History*, Yale University Press, 1953.

[8] In fact, Jasper's notion was not altogether different from the one Hegel proposed in his lectures on the philosophy of history, although in Hegel's case the ascription, as in the case of Iran, and denial—as in his statement that India does not have a history—of such a capacity was heavily imbued with an empirical bias that cannot but be called Eurocentric.

[9] *Daedalus*, 104:2 (Spring 1975).

Eisenstadt who, with Wolfgang Schluchter as the other principal investigator, made it the focus of a sustained research programme. In collaboration with a large number of historians and linguists Eisenstadt extended the analysis considerably. It has, without achieving universal acclaim but also without being convincingly refuted, been the subject of two decades of intense scholarly debate, involving ancient historians, historians of religion and philosophy, and linguists.[10] In a recent volume an effort is made to take stock of this debate but also to indicate the long-term consequences and relevance of this debate to key problems in present-day historically orientated scholarship on major transformations of societies and, indeed, civilizational legacies.[11]

The concept of the Axial Age encompasses deep-seated intellectual and cosmological shifts that occurred in different forms but with striking, if relative, simultaneity, across the Eurasian hemisphere. These shifts were manifested in such different forms as the thought of Confucius and, two centuries later, Mencius in China, Buddha in India, the Hebrew prophetical movement and the classical age in Greek philosophy. Neither in the early formulations of Jaspers, nor in the more recent ones by scholars collaborating with S. N. Eisenstadt, has there been an entirely successful effort to relate these cosmological shifts to other types of human activities. Maybe the most important direction in future research directions is to spell out the links between the set of intellectual and cosmological breakthroughs and sea-changing institutional transformations that a limited sense of the concept of the Axial Age denotes.

Jaspers' position rests on the assumption that in the centuries around the middle of the first millennium BCE a major shift occurred in the way reflectively articulate human beings in some of the high cultures in the Eurasian hemisphere reconceptualised their existential position. The breakthrough was manifested in different ways in the different civilizations of the Eurasian hemisphere. However in all forms it involved the textual articulation of an increasing human reflexivity and *reflexive consciousness*. This is what Jaspers saw as the most basic feature: an abil-

---

[10] Among these publications the following ones by S. N. Eisenstadt may be specially mentioned, 'The Axial Age: The Emergence of Transcendental Visions and the Rise of Clerics', *European Journal of Sociology* 1982, 23(2): 294-314; *The Origins and Diversity of Axial Age Civilizations*. Albany, N.Y.: State University of New York Press, 1986; *Kulturen der Achsenzeit. Teil 1 und 2*. Frankfurt/M: Suhrkamp, 1987; *Kulturen der Achsenzeit II.Teil 1, 2 und 3*. Frankfurt/M: Suhrkamp, 1992.

[11] Johann P. Arnason, S. N. Eisenstadt, and Björn Wittrock (eds), *Axial Civilizations and World History* (Leiden: Brill, 2004).

ity to use reason to transcend the immediately given. This reflexivity was manifested in dramatic shifts in four major dimensions, namely the following:

Firstly, an elaboration of more reflective cosmologies in terms of either the immanence of human existence or a shift in the direction of the positing of a fundamental and discursively argued separation between a *mundane* and a *transcendental sphere*. This also involved an *articulation* and *interpretation* of such cosmologies in terms not only of their oral mediation but also of their textual *inscription* and the emergence of a set of rules for the authoritative interpretation of such texts. Such processes of codification and standardisation inevitably entailed breaches with some previously co-existing set of beliefs and practices. They also entailed the potentials for new interpretative contestations. Thereby, of course, the stage was set not only for the articulation and diffusion of orthodoxy but also for heterodox challenges.

Secondly, the articulation and inscription of an increasing *historical consciousness*, an awareness of the temporal location and the limitations of human existence and thereby also a sense of relative contingency;

Thirdly, new conceptualisations of social bonds and connectedness, i.e. imaginations of what might be called sociality.

Fourthly, an increasing awareness of the *malleability* of human existence, of the potentials of *human action* and human agentiality within the bounds of human mundane temporality or, as in the case of Iranian culture, with respect to the relationship between actions in a mundane and a transcendental sphere. Conceptualisations of agentiality tended during the axial transformations to become increasingly premised on what might be termed more individualistic assumptions than had previously been the case.

This, I maintain, is the core of the meaning of the Axial Age in its original formulation, and it is this core that has subsequently been elaborated in various ways. It is to my mind important to see that any particular articulation of a position on any of these existential dimensions will inevitably involve some assumptions that are contextually bound and culturally specific. It would for instance be illegitimate to tie the meaning of the Axial Age to an insistence on the occurrence of some specific cosmology, say one been premised on notions of transcendence as opposed to immanence, or on some specific account of the dramatic increase in historical consciousness that we associate with the Axial Age.

What is not culturally specific is the idea that the Axial Age is a period of deep change on fundamental dimensions of human existence, namely radical shifts, as textually manifested, in reflexive consciousness concerning *cosmology, historicity, sociality and agentiality.*

The change is broadly cotemporaneous across vast regions of the Old World. The Axial Age is then an epoch, but not the only one, of a profound cultural crystallisation that affects these inevitable existential dimensions in some of the high cultures across Eurasia. These shifts entail the consolidation or the emergence of a set of different cosmologies and make possible a set of different institutional paths of development of lasting importance.

For all contestations about historical accounts, such a delimitation of the notion of the Axial Age provides not only a fruitful starting point for the study of global history and for an understanding of its relevance to the social and human sciences at large. It is, I claim, the only possibility of giving the notion of the Axial Age a meaning that does not entail an unjustifiable teleology and some form of cultural imposition.

One problematic question is that of the relationship of political and societal formations before and after what is often termed the axial breakthrough. It seems undeniable that Jaspers argues that the Axial Age constitutes the origin of history, in the sense of the history of human beings who have consciously reflected about their own location in temporal and cosmological terms and tried to form their own existence from the vantage point of such reflections. This is an argument that tends to deny the historicity of previous civilizations in a way that cannot be made compatible with available historical research.

Contrary to Jaspers' assertions, several of the contributors to the Arnason, Eisenstadt, Wittrock volume[12] highlight the fact that in China, Greece and the Near East a key factor behind the dramatic increase in reflexivity and critical discussion may have been precisely the breakdown of the established practices and assumptions prevailing in earlier civilizations. Whether we look at Egypt, Greece, Mesopotamia or China during the Shang and Zhou empires, it is simply not possible to defend what Jaspers seems to assert, namely that these civilizations somehow fall outside of history, even in the specific sense of the word employed by Jaspers himself.

The important question is rather to what extent the axial transformations did or did not involve continuities relative to these earlier civilizations. Maybe the most fruitful way to approach this problematique

---

[12] Op. cit. 2004.

is to focus on the relationship between two types of components: firstly the interpretation and redefinition by key Axial Age writers of an imagined legacy of their own societies and civilizations; secondly their own linguistic strategies and conceptual innovations that often involve the generalisation, or rather universalisation, of key characteristics in their interpretations of these traditions. Thus the Confucian ethic involves not so much completely new conceptualisations, but rather an articulation of a tradition, synthetic in its own ways, and the universalisation of some of the most important virtues, which had traditionally been seen as limited to the aristocratic strata. In this case, as in several of the others, axiality is a form of reaction to a new type of human condition where neither the structures of kinship and physical proximity, nor those of a self-legitimising empire, suffice any longer to embed the individual in a context of meaning and familiarity. The emergence of the world religions is also part of this problematique.

The relationship between the Axial Age and the emergence and diffusion of the great world religions has been extensively examined. The idea of such a relationship has been at the core of much reasoning concerning the Axial Age hypothesis. Again, it seems undeniable that the intellectual and ontological shift, described in terms of a breakthrough, has important links to deep-seated shifts in religious practices. It is however also clear that the exact nature of such links is in many cases open to quite different interpretations.

In most interpretations of the Axial Age, a relationship is discerned between the Axial Age as a shift in cosmology and ontology on the one hand, and the emergence of imperial-like political orders on the other. This raises three questions that concern *firstly* the imagined nature of axial- and pre-axial age political orders, *secondly* the continuities of such orders and, *thirdly*, the consequences of the axial breakthrough for political orders.

As to the *first* question, clearly, as argued by Arnason, Jaspers' characterisation of pre-Axial political orders in terms of 'small states and cities' is not tenable.[13] It is, as already argued, possible to delineate a meaningful conceptualisation of the Axial Age as an epoch in global history that involved profound shifts in at least four fundamental and inescapable dimensions of human existence, namely cosmology, historicity, sociality and agentiality. The Axial Age is not the only period

---

[13] Johann P. Arnason, 'The Axial Age and its Interpreters: Reopening a Debate', in Arnason, Eisenstadt, and Wittrock (2004), 19-48.

where deep-seated shifts of this type occur. It is, however, probably the most consequential cultural crystallisation before the Common Era.

The redefinitions, characterising a period of cultural crystallisation, will always occur in a given historical context and the practical and institutional implications of the shifts mean that a range, but certainly not an unlimited range, of new horizons of human practice open up. Thus while there is no one-to-one relation between a given shift in culture and cosmology and a particular institutional path of development, it is still possible to argue that in a given context some institutional paths are made conceivable, in a literal sense of the word, and others are not.

There are five distinctly different paths of axial transformations linking cultural and cosmological shits to institutional transformations, none of which should be given either empirical or normative preferred status. In the present context, I shall only outline their differences by the briefest indication.

Firstly, there is the development in the Near East whereby, in a complex process of influence and juxtaposition, the Mosaic distinction (to use Jan Assmann's terminology) between true and false in religion and, as a consequence, a distinction between religion and politics, is being drawn not, despite several preparatory steps, in Ancient Egypt but in Ancient Israel. Eventually this distinction, in the prophetic age and in second temple Judaism gives rise to a path of development that may perhaps be termed transcendental-interpretative.

Significant elements include processes of textual inscription and standardisation as well as interpretative contestation and the interplay between carriers of orthodoxy and heterodoxy. The participants in these contestations exhibit a remarkable independence relative to political power. Sometimes this reflects a withdrawal from it. However, more often their activities impinge upon the world of rulership, sometimes explicitly, sometimes inadvertently, sometimes as heterodox dissent or even rebellion, and sometimes as support for established power.

Secondly, there is a related path, fundamentally influenced by Near Eastern developments, but in key respects distinctly different. It is a tradition that gradually emerges in the Greek world and that may be termed a philosophical-political path of development. It involves contestation and deliberation that exhibit intense concern about human potentials and action, about the location of human beings in history and constant reflection on the human condition.

However, in this case, a clear distinction between a transcendental and a mundane sphere, something absolutely central to the transcendental-interpretative tradition, is relatively insignificant. Nor can one speak of a standardised religious cosmology inscribed in codified texts. Instead contestation is dialogical, if often textually transmitted, and has a philosophical and largely pragmatic character with the political and moral life of a given community, a polis, as an inevitable reference point. The key protagonists in these contestations act in a context that is characterized by a previously unknown combination of intellectual independence, institutional autonomy and political engagement.

Thirdly, there is the particular Chinese path that involves, at least from a period a millennium earlier than the Axial Age proper, the gradual merging and synthesis of different regional ritualistic practices and political orders in a broad synthetic cultural tradition that may be termed universal-inclusive. Key features of not only cultural but also political order are clearly articulated hundreds of years before the Axial Age and in some respects, Confucius, Mozi and later Mencius and the legalists write against the background of a perceived loss of cohesion, and indeed the demise, of this earlier order and seek a renewed articulation of it. Cultural and scientific developments can be and have been (as by Harbsmeier in this volume) described by a wide set of stepwise shifts but nevertheless exhibit important ruptures and advances in the period of the Axial Age, as do certain political and social thought with a renewed emphasis on both tradition, history and human agency.

A fundamental feature of this path of axiality is that it is universal-inclusive but at the same time characterised by a high degree of contingency even in the political sphere. Thus already in pre-axial Zhou political thought the Mandate of Heaven transfers the ultimate legitimacy to political order. However, it is a revocable mandate and improper conduct is incompatible with the maintenance of this mandate. Therefore Heavenly sanctioned imperial rule is nonetheless contingent and open to doubt, critique and potentially revolt. Similarly, there is a synthetic cultural order composed of highly different original traditions, some of which may perhaps best be understood as forms of moral philosophy, and two of which, Confucianism and Daoism, have little if any concern for a distinction between transcendental and mundane spheres. Precisely for this reason the universal-inclusive path of the Sinic world allows for and involves constant philosophical contestation between different traditions. In a sense, a Mosaic distinction need not be drawn in a context where the relationship between political and religious order has always been much more open-ended than in the early Near East polities of Egypt and Mesopotamia.

Fourthly, in India early Buddhism constitutes an axial challenge to Vedic religion. As discussed by Sheldon Pollock,[14] this challenge involves, through a process of semantic appropriation, transvaluation and contestation, a focus on those aspects that have here been delimited as central to the Axial Age, namely a focus on history and agentiality, and thereby, brings out the potentials of a critical stance towards what are no longer semi-naturalistic practices, but rather conventions that may be transgressed.

It is precisely in reaction to this challenge that an articulation of Vedic religion occurs. The Indic world of Vedic religion may have been distinctly non-axial, but Vedic religion could not avoid an engagement with the cultural systems that grew out of the early axial transformations. Whereas, both the philosophical-political axiality of Greece and the universal-inclusive axiality of the Sinic world had political order as its explicit or implicit centre of attention, the political implications of the Indic path—let us call it pluralistic-semantic—largely, and with the possible exception of the Maurya Empire under Ashoka, remained potentials or entirely contingent.

Fifthly, the geographical and political space where all of the major traditions of Eurasia actually interacted is the area of the Achaemenid Empire and its Hellenistic and Iranian successors. In many ways, cultural traditions in the Iranian lands came to serve as direct or indirect sources of inspiration for several of the world religions and imperial orders. However, knowledge of key aspects religious, and even political, practices not only in the Achaemenid Empire but also the Sassanian Empire is lacking. Nevertheless the path of development in the Iranian lands may perhaps be termed one of a dualistic-agential tradition, where the relationship between political and religious order is seen as one of mutual dependence and close interaction, where there is a distinction between a transcendental and a mundane sphere but where the battles within these spheres have direct implications for all actions in the mundane sphere.

It is therefore at the same time a tradition with an articulated cosmology but in its dualistic conceptualisation of this cosmology it differs fundamentally from the cosmology of the mainstream of Judaism,

---

[14] In Arnason et al. 2004.

Christendom and Islam. This however, also means that the cosmological distinction between a transcendental and a mundane sphere is consistent with a strong this-worldly orientation of practical engagement and action in the realm of political order. The relationship of the main intellectual-religious carriers of this cosmology to political power is characterized by proximity and reciprocal dependence. As in other forms of axiality, there are also forms of heterodoxy and dissent. However, on the whole, there is a more explicit and direct link to imperial power here than found along the other paths of axiality.

The Achaemenid Empire came to exert a far-reaching influence on later types of imperial orders in the region of the Mediterranean and the Near East. In the first millennium CE the Sassanian Empire was in its own self-conception the legitimate heir of the Achaemenid Empire.

The Byzantine Eastern Roman Empire—for half a millennium the main competitor of the Sassanian Empire in the Eastern Mediterranean and Near Eastern region—with its Hellenistic and urban legacy was structurally different from the Sassanian Empire. However from the seventh century onwards it increasingly, not least as a result of the loss of rich urban centres in Syria and Egypt in the wake of the original Islamic onslaught, came to exhibit many features reminiscent of the Iranian Imperial model. This was so in terms of changes in military-territorial organisation in a direction that in medieval Western Europe came to be called feudal. It was also the case in terms of a gradual change in relationships between political and religious order.

The Achaemenid Empire was the first imperial political order to be premised on a cosmology that was axial and at the same time involved a close reciprocal, but not symmetric, relationship between the leading representatives of political and cosmological-religious order. The same is true for the Sassanian Empire and for the successor of that Empire, namely the new Islamic political order, at least as it emerged with the establishment of the Abbasid Caliphate.

As was the case with the Roman Empire, the Achaemenid Empire was characterized by a tolerance of minority cultures and languages. Unlike the Roman Empire, it did not engage in efforts to promote the language of the rulers, i.e. Old Persian, relative to the language of other peoples of the Empire. However, the Iranian Empires, as well as the classical Roman Empire, involved elements of, to use Sheldon Pollock's expression, ethno-transcendence, i.e. the assignment of a crucial place in the imperial project to an ethnically defined people that is linked both to the temporal extension of empire and to its divine protection.

Both the Roman and Iranian imperial patterns are distinctly different
from that of India, but also from the cultural-political order of Ancient
Israel and Ancient Greece during the early Axial transformations—and
of course also from that of non-Roman and non-Axial Europe. In both
Ancient Greece and Ancient Israel the position of the intellectual carriers of interpretative elaborations was characterized by greater independence relative to the holders of political power. This is again one
reason why it would be erroneous to assume a necessary relationship
between axiality and imperial order. One may indeed argue, that the
post-Axial imperial orders, while often embracing a cosmology of Axial
origins, often involved severe institutional constraints and a reduction
in intellectual autonomy for the carriers of axial thought.

Perhaps we may summarize, with all inevitable simplifications, some
of the points above in a figure.

If anything, this figure highlights three conclusions indicated above:

Firstly, a qualitative increase in reflexivity, historicality and agentiality is characteristic of the Axial Age and is the very premise for any
reasoned distinction between political order and religious-cultural order
and hence for the opening up of the possibility of a challenge to cultural claims of legitimacy of political order. Once this possibility has
been conceptually permitted, it is a potential that can never henceforth
be 'unthought', i.e. the potential of a fundamental challenge of established order can never again be permanently removed. However, the
cultural-cosmological construct that allows for such a distinction may,
but does not need to, rest on a crucial distinction between a transcendental and a mundane sphere. In fact in four of the five paths of axiality, this is not the case.

Secondly, the institutional position of the interpreters of a given cultural-religious cosmology determines whether the potentials of the increases
in reflexivity are being realized or not. Within each of the five paths
of axiality there was always interplay between orthodoxy and heterodoxy, and there were always contending articulations of a given cultural-cosmological order. Often, as in the cases of both India and China,
there was also always contention between deeply different cosmologies.
Even in the case of Sassanian Iran, Zoroastrian orthodoxy had always
to contend with heterodox interpretations (Zurvanism, Mazdakism).

Thirdly, there are fundamental differences in terms of the ethno-lin-
guistic force of the different paths of axiality. From the perspective of
our own age, it is difficult not to reflect upon the fact that virtually all
modern imperial orders reflect a form of Roman-Eastern Mediterranean

Figure 1. Five Paths of Axiality

Region of Emergence	Cultural-Cosmological Focus	Relation to Political Power	Ethno-linguistic Force
Ancient Israel	transcendental-interpretative	strong independence	autonomous
Greece	philosophical-political	strong independence	weakly ecumenical
China	universal-inclusive	weak dependence	strongly ecumenical
India	pluralistic-semantic	strong independence	weakly ecumenical
Iran	dualistic-agential	strong dependence	Ethno-transcendence cum linguistic pluralism

path rather than the less impositional ones of some of the other axial paths or the more ecumenical path of one of them, i.e. China. From the point of view of modern social thought and with the newly awakened interest in imperial orders, it seems that the study of the Axial Age, if nothing else, might serve an urgent need to broaden the range of imagination of modern social and political thought.

The Axial Age involved a series of momentous transformations that affected a number of cultures across Eurasia within a relatively limited range of time (from a global historical perspective). These transformations came to have far-reaching implications. They involved, as emphasized earlier, deep-seated shifts along the key existential dimensions of cosmology, historicity, sociality and agentiality and constitute a period of profound cultural crystallisation in world history by determining important parameters for cultural and political developments for centuries to come.

However, this does not commit us to either a belief in the end of history, nor to a hypothesis that the particular reconfiguration of positions on these dimensions would have to be the same or even similar in different cultures or civilizations. There are also momentous reconfigurations of such positions. The transformations of the eleventh to thirteenth centuries—what in another context I have termed a period

of Ecumenical Renaissances[15]—constitutes another such period of reconfiguration and should also be examined in comparative terms both
relative to the Axial Age and to the age of modernity in the latter half
of the second millennium CE.

The Cultural Crystallizations of the Tenth to Thirteenth Centuries: An Age of Ecumenical Renaissances?

At the turn of the first millennium CE the imperial orders, which had
emerged in the wake of the Axial Age, had all withered or been fundamentally transformed. Trade routes across the Old World were more
important than in the Axial Age, but still in the context of Western
Europe, as argued by R. I. Moore (in this volume), of subordinate
importance relative to local trade. However the political and cultural
orders of the high civilizations across the hemisphere were all in process
of challenge and deep-seated change. Some of them—most prominently
perhaps China and the Byzantine world and least prominently perhaps
Japan and Western Europe—were threatened, if not overwhelmed, in
their engagement with the peoples of the nomadic regions of the hemisphere. More generally, the empires that had emerged in the wake of
the Axial Age, the Roman and the Han Empires, but also the Maurya
Empire, had long succumbed. Even the Sassanian Empire, that had
overcome and succeeded the Parthian, and which had successfully with-
stood incursions of Central Asian nomadic peoples, had itself succumbed
as a result of the conquest of Islam.

Only China (of the Tang and the Song dynasties) and the Byzantine
Empire represented exceptions and could lay claim to more sustained,
if truncated and reformulated, paths of some continuity in cultural and
even institutional terms. A more general pattern of decline or conquest
through civil war or external invasion is however true both for Western
Europe of the Carolingian and Ottonian Empires and of the Islamic
world of the Abbasid Caliphate and later of the Seljuk Sultanate. Much
later, it was of course to be exemplified in the emergent power of the
Ottomans, the Safavi and the Mughals.

For all the high civilizations of the later centuries of the first millennium and the first centuries of the second millennium there was the
parallel phenomena of economic expansion, trade and interactions amidst

---

[15] Björn Wittrock, 'Social Theory and Global History: The Three Cultural Crystallizations', *Thesis Eleven*, Number 65, May 2001, pp. 27-50.

processes of elite contestation reshaping the political order, alongside the more or less serious threats of external incursions. By the turn of the first millennium such threats in the far West of Europe, had largely subsided. The earlier peripheries of the North and East had become parts of Christendom and attacks from across the Mediterranean had gradually subsided. In the Islamicate, Hindu and Chinese civilizations, however, waves of incursions originating in Central Asia, were prominent. In parallel to patterns of commerce, conquest and conversion, processes of deep-seated cultural engagement and reinterpretation also occurred across all of the high civilizations of the Old World. This engagement took place in terms of reconceptualisations along the same dimensions as during the Axial Age. An important consequence was a series of efforts to form a synthesis of the fundamental features of the tradition of a civilization with the emergent challenges to it.

In Europe this entailed intense deliberations and controversies about the relationship between the tradition of Latin Christendom and the philosophical and linguistic tradition of classical antiquity. In China it ushered in the neo-Confucian movement, the reassertion of the virtues of that tradition and, consequently, the preservation of Sinic civilization as a cultural and linguistic ecumene. In Hindu civilization the encounter with the cultural and also political influence of Islamic civilization led to reformulations and rearticulations of Hindu tradition in the light of these challenges. Whereas the neo-Confucian movement and the preservation of an all-encompassing political order in China—and here the interlude of the Yuan dynasty represented a rupture only to a marginal extent—entailed the preservation of an ecumenical language, both India and Europe experienced what might be termed the first steps in a secular shift towards vernacularisation of linguistic practices and, particularly in the Indian context, a localisation of religious practices. In both contexts ecumenical and vernacular linguistic practices would co-exist for centuries to come but processes of a fundamentally transforming nature had emerged. In Europe the emergence of religious practices tied to new monastic orders entailed closer links to local communities, but also served as a powerful instrument for homogenizing efforts—as was the case with e.g. the activities of the Cistercian order in the newly Christianized parts of Northern and Eastern Europe.[16]

---

[16] See e.g. Klaniczay in this issue but also his volume *Holy Rulers and Blessed Princesses: Dynastic Cults in Medieval Europe* (Cambridge: Past and Present Publications, Cambridge University Press, 2002).

In the latter part of the first millennium CE and in the beginning of the second one there is in Western Europe but also across the hemisphere an emerging effort to recreate ecumenical and imperial orders, often linked to urban and commercial advances. Beside the Ottonian Empire in Western Europe, both the Song dynasty in China and the Fatimid in Egypt as well as the revival of the Byzantine Empire under the Macedonian dynasty fall within this pattern. What occurs is a hemispheric-wide movement where all the high civilizations are confronted by not only practical challenges but also by challenges to deeply held presuppositions and cosmologies. In this process the different transregional cultural ecumenes had to articulate and synthesise core components of their ecumenes in the face of both expansion and challenge.

Processes of agricultural growth, urban expansion, elite contestation and state-formation were closely related to cultural processes that involved an articulation of forms of cultural as well institutional attachment. Jointly these processes set the stage for long-term trajectories of the agro-literate societies of the Old World and in the last instance also for the world of multiple modernities and global interactions and encounters in which we ourselves live.

The contributions to this issue highlight seven interlinked processes that were operating, if in different degrees, across the civilizations of the hemisphere at the turn of the first millennium CE, namely:

- *Agricultural growth*, a phenomenon that occurred as a result of changes in production techniques, including new types of ploughing, new types of crops as well as demographic changes (not least in China during the Tang-Song transition).
- Agricultural growth in turn allowed for the emergence of *new cities* and new types of *urban life*, but also to the emergence of guilds of artisans. Urban developments are furthermore related to efforts at articulating notions of rights both in agriculture and in urban life.
- This increasing role of urban life is also related to growth in commerce, to some extent long-range commerce but predominantly local and regional commerce.
- In most civilizations, processes of *elite formation* and *elite contestation*, particularly between traditional and clan-like older elites, often with relationships to imperial courts, and new military and clerical elites.
- The emergence of these new types of elites as well as that of guilds and other new orders are closely related to the emergence of new types of *institutions for the training of clerical and religious elites*, capable of articulating an interpretation of often quasi-judicial rules and laws.

The emergence of universities in Europe, of neo-Confucian academies in China and the growing support for madrasas in many parts of the Islamicate world are examples of this.

- The rise of new elites had important implications for the overall social order as well as for the nature and regulation of social interactions outside of the realm of government proper, what might even be termed a *civil society*. Contrary to the assumptions of Whiggish literature on the history of civil society—a concept which incidentally is introduced into European discourse from translations of Aristotle— the constitution of a new civil society is almost invariably associated with the decline or disappearance of earlier forms of social interactions, often of a more fleeting and less regulated kind.

- Elite contestations tend to focus on what modern social science would describe as processes of *state-formation* but what might better be termed contestation about the nature and control of *political order*. Across all of Eurasia imperial orders are fundamentally transformed in the tenth to thirteenth centuries.

With much simplification we may discern paths of development of some of the major successors of the five types of axial civilizations characterized above. However, there are, as already argued, no unbroken continuities. Furthermore while axial transformations originated in some relatively clearly delimited regions of the Old World, while others, including the old civilizations of Mesopotamia and Egypt were not part of these transformations, axial civilizations came to have lasting consequences for wide regions of Eurasia far beyond their places of emergence. Therefore any examination of the transformations in the early second millennium CE and their links to axial and non-axial traditions must be highly selective. In the present context, I will limit my brief comments to a juxtaposition of paths of development in the West and East of Eurasia and only add some comments about other regions. In practical terms the focus will be on three, to a limited extent four, regions of the hemisphere—the worlds of Western, and to some extent, Eastern Christendom, as well as of China and Japan—which may be said to mainly draw on the legacies of two, or rather three, of the five axial civilizations discerned earlier, namely those of the Hellenistic and the Sinic worlds and to some extent that of ancient Israel. Needless to say, inspiration from the two other axial civilizations may also have been of importance in the far West and East, but to a more limited extent. It is difficult to imagine cultural evolution either in the Mediterranean or the Sinic world without influences from Zoroastrianism and Manichaeism extending over many centuries. Similarly, of course, the entire history of Buddhism in East Asia is premised on complex links to the Indic world, and it is hardly coincidental that the probably most well known and popular literary work in the Sinic world till this day is the famous tale from the Tang period, Journey to the West, i.e. India.

The Standard View of the Rise of the Western World: A Reinterpretation

In such a wide context we may briefly highlight key features of the traditional Weberian interpretation of the emergence of a distinctly European trajectory that in the last instance is held to explain Europe's path to modernity. There can be no doubt that for an understanding of the particular European development, the standard Weberian account provides a highly suggestive and useful interpretation. This interpretation emphasises four coterminous transformations that occurred in the beginning of the first millennium CE.[17]

A key element was the increasing recognition, in the wake of the so-called *Papal Revolution*, of a de-facto separation of ecclesiastical and mundane power. In the political praxis of Western Europe, this bifurcation excluded two other forms of political order, namely those of theocracy and of caesaro-papism. It also set the stage for the institutionalisation of forms of contestation and pluralism in matters of the utmost importance to a society.

Equally important was what has come to be termed the *Feudal Revolution*, involving an articulation of a variety of rights and obligations that could be claimed and upheld in various public fora. Thus we may say an incipient society had been created, where the rule of law has been trans-

---

[17] A sophisticated recent formulation of the Weberian position is provided by Wolfgang Schluchter in his book *Paradoxes of Modernity: Culture and Conduct in the Theory of Max Weber* (Stanford, Ca: Stanford University Press, 1996). See in particular chapter 4, pp. 179-243. In two issues of the journal *Daedalus* on the themes of *Early Modernities* (Summer 1998, Vol. 127, No. 3) and *Multiple Modernities* (Winter 2000, Vol. 129, No. 1) results are reported from a long-term research programme that tries to look at global historical developments and to rethink key concepts in contemporary social theory; both issues have subsequently been reprinted in book format as S. N. Eisenstadt, Wolfgang Schluchter and Björn Wittrock (eds), *Public Spheres and Collective Identities* (New Brunswick, N.J.: Transaction Press, 2001) and S. N. Eisenstadt (ed.) *Multiple Modernities* (New Brunswick, N.J.: Transaction Press, 2002) respectively. Two relatively recent issues of the journal *Thesis Eleven* on civilizational analysis (May 2000, and August 2000) are also highly relevant to such efforts.

formed from the oral adjudication—familiar in many European societies, not least the Scandinavian ones—to a new type of society. That is a society where the idea has taken root that rights and obligations may be textually inscribed and require interpretation, articulation and competent adjudication by legal scholars.

The growth of urban life, the *Urban Revolution*, did not only entail a stimulus for trade and economic activities. It also tended to be associated with wide-ranging municipal self-government. In some parts of the Holy Roman Empire where effective imperial power had become greatly weakened, such as Northern Italy, new forms of city republican rule took shape. Originally sometimes modelled on an association for common trade purposes, models of city republican government came to exert a deep influence on notions of political rulership in Europe.

This set the stage for an *intellectual revolution* both in scholarly activities themselves and in making possible the existence of multiple fora for intellectual activities, nested in a multiplicity of political and institutional arenas across a Europe that yet formed part of one ecumenical order: Western Christendom. Thus universities were formed as a particular type of self-governing corporation with at least partial autonomy from the Church. This revolution was inherent in the emergence of European universities and in the synthesis of the traditions of Western Christendom and the philosophy of classical antiquity. It also meant that both universities and monastic orders emerged as key institutions in European history.

These processes entailed the emergence of political and intellectual pluralism. They were also related to changes that occurred and that concerned reconceptualisations of notions of cosmology, of history, of social order and of the malleability of mundane existence in terms of human actions. These shifts seem to have been of the greatest importance for the economic transformations of Europe, including such shifts as a radical revaluation—or rather devaluation—of the assessment of usury among the mortal sins. In the reading of Douglass North, the institutional changes most of all entailed that market imperfections were reduced.[18] However, although these changes in Europe were unique, contrary to what most classical social science has tended to assume, they must be seen in the light of analogous changes along similar dimensions of revaluation that were equally prominent in other parts of the

---

[18] Douglass C. North and Robert P. Thomas, *The Rise of the Western World: A New Economic History* (Cambridge: Cambridge University Press, 1973), 5ff.

hemisphere. These shifts outside of the European context came, however, to have radically different consequences in these different contexts.

It should therefore be possible to set the stage for a more truly comparative understanding of the processes occurring outside of the European context, a context that has to date almost exclusively informed the social sciences in their formation of analytical categories. There are for instance striking differences in the formation of collective identities, in the nature of public spheres, in the development of linguistic practices, across the civilizations of Eurasia. Thus in Europe there tends to be, to give but one example briefly referred to above, a slow but secular growth in the use of vernacular languages and a concomitant shift from imperial towards more nationally conceived forms of political order. In the different parts of the Indian subcontinent, on the other hand, Indologists identify a growth of secular literature—but complementing rather than replacing Sanskrit literature. However, as argued by Pollock[19] there was no emergence of clearly territorially bounded, not to speak of national, forms of polities, at least in a European sense of the term. In the Far East, to take but one other example, both classical Chinese and the form and the ideal of imperial order were maintained in spite of the vagaries and turmoil over these centuries.

The contributions to this issue highlight the institutional and social manifestations of the transformations in Europe in the tenth to thirteenth centuries. R. I. Moore effectively demonstrates the extent to which there is a profound transformation of the older types of elites basing their position on violent appropriations internally and externally in a context of permeable borders and vaguely defined rules of ownership and inheritance.[20] In the situation of increasing regulation of the rights and borders attached to land and the possibility of an increasing productivity of agriculture, elites transform themselves into estates with articulated rights, basing their position on extracting revenues from the land and securing the reproduction of family wealth by laws that drastically and suddenly exclude previously legitimate heirs from inheritance, and thereby creating a need to tend for the daughters and second and third sons of elite families. In one sense, the result is a form of histor-

---

[19] In Arnason, Eisenstadt and Wittrock, 2004 and in this issue.

[20] An interesting account that focuses on the intellectual transformations is Marcia L. Colish, *Medieval Foundations of the Western Intellectual Tradition* (New Haven, Conn.: Yale University Press, 1997). An authoritative overview is Robert Bartlett, *The Making of Europe: Conquest, Colonization, and Cultural Change, 950-1350* (London: Allen Lane, The Penguin Press, 1993).

ical compromise, where the newly regulated aristocratic groupings agree to give very substantially to monasteries and other forms of charitable endowments on the crucial condition that these endowments never be used to threaten the position of the donors or their legitimate descendents. The great geographical increase of Western Christendom at the turn of the first millennium CE entailed, as argued by Klaniczay (in this issue), not only a numerical and spatial enlargement as well as the pacification of peoples, the Norsemen and Vikings from the North and the Magyars from the East, who had earlier posed a considerable threat to the central and western regions of the continent. It also involved energetic efforts on the part of the Papacy to strengthen its relative position through the activities of monastic orders, which were themselves innovated and transformed in the process. Similarly and more or less simultaneously, Byzantine Christendom was able to extend its cultural sphere in Eastern Europe by conversions of peoples in the Balkans and, most importantly in the long run perhaps, of the Kievan Rus.

In sum, in the Europe of Latin Christendom a new type of social order emerges, where landed elites control the exercise of violence and where new rules of marriage, inheritance and chastity guarantee the preservation of profitable estates over time. One element of this transformation is the emergence of a stratum of professional military men, knights, seeking the favour of greater or lesser lords for shorter or longer times. However, an ultimately more profound change is the formation of a new kind of governing class, based on clerical skills. All rulership henceforth depends on the competence of new clerical elites that possess the necessary abilities to count, record and adjudicate, and the institutions that provide the necessary skills and training for this. This is, as pointed out by Moore, also a point where developments in the European and Chinese contexts, present both striking analogies and elements of divergence.

East Asian Transformations

There is a long-standing debate in Chinese historiography on the continuities and discontinuities of the period starting with the rise of the Tang Dynasty and ending with the demise of the Dynasty of Southern Song. This debate has to some extent reflected disagreements both concerning interpretation and evaluation. The fact that China achieved its greatest extension during the Tang Dynasty and conversely the history of the Song ended with the Mongol conquest is one such factor that has inevitably influenced perceptions in earlier periods. Scholarship, however, has long since fully recognized the remarkable cultural and economic achievements of China during the Song and the degree to which this period from the late tenth to the late thirteenth centuries was formative of China's intellectual and institutional history. In more recent years scholars such as Paul Jakov Smith have highlighted the extent of continuities across this entire period and even across that from the late Song over the Mongol rule of the Yuan Dynasty to the Ming.[21]

As in the context of Europe, but on a larger scale and earlier in time, there are the parallel developments of an expansion of agricultural production—linked to a demographic shift towards South China—and a growth of urban centres, but also the decline of an old elite of aristocratic clans with close ties to Imperial rule, and even elements of an incipient industrial revolution. The social and economic transformations were contemporaneous with the rise of more organized and increasingly threatening political orders at the western and northern borders of China. As a consequence processes of elite contestation and state formation—or rather renewal of political order and the search for more efficient means of resource mobilization—interact and shape the conditions for the social and cultural transformations.

As in the context of Western Europe, however, one crucial aspect of these transformations is the rise of a governing clerical elite, needless to say with its roots in the old aristocracy but based on an ethic that put a premium on service to the political order and on selection via a far more stringent examination system than any similar grouping elsewhere. It is this elite of Mandarins that at the turn of the first millennium, amidst growing territorial threats, came to embrace ever more ambitious and activist policies designed to enact a programme of comprehensive reform to stave off invasions and to regain territories lost, policies that could not but provoke opposition and critique from parts of the social elites.

The periods following the loss of a substantial part of the Empire in the early twelfth century and the transition from the Northern to the Southern Song were marked by efforts to strengthen central political rule that tended to be thwarted by the lack of efficient control and fiscal authority at the local level. As a result clerical elites tended to

---

[21] A monumental work is Paul Jakov Smith and Richard von Glahn (eds), *The Song-Yuan-Ming Transition in Chinese History* (Cambridge, Ma: Harvard East Asian Monographs, 221; distributed by Harvard University Press, 2003); also see Smith in this volume.

withdraw from the political centre and focus on other more localized arenas, including the family.

One manifestation of these tendencies towards a separation between clerical elites and central political rulership was the articulation of a reform movement from within the clerical elites striving for a renewal based on a revitalization of a core tradition of Confucianism. This so-called Neo-Confucianism, or Learning of the Way (*daoxue*), reflects both resentment over the loss of Chinese heartlands and dissatisfaction with imperial and ministerial rule. It also—and here it is difficult not to think of analogies in the context of Western Europe in roughly the same time—included a focus on family structure and proposals for inheritance and control of property designed to strengthen patrilineal ties and, conversely, to curtail the situation of women. Ironically, these views on women and property only became realisable and institutionalised after the conquest of the Mongol 'barbarians', a created tradition that became further strengthened during the Ming Dynasty.

During in the last years of the Southern Song, what had emerged as a movement of critique and reform came to be embraced, if too late to have any immediate impact, by the political centre, and then, after the fall of the Southern Song, survived at the local level to find a place in local schools and academies in Southern China. As an effective ideology of the educated elite, Neo-Confucianism became predominant only after the fall of the Song and during the new Mongol Dynasty of the Yuan. By then the Chinese educated elite had achieved sufficient autonomy to serve as a carrier of social and political practices irrespective of Dynastic order, and hence also to survive as a ruling stratum under the Ming—and subsequently also under the Qing—thereby providing a unique degree of continuity in the exercise of political and bureaucratic power.

Japanese developments in the beginning of the second millennium CE exhibit many of the features discerned initially in this section as characteristic of developments both in Europe and in China during this period of time. Thus in Japan there was also rapid growth in agricultural production, growth of urban life, increasing commerce both domestically and externally (with China), a movement towards restructuring the basis of traditional elites with less reliance on direct imperial patronage, a deep-seated restructuring of what might be termed civil society as well of the nature of political order. Yet there were, as strongly argued by Adolphson, continuities in the sense of a continued mutually reinforcing relationship between the imperial political elite and religious elites.[22] The rise of a warrior class out of older elites, more directly tied to the imperial order, is also a gradual development that only in the fifteenth century leads to its clear predominance as the ruling class. Rather the persistent pattern is one of continuity between the old imperial order of the Heian period and the power-sharing between imperial political-administrative, religious and military elites of the Kamakura period (from the late twelfth to the mid-fourteenth centuries).

In one sense, economic developments and the need for increased reliance on private assets for the maintenance of elite status paved the way for the emergence of a triangular mode of power-sharing between clerical, religious and military elites during the Kamakura period, in place of an older pattern of imperial rule relying on bureaucratic control for the management and revenues of agricultural land and on religious elites for legitimacy. However, the new commercial and urban elites that grew as a result of economic developments were becoming ever wealthier, but were also consistently excluded from political power. Even so, the economic needs of society were such that the interests of merchant and commercial interests had to continuously be taken into account as a major variable by the politically dominant groups throughout the second millennium CE, i.e. even during the near-absolutist Tokugawa Shogunate from the seventeenth century onwards.

Eurasian Transformations and the Idea of an Age of Ecumenical Renaissances

The period from the tenth to the thirteenth centuries is a time of crisis, but also of the reassertion of cultural legacies in all of the major civilizations and agro-literate societies of Eurasia. In terms of institutional developments, it is clear that interlinked processes of agricultural expansion, urban and commercial growth and changes in military technology give rise to elite contestations and efforts to rearrange the struc-

---

[22] See Mikael S. Adolphson in this volume and *The Gates of Power: Monks, Courtiers, and Warriors in Premodern Japan* (Honolulu: University of Hawai'i Press, 2000). Adolphson's analysis constitutes a break with an earlier view which sees the transition in the late twelfth century from the imperial order of the Heian period to the Kamakura period as a decisive rupture. An interesting example of such a view is represented by Pierre François Souyri, *The World Turned Upside Down: Medieval Japanese Society* (New York: Columbia University Press, 2001). Interesting examples of civilizational analyses of Japan are S. N. Eisenstadt, *Japanese Civilization: A Comparative View* (Chicago, IL: The University of Chicago Press, 1998) and Johann P. Arnason, The Peripheral Centre: *Essays on Japanese History and Civilization* (Melbourne: Trans Pacific Press, 2002).

ture of the political order. It is also clear that these processes are interpreted and legitimated with recourse to long-standing cultural legacies within different civilizations.

Of course, the degree of cultural pluralism varies across, and within, civilizations. On the whole the degree of toleration of cultural and religious pluralism is probably lower throughout this period in both Western and Eastern Christendom, as well as in Japan, than it is in China or India—and later in the Mongol Empire. In China, Confucianism and Daoism had been part of the Sinic cultural ecumene since the Axial Age and in the first half of the first millennium CE were joined by Buddhism in its Mahayana variety and others, not least Lamaism. During some periods—and the Yuan Dynasty is one of them—'Iranian' religions, meaning Nestorian Christianity, Zoroastrianism and Manichaeism, also played a fully accepted and sometimes prominent role.

Generally, however, what tends to happen towards the end of the first millennium and the beginning of the second millennium CE is that even in the most tolerant contexts, cultural and religious ideas and schools with their roots elsewhere become subject to processes of domestication and integration into the cultural mainstream of a given civilization. In this respect, Japanese developments provide interesting examples of the reinterpretation of Chinese variants of schools of Buddhism and their transposition into forms that appear as distinctly Japanese, of which Zen Buddhism is but one. In the Chinese context, an even more successful cultural embrace occurs e.g. with Nestorian Christianity which in this period gradually becomes indistinguishable from Mahayana Buddhism.

In institutional terms, the rise of new types of clerical elites means that two potential cleavages are of central importance. One has to do with the nature of the relationship between clerical and political elites, in particular the degree of autonomy in the formation of the clerical elites. The other has to do with the relationship between the social and political order, in particular the degree to which social groupings are included or excluded from wielding power in the political arena.

If we compare the major civilizations across Eurasia in terms of the first dimension, it seems clear that Western Europe and China are the only civilizations where clerical elites become subject to a demanding formal training and yet enjoy a high degree of autonomy from political power during their formation. In Constantinople, efforts to train new clerical elites in the beginning of the second millennium CE were tried but seem to have failed largely because the ties between these incipient elites and traditional social elites remained too close. In Japan, the entourages of the Imperial court and the local lords seem to have enjoyed a no more subjugated position than their peers in Europe. However institutionalised autonomy for the formation of clerical elites did not exist to the same degree as in Western Europe or China.

The second dimension concerns relationships between social and political order. In Japan, a new consensus of power-sharing can be seen to have evolved between the three regrouped traditional elites of society, maintaining an exclusion of the newer commercial and urban elites. Something similar may be true of China although it seems that the overt position of imperial rule remains paramount in this context. In Western Europe, there is a real sharing and, to some extent, spatially defined division of power between different social groupings, including new urban elites and traditional elites. What is different in the European context, compared to the Byzantine Empire, China and Japan, is the absence of a long-standing imperial political order. To some extent the Church represents the heritage of empire but it can never assert a generally accepted claim to such a position. Maybe we can say that Western Europe therefore comes to represent an institutionalised articulation of what S. N. Eisenstadt has always seen as the most important characteristic of an Axial civilization, namely a belief in the existence of a chasm between a transcendental and a mundane sphere. In practice such a chasm becomes institutionally articulated with the division between a domain of the Church and another of the secular political order and their continuing coexistence in institutional pluralism.

At the same time, there emerges a new type of historical consciousness both in the core areas of Western Christendom and in the newly Christianized lands of Northern and Eastern Europe. Europe also witnesses new articulations of agentiality; commercial growth would have been all but impossible if a widening of the forms of accepted agentiality had not occurred, e.g. by the devaluation of usury in the list of sins. Analogously, new forms of sociality become articulated both within emerging city republics and with the introduction, through translations of Aristotle, of new ideas about political community and civil society. The transformations in the beginning of the second millennium CE are crucial for the formation of new institutional and intellectual legacies and paths of development. What occurs in these centuries is not a mere shift in ideas. It is the articulation and institutional entrenchment of different deep-seated cultural legacies in Europe and across the Eurasian hemisphere.

Figure 2. Institutional Paths of the Six Ecumenical Renaissances

Region	Cultural Order	Political Order	Social Order	Clerical Class
Western Europe	Unitary-integrative	Dualistic-hierarchical	Structured duality and hierarchical pluralism	Autonomous formation, heteronomous service
Byzantium	Unitary-encompassing	Unitary-hierarchical	Regimented but contested hierarchy	Heteronomous
China	Pluralistic-encompassing	Unitary and conditionally hierarchical	Hierarchical pluralism	Autonomous formation, movement to more autonomous service
Japan	Unitary-integrative	Movement from unitary imperial hierarchy to de facto coalition of hierarchies	Structured parallel hierarchies	Heteronomous
Indic World	Pluralistic	Politico-symbolic order	Historically evolving hierarchical order	Heteronomous
Islamic World	Encompassing-integrative	Contested religio-military	Normatively prescr. order	Heteronomous

Conclusion

Finally we may then first highlight, with the help of a simple figure, some of the main empirical statements argued above, and then, in another equally simplified figure, relate these arguments to the conceptual categories initially proposed. The first figure will refer to key features in the cultural, political and social order of the different civilizations that form the focus of this issue. The second figure will relate these phenomena to the four basic analytical categories introduced already in the section above on the Axial Age.

Despite the inevitable simplifications the overview nevertheless highlights important features that have been briefly alluded to above. The standard view of the European trajectory tends to focus on the emerging pluralism of the Western European political order and hypothesize this feature as unique and crucial for the future ascendancy of Europe. However, such accounts tend to overlook vitally important characteristics of other trajectories. In the case of China, to take a prominent counterexample, there can be little doubt that the Chinese cultural order had long been characterized by a high, if varying, degree of pluralism and openness towards a range of religious and cultural traditions of different origins but all of which could be accommodated within a Sinic cultural ecumene. Even if the Northern, and even more so Southern, Song was overtly less hospitable in this respect than the Tang—and for that matter the coming Yuan—Dynasty, the basic feature does not change, namely that Chinese cultural order has a tradition of pluralism and openness to diversity and contestation that the European one did not have to even remotely the same extent. Furthermore, even if Chinese political order was unitary and hierarchical, the cosmological underpinnings of political order were explicitly conditional, i.e. while service to the incumbent of the Mandate of Heaven was seen as obligatory in Confucian tradition, this Mandate could also be forfeited and an unworthy or inefficient holder of it could invoke no further transcendental legitimacy.[23] What happens at the turn of the first millennium CE is that these elements of conditionality, pluralism and contestability become greatly enforced in institutional terms through the growing autonomy of the key clerical class. This autonomy is furthermore increasing both in terms of the formation of this ruling class, as it were, and in terms of its actual service which, as a result of the territorial losses in the North, the subsequent downfall of Northern Song, and the relative inefficiency of the political order of the Southern Song, increasingly comes to focus on a local rather than a central level. To some extent one may even describe these events in terms of the emergence of a kind of localized civil society. In this respect, it is of great importance that the Mongol conquest and the establishment of the interlude of the Yuan Dynasty is not able to change this basic pattern; in fact this dynasty turns out to be entirely dependent on the newly reformed clerical class for its exercise of power.[24]

---

[23] A brief but important discussion about the centrality of political order in Chinese thought is found in Benjamin I. Schwartz, "The Primacy of the Political Order in East Asian Societies: Some Preliminary Generalizations", in Stuart R. Schram (ed.), *Foundations and Limits of State Power in China* (European Science Foundation, SOAS, London, and The Chinese University Press, Hong Kong, 1987), 1-10.

[24] See also Peter K. Bol, "Examinations and Orthodoxies: 1070 and 1313 Compared", in Theodore Huters, R. Bin Wong, and Pauline Yu (eds), *Culture and State in Chinese History* (Stanford, Ca: Stanford University Press, 1997), 29-57.

In this respect, the consequences of Mongol conquest, although not so different between the Sinic and the Islamic world in terms of the length of conquest—or rather perhaps the brevity of time before the conqueror had become converted or assimilated into the regional religious and cultural ecumene—were significant. While both worlds came to preserve their ecumenical cultural languages, it is only in the Chinese context that it is possible to speak also of continuity in the nature of political order.[25]

Japan, on the other hand, while possessing a cultural order with different layers of tradition and religious practice integrated into a coherent unity, is characterized in the beginning of the second millennium CE by important shifts in important respects in the social and political order. These shifts generally mean that the political order becomes shaped by the contests of three parallel hierarchies, one imperial, another military and a third one religious. These hierarchies themselves also become more structured in ways that for some of the classics of social science seemed reminiscent of the structuring of feudal rights in Europe. Another feature that is somewhat reminiscent of Europe is the concomitant emergence of what might be termed a new kind of civil society, where commercial and urban interests come to play an important role socially and culturally while, however and contrary to Europe, being excluded from real political power for centuries to come.

In Japan, as in Europe—where of course this is precisely the time when an explicit articulation of the meaning of civil society emerges with the introduction of Aristotelian political writings into Western Europe—this new structured civil society also meant that an earlier set of social interactions waned. In the colourful language of Souyri, pressures now mounted on "a marginal and wandering population beyond the state's control," a population of fishermen, peddlers, storytellers, puppeteers, jugglers, magicians, prostitutes and itinerant artists and artisans. This "wandering world (*henreki no sekai*)—an almost nomadic population with no close ties to the land"—were related to a pre-feudal social order of imperial rule and services of the court of the old order. It helped "spread folk culture, throughout Japan, disseminated beliefs

---

[25] It seems also clear that whereas the Chinese cultural order remained pluralist, one unforeseen effect of the Mongol conquest of Baghdad and central lands of the Islamic world, was that the relative benevolence of the Mongols towards the then still substantial Nestorian and Monophysite Christian populations came to engender suspicions and distrust and eventually lead to the numerical decline of Christian minority populations in this region.

and fashions, and ultimately helped make the peoples who live on the archipelago a group more homogeneous than fragmented".[26] In this respect the new political and social order, which emerged in the beginning of the first millennium CE and most dramatically perhaps from the late twelfth century onwards, was a significantly more regulated one.

It then only remains to summarize some of these institutional and structural developments in terms of the four basic analytical dimensions discussed earlier. While these dimensions form an inescapable part of human life in any textually articulated form of historical and cosmological consciousness, the relative positions on them may of course vary greatly across time and space.[27]

What happens in the beginning of the second millennium CE however is that new articulations emerge in some of the major civilizations of Eurasia that make new practices and institutions conceivable. I have already at some length dwelt upon this in terms of the emergence of new forms of sociality. Analogously there are important shifts in terms of historical time in the European context. The dramatic expansion of Western Christendom which occurs in this period (and which forms the focus of the contribution to this issue by Gábor Klaniczay) entails that a biblically inscribed historicality is equally extended and comes to replace a number of previously existing forms of historical consciousness. This process has somewhat different characteristics in different parts of the newly Christianized European peripheries. However, it ultimately leads to a kind of standardization of historical consciousness of a trans-European kind, which in turn is then used in the construction of a variety of different locally based accounts. In the Indic world transpositions of literary accounts occur across different media, but there are also contestations between the historicalities of different cultural and religious traditions. In the Sinic world Neo-Confucianism likewise involves new constructions of sociality and the position of the literati in relation

---

[26] Souyri (2001) op. cit., 14. A brief account of the role of the concept of feudalism in Japanese historiography and of its relationship to German historiography is provided by Ishi Shiro, "Zur Anwendung des Feudalismus-Begriffs auf die japanische Geschichte," *Japan Review* 9 (1997), 75-85.

[27] These dimensions are then also inherent in any "civilization" as the term is often employed. Interesting entries on this concept can be found in articles written by Johann Arnason, Aziz Al-Azmeh, and S. N. Eisenstadt in Neil Smelser and Paul Baltes (eds), *International Encyclopedia of the Social and Behavioral Sciences* (Amsterdam, New York, Oxford: Elsevier, 2001). See also J. M. Roberts, *History of the World* (London: Penguin, 1995), 41-7, and Johann P. Arnason, *Civilizations in Dispute: Historical Questions and Theoretical Traditions* (Leiden: Brill, 2003).

Figure 3. Dimensions of Human Existence as Culturally Defined

Region	Cultural-Cosmological Focus	Historicality	Sociality	Agentiality
Western Europe	Axial-political	religiously transposed/ imposed	increasingly structured soc.	extended, redefined
Byzantium	Axial-liturgical	traditional	impero-centric	contested, heteronomous
China	Axial-inclusive	naturally evolved	impero-centric but increasingly autonomous	normatively def.
Japan	Semi-axial, autonomous	naturally evolved	increasingly structured soc.	extended
Indic World	Semi-axial, Pluralistic-semantic	naturally evolved	layered	multiple
Islamic World	Axial-normative	religiously transposed/ imposed	rule-ordered	normatively def. foci of ag.

to historical tradition and society that in turn justify new—and future-orientated—claims in the name of tradition.

Different forms of redefining conceptualisations of time and belonging ultimately make possible new ways of being and intervening in the world. In the context of Western Europe, this is directly related to processes of urban and commercial growth and has links to the interpretation of biblical accounts of sins and vices. It is only when usury is no longer seen as the pre-eminent sin that such growth is at all conceivable. Similarly the emergence of a new clerical class, autonomously formed, is only possible once the interpretability of different textual accounts is seen as a legitimate and institutionalised procedure.

These brief examples can only serve to illustrate various ways in which profound redefinitions of the cosmological and existential dimensions occur in different high cultures in the Eurasian hemisphere in the beginning of the second millennium CE. This occurred in ways which invoked deep-seated cultural traditions of given societies and which came to have lasting effects by making possible new institutions and practices that defined the trajectories of these different civilisations for the major part of the millennium to come.

II. EUROPE AND BEYOND

THE TRANSFORMATION OF EUROPE
AS A EURASIAN PHENOMENON[1]

ABSTRACT

That the period c. 1000-1300 CE was one of transformation in Europe, amounting to "the birth of Europe", is widely agreed among specialists in the region. The present paper argues not only that this transformation can be described in terms analogous to those held to amount to the "Axial Age" around 500 BCE or the "cultural constitution of modernity" around 1800, but that comparable transformations can be discerned in the other literate civilizations of Eurasia at the same epoch. It maintains, however, that these transformations were precipitated not by contacts between the civilizations, but by internal developments within each of the civilizations, arising from common exposure to the social and economic consequences of intensive economic growth, in particular as they affected the position and influence of the clerical elites. This common transformation has been less noticed and is more difficult to describe than those of the "Axial Age" or "modernisation" because the contrasting responses of the respective elites to these challenges sharpened the social, cultural and political differences between the civilizations and set them on diverging historical trajectories: its leading characteristic and consequence, therefore, was differentiation, rather than integration or homogenization.

The recognition of the emergence of Latin Christendom—to which western historians often refer as "medieval civilization"—as a distinctive artefact of the eleventh and twelfth centuries is relatively recent and not wholly uncontroversial, a piecemeal achievement of twentieth-century historiography.[2] Regional specialists naturally describe the changes which

---

[1] The title echoes that of an earlier paper, R. I. Moore, "The Birth of Europe as a Eurasian Phenomenon", *Modern Asian Studies* 31/3 (1997), pp. 583-601, reprinted in V. Lieberman, ed., *Beyond Binary Histories: Re-imagining Eurasia to c. 1830* (Ann Arbor, 1999), pp. 139-59, a valuable symposium on comparative state formation in early modern Eurasia.

[2] The construction of the paradigm has yet to be satisfactorily chronicled, Norman F. Cantor *Inventing the Middle Ages* (New York, 1991) notwithstanding. Among the names that will figure prominently when it is are: Henri Pirenne (*Medieval Cities*, Princeton, 1925), Charles Homer Haskins (*The Renaissance of the Twelfth Century*, Cambridge, MA 1927), Ernst Kantorowicz (*Kaiser Friedrich der Zweite* Berlin 1927, = *Frederick II*, London 1931, Gerd Tellenbach (*Libertas: Kirche und Weltordnung im Zeitalter des Investiturstreites*, Stuttgart 1936, = *Church, State and Christian Society at the time of the Investiture Contest*, Oxford 1940),

took place in north-western Europe during that period very differently, according to their philosophical and historiographical persuasions. Nevertheless, they are to all intents and purposes unanimous that those centuries saw the completion of a set of interlinked changes in economy, society and culture amounting to a transformation of the quality and conditions of social and political life.[3] Many of them would be happy to describe that transformation as, or as involving, a deep-seated cultural crystallisation, and, taking a step further, to agree that it issued in long-term historical processes—since it is from this point that the continuous history of Europe as a single distinctive cultural formation is readily discernible—or even, taking another, that it constituted a turning point in world history, since it set Europe on the path towards the breakthrough to modernity which (as most European historians take for granted) was essentially a European development. There is currently acute disagreement as to whether these changes resulted from an eleventh-century crisis, which has until recently been the consensus, or from gradual, cumulative changes in economy, society and culture which had been in train at least since the ninth century.[4] However, that question is not immedi-

---

Marc Bloch (*La société féodale*, 2 vols, Paris, 1939, 1940, = *Feudal Society*, London 1961), R. W. Southern (*The Making of the Middle Ages*, London, 1953), Georges Duby (*Hommes et structures du moyen age: receuil d'articles*, Paris, 1973, approx. = *The Chivalrous Society*, London, 1977), M.-D. Chenu (*La théologie au xiie. siècle*, Paris, 1957, = *Nature, Man and Society in the Twelfth Century*, Chicago 1968), Robert S. Lopez (*The Commercial Revolution of the Middle Ages*, Englewood Cliffs NJ, 1971), Alexander Murray, (*Reason and Society in the Middle Ages*, Oxford, 1978), Brian Stock, (*The Implications of Literacy*, Princeton, 1983), Robert Bartlett (*The Making of Europe: Conquest, Colonization and Cultural Change, 950-1350*, London, 1993) and Dominic Iogna Prat, (*Ordonner et exclure: Cluny et la société chrétienne face à l'hérésie, au judaïsme, à l'Islam 1000-1150*, Paris, 1998, = *Order and Exclusion*, Ithaca 2002).

[3] Influential syntheses include, in addition to the above, Louis Halphen, *L'essor de l'Europe* (Paris, 1932), Jacques Le Goff, *La civilisation de l'occident médiévale* (Paris, 1964 = *Medieval Civilization*, Oxford, 1988), John H. Mundy,*Europe in the High Middle Ages* (2 ed. London, 1991), Robert Fossier, *Enfance de l'Europe, X^e-XIIe siècle: aspects économiques et sociaux* (2 vols, Paris, 1982), J.-P. Poly, and E. Bournazel, *La mutation féodale, x^e-xiiie siècles* (Paris, 1981, = *The Feudal Transformation 900-1200*, New York, 1991). My own views are defended in R. I. Moore, *The First European Revolution, c. 970-1215* (Oxford, 2001), cited below as Moore, *FER*. I have not yet seen M. Borgolte, *Europa entdeckt seine Vielfelt* (Stuttgart, 2002) or Michael Mitterauer, *Warum Europa? mittelalterliche Grundlagen eines Sonderwegs* (Munich, 2003).

[4] Dominique Barthélemy, "La mutation féodale, a-t-elle eu lieu?", *Annales ESC 47* (1992), 767-77, and several subsequent papers, collected and amplified in Barthélemy, *La mutation féodale, a-t-elle eu lieu? Servage et chevalerie dans la France des xe. et xie. siècles* (Paris, 1997), directed in the first instance against the views developed by Georges Duby from the 1940s. Duby's fundamental arguments are most clearly presented in the papers collected in *Hommes et structures* (Paris, 1974, substantially translated as *Chivalrous Society*, London, 1977); see also his *Guerriers et paysans* (Paris, 1973, = *The Early Growth of the European Economy* (London 1974) and *Les trois ordres* (above, n. 2). On Duby's work see

ately germane, though it may have a bearing on the relationship, if there was one, between these European developments and the wider history of Eurasia.

The question presented by the current inquiry is whether this transformation is to be seen within "the contours of a global [or at least Eurasian] historical development" which might have constituted a turning point in world history analogous to (but not necessarily directly comparable with) those conventionally characterised as "the Axial Age", fifteen hundred years or so earlier, or as the "breakthrough to modernity" of the eighteenth and nineteenth centuries CE. It is certainly a question worth asking. At first sight, for example, the extent to which eleventh and twelfth century analogies can be found to Wittrock's account (following Koselleck) of "the cultural constitution of modernity" is very striking.[5] If a sense of "new expectations and new imaginations running much deeper than change of practice" was captured by Browning's "Bliss was it in that dawn to be alive", equivalents are not difficult to identify in the earlier period, the cliché of medieval pessimism notwithstanding.[6] Odilo of Cluny was said (in a quotation, typically of the age, from Suetonius' *Life* of Augustus) to have found his monastery brick when he succeeded to the abbacy in 994, and left it marble when he died in 1048, the most splendid of the "white cloak of churches" with which

---

further R. I. Moore, "Duby's Eleventh Century", *History* lxix (1984), 36-49; Claudie Duhamel-Amado et Guy Lobrichon, eds, *Georges Duby: l'écriture de l'histoire*, (Brussels, 1996), and for an illustration of the debate on his views, which continues, Thomas N. Bisson, "The Feudal Revolution", *Past & Present* 142 (1994), 6-42, and ripostes by Barthélemy and others, "Debate: The Feudal Revolution", ibid. 152 (1996), 196-223 and 155 (1996), 177-225.

[5] Bjorn Wittrock, "Cultural Crystallization and Conceptual Change: Modernity, Axiality and Meaning in History" in Jussi Kurunmäki and Kari Palonen eds *Zeit, Geschichte und Politik. Zum achtzigsten Geburtstag von Reinhart Koselleck* (Jyväskylä 2003), pp. 105-34; "Social Theory and Global History: The Three Cultural Crystallizations", *Thesis Eleven*, 65, (2001), 27-50.

[6] Heightened consciousness of human capacity to change the world does not necessarily imply a shared optimistic assessment of the outcome: for example, many historians now agree with pessimists of the period—most notoriously Malthus—that at the moment of the perceived "breakthrough to modernity in the late eighteenth and early nineteenth centuries" the world was headed for stagnation (at best) stemming from ecological constraints which were unforeseeably (and temporarily?) averted only some generations later: cf., e.g. E. L. Jones, *Growth Recurring* (Oxford, 1988); E. A. Wrigley, *Continuity, Chance and Change* (Cambridge, 1988); Kenneth Pomeranz, *The Great Divergence* (Princeton, 2000), especially at pp. 69-107. On this view "modernisation" is to be distinguished from "industrialization" not only thematically but chronologically; it follows that in the present discussion we are comparing Europe at the emergence of a new mode of production and at the apex, if not in the decline, of an old one.

the Cluniac chronicler Radulphus Glaber saw the world covered in his time.[7] The extension of cultivation with its attendant institutions was celebrated by the Norman chronicler Ordericus Vitalis, writing in the 1120s, when he remarks that his fellow Benedictines "cut down dense woods, and now give praise in the high-roofed monasteries and spiritual palaces built there, chanting to God with peace of mind in places where formerly robber outlaws used to lurk to perform evil deeds".[8] The resulting social and cultural transformation was clearly recognised by his contemporary Hugh of St. Victor: "In antiquity men used to eat mainly by hunting, as they still do in certain regions where the use of bread is extremely rare, where flesh is the only food, and water and mead the drink".[9] The authority of tradition was not often dismissed with the frankness of Arnold of Regensburg's, "if the old is disordered it should be entirely thrown away, or if it conforms to the proper order of things but is of less use it should be buried with reverence" (c. 1030),[10] but Chrétien of Troyes is widely accepted as a spokesman of his time when he wrote, c. 1170:

> Our books have informed us that the pre-eminence in chivalry and learning once belonged to Greece. Then chivalry passed to Rome together with that highest learning which now has come to France. God grant that it may be cherished here, that the honour which has taken refuge with us may never depart from France. God has awarded it as another's share, but of Greeks and Romans no more is heard; their fame is past and their glowing ash is dead.[11]

If dismissals of the old world were seldom so explicit as these, they were nonetheless implicit in and inseparable from the great synthetic projects in which, to echo Wittrock again, the twelfth and thirteenth centuries witnessed the unfolding of clerical society, "which saw itself as the new world, laying intellectual claim to the whole world and simultaneously denying the old"[12]—Gratian's *Decretum* of canon law, the *Ordinary Gloss*

---

[7] John France, Nithard Bulst and Paul Reynolds, eds *Rodulfus Glaber Opera* (Oxford, 1989), pp. 117, 127.

[8] Orderic Vitalis, *Ecclesiastical History* x. 16, ed. Marjorie Chibnall (6 vols Oxford, 1968-80), v. 294-7.

[9] *Didascalicon*, 2.25, trans. Jerome Taylor (New York, 1961) p. 99 (late 1120s). On the stereotyping of the less by the more developed in the following generations see John Gillingham, "The Beginnings of English Imperialism" *Journal of Historical Sociology* 5/4 (1992), 392-409; Moore, *FER* pp. 147-8.

[10] Quoted by Patrick Geary, *Phantoms of Remembrance* (Princeton 1994), p. 8.

[11] *Cligés*, lines 30-44.

[12] Wittrock (2003), p. 108.

on the Bible, the *summa* of Aquinas. Not only did each of them aspire, with remarkable and durable success, to a definitive, detailed and over-arching account of its respective facet of divine revelation, but each did so by means of collecting the vast and contradictory accumulation of texts and precepts since antiquity, subjecting it to the human test of Aristotelian dialectic and discarding, or in Arnold of Regensburg's phrase, burying with reverence, what failed to meet it. These were the most abstract, and perhaps the most ambitious expressions of the articulate and conscious construction of a new world which, concretely, was consciously and magnificently represented in its technically and aestheti-cally revolutionary churches. It is no coincidence that the twelfth century was Europe's greatest age of construction before the nineteenth. The same spirit was manifested institutionally in religious houses, urban communes, merchant guilds and so on, as well as in their cognitive realisation as new orders of society—including, of course, that of chivalry—each with the written rule appropriate to it. The composition and recording of rules was one of the age's most regular if often humdrum expressions of social organisation and leadership.

Much of this had its immediate origin in the set of events which, in the second half of the eleventh century, saw the emergence of the Roman papacy as not merely the titular but the active and increasingly effective directorate of the Catholic Church, a movement which has often, and with good reason, itself been described as revolutionary.[13] Certainly it was so in most of the usual senses. It was, in the first instance, the work of a tightly knit and ideologically motivated group of clerics, its leaders originally brought to Rome in the entourage of Pope Leo IX (1048-54). They were driven by a conviction of the absolute corruption of the existing church and its prelates, to such an extent that (under the impulsion of Humbert of Moyenmoutier's *Books against the Simoniacs* (1058) which attributed the present evils of the church and the world to commerce in spiritual office), they came close to breaking the apostolic succession by denouncing as irretrievably invalid the orders of all who were tainted by the sin of simony, and thence of those who had in turn been ordained by simoniacs. Their vision, resoundingly proclaimed in the correspondence of Pope Gregory VII (1073-83, formerly Cardinal Hildebrand),[14] by either of whose names the movement is most

---

[13] For a classic statement, Karl Leyser, "On the Eve of the First European Revolution", in his *Communications and Power in Medieval Europe: 2, The Gregorian Revolution and Beyond* (London, 1994), pp. 1-19.

[14] H. E. J. Cowdrey, trans., *The Register of Pope Gregory VII, 1073-1085* (Oxford, 2002).

commonly known, demanded an entire reordering of human society under papal authority and a clergy separated from the world by celibacy. To achieve it Gregory did not hesitate, in classic revolutionary fashion, repeatedly to engineer the ousting by popular agitation of "corrupt" bishops who constituted the hierarchy over which he himself presided. Gregory and his associates wrote, to borrow another phrase from Wittrock, the promissory notes which shaped the agenda of European politics, local and cosmopolitan, for three generations at least, and whose under-takings, counterfeitings and defaults coined the language of aspiration and betrayal until the time of Luther and beyond. In doing so they articulated a vision of "right order in the world"[15] that was the counter-part of Polanyi's "discovery of society", reformulating and entrenching the religious representation of the social order from which disengagement would be a condition of modernity.

Economic Growth and its Consequences

At the root of all these changes was that from an economy of predation to one of exploitation—from an economy in which a warrior aristocracy supported itself mainly by the profits of external and internal plunder and warfare to one in which its descendants did so mainly on the surplus of agricultural production. Of course, this was a long process, highly differentiated regionally, and the formulation risks obliterating the often highly developed long distance exchanges and busy local markets of the Carolingian (ninth century) world. Nevertheless, it is from the later decades of the tenth century, and especially the early ones of the eleventh, that we see the aristocracy of western Europe so urgently determined to annex and maximise the profits of agriculture as to undertake a rad-ical revision of their land-holding practices and family structures in order to do so. Ill-defined tracts of land roamed over by kin-based warrior bands were broken into precisely bounded estates, typically controlled from castles or monasteries and cultivated by a newly enserfed peas-antry. Cereal crops became the staple, supporting a proportionately much larger non-agrarian population, a market economy and a reor-ganised and reinvigorated high culture. In consequence the area under cultivation was hugely increased, and new regions that had not previously been capable of sustaining complex, citied civilization and the specialised,

---

[15] The sub-title of Tellenbach's classic study, above n. 2.

hierarchically organised social order that went with it, including the whole of northern and eastern Europe, now became capable of doing so. This intensification and expansion completed a permanent extension of citied civilization far beyond the areas which had been able to support it in antiquity that was the crucial achievement not only of European but of Eurasian history in the later centuries of the first millennium CE.

The essential consequences of intensive economic growth were that by making greater resources available to those who could command its sources it sharpened social differentiation and upset the existing balance between local and central power. Some of the character and results of the ways in which it did so in eleventh-century Europe may be illustrated through an incident in 1038, when the knights of vicomte Eudo of Déols routed a militia—*multitudo inermis vulgi*—which had been raised by Archbishop Aimo of Bourges to make the nobility of the Berry subscribe to the oath of the Peace of God—that is, to abstain in various ways and circumstances from private warfare, including the oppression of the peasantry. On the following day the River Cher ran red with blood, and was almost blocked by discarded weapons and dead bodies.[16] The episode is often cited as marking the decisive supremacy of highly trained and expensively armed professional soldiers over the peasant levies which had constituted the armies of the Carolingian world. The frequency with which our scanty narratives of the tenth and very early eleventh centuries describe or suggest the activity of assemblies and levies of free cultivators clearly implies that the specialists had not yet established a clear monopoly of effective violence. Indeed the very ease of the victory by the Cher might suggest that the Archbishop and his followers had under-estimated the overwhelming superiority of the knights. That would be consistent with the recent appearance of the more elaborate body armour and more expensive weaponry, including the lance, which sharply increased the cost of equipping and training a knight.[17] Again, by the 1030s we find the meaning of the word *miles* itself restricted to refer specifically to a mounted warrior, which is implicit but not certain in the chronicle of Richer, written at the very end of the tenth century,[18] for example, but plainly not the case at all only a few years before that in the chronicle of Le Puy to which we shall refer

---

[16] T. Head in Thomas Head and Richard Landes, eds *The Peace of God: Social Violence and Religious Response around the Year 1000* (Ithaca, 1992), pp. 225-6; also Guy Devailly, *Le Berry du xe. siècle au milieu du xiie.* (Paris, 1973), pp. 142-8.

[17] Bartlett, *Making of Europe* pp. 60-84.

[18] Philippe Contamine, *War in the Middle Ages* (Oxford, 1984), p. 31.

below. On the other hand, if the technology was new in 1038 there is
no doubt that it had developed and spread very rapidly, that *miles*
became simultaneously a synonym for illicit and unrestrained power,
and that the standing of a lord was clearly and absolutely measured by
the number of knights that he could command, whether from his own
retinue or as mercenaries, who were readily available on demand by
the middle of the eleventh century. By its end they were so clearly to
be preferred to enlisted men that on a famous occasion in 1094 Ranulf
Flambard, chief minister of William II of England and Normandy, sent
the levies of the English shires home again after collecting, on Dover
Beach, the ten shillings which each man had brought with him to buy
provisions while on campaign.[19]

The victory on the Cher illustrates how in Europe the transformation
of society was accompanied (in its first phase) by the fragmentation of
public authority and the inextricable entanglement of such authority
with the possession of landed property which classically defines feudalism
for institutional historians, as well as by the predominance of the seignurial
or manorial mode of production which did so for Marx. But the episode
on Dover Beach underlines how it depended no less fundamentally on
the possibilities of counting, reckoning and recording, and of abstracting,
generalising and legitimizing the principles of extraction—or extortion—
which the literate, and only the literate, possessed.[20] "Clerical" is a more
apt description than the conventional "feudal" society, at least for the
purpose of the present argument, not simply because the latter is con-
tentious in itself, and open to the confusion that arises from widely varying usage, and certainly not because the papacy achieved the monopoly
of authority to which the Gregorians aspired—it did not—but because
clerical skills and with them clerical culture now became fundamental
to all exercise of power in the secular as much as in the religious sphere.
In saying so, however, it is essential to insist that this does not imply
that those skills, the power that flowed from them and the mentalities
associated with them were at any time exclusively located in, still less

---

[19] C. W. Hollister, *The Military Organisation of Norman England* (Oxford, 1965), pp.
232-3.

[20] That is, functionally literate: we cannot assess to what extent these skills extended
informally beyond the ranks of the formally educated (*literati*), but we can be sure that
the *literati* defended their formal monopoly with increasing ruthlessness and determination from about this time: R. I. Moore, "Heresy and the Making of Literacy, c. 1000-
1150" in Peter Biller and Anne Hudson eds, *Heresy and Literacy in the Middle Ages* (Cambridge
University Press, 1994), pp. 19-37.

directed by, any single institution (least of all "the Church") or sector of society more precisely defined than the whole body of the privileged, or as they said, the free. To understand both the reasons for this and its implications a broader account of the great transformation is necessary.

I do not share the view that these developments in Europe were to any significant degree the outcome of "formative intercivilizational encounters". On the contrary, the contribution of the Byzantine and Islamic worlds to the cognitive transformation of the Latin West was mainly passive, as the sources of texts which Latin clerks appropriated to their own uses (though their long term importance, of course, was far broader than that implies), and as providing two of a series of *others* whose construction and denigration enabled those clerks to define and develop their own collective identity, and to bolster their claim to cultural hegemony against real and imagined rivals within the Latin West.[21] The cessation of invasion from Vikings, Slavs and Arabs around the middle of the tenth century, whose contribution to the "takeoff" is grotesquely exaggerated in text-book accounts, was largely the result of developments within Christian Europe—conversion and the assimilation that followed it on the one hand, more effective military organisation and preparedness on the other.

Western Europe certainly benefited greatly, indeed indispensably, from the general growth of long distance and intercivilizational commerce in these and the preceding centuries, but the indications are that its economic transformation was stimulated in the first instance by the intensification of local production and exchange. Such intensification was by far the most important element in the first condition that had to be satisfied if the great transformation was to take place—the conquest of hunger. Signs of growing pressure on the agrarian system were mounting at least from the middle of the ninth century, such as the reluctant decision of the monks of Bobbio in the 860s and 870s to clear forest for new farms "out of necessity",[22] and the eleventh century saw more general famines than any other in European history. But it also saw the rapid and universal adoption in lowland Europe of a system of production hitherto employed only on a very limited scale, the intensive cultivation (especially) of cereal crops, which demanded a social revolution that enserfed the peasantry to entrench privilege and enrich its

---

[21] Moore, *FER*, 146-59; Iogna Prat, *Order and Exclusion* passim.
[22] Massimo Montanari, *The Culture of Food* (Oxford, 1994; 1993), p. 38.

possessors—and which made it possible to sustain for the next eight centuries a population larger, more concentrated and more specialised by far than it had been before.[23]

Warriors and Clerics

Beyond the threat of hunger this intensification had been prompted in large part by another problem which posed a fundamental challenge to the organisation of Frankish society. From the later part of Charlemagne's reign onwards the loss of the open frontier which he and his forebears had exploited so brilliantly deprived the Frankish warriors of the opportunities of plunder afforded by regular expeditions against less developed neighbours, and forced them to turn upon each other to sustain their reputations and maintain their retinues.[24] The availability, or not, of such a frontier was undoubtedly an important factor in shaping the nascent political structures of western Europe in the earlier part of our period—and in accounting, for instance, for some of the differences that developed between those to the west and those to the east of the Rhine— as it was at this time in north China and perhaps in the central Islamic lands: this is a complex issue, but one seriously under-explored from a comparative point of view.[25]

The diminishing profits of warfare as the opportunities of plunder and booty moved eastward with the frontier, and the increasing cost of securing and maintaining a following, are certainly to be counted among the principal reasons for the immediate cause of the crisis of the late tenth century, namely intense, and greatly intensified, competition for land among the Frankish nobility. The search for wealth turned inwards, no doubt stimulated by the example of the churches, which by the mid-tenth century were beginning to discover, or rediscover, the benefits of consolidating estates, clearing land and extending cultivation. In those circumstances, however, the multiple claims which arose from partible inheritance, in which all a man's children were entitled to a share, lead-

---

[23] Moore, *FER* pp. 30-42.

[24] T. A Reuter, "Plunder and Tribute in the Carolingian Empire" *Transactions of the Royal Historical Society*, 5/35 (1985), 75-94.

[25] Ibid. pp. 42-44. For Europe, Robert Bartlett and Angus Mackay eds, *Medieval Frontier Societies* (Oxford, 1989) and more broadly Daniel Power and Naomi Standen eds, *Frontiers in Question: Eurasian Borderlands 700-1700* (London, 1999). In a vast literature Thomas J. Barfield, *The Perilous Frontier: Nomadic Empires and China* (Oxford, 1989) offers an analysis that cries out for comparative application.

ing to the fragmentation of patrimonies and the instability of holdings, became intolerably irksome. Intense and prolonged intra-familial feuding, frequently marked by the infliction on the losers of mutilations, blinding and castration obviously designed to remove them from the struggle for succession, was a natural consequence. It was accompanied both by frequent and loudly bewailed annexations of ecclesiastical property and by the placing of property under ecclesiastical protection through the medium of monastic foundation and endowment. It is particularly striking that the renewal of attacks on church land—"usurpations"— which is a notorious feature of these disorders seems often to have been designed not so much to secure the land itself as, through the process of settlement and reconciliation, to bring the "usurper" within the social ambit of the church. It is, for example, a frequent element in the settlement of these disputes that he will be buried in the church or the monks' cemetery. In other words, we are concerned here with a search not only for wealth, but for status and stability.[26]

To secure the profits of lordship over land in the long term violence was not enough. It was necessary to transform the structures both of landholding and of family, and therefore to redraw mental horizons, implanting, for example, a horror of incest and an ideal of delayed fulfilment, to buttress acceptance of undivided inheritance and the monogamous and exogamous model of matrimony which would secure the integrity and continuity of the holding over successive generations. The terms upon which the conflicts between churches and their neighbours that resounded throughout the eleventh and early twelfth centuries were resolved secured both the economic future and the political subordination of the warrior aristocracy in Europe, the first in some degree by design, the second assuredly not. They are foreshadowed as early as 975, when Bishop Guy of Le Puy used a sharp combination of diplomacy and force to secure the restoration to his church of the lands of which it had been despoiled by the local *milites ac rustici*—a phrase, incidentally, which confirms that we are here still on the threshold of differentiation, for the bracketing would be almost inconceivable even a generation or so later, when the word *miles* had begun to imply privilege, and *rusticus* to acquire an equally distinct connotation of unfreedom. The paragraph of the chronicle immediately following that which describes this triumph

---

[26] Barbara Rosenwein, *To Be the Neighbor of St. Peter: The Social Meaning of Cluny's Property, 909-1049* (Ithaca and London, 1989); see also S. D. White, *Custom, Kinship and Gifts to Saints* (Ithaca and London, 1988).

records that the Bishop made a division between his own revenues and those of the church, and required his canons to embrace the common life—that is to renounce individual property and make vows of chastity. In other words, the leading families of the diocese had handed over land for the support of their scions who occupied the cathedral stalls—on condition that it would remain the property of the church in perpetuity, and could not become the patrimony of new dynasties to rival their own. For two centuries and more to come, through the great upheavals of the Gregorian Reform and beyond, this was the pattern of innumerable settlements great and small, gradually reinforced by increasingly precise and stringent stipulations about the life, demeanour and recruitment of both clergy and monks, which always ensured that the price of their endowment was an ever wider and more unbridgeable gulf between their lives and property and those of their brothers in the world.[27]

The bargain was not a one-sided one, however. No doubt the warriors valued the prayers of their brothers above all else, but prayer was not the only benefit which their generosity secured. Quite suddenly, from the early eleventh century, land began to be passed from one generation to the next by primogeniture in the male line, as we can see from the fact that it is from this time that we can describe the aristocratic families of much of western Europe by drawing diagrams of their (dynastic) family trees. Thus the patrimony could remain undivided. It was a sudden and dramatic change, which, though never universal and after a century or so considerably softened in its effects by the greater availability of cash revenues, established one of the elementary structures of western European society. To achieve it meant to overthrow, within a few years, the most fundamental rights and customs of aristocratic society. It was often a violent and brutal process, frequently involving the precipitate ejection of vigorous young men from their homes and expectations, and giving rise everywhere to prolonged and bitter feuds. But it was done. No less essentially, it was accepted, legitimised and internalised, so that within two or three generations this appears through much of northern Europe as the ordinary and proper way of doing things. And it was achieved, quite simply, by preventing those who were to be excluded, of either sex, from marrying, and so postponing indefinitely the moment when they would lay claim to their natural inheritance.

---

[27] Moore, *FER* pp. 81-101.

To make that possible the contribution of the church was indispensable. First, it provided and enforced with increasing vigour in the new millennium a model of Catholic marriage which established a clear distinction between legitimate and illegitimate offspring. Second, it propagated an ideal of virginity which gave status and respectability to those excluded from the breeding cycle, either permanently or temporarily (for knights too were chaste, in principle, until they escaped from bachelordom). Third, and most remarkably, by suddenly adopting in the middle of the eleventh century, and without the slightest scriptural or canonical foundation, the view that a marriage between partners with a common ancestor in seven generations was incestuous, it provided a virtually infallible instrument for preventing or annulling any marriage which was inconvenient to the dynastic interest, or for that matter any other interest, of the families concerned.[28] The newly-stigmatised bastards, daughters, and younger sons at the expense of whose traditional claims this resolution was achieved were compensated through the massive endowment of monasteries, cathedrals and other churches with land and its revenues—up to a third of all land in some regions—and took the lead in opening it up for profitable cultivation. The clergy—and, crucially, not only the monks—paid for it by underwriting the legal, moral and cognitive transformations which sustained the new order. They secured in return not only the material but the social basis for a renewed and reinvigorated ecclesiastical hierarchy which laid secure foundations for its own authority and its own perpetuation in new systems of university education, and new syntheses of learning, the law and theology, to assume its leading place among the restored and aggressive monarchies of Latin Christendom.

In this way Western Europe was provided with a dual structure of landholding, by right of blood on the one hand and of profession and ordination on the other, elegantly articulated in such a way that a claim to either could be asserted only by disclaiming all interest or right in the other. There was, however, a price. The son who abandoned his claim on the family patrimony qua son still had to live, and discovered

---

[28] The first and second of these strategies were clearly identified by Georges Duby, especially in "Lignage, noblesse et chevalerie au xiie. siècle: une révision", *Annales: Economies, sociétés civilisations* (1972), also in *The Chivalrous Society* (above, n. 2), pp. 59-80, and *The Knight, the Lady and the Priest* (London, 1984); the third pointed to by Goody, *Development of the Family and Marriage in Europe* (Cambridge, 1983); see also Moore, "Duby's Eleventh Century", *History*, lxix (1984), 36-49.

a new basis for demanding his portion in the tonsure which he had been persuaded or compelled to adopt. The logic of reform was elegantly completed by granting it to him on the condition of celibacy— that is, not necessarily on his having no children, but certainly on his having no heirs. The elder brother who agreed to restore to the "reformed" church the property which his father or grandfather was said to have usurped might do so with the knowledge that it would not become the patrimony of a rival dynasty, and that the monastic stall or prebendary which it supported would not be claimed by the offspring of its present holder, but would regularly be vacated with a reasonable expectation that it would become available to the future siblings of his own successors.[29]

The establishment of the dynastic family and of the dual system of proprietorship characteristic of Latin Christendom entailed the creation of a new, and large, class of disinherited. Paradoxically, this class, to my knowledge, has never as such been the subject of a unified study or analysis, though its members and their activities produced virtually all the sources, and have been the subject of the bulk of the historiography, of the European middle ages. Indeed, one of the most puzzling and elementary questions associated with it is whether the eleventh— and twelfth-century aristocracy could have produced enough younger and illegitimate sons, and daughters, to have performed all the functions that are attributed to them by modern scholarship. Many, as we have just said, were placed in monasteries, and this was the period of by far the greatest efflorescence of monasticism, both male and female, in European history.[30] Many more found places as canons of cathedrals and great churches, in the rapidly expanding households of bishops, and as senior diocesan clergy. Yet more performed equivalent functions, military but also increasingly administrative and clerical, in the retinues of secular or ecclesiastical lords—or, when their activities were not approved by princes or chroniclers, as the feared and execrated mercenaries who increasingly made up the cavalry which was the core of every army. And last, if certainly not least, they were frequently prominent among the earliest *primores* or consuls who led the emergent urban communities.[31]

---

[29] This strategy was not undermined by the well-known phenomenon of the formation of clerical dynasties, since the illegitimacy of the sons barred them both from taking orders and from claiming benefices—unless, of course, their patrons chose to overlook it.

[30] Bruce Venarde, *Women's Monasticism and Medieval Society: Nunneries in France and England, 890-1215* (Ithaca and London, 1997), especially at pp. 28-75.

[31] David Nicholas, *The Growth of the Medieval City* (London, 1997), pp. 115-25.

In all of these roles the disinherited were pre-eminently the drivers of change. An interesting characteristic of those with whom we are particularly concerned in this paper, the "new men", as they were proverbially called, who made their ways in the service of great lords, is that they do not fit neatly into any one of the conventional social categories, as *oratores, pugnatores* or *laboratores*, or indeed into the contemporary accounts of the social order which they themselves provided.[32] They were the men (and I do mean men) who made the new world work— who possessed the skills, of literacy, of legal and administrative acumen, of counting and accounting and knowing the ways of money and how to make and use it, at all sorts of levels and in all sorts of milieus, from the chancellors of popes and emperors to the chaplains and household knights of lords of the manor. Throughout our period, and for obvious reasons, they were in great and increasing demand. We see it most easily in the creation of the universities. In the eleventh century a student wandered from one place and master to another (as he would have done in the Islamic world) to pick up more or less at random what might be offered. The young Abelard (born in 1079) could not secure all the instruction he needed at Paris in the 1090s, but by the 1130s Paris so far surpassed other cities in the number of its schools and the fame of its teachers that students might pursue courses in all seven of the liberal arts there, and then proceed to theology—when they had secured the approval of the masters to do so. By the 1170s the Bishop could be forbidden to grant his *licentia docendi* to anyone who had not been accepted by the masters as one of their number, or to withhold it from anyone who had, the most fundamental of the liberties secured by charter in 1200. By then the popularity of Paris had already been surpassed by that of Bologna, whose specialism in law, ecclesiastical and civil, gave it a decided vocational advantage, and which secured its institutional foundations at roughly the same time, though in somewhat different fashion. Oxford, granted its first statutes in 1215, was the first of many universities established in the thirteenth century to mark the enthusiasm of every sovereign in Europe (including the Pope) to assure a steady supply of suitably trained functionaries.[33]

---

[32] Cf. Georges Duby, *The Three Orders: Feudal Society Imagined* (Chicago and London, 1980) especially pp. 73-92, 232-307—but he does not discuss this anomaly.

[33] Jacques Le Goff, *Intellectuals in the Middle Ages* (Oxford, 1993); R. W. Southern, *Scholastic Humanism and the Unification of Europe I: Foundations* (Oxford, 1995).

Not all masters, by any means, became functionaries, and by no means all functionaries were masters, though the proportion of those who were increased rapidly, especially after the middle of the twelfth century. The young man who sought his training as a knight in the household of some great lord famously underwent arduous training in the skills of the courtier as well as the soldier, and might quickly find that he could harass his lord's enemies as well with his tongue as his lance. The formal distinction between clerks and knights rapidly dissolved in the competition for favour, and by the end of the twelfth century was not much more clearly marked by practical literacy than it was scrupulously observed in dress or behaviour. The situation of both was the same: with nothing to depend on from the resources of their family all their hopes depended on the favour of their lord, including ultimately the only sure escape from this precarious dependency—for the knight a rich wife, and for the clerk a benefice, which he habitually referred to as his longed for bride.

Strengthening Authority

The consequences of the courtiers' absolute dependence on their ability to win and retain the favour of their lords were most painfully apparent at royal courts, where the greatest opportunities and rewards could be found. The English chronicler Henry of Huntingdon tells us how he found Bishop Robert Bloet of Lincoln, no tender plant, in tears, his retinue dressed in wool instead of silk, his men fined by justices of low birth, and bits of his land transferred to others as his lawsuits went wrong, because he had lost the king's favour.[34] No wonder Robert's fellow courtier of King Henry I, Nigel d'Aubigny, believing himself to be dying, wrote in 1118 to his master:

> I beg you my dearest Lord in whom after God lies my whole trust, to have pity on me in my great need...... I have been yours while I could, and I have loved you most truly and served you most faithfully. In your service and in my own affairs I have committed many great sins and I have done few if any good deeds....[35]

Henry 'Beauclerc' had a reputation as a great patron of scholars, and Nigel—no scholar, but a highly effective administrator—owed every-

---

[34] R. W. Southern, *Medieval Humanism and other Studies* (Oxford, 1970), pp. 224-5.
[35] Ibid. pp. 220-1.

thing to his king. Unlike his Chinese counterparts who had been sustained through the long and costly march through the imperial examination system by a family justly confident that his success would secure their position for three more generations, he owed nothing to his kin—nothing to the monopoly of the warriors, everything to the state, to the creation of whose monopoly he and hundreds like him throughout Latin Europe in the following centuries wholeheartedly devoted his career and his talents. The claims with which the *clerici* of Latin Europe rationalised and justified the power of their masters, and which they extended rapidly and ingeniously during the twelfth and thirteenth centuries, to the effect that the business and responsibilities of government were entrusted to them, to be exercised with due concern for justice, the protection of the weak and so on, but nevertheless by arbitrary will and absolute right, are of a kind familiar among Eurasian traditional elites. "There is no power but of God", as the Treasurer of Henry II of England put it. "There is clearly therefore nothing incongruous or inconsistent with the clerical character in keeping God's laws by serving Kings as supreme".[36] In practice, however, such assertions by no means always implied an effective claim to a monopoly of violence. The anxieties of Robert Bloet and Nigel d'Aubigny illustrate how, and why, the difference in western Europe was that the aggrandisement of central authority, royal or papal, in the twelfth and thirteenth centuries did not rest upon an unspoken accommodation with local magnates such as obtained, under various guises, in other Eurasian polities throughout the traditional period. On the contrary, the precarious rewards of favour and influence at secular and ecclesiastical courts alike fell to those with the ingenuity to devise legitimate and effective means of penetrating the hard shell of local hegemony and the ruthlessness to implement them not always or everywhere, but often enough and widely enough to tip the balance, in the long run, decisively towards the aggrandisement of the state at the expense of the kin.

Such an ethos, of course, needed cultural as well as political roots. Twelfth-century clerical culture was, as we have already seen, the creation of an educational system much more highly structured than its predecessor. As might be expected, the process involved a standardisation of the curriculum and the definition and dissemination of a canonical body of texts, and of approved commentaries on them, drawn both

---

[36] Richard FitzNigel, *Dialogus de scaccario* ed. Charles Johnson (London, 1950), p. 1.

from the patristic period of late antiquity (fourth and fifth centuries CE) and from the twelfth and thirteenth centuries themselves. Less familiar in the textbook accounts is the concentration of intellectual and religious authority in these institutions and the people who were licensed by them. From the middle of the eleventh century every possible source of such authority other than the prelates and masters of the Latin church was subjected to an increasingly ruthless process of vilification and demonization, depicted and persecuted as a source of moral, physical and doctrinal pollution. The Celtic and Orthodox Christian Churches, Islam, the Jews and Judaism, were assaulted in turn, in the last case creating the stereotype, and inaugurating the long and terrible history, of European antisemitism. The acclamation of holy men by the faithful which had played an important part in bringing popular support to the struggle for ecclesiastical land and liberty in the eleventh century was viewed with increasing suspicion, and effectively snuffed out, in the twelfth, when the recognition of saints and miracles became a centralised and highly formalised procedure, and veneration for relics was carefully controlled and sanitised in pilgrimages to approved shrines. The accusation of heresy was turned more often and more ruthlessly, especially from the middle of the twelfth century, against unauthorised preachers, or anybody else who seemed to threaten or might conveniently be alleged to threaten to command influence among the unprivileged, and the thirteenth century saw the panoply of religious persecution developed to the full.[37]

Eurasian Perspectives

The crucial result of the transformation of Western Europe during our period, then, was the creation of a governing class (governing, that is, in practice though and essentially not in theory) whose members identified with the interests of their lords and patrons, and not their kin. It was, of course, not the end, but the beginning (in the modern history of Europe) of a conflict which continued throughout the ancient regime and beyond—a conflict which, for all its vicissitudes, always underlay the growth of public institutions and the expansion of their sphere, with all the attendant consequences. On a superficial view, which is all that

---

[37] *FER* pp. 146-80, developing the argument of R. I. Moore, *The Formation of a Persecuting Society: Power and Deviance in Western Europe, 950-1250* (Oxford, 1987).

I can offer, some of the same issues were at stake in other civilizations of Eurasia in our period, but the outcome was different.[38] China offers the most obvious analogy. The growth of the examination system, with the accompanying canonisation of texts, commentaries and methodology—probably even stricter and certainly in the long run more successfully monopolistic than in Western Europe—seems to have arisen from similar causes, in the need for an old aristocracy to transform itself in order to renew its access to power and wealth—here through imperial office rather than land—and for a new regime to create and reward its own cadre of supporters.[39] The link between the officials and their families, however, remained unbroken, despite formal recognition (for example, in the rule that imperial officials should not serve in their home district) of the danger it held.[40] This ensured that the wonderfully intricate and imposing structure of Chinese imperial government (the number of whose officials and the scope of whose responsibilities, in striking contrast to its Western European counterparts, remained more or less static for the next seven hundred years)[41] was little more than a mechanism for discreetly sustaining the wealth and position of the gentry.[42]

It seems that a similar explanation accounts for the failure of the attempts of the Comnenian emperors in Byzantium to reinvigorate their governmental machinery by way of supporting advanced teaching in Constantinople.[43] In the Islamic world, on the other hand, teaching was not institutionalised; reputation continued to rest upon individual charisma—that is, popular acclamation—and the progress and dissemination of learning was therefore subject to the approval of the com-

---

[38] I have set out this argument more fully in "The Eleventh Century in Eurasian History: A Revisionary Approach to the Historiography of Ancient and Medieval Civilizations", *Journal of Medieval and Early Modern Studies*, 33.1 (2003), 1-21.

[39] Peter Bol, *'This Culture of Ours': Intellectual Traditions in Tang and Sung China* (Stanford, 1992), especially pp. 128-92.

[40] Robert P. Hymes, *Statesmen and Gentlemen: The Elite of Fu-Chou, Chinag-Hsi, in Northern and Southern Sung* (Cambridge, 1986), pp. 62-81.

[41] John King Fairbank, *A New History of China* (Cambridge MA, 1992), pp. 93-5.

[42] Hilary J. Beattie, *Land and Lineage in China* (Cambridge, 1979), pp. 57-87; Chang Chung-li, *The Income of the Chinese Gentry* (Seattle, 1962), pp. 97-8; Ho Ping-ti, *The Ladder of Success in Imperial China: Aspects of Social Mobility 1368-1911* (New York and London, 1962), pp. 92-125.

[43] See especially A. P. Kazhdan and Ann Wharton Epstein, *Change in Byzantine Culture in the Eleventh and Twelfth Centuries* (Berkeley, Los Angeles, 1985), 120-33, 192-5; Paul Magdalino, 'Enlightenment and Repression in twelfth-century Byzantium: the evidence of the canonists' in N. Oikonomides, ed. *Byzantium in the Twelfth Century: Canon Law, State and Society* (Athens, 1991), 359-73.

munity or whoever could sway it—the same conditions that produced 'monkey trials' in early twentieth-century Tennessee. And the reason for this, at least in part, was that the tournament-like conditions of disputation produced in that way were the product of the widespread establishment of *madrasa* institutions in the eleventh and twelfth centuries which arose from the efficacy of *waqf* (charitable) foundations to assist the survival of learned elites which lacked the secure mechanisms of their Western and Chinese counterparts for the transmission of wealth and status.[44] Finally, to mention the uses of competitive altruism is to call to mind the role of monastic and other religious foundations not only in Latin and Greek Christendom, where it has been the subject of a great deal of attention, but in China, in Southeast Asia and in India—especially in the south, where the eleventh century was one of the great ages of temple foundation and direct analogies with monastic patronage in Francia are clearly visible in the efforts of local grandees and more distant lords to secure the allegiance of new and prosperous territories by means of competitive patronage.[45] More generally, the pattern of alternating munificence in religious endowment and reaction against it is at least superficially observable, and for similar reasons, in most if not all of the Eurasian civilizations. This is an obviously feasible and potentially fruitful subject for comparative study.[46]

These are some indications, possibly not the most obvious, that the period from around the beginning of the tenth to the middle of the thirteenth century CE did indeed see a "phase of socio-cultural crystallization" in Eurasia. It appears more difficult to describe than those of the "Axial Age" or "modernisation" because—and perhaps only because—its leading characteristic and consequence was social and cultural differentiation, and not integration or homogenization. It was now, rather than in the early and middle centuries of the first millennium CE as current paradigms tend to assume, that the Eurasian civilizations took the distinctive forms which characterized them for the greater part

---

[44] Michael Chamberlain, *Knowledge and Social Practice in Medieval Damascus 1190-1350* (Cambridge, 1994). Notice especially the comparative discussion on household survival at pp. 66-8.

[45] Compare Hermann Kulke and Dietmar Rothermund, *A History of India* (2 ed., London 1990), pp. 136-8 with George W Dameron, *Episcopal Power and Florentine Society, 1000-1320* (Cambridge, MA, 1991), chapter 1.

[46] For which Barbara Rosenwein, *Negotiating Space: Power, Restraint and Privileges and of Immunity in Early Medieval Europe* (Ithaca and London, 1999) provides some fundamental questions and stimulating approaches.

of the second millennium.[47] The changes stemmed from a series of crises within the governing (clerical) elites of each civilization which arose from analogous but not directly related causes. The common element was that the families which constituted the governing elites found that the strategies that had sustained their wealth and position since the end of antiquity were no longer adequate to do so. In each case the particular response entailed a reformulation of the interpretation and transmission of the high culture, and with it of the means of recruitment to the clerical elite, and hence of the relationship of that elite both to government and to society at large. Although these changes occurred in a context of increasing commercial and other inter-civilizational contacts they arose primarily and predominantly from intensive economic growth and the social tensions to which it gave rise within each civilization, and are to be understood first in terms of these and related local and domestic developments. Indeed the tendency of social theorists and historians interested in the "big picture" (Weber excepted), or in the relations between civilizations, to address contacts rather than comparisons is an important reason for their relative failure to identify, let alone explain, the transformations of the eleventh, twelfth and early thirteenth centuries as a single, and crucial, phase of Eurasian history. Conversely, the notion of a "general crisis of elites" is capable of accommodating a variety of causes, responses and outcomes within a common frame of discussion and analysis.

I make these comments not through any chauvinistic desire to deny non-Europeans a role in European development, but by way of suggesting that historians have too often been seduced by the glamorous and accessible into paying insufficient attention to the local, the humdrum and the obscure, and that comparative social, cultural and institutional history is more germane to the present project than the history of contacts. I have, in conclusion, no suggestion to offer as to the reason for the chronological coincidences between the developments discussed above, which are striking though not always precise. Proponents of the centrality of inter-civilizational contacts and of world systems will

---

[47] In this paper a civilization is defined as the set of the peoples and communities under the hegemony of a single literate culture, as described by Ernest Gellner's model of the "agro-literate polity": Ernest Gellner, *Nations and Nationalism* (Oxford, 1983), pp. 8-13. Hence, though I firmly agree with the view (of, e.g., Pomeranz) that large scale comparison is too often vitiated by the inappropriate use of the "civilization" as the unit of comparison, when carefully identified regional comparison is what is required, it is appropriate when what we are comparing is the nature and vicissitudes of high cultures and their relationships with society at large.

be unsurprised. But I remain sceptical, with some confidence in the case of Western Europe, and to the very limited extent of my competence in other cases. It does appear that rich as the rewards of comparing them more closely and with greater sophistication will unquestionably be, these transformations moved very much according to their own rhythms, though also, it may appear, with something like a common momentum.

THE BIRTH OF A NEW EUROPE ABOUT 1000 CE: CONVERSION, TRANSFER OF INSTITUTIONAL MODELS, NEW DYNAMICS

GÁBOR KLANICZAY

ABSTRACT

The spread of Christianity, the new state formation processes, the economic, social and cultural evolution, and the development of ecclesiastical and political institutions in East Central and Northern Europe after the turn of the first millennium provide an excellent subject for a broad comparative enterprise dealing with the transmission of institutional and cultural models. This period was a noteworthy and well articulated phase of Euroepan history as a whole, described by Marc Bloch as the "deuxième âge féodal"; this was the "age of the cathedrals" for Georges Duby and the high point of the "civilization of the medieval West" for Jacques Le Goff. More recently, it has been characterized by Robert Bartlett as the "making" and the "Europeanization" of Europe, and by R. I. Moore as "the first European revolution". If any model can be identified in the evolution of medieval Europe, this period is the best place to look for it. And if one is trying to observe the transfer of models, what better territory can there be than East Central and Northern Europe, whose people opted, precisely in this period, to follow the example of *Europa Occidens?* In my essay I provide a brief overview of the studies related to four aspects of this process: the conversion to Christianity, the extension of ecclesiastical structures and of religious orders, the formation of dynastic cults, and the evolution of social categories in the High Middle Ages, looking for similarities and differences in the evolution of these two regions.

The two centuries around the turn of the first millennium brought the most significant expansion of *Europa Occidens*, also identified as the world of Latin Christianity, in the early Middle Ages. Two formerly dangerous and aggressive enemies, the Scandinavian Vikings (Danes, Norwegians, and Swedes) on the northern borders and the Hungarians on the eastern, adopted Christianity and founded kingdoms that sought a place among the European states.[1] The most outstanding event of the

---

[1] Carole M. Cusack, *The Rise of Christianity in Northern Europe, 300-1000* (London: Cassell, 1999); Guyda Armstrong and Ian Wood (eds), *Christianizing Peoples and Converting Individuals* (Turnhout: Brepols, 2000), 61-102; András Róna-Tas, *The Hungarians and Europe in the Early Middle Ages. An Introduction to Early Hungarian History* (Budapest: CEU Press, 1999).

"cooptation" of a new group of nations to Europe was, however, related to the largest and most peaceful ethnicity converted in this period, the Slavs, and to the young emperor, Otto III, who was acclaimed according to the *Annales Quedlinburgenses* as the ruler not only of *"populus Romanus"* but of *"quasi tota Europa"*.[2] As a symbolic expression of the new vision of Europe, the *Evangelistary* of Otto III prepared in Reichenau at the end of the tenth century shows four symbolic female figures rendering homage to him: besides *Roma, Gallia*, and *Germania*, the "newcomer" *Sclavinia* now figures as well.[3]

Incorporation of the Slavs had already begun earlier. After the Bulgarians and the Moravians had been converted in the ninth century by the Cyrillo-Methodian mission,[4] Latin Christianity was also firmly anchored among the Czechs[5] and the Croatians.[6] Still, the conversion of the Poles—especially the famous meeting of Otto III and Bolesław Chrobry at the relics of St. Adalbert in Gniezno in March 1000—could be considered as the representative event announcing that a new, extended Europe had been born. The Holy Roman Emperor won in the person of the Polish ruler a new *"frater et cooperator imperii, populi Romani socius et amicus"*.[7] The eastern, orthodox part of Christianity, Byzantium, was on a similarly expansive course at precisely this time. The conversion of Vladimir, Grand Duke of the Kievan Rus, in 988 added another significant eastern Slavic territory to the domain of *Christianitas*.[8]

The birth of this "new Europe" also brought a series of lasting regional differences to the already existing structures of *Europa Occidens*, and the historical dynamics caused by the transfer of institutional and cultural

---

[2] Knut Görich, *Otto III. Romanus Saxonicus et Italicus* (Sigmaringen: Thorbecke, 1993); Gert Althoff, *Kaiser Otto III*, (Darmstadt: WBG, 1996).

[3] Percy Ernst Schramm, *Die deutschen Kaiser und Könige in Bildern ihrer Zeit. 751-1190* (1928), (München: Prestel, 1983), Fig. 110, pp. 205, 362.

[4] Francis Dvornik, *Byzantine Missions among the Slavs* (New Brunswick: Rutgers University Press, 1971); A. P. Vlasto, *The Entry of the Slavs into Christendom* (Cambridge: Cambridge University Press, 1970); Henrik Birnbaum, "The Lives of Sts. Constantine-Cyril and Methodius. A Brief Reassessment", *Cyrillomethodianum* XVII-XVIII (1993-1994), 7-14.

[5] Marvin Kantor (ed. tr.), *The Origins of Christianity in Bohemia. Sources and Commentary* (Evanston, Ill.: Northwestern University Press, 1990).

[6] Neven Budak, "Frühes Christentum in Kroatien", in *Karantanien und der Alpen-Adria-Raum im Frühmittelalter*, ed. by Günther Hödl and Johannes Grabmayer (Vienna-Cologne-Weimar: Böhlau, 1993).

[7] Johannes Fried, *Otto III. und Boleslaw Chrobry. Das Widmungsbild des Aachener Evangeliars, der "Akt von Gnesen" und das frühe polnische und ungarische Königtum* (Stuttgart: Steiner, 1989); Michael Borgolte (ed.), *Polen und Deutschland vor 1000 Jahren. Die Berliner Tagung über den "Akt von Gnesen"* (Berlin: Akademie Verlag, 2002).

[8] Andrzej Poppe, *The Rise of Christian Russia* (London: Variorum, 1982).

models from one European region to another remained a crucial factor of European history up to the modern age. The emergence of this scheme is the topic of this essay.

Historical Interpretations

Let me first consider how the problem of regions and borders was formulated in historiography. "Where do the internal borders of Europe run?" The question with which the Hungarian medievalist Jenő Szűcs started his essay on the three historical regions of Europe twenty years ago[9] has occupied the thoughts of historians ever since the notion of Europe was formulated in Antiquity: Tacitus was well aware of the North/South divide, and the partition of the Roman Empire (also based on the duality of Latin and Greek cultures) had made the East/West divide apparent, at least since the time of Diocletian.[10] These European dividing lines subsequently became more complicated and nuanced after *Europa Occidens* reasserted itself in Carolingian times, and they constituted, along the river Elbe, a new and lasting East-West boundary.[11]

All the erstwhile borders, however, could be (and were) resurrected in the course of history. The political and cultural geography of Europe witnessed the repeated restatement of the quadruple division each time the continent was contemplated in terms of polar oppositions. Medieval Christianity saw Western Latinity in opposition to the "schismatic" Greek and Slavonic Eastern Orthodox Churches. The "barbarian" North was contrasted to the Mediterranean South in Renaissance times, and the Enlightenment reinvented the "exotic" Eastern Europe.[12] In the

---

[9] Jenő Szűcs, "The Three Historical Regions of Europe. An Outline", *Acta Historica Academiae Scientiarum Hungaricae*, 29 (1983), 131-84; also published in *Civil Society and the State: New European Perspectives*, ed. by John Keane (London: Verso, 1988), 291-332.

[10] On the evolution and the differentiation of the notion of Europe, see Federico Chabod, *L'idea di Europa* (Bari: Laterza, 1958); Oskar Halecki, *The Millennium of Europe* (Notre Dame, Indiana: University of Notre Dame Press, 1963); Jean-Baptiste Duroselle, *L'idée d'Europe dans l'histoire* (Paris: Denoël, 1965); Denis Hay, *Europe. The Emergence of an Idea* (Edinburgh: Edinburgh University Press, 1968); Jacques Le Goff, *La Vieille Europe et la nôtre* (Paris: Seuil, 1994); Norman Davies, *Europe. A History* (Oxford-New York: Oxford University Press, 1996); Heinz Duchhardt and Andreas Kunz (eds.), *"Europäische Geschichte" als historiographisches Problem* (Mainz: Verlag Philipp von Zabern, 1997); Michael Mitterauer, *Warum Europa? Mittelalterliche Grundlagen eines Sonderwegs* (München: Beck, 2003).

[11] Jürgen Fischer, *Oriens-Occidens-Europa. Begriff und Gedanke 'Europa' in der Spätantike und im frühen Mittelalter* (Wiesbaden: Steiner, 1957).

[12] Larry Wolff, *Inventing Eastern Europe. The Map of Civilization on the Mind of the Enlightenment* (Stanford: Stanford University Press, 1994).

nineteenth and twentieth centuries, one could observe the gradual formation of the idea of an intermediary region of Central Europe.[13] The noteworthy success of this modern *Mitteleuropa* subsequently prompted research in the historical genealogy of this fascinating but problematic geographic unit.

Polish, Hungarian, and Czech historians have been engaged in this regional inquiry since the 1920s. I should mention among the Polish the work of Marceli Handelsman and Oskar Halecki, who founded, in 1927, the Federation of Historical Societies in Eastern Europe, and who dealt for decades with the definition of an East Central region throughout European history.[14] Halecki formulated the problem some decades later, in his synthetic work *The Borderlands of Western Civilization*. He characterizes historical interest as either dedicating its attention to Western Europe ("frequently identified with the whole continent") or completing the vision of Europe as a whole by rediscovering Byzantium, the Ottoman Empire, or Muscovy. He then goes on to say: "There remained, however, a vast *terra incognita* of European historiography: the eastern part of Central Europe, between Sweden, Germany, and Italy, on the one hand, and Turkey and Russia on the other. In the course of European history a great variety of peoples in this region created their own independent states, sometimes quite large and powerful; in connection with Western Europe they developed their individual national cultures and contributed to the general progress of European civilization". Subsequently he points to the "difficulty of giving to that part of Europe a truly fitting name . . . If only two parts, Western and Eastern Europe, are distinguished, it is impossible to find a proper place for a territory which does not belong *in toto* to either part. If the conception of a Central Europe is added, it must be specified at once that there is an inherent dualism in that central region. Leaving aside its western, homogeneously German section, only the eastern section can be roughly identified with the 'new' or 'unknown' field of study which is being introduced here into the general framework and pattern of European history. For that very reason the name East Central Europe seems most appropriate".[15]

---

[13] G. Beauprêtre (ed.), *L'Europe Centrale. Réalité, mythes, enjeu XVIIIᵉ-XXᵉ siècles* (Warsaw, 1991).

[14] All this is described by Jerzy Kłoczowski, *East Central Europe in the Historiography of the Countries of the Region* (Lublin: Institute of East Central Europe, 1995).

[15] Oscar Halecki, *The Borderlands of Western Civilization. A History of East Central Europe* (New York: Ronald, 1952), pp. 3-4.

In Hungarian historiography, after the 1920s, István Hajnal distinguished historical regions within medieval and early modern Europe on the basis of the spread of the practice of writing.[16] The emerging new historiographic interest was signalled by the publication, between 1935 and 1944, of the review *Archivum Europae Centro-Orientalis*, edited by Emil Lukinich. Among Czech historians the achievements of Francis Dvorník must be mentioned; he concentrated on a comparative presentation of the processes of state formation and conversion to Christianity in the region.[17]

After World War II, the historical problem of Central Europe came to be reformulated by economic and social historians. In Hungary Zsigmond Pál Pach raised the issue in agrarian history, positing a Central European "deviation" in the early modern period from European, Western patterns,[18] as did Jenő Szűcs in connection with the early modern "halt" of urban evolution.[19] Their colleague László Makkai integrated the various regional indices into a coherent picture of the *"caractères originaux"* of this region (using a category once coined by Marc Bloch). He described Central Europe as building social and political modules structurally similar to those of the West, but from very different raw material.[20]

This is the context in which Jenő Szűcs turned to another field of comparative regional history—to the problem of identity and national/tribal consciousness (*Gentilismus*). Here he could identify a neat Central European regional pattern: the common traits distinguishing Central Europe's freshly converted "new barbarians" around the year 1000, both from

---

[16] István Hajnal, *Technika és művelődés* (Technology and Civilization) ed. by Ferenc Glatz. (Budapest: História; 1993); idem, *L'enseignement de l'écriture aux universités médiévales* (Budapest, 1954).

[17] Francis Dvornik, *The Making of Central and Eastern Europe* (London: The Polish Research Centre, 1949); idem, *The Slavs in European History and Civilization* (New Brunswick: Rutgers University Press, 1962).

[18] Zsigmond Pál Pach, *Nyugat-európai és magyarországi agrárfejlődés a XV-XVII. században.* (West European and Hungarian Agrarian Evolution in the Fifteenth to Eighteenth Centuries) (Budapest: Kossuth 1963); idem, *Hungary and the European Economy in Early Modern Times* (Aldershot: Variorum, 1994).

[19] Jenő Szűcs, *Városok és kézművesség a XV. századi Magyarországon* (Towns and Crafts in Fifteenth Century Hungary) (Budapest: Művelt nép, 1955); idem "Das Städtewesen in Ungarn im 15-17. Jahrhundert" in György Székely (ed.), *La Renaissance et la Réformation en Pologne et en Hongrie.* (Budapest: Akadémiai, 1963), 97-164.

[20] Marc Bloch, *Les caractères originaux de l'histoire rurale française* (Oslo, H. Aschehoug; Cambridge, Mass., Harvard University Press, 1931); László Makkai, "Les caractères originaux de l'histoire économique et sociale de l'Europe orientale pendant le Moyen Age", *Acta Historica Academiae Scientiarum Hungaricae*, 16 (1970), 261-87.

the Latin and Germanic peoples that had taken up Christianity centuries earlier, and from the Russian Orthodox East, later partly subdued by the Mongol, and also from the Byzantine, Bulgarian, Serbian Southeast, which later came under Ottoman rule.[21] The long-term evolution of this Central European model, initiated by his studies on national consciousness, was carried forward in Szűcs's previously quoted essay on the three historical regions of Europe.[22] He points out that after an initial similarity between the new East Central European states and Kievan Russia in the eleventh to thirteenth centuries, the Mongol attack introduced a breach and pushed Central Europe toward more intensive assimilation to the West. Yet the hastened, centrally promoted and thus necessarily inorganic modernization produced several side-effects (e.g., the disproportionately large nobility and the relative weakness of urban development in Hungary and in Poland) and allowed the subsequent reversal of this Western orientation several times. A kind of pendulum swing (or, to echo the great Hungarian poet, Endre Ady, a "ferry-like" movement) can be observed in the changing alignments of the countries in this region. At times they moved closer to the West, at other times to their eastern neighbours.

The most recent synthetic overviews of this problem are by Pál Engel, who first analyzed how the new Christian state created by the converted Hungarians found its place among the kingdoms of Christian Europe after the year 1000.[23] In a second monograph, he concentrated mainly on the organization of the political structures of the "realm of Saint Stephen"; the evolution of the institutional, administrative, and social structures behind this important medieval state from the eleventh to the thirteenth centuries; and their successful reorganization and modernization by the newcomer Angevins in the fourteenth century.[24]

---

[21] This book, written in the 1970s, was published posthumously: Jenő Szűcs, *A magyar nemzeti tudat kialakulása. Két tanulmány a kérdés előtörténetéből* (The Formation of the Hungarian National Consciousness. Two Studies from the Prehistory of the Question) (Szeged: Magyar Őstörténeti Könyvtár, 1992); see also my review of it in *Budapest Review of Books* 4 (1994), 25-9; idem, "Zwei Fragmente", in *Studien zum Nationalen Bewußtsein: Mittelalter und Gegenwart*, ed. by János M. Bak, Special Issue of *East Central Europe—L'Europe du Centre-Est. Eine wissenschaftliche Zeitschrift* Vol. 20-23, pt. 2 (1993-1996), 55-90.

[22] Szűcs, "The Three Historical Regions".

[23] Pál Engel, *Beilleszkedés Európába a kezdetektől 1440-ig* (Finding one's place in Europe from the beginnings to 1440) (Budapest: Háttér Lap- és Könyvkiadó, 1990); cf. my review of it, "Incursions into Europe", in *Budapest Review of Books* 2 (1992), 16-20.

[24] Pál Engel, *The Realm of St. Stephen. A History of Medieval Hungary 895-1526*. Translated by Tamás Pálosfalvi. English edition edited by Andrew Ayton (London-New York: I. B. Tauris Publishers, 2001).

In Poland, post-World War II historians also took a new look at social and economic topics. The work of Aleksander Gieysztor stands out here. He wrote a number of studies of Polish and regional urban development and early state formation.[25] The model was set by the comparative economic studies carried out by Marian Małowist[26] and Witold Kula.[27] Meanwhile, many Polish medievalists were striving to situate Polish history in a broad comparative European context: Aleksander Gieysztor,[28] Bronisław Geremek [29] and Henryk Samsonowicz[30] should be mentioned here.

One last significant group of historical investigations has to be added to this enumeration of mainly Polish and Hungarian studies: German (and partially Czech) historiography crystallizing around the notion formulated by Ferdinand Seibt: *Westmitteleuropa*.[31] Seibt, and the whole tradition of German and Austrian *Ostforschung*, proposed this term principally for the analysis of the economic, social, and cultural influence of Germany on this region in commercial contacts, urban structures, and religious orders. The western (principally German and Austrian, but also partly

---

[25] Aleksander Gieysztor, "Le origini delle città nella Polonia medievale", In *Studi in onore di Armando Sapori*. (Milan, 1957), t. 1, 129-46; idem "Les stuctures économiques en pays slaves à l'aube du Moyen Âge jusqu'au XIe siècle et l'échange monétaire", in *Moneta e scambi nell'alto medioevo*, Settimane di studio del Centro italiano di studi sull'alto medioevo, 8, 21-23 aprile 1960 (Spoleto: Centro italiano di studi sull'alto medioevo, 1961), 455-84; idem, "Trade and Industry in Eastern Europe before 1200", in *The Cambridge Economic History*, vol. 2, ed. by M. M. Postan and E. Miller (Cambridge: Cambridge University Press, 1987), 474-524, 912-17.

[26] Marian Małowist, *Croissance et régression en Europe XIVe-XVIIe siècles. Recueil d'articles* (Paris: Armand Colin, 1972).

[27] Witold Kula, *Théorie économique du système féodal. Pour un modèle de l'économie polonaise XVIe-XVIIIe siècle* (Paris-La Haye: Mouton, 1970).

[28] Tadeusz Manteuffel and Aleksander Gieysztor (eds), *L'Europe aux Xe-XIe siècles. Aux origines des états nationaux* (Warsaw, 1968); Aleksander Gieysztor, "La Polonia medioevale tra Occidente ed Oriente europeo", *Studi storici*, 9 (1968), 247-60; idem, "L'Europe médiéval du Centre-Est: frontières mouvantes de cultures", in *Europa medievale e mondo Bizantino. Contatti effettivi e possibilità di studi comparati*, ed. by Girolamo Arnaldi and Guglielmo Cavallo (Rome, 1997), 213-20.

[29] Bronisław Geremek, *The Common Roots of Europe* (Cambridge: Polity Press, 1991). First published in Italy under the title *Le radici comuni dell'Europa*, by Arnaldo Mondadori Editore.

[30] Henryk Samsonowicz, *Miejsce Polski w Europie* (The Place of Poland in Europe). (Warsaw: Bellona, 1995).

[31] Ferdinand Seibt, "Von Prag bis Rostock. Zur Gründung der Universitäten in Mitteleuropa", in *Festschrift für Walter Schlesinger*, ed. by Helmut Beumann (Cologne-Vienna: Böhlau, 1973), 406-26; Winfried Eberhard, Hans Lemberg, Heinz-Dieter Heimann, and Robert Luft (eds.), *Westmitteleuropa—Ostmitteleuropa. Vergleiche und Beziehungen. Festschrift für Ferdinand Seibt zum 65. Geburtstag* (Munich: Oldenbourg, 1992).

Italian) neighbors of the new Central European nations indeed developed a lasting cooperation and symbiosis with this region. They were instrumental in introducing and maintaining "western" models in these countries, and they represented the changing "universal" tendencies of the various ages, but they also developed a special Central European "regional character"[32] themselves.

At the same time Central Europe also received stimulation from a number of influences from the other side, from Byzantium and from *Slavia orthodoxa*.[33] While frequently menaced with becoming the clash zone and the prey of the Western and Eastern superpowers (the Holy Roman Empire, Byzantium, the Mongols, the Ottoman Empire, Russia), in the Middle Ages this region was also unique as a meeting place of Western and Eastern, Northern and Mediterranean cultures.

The last book written by Aleksander Gieysztor gives an elegant synthesis of recent research on the birth of medieval Central Europe: *The New Europe of the Year 1000. The Papacy, the Empire and the "Newcomers"*.[34] Gieysztor presents a systematic comparative panorama of these transforming tribal societies, unified by emerging new elites and dynasties taking up the Christian faith. He describes in detail the formation of the three Christian states of Central Europe—the Czech, the Polish, and the Hungarian—and then shows how the specific personal impact of some of the great historical personalities contributed to the integration of this region in the structures of Europe. He starts his book with a description of the Rome-based all-European network developed by the martyr missionary bishop St. Adalbert,[35] who worked toward the better incorporation of his native Bohemia and its two neighbors, Hungary and Poland, into the world of *Christianitas*. We meet the learned pope of the year 1000, Gerbert d'Aurillac (Sylvester II), who allegedly sent

---

[32] Hagen Keller, *Zwischen regionaler Begrenzung und universalem Horizont. Deutschland im Imperium der Salier und Staufer 1024-1250* (Berlin: Propylaen, 1986).

[33] Cf. Arnaldi and Cavallo, *Europa medievale e mondo Bizantino*; Evelyne Patlagean, "Les Etats d'Europe centrale et Byzance, ou l'oscillation des confins", *Revue historique*, 302/4 (2000), 827-68.

[34] Aleksander Gieysztor, *L'Europe nouvelle autour de l'An Mil. La Papauté, l'Empire et les «nouveaux venus»* (Rome, 1997).

[35] František Graus, "St. Adalbert und St. Wenzel. Zur Funktion der Heiligenverehrung in Böhmen", in Klaus-Detlev Rothusen and Klaus Zernack (eds.), *Europa Slavica—Europa Orientalis. Festschrift H. Ludat* (Berlin: Duncker & Humblot, 1980), 205-231; Sławomir Gawlas, "Der hl. Adalbert als Landespatron und die frühe Nationenbildung bei den Polen", in Borgolte (ed.), *Polen und Deutschland*, 193-234.

the crown to St. Stephen, and his disciple, the "marvel of the world", the grand emperor, Otto III who decided to convert and co-opt this region rather than try to conquer it, but who left his utopian plan unfinished when he died at the age of twenty-two.[36]

Inventing Central Europe in the years around 1000 allowed the extension of *Europa Occidens* toward the East and the constitution of the Holy Roman Empire as the centre of *Christianitas*. What was unforeseen then, in the times of Emperor Otto III, was that this extension would soon clash against various forms of resistance from the East, and the Eastern part of this "central" region would acquire its specific identity by remaining a conflict-ridden intermediary zone between West and East, an "*antemurale*", a buffer region with recurrent existential insecurities and frequently resurgent split consciousness.

Another round of considerations should follow here on the problem of the formation of the Scandinavian "periphery",[37] whose rhythm and characteristics were in many respects similar to Central Europe's. True, the problem of the relationship of Scandinavian evolution to all-European models is not researched in such an obstinate manner as the similar problem in Central Europe (maybe because Scandinavia feels less excluded from the development of the West). This consideration was, however, present here as well. In a few cases, such as the problem of the relations with the papacy studied by Wolfgang Seegrün,[38] or the problem of the "categories of medieval culture" and "feudalism" studied by Aaron J. Gurevich, it has already been considered.[39] The comparative point

---

[36] Cf. also: Pierre Riché, *Gerbert d'Aurillac, le pape de l'an mil* (Paris: Fayard, 1987); idem, *Les grandeurs de l'an mil* (Paris: Bartillat, 1999).

[37] I will not dwell here on the discussion of the notions of "core" or "centre" and "periphery", as introduced into the discussion of economic history by Immanuel Wallerstein, *The Modern World System: Capitalist Agriculture and the Origins of the European World Economy in the Sixteenth Century*, (New York: Academic Press, 1974), following the incentives of Fernand Braudel; my use of the notion of "periphery" will purely indicate the geographic position of the two discussed regions in relation to two ecclesiastical centres: Rome and Byzantium.

[38] Wolfgang Seegrün, *Das Papsttum und Skandinavien bis zur Vollendung der nordischen Kirchenorganisation (1164)* (Neumünster: Wachholz, 1967).

[39] Aaron J. Gurevich, "Die Freien Bauern im mittelalterlichen Norwegen", *Wissenschaftliche Zeitschrift der Universität Greifswald*, 14 (1965), 323-36; idem, "Space and Time in the Weltmodell of the Old Scandinavian People", *Medieval Scandinavia* (1969), 42-53; idem, "Saga and History: The Historical Conception of Snorri Sturluson", *Medieval Scandinavia* (1971), 42-53; idem, *Le origini del feudalesimo*, pref. di Raoul Manselli (Roma, 1982).

of view is also recognizable in recent studies by Birgit and Peter Sawyer,[40] Sverre Bagge,[41] Tore Nyberg[42] and Brian Patrick McGuire.[43] The analogy between Central European and Scandinavian evolution has recently been examined more thoroughly by historical researchers. A few examples: the comparative enquiry on ecclesiastical history in both regions organized by André Vauchez in 1989;[44] the conference in the Collegium Budapest in 2001 on the comparison of saints' cults and canonization trials in Scandinavia and Central Europe;[45] the new research project launched by Sverre Bagge, his colleagues in Bergen, Nora Berend (Cambridge), and several Central European research centres on "Periphery and Centre in Medieval Europe", and finally, another comparison between Northern and East-Central Europe was attempted in connection with the recent insights into the papal penitentiary archives, where, after the important initiatives of Ludwig Schmugge,[46] a project for the former region was launched by Christian Krötzl, and by Gerhard Jaritz and Piroska Nagy for the latter.[47]

All this work, however, will only be tangentially mentioned in the following suggestions for a comparative overview of the transfer of institutional models. Because of my particular competencies, I will mainly consider the case of Central Europe.

---

[40] Birgit and Peter Sawyer, *Medieval Scandinavia. From Conversion to Reformation, circa 800-1500* (Minnesota-London: The University of Minnesota Press, 1993).

[41] Sverre Bagge, *The Political Thought of The King's Mirror* (Odense: Odense University Press, 1987), idem, "The Scandinavian Kingdoms", in *The New Cambridge Medieval History*, vol. 5 (Cambridge: Cambridge University Press, 1999), 720-42. See also his contribution to this volume.

[42] Tore Nyberg, *Die Kirche in Skandinavien. Mitteleuropäischer und englischer Einfluss im 11. und 12. Jahrhundert: Anfänge der Domkapitel Børglum und Odense in Dänemark* (Sigmaringen: Thorbecke, 1986); idem, *Monasticism in North-Western Europe, 800-1200* (Aldershot: Ashgate, 2000); Lars Bisgaard (ed.), *Medieval spirituality in Scandinavia and Europe: A collection of essays in honour of Tore Nyberg* (Odense: University Press, 2001).

[43] Brian Patrick McGuire (ed.), *The Birth of Identities. Denmark and Europe in the Middle Ages* (Copenhagen: C. A. Reitzel, 1996).

[44] *L'Eglise et le peuple chrétien dans les pays de l'Europe du Centre-Est et du Nord (XIVᵉ-XVᵉ siècles)*, Actes du colloque . . . de Rome (27-29 Janvier 1986) (Rome: École Française de Rome, 1990).

[45] Gábor Klaniczay (ed.), *Procès de canonisation au Moyen Age—Aspects juriqiques et religieux, Medieval Canonization Processes—Legal and Religious Aspects* (Rome: École française de Rome, 2004).

[46] Ludwig Schmugge, "Centro e periferia attraverso le dispense pontificie nel secolo XV", in *Vita religiosa e identità politiche. Universalità e particolarismi nell'Europa del tardo Medio Evo*, ed. by Sergio Gensini (SanMiniato, 1998), 33-58.

[47] In October 2003 there was a conference on this theme in Bergen organized by Thorstein Jorgensen, in January 2004 another one was organised by Piroska Nagy in Budapest with the title: *Ad Confines. The Papal Curia and the Eastern Peripheries of Christendom in the Later Middle Ages (14th-15th c.)*.

Conversions

The religious conversion, the state formation processes, the economic, social, and cultural evolution, and the development of ecclesiastical and political institutions in East-Central and Northern Europe after the first millennium provide an excellent subject for a broad comparative enterprise dealing with the transmission of institutional and cultural models. This period was a noteworthy and well articulated phase of European history as a whole, described by Marc Bloch as the *"deuxième âge féodal"*;[48] this was the "age of the cathedrals" for Georges Duby[49] and the high point of "the civilization of the Medieval West" for Jacques Le Goff.[50] This period has been characterized more recently by Robert Bartlett as the "making" and the "Europeanization" of Europe,[51] and by Robert Moore as the "first European revolution".[52] If any model can be identified in the evolution of medieval Europe, this period is the best place to look for it. And if one is trying to observe the transfer of models, what can be better territory than the eastern and northern regions, whose people opted, precisely in this period, to follow the example of *Europa Occidens?* In the second half of my essay I will provide a brief overview of the studies related to some aspects of this process.

Before starting, we need a brief note on the terms of this comparison, and the prudence with which one should diagnose historical phenomena as replicas of institutional and cultural models elsewhere. Much of the Central and East European historiography described above aimed to uncover precisely this component in the historical evolution of the region, measuring the degree of success by the recognizable accuracy and speed of the adaptation of these models, or, on the other hand, complaining about the imperfection and sluggishness of their adoption as a sign of "backwardness". Comparative analyses of this medieval period, however, have recently been reconsidered in several important conferences, which restated the stimulating plea of Marc Bloch for the "comparative history of European societies"[53] in the light of the achievements of the

---

[48] Marc Bloch, *Feudal Society*. Vol. 1. *The Growth of Ties of Dependence*; Vol. 2. *Social Classes and Political Organization* (Chicago: University of Chicago Press, 1964).

[49] Georges Duby, *The Age of the Cathedrals: Art and Society, 980-1420* (Chicago: University of Chicago Press, 1981).

[50] Jacques Le Goff, *La Civilisation de l'Occident médiéval* (Paris: Arthaud, 1984).

[51] Robert Bartlett, *The Making of Europe. Conquest, Colonization and Cultural Change 950-1350* (Harmondsworth: Penguin Books, 1993).

[52] Robert Moore, *The First European Revolution* (Oxford: Blackwell, 2000).

[53] Marc Bloch, "Pour une histoire comparée des sociétés européennes", *Revue de Synthèse*

Annales historians and other schools of comparative European historiography.[54] As Marc Bloch had done in his *Feudal Society*, the studies and
discussions initiated by S. N. Eisenstadt (among them the workshop
feeding into the present volume) strove to situate European civilization
in a world-wide comparative perspective.[55] As for the internal characterization of the "European model", the stress is put nowadays on the
"irreducible plurality of cultures"[56] and on a re-examination of the terms
of comparison in the light of recent findings in social theory.[57] A useful
corrective to the traditional comparative approaches and the study of
the transfer of cultural models is what Michael Werner and Bénédicte
Zimmermann labelled *"histoire croisée"* or *"Verflechtungsgeschichte"*.[58] This
approach points to mutual influences at each major political, social or
cultural encounter which constantly transform the model as well as its
presumed replica, and emphasizes rather a dynamic relationship emerging
from these processes, instead of a mechanical transfer and a passive
reception of crystallized and unchanging artefacts.

Bearing all of this in mind, let me exemplify my argument with brief
sketches of four subjects: the process of conversion to Christianity, the
extension of ecclesiastical structures and of religious orders, the formation of dynastic cults, and the evolution of social categories in East-
Central and Northern Europe.

historique (1928), repr. in idem, *Mélanges historiques* (Paris: S.E.V.P.E.N., 1963) vol. I,
16-40.

[54] *Marc Bloch aujourd'hui. Histoire comparée et sciences sociales*, ed. by Hartmut Atsma and
André Burguière (Paris, EHESS, 1990).

[55] Bloch, *Feudal Society*; S. N. Eisenstadt, *European Civilization in a Comparative Perspective.
A Study in the Relations Between Culture and Social Structure* (Oslo: Norwegian University Press,
1987).

[56] Michael Borgolte (ed.), "Unaufhebbare Pluralität der Kulturen? Zur Dekonstruktion
und Konstruktion des mittelalterlichen Europa", in *Historische Zeitschrift*, Beiheft 32
(München: Oldenbourg, 2001); Michael Borgolte, *Europa entdeckt seine Vielfalt 1050-1250*
(Stuttgart: Verlag Eugen Ulmer, 2002).

[57] Patrick Geary, "Vergleichende Geschichte und sozialwissenschaftliche Theorie", in
Michael Borgolte (ed.), *Das europäische Mittelalter im Spannungsbogen des Vergleichs* (Berlin:
Akademie, 2001), 29-38.

[58] Michael Werner and Bénédicte Zimmermann, "Vergleich, Transfer, Verflechtung:
Der Ansatz der Histoire croisée und die Herausforderung des Transnationalen", *Geschichte
und Gesellschaft*, 28 (2002), 607-36; idem, "Penser l'histoire croisée: entre empirie et
réflexivité", *Annales HSS*, 58 (2003), 7-36.

The "rise of Western Christendom",[59] the "conversion of Europe",[60] the "evangelization of Europe",[61] "christianizing peoples",[62] a historical process that is by its nature related to the transfer of a set of cultural and institutional models, is a good subject for the illustration of the basic problems in these processes. In the first place, it seems convenient, following Ian Wood, to distinguish between the missionary activity of converting pagans and Christianization in a country where the Christian Church already had the support of secular power and was trying to intensify its publicly uncontested domination in the sphere of religion.[63] These two types roughly corresponded in Europe to two historical phases: individual missionary activity coming from various directions preceded the decision of the rulers to take up Christianity and to support the expansion of the ecclesiastical organization. With a series of slight variations, this had been the pattern in the early Middle Ages, with the conversion of the Visigoths, the Franks, the Anglo-Saxon kingdoms, and various Germanic tribes.[64]

It might be worth underlining that in this first phase of Christianization many rivalries developed between missionary centres: Rome and the Arians among the Visigoths, Franks and other Germanic tribes, Rome and the Irish on Anglo-Saxon ground.[65] The conversion of East-Central and Northern Europe followed an analogous pattern. In the conversion of Scandinavia around the tenth and eleventh centuries missionaries coming from the Anglo-Saxon domains were fiercely competitive with others from the regions of Hamburg and Bremen.[66] As for East-Central Europe, besides the three principal centres sending converting missions (Italy and Bavaria for Latin Christianity and Byzantium for the Greek variety), a Slavonic tradition emerged after the successful missionary

---

[59] Peter Brown, *The Rise of Western Christendom: 200-1000 AD* (Oxford: Blackwell, 1996).

[60] Robert Fletcher, *The Conversion of Europe: from Paganism to Christianity 371-1386* (London:Harper Collins, 1997).

[61] Ian Wood, *The Missionary Life. Saints and the Evangelisation of Europe, 400-1050* (Harlow: Pearson Education, 2001).

[62] Armstrong and Wood, *Christianizing Peoples and Converting Individuals.*

[63] Wood, *The Missionary Life,* 3-4.

[64] E. A. Thompson, *The Visigoths in the Time of Ulfila* (Oxford: Clarendon, 1966); Walter Goffart, *The Narrators of Barbarian History. Jordanes, Gregory of Tours, Bede, and Paul the Deacon* (Princeton: Princeton University Press, 1989); Henry Mayr-Harting, *The Coming of Christianity to England* (London: B. T. Batsford, 1972).

[65] R. A. Markus, "Gregory the Great and a papal missionary strategy", in *The Mission of the Church and the Propagation of the Faith,* ed. by G. J. Cuming, (*Studies in Church History,* 6) (Cambridge, 1960), 29-38; Wood, *The Missionary Life,* 25-53.

[66] P. H. Sawyer, "The process of Scandinavian Christianization in the tenth and eleventh centuries", in Birgit Sawyer, Peter Sawyer, Ian Wood (eds.), *The Christianization*

activity of Cyril-Constantine and Methodius in Bulgaria and Moravia.[67] The Christianization of the Czechs was claimed both by Bavarian missionaries (who may have converted Duke Spytihněv at the beginning of the tenth century, and who ultimately defined the Latin character of Czech Christianity) and by the Cyrillo-Methodian tradition (Methodius, coming from the Moravians, allegedly baptized the father of Spytihnev, Bořivoj).[68] As for Hungary, the Greek missionaries reached its southeastern confines somewhat earlier than the ones coming from Germanic (Bavarian, Saxon) territories, in the second half of the tenth century. Though the Latin orientation quickly prevailed, the presence of Greek Orthodox Christianity persisted in Hungary till the end of the Middle Ages.[69]

The most emblematic case was the Kievan Rus: according to the narrative of the Russian chronicle "of the olden times" (*Povest vremennykh let*), before deciding which religion to convert to, Grand Duke Vladimir in 986 invited representatives of Latin and Greek Christianity and also some Jewish rabbis. He listened to how they exposed the basic tenets of their faith and opted eventually to align with the Orthodox Church of Byzantium.[70] A point to be retained from all these competing, parallel influences is that one cannot identify a single model transferred to this region. The Christian faith expanded from a multitude

---

of Scandinavia (Alingsås: Viktoria Bokförlag, 1987), 68-87; Lesley Abrams, "The Anglo-Saxons and the Christianization of Scandinavia", *Anglo-Saxon England* 24 (1995), 213-49.

[67] Francis Dvornik, "Byzantium, Rome, the Franks and the Christianization of the Southern Slavs", in *Cyrillo-Methodiana. Slavistische Forschungen* 6 (1964), 85-125; Vlasto, *The Entry of the Slavs into Christendom*; Richard E. Sullivan, "Khan Boris and the Conversion of Bulgaria: A Case Study of the Impact of Christianity on a Barbarian Society", *Studies in Medieval and Renaissance History* 3 (1966), 55-139; Vladimir Vavřínek (ed.), *Byzantium and Its Neighbours from the Mid-9th to the 12th Centuries*. Papers read at the Byzantinological Symposium Bechyně 1990 (Praha: Byzantinoslavica, 1990).

[68] These claims, stemming partly from the contradictory hagiographic tradition of St. Wenceslas (the Slavonic influence was claimed by the controversial Christian legend), are summarized by Kantor, *The Origins of Christianity in Bohemia*.

[69] Gyula Moravcsik, "The role of the Byzantine Church in medieval Hungary", *American Slavic and East European Review* 18-19 (1947), 134-51; idem, *Byzantium and the Magyars* (Amsterdam, 1970); György Györffy, "A szávaszentdemeteri görög monostor XII. századi birtokösszeírása" (The chartulary of the Greek monastery of Sremske Mitrovica from the 12th century), *A Magyar Tudományos Akadémia Társadalmi-történeti tudományok osztályának közleményei* (1952), 325-62, (1953), 69-104.

[70] *Povest' vremennykh let*, ed. V. P. Adrianova-Peretc (Moscow/Leningrad, 1950); Dmitri Obolensky, *The Byzantine Commonwealth. Eastern Europe 500-1453* (London: Sphere Books, 1974); Ihor Ševčenko, *Ukraine between East and West: Essays on Cultural History to the Early Eighteenth Century* (Edmonton—Toronto: Canadian Institute of Ukrainian Studies Press, 1996), 27-53.

of centres, frequently in conflict with each other, coming from "above" as well as "below", and from all directions along the trade routes.

The second phase of Christianization, following the conversion of the rulers and their support given to the Church, worked through two cultural mechanisms: a triad of conflict-repression-resistance, giving way sooner or later to the "melting pot" effect.

The conversion of the barbaricum was certainly disrupting. It destroyed older social and cultural structures, creating a set of new dependencies and frequently also generating a lasting resistance to the West.[71] The hostility is illustrated by the tragic outcome of the missionary journeys of Saint Adalbert (†997), the "Five Brothers" (†1002) and then of Bruno of Querfurt (†1009) on the Prussian fringes of Poland. Their violent massacre by the local pagans shows the degree of "barbarian" hostility to the spreading of the new faith.[72]

The Hungarian Christianization could hardly be labelled a peaceful one either. Duke Géza (c. 970-997) and his son, Stephen I, crushed the resistant rival chieftains in a series of bloody internal wars, frequently with the help of German knights.[73] The nature of the repression is well illustrated by a passage from the *Legenda Minor* of Saint Stephen (written toward the end of the eleventh century):

> The king spoke to them, saying: 'Why did you transgress the law ordained by God? Why did you punish the innocent and know no mercy? . . . As you have done, so shall the Lord do unto you through my person.' Having received their sentence, they were led away, and perished, hanged two by two along the roads of every province of the country. Thus it was that he wanted to make people understand that the same would be done to whoever did not abide by the just law promulgated by God. The people of the earth heard the judgement that the king had passed, and were filled with fear.[74]

---

[71] Ian Wood, "Pagan religions and superstitions east of the Rhine from the fifth to the ninth century", in G. Ausenda (ed.), *After Empire: Towards an Ethnology of Europe's Barbarians* (Woodbridge: Boydell Press, 1995); Karol Modzelewski, "Europa romana, Europa feudale, Europa barbara", *Bullettino dell'Istituto Storico per il Medio Evo e Archivio Muratoriano*, 100 (1995/96), 377-409.

[72] Aleksander Gieysztor, "Sanctus et gloriosissimus martyr Christi Adalbertus. Un État et une Église missionnaires aux alentours de l'an mille", in *La conversione al cristianesimo nell'Europa dell'alto medioevo*. Settimane di studi sull'alto Medioevo, vol. 14 (Spoleto, 1969), 611-47; Wood, *The Missionary Life*, 207-43.

[73] György Györffy, *Saint Stephen the King* (Boulder, Col.: Atlantic Publications, 1986).

[74] *Legendae Sancti Stephani regis maior et minor atque legenda ab Hartvico conscripta*, ed. by Emma Bartoniek, in: *Scriptores Rerum Hungaricarum tempore ducum regumque stirpis Arpadianae gestarum*, ed. by Emericus Szentpétery (Budapest: Academia Litter. Hungarica, 1938), vol. II, 398-9.

No wonder that the reprisals soon provoked two forceful "pagan" upheavals (in 1046 and 1072). One of the leading figures of the Hungarian church, Bishop Gerard (Gellért) of Csanád, was killed in the first one.[75]

Yet the new Christian kingdom of Hungary managed to become a "host-country", open to absorbing all kinds of interesting or useful novelties (Saint Stephen's harsh measures were also aimed at securing the protection of foreigners). "Guests" (Bavarian missionaries, Italian pilgrims, Byzantine monks, travelling German churchmen, Jewish and Muslim merchants, French and English wandering knights) had to be welcomed and were protected by the king.[76] This was one of the principal recommendations stressed in the "mirror of princes" attributed to Saint Stephen, the *Libellus de institutione morum* addressed to his son Emeric: "A country with a single language and a single custom is weak and vulnerable".[77] Absorption of the cultural and institutional patterns of Latin and Greek Christianity was also furthered by incorporation: at the end of the eleventh century Ladislas I and Coloman, while extending the borders of their kingdom toward the Orthodox territories of Bulgaria and Serbia, attached previously converted Croatia to the Crown of Hungary (this personal union lasted until WWI), and the latter extended similar status to Dalmatia in 1108. These conquests established the *regnum Hungariae* as a meeting point and melting pot of traditions from many different nations and cultures, and as an expansionist power in the Balkans and Eastern Europe.

This mixing can also be observed in other new kingdoms in the East and the North: the Germanic (and Latin) traditions mingled in Czech Christianity with the (Christian or pagan) Slavonic ones till the end of the Middle Ages.[78] Though Poland lost its political unity in the twelfth

---

[75] László Szegfü, "La missione politica ed ideologica di San Gerardo in Ungheria", in Vittore Branca (ed.), *Venezia ed Ungheria nel Rinascimento* (Firenze: Sansoni, 1973), 23-36.

[76] Erik Fügedi, "Das mittelalterliche Königreich Ungarn als Gastland", in Walter Schlesinger (ed.), *Die deutsche Ostsiedlung des Mittelalters als Problem der europäischen Geschichte* (Sigmaringen: Thorbecke, 1975), 471-507; the status of "foreigners" in medieval Hungary was recently analyzed by Nóra Berend, *At the Gate of Christendom. Jews, Muslims and 'Pagans' in Medieval Hungary, c. 1000-c. 1300* (Cambridge: Cambridge University Press, 2001).

[77] Josephus Balogh (ed.), "Libellus de institutione morum", in Szentpétery, *Scriptores Rerum Hungaricarum*, Vol. II, 614-21. Jenő Szűcs, "König Stephans 'Institutionen'—König Stephans Staat", in idem, *Nation und Geschichte. Studien* (Budapest: Corvina, 1981), 245-62.

[78] František Graus, "Kirchliche und heidnische (magische) Komponenten der Stellung der Přemyslidensage und St Wenzels-Ideologie", in *Siedlung und Verfassung Böhmens in der Frühzeit*, eds. František Graus and Herbert Ludat (Wiesbaden: Harrassowitz, 1967), 148-61.

century and regained it only in the fourteenth, its situation between Germanic West and Kievan (later Mongolian) East, Baltic, Scandinavian, and Teutonic North, and Hungarian and Czech South was a colorful one.[79] And as for Scandinavia itself, the coexistence and the changing political hegemony of the three states of Denmark, Norway, and Sweden, and their expansive attempts toward the West (to Iceland and England) and to the East (Finland, Russia), created a similar melting pot.[80]

The absorption of a variety of western or eastern Christian elements did not mean, however, the disappearance of Slavic, Hungarian, Germanic, and old Norse pre-Christian beliefs and customs. Though we hear little of all these in the first centuries after the conversion, except for occasional ecclesiastical complaints about the persistence of "paganism", the resurgence of these beliefs and mythologies can be observed in the chronicles of the subsequent centuries.[81] In the later Middle Ages, the opposition of a learned clerical culture trying to uproot "popular superstition" and "magic" developed there in a similar manner as in the West in the early Middle Ages.[82] But whereas in the West the appearance of the mendicant orders in the thirteenth century started a

---

[79] *Christianity in East Central Europe: Late Middle Ages*. ed. by Jerzy Kłoczowski, Paweł Kras, Wojciech Polak (Lublin: Instytut Europy Srodkowo-Wschodniej, 1999); Jerzy Kłoczowski, *A History of Polish Christianity* (Cambridge: Cambridge University Press, 2000).

[80] Nyberg, *Die Kirche in Skandinavien*; Jürgen Petersohn, *Der südliche Ostseeraum im kirchlich-politischen Kräftespiel des Reichs, Polens und Dänemarks vom 10. bis 13. Jahrhundert* (Vienna-Cologne: Böhlau, 1979); Michael Müller-Wille, *Rom und Byzanz im Norden. Mission und Glaubenswechsel im Ostseeraum während des 8.-14. Jahrhunderts* (Mainz: Akademie der Wissenschaften und der Literatur, 1995).

[81] József Deér, *Heidnisches und Christliches in der altungarischen Monarchie* (Darmstadt: WBG, 1969); Graus, "Kirchliche und heidnische (magische) Komponenten"; Jacek Banaszkiewicz, *Podanie o Piascie i Popielu. Studium porównawcze nad wczesnosredniowiecznymi tradycjami dynastycznymi /*The Piast and Popiel traditions: a study in early medieval dynastic traditions/ (Warszawa: Panstwowe Wydawnictwo Naukowe, 1986); idem, "Königliche Karriere von Hirten, Gärtnern und Pflüger. Zu einem mittelalterlichen Erzählschema vom Erwerb der Königsherrschaft (die Sagen von Johannes Agnus, Premysl, Ina, Wamba und Dagobert)", *Saeculum*, 3/4 (1982), 265-286; Sverre Bagge, *Society and Politics in Snorri Sturluson's Heimskringla* (Berkeley: The University of California Press, 1991); idem, "Icelandic Uniqueness or a Common European Culture. The Case of the Kings' Sagas", in *Scandinavian Studies* 69 (1997), 418-42; Niels Henrik Holmquist-Larsen, "Saxo Grammaticus in Danish Historical Writing and Literature", in McGuire, *The Birth of Identities*, 161-88.

[82] Dieter Harmening, *Superstitio. Überlieferungs- und theoriegeschichtliche Untersuchungen zur kirchlich-theologischen Aberglaubensliteratur des Mittelalters* (Berlin: Schmidt, 1979); Aaron J. Gurevich, *Medieval Popular Culture: Problems of Belief and Preception* (Cambridge: Cambridge University Press, 1990); Valerie Flint, *The Rise of Magic in Early Medieval Europe* (Princeton: Princeton University Press, 1991).

new campaign against superstition,[83] a similar critique of "popular magic" in East Central Europe came only in the fourteenth and fifteenth centuries; its foremost representatives were Observant Franciscans—but all this is beyond the chronological range discussed here.[84]

Ecclesiastical Institutions

The second topic I propose, the development of ecclesiastical structures and monastic orders, is the immediate continuation of the conversion process. In the Hungarian case, the quick development of ecclesiastical institutions (bishoprics, abbeys, parishes) and state administrative structures (counties, castles) is fairly well documented in the Laws of Saint Stephen (†1038), Saint Ladislas (†1095), and Coloman the 'Learned' (†1116).[85] After the relatively slow rise of the number of bishoprics in the Czech and Polish lands (Prague, Olomouc, Poznań, Gniezno, Cracow, Wrocław, Kołobrzeg, Plock),[86] the territory of the Hungarian kingdom quickly witnessed the foundation of ten bishoprics (Esztergom, Kalocsa/Bács, Pécs, Györ, Veszprém, Csanád, Eger, Vác, Bihar, Transylvania).[87] As for Scandinavia, the Danish bishoprics began to multiply during the reign of Otto I (Hedeby/Schleswig, Ribe, Århus, Viberg, Børglum, Odense, Roskilde, Lund), soon followed by the Swedish and Norwegian bishoprics (Skara, Uppsala, Sigtuna, Linköping, Nidaros/Trondheim, Oslo, Stavanger Selje).[88]

The establishment of bishoprics and the development of ecclesiastical

---

[83] Jean-Claude Schmitt, *The Holy Greyhound: Guinefort, healer of children since the thirteenth century* (Cambridge: Cambridge University Press—Editions de la Maison des Sciences de l'homme, 1983); idem, "Les superstitions", in Jacques Le Goff (ed.), *Des dieux de la Gaule à la papauté d'Avignon (Histoire de la France religieuse,* Vol I.) (Paris: Seuil, 1988), 419-551.

[84] Stanisław Bylina, "Magie, sorcellerie et culture populaire en Pologne aux XVe et XVIe siècles", in *Witch Beliefs and Witch-hunting in Central and Eastern Europe* (Conference in Budapest, Sept. 6-9, 1988), Special issue of *Acta Ethnographica Hungarica. An International Journal of Ethnography,* 37 (1991), 173-90; Krzysztof Bracha, *Teolog, diabeł i zabobony: Świadectwo traktatu Mikołaja Magni z Jawora De superstitionibus* (The Theologian, the Devil, and the Superstitions: The Testimony of the Treatise of Nicolaus Jawor, *De superstitionibus*) (Warsaw: Instytut Historii PAN, 1999).

[85] János M. Bak, György Bónis, and James Ross Sweeney (eds. tr.), *The Laws of Medieval Hungary. Decreta regni mediaevalis Hungariae* (Bakersfield: Schlacks, 1989); János M. Bak, "Signs of Conversion in Central European Laws", in Armstrong and Wood (eds), *Christianizing Peoples and Converting Individuals,* 115-24.

[86] Kłoczowski, *A History of Polish Christianity,* 14-20.

[87] György Györffy, "Zu den Anfängen der ungarischen Kirchenorganisation auf Grund neuer quellenkritischer Ergebnisse", *Archivum Historiae Pontificae* 7 (1969), 79-113.

[88] Nyberg, *Die Kirche in Skandinavien,* 23, 77; Bartlett, *The Making of Europe,* 5-23.

structures were closely related to the evolution of the relations of these regions with the Papacy. The question had special political significance in the period of the emerging political conflicts between the Papacy and the Empire—the alignment of these new Christian kingdoms was very important for both. In general the intensive papal diplomacy had considerable success in Hungary, Poland, and Sweden, whereas the loyalties of Bohemia and Denmark were continually disputed between the Pope and the partisans of the Empire.[89] The papal legates frequently interfered in dynastic conflicts in all these countries and tried to introduce their up-to-date centralizing reforms in these recently Christianized countries, where they expected less resistance to their initiatives. The long pontificate of Alexander III (1151-1181) is a good example for this model. He was one of the great artisans of "papal government", and his attention was alert to the development of ecclesiastical structures on the periphery.[90] In his famous letter addressed in 1171 or 1172 to "*carissimi in Christo filio K. illustri Suevorum et Gothorum regi*",[91] where he gives long instructions on the nature of Christian marriage (opposing alleged practices of pagan polygamy),[92] he writes about the honor to be shown to the bishops and other ecclesiastics, recommends the payment of tithes, and finally reprimands the Swedes for venerating as a saint a man who was killed while drunk. This last passage of the letter, starting with the exclamation "*Audivimus*", became the cornerstone of the Papacy's claim to have the exclusive right to canonize saints. This right, previously exercised by the bishops, subsequently became a papal monopoly in the early thirteenth century.[93]

---

[89] Walter Ullmann, *The Growth of Papal Government in the Middle Ages* (Routledge & Kegan Paul, London, 1955); Colin Morris, *The Papal Monarchy. The Western Church from 1050 to 1250* (Oxford: Clarendon Press, 1989); József Gerics and Erzsébet Ladányi, "A Szentszék és a magyar állam a 11. században" (The Holy See and the Hungarian State in the eleventh century), and Kornél Szovák, "Pápai-magyar kapcsolatok a 12. században" (Papal-Hungarian contacts in the twelfth century), in *Magyarország és a Szentszék* (Hungary and the Holy See), ed. Zombori István (Budapest: METEM, 1996), 9-46; Seegrün, *Das Papstum und Skandinavien*; Werner Ohnsorge, *Päpstliche und gegenpäpstliche Legaten in Deutschland und Skandinavien 1159-1181* (Vaduz: Kraus Reprint, 1965).

[90] Johannes Laudage, *Alexander III. und Friedrich Barbarossa* (Cologne: Böhlau, 1999); the relations of Alexander III with the "periphery" are examined in the MA thesis by Márta Kondor at the Central European University: *Case Studies to the Problem of Centre-Periphery in Western Christendom: Uppsala and Spalato in the Time of Pope Alexander III*. Budapest, 2004.

[91] Migne, *Patrologia Latina*, vol. 200, col. 1259.

[92] On this problem see Georges Duby, *Medieval Marriage: Two Models from Twelfth-century France*. (Baltimore: Johns Hopkins University Press, 1991).

[93] Eric Waldram Kemp, "Pope Alexander III and the Canonisation of the Saints", *Transactions of the Royal Historical Society*, 4th series, 27 (1945), 55-62; idem, *Canonization*

Besides the bishoprics and parishes supported and monitored by both the secular power and the Papacy, the most important agents in the process of Christianization were the religious orders. The first monastic foundations went in tandem with the missionary activity; they were principally Benedictine monasteries in the East-Central European territories.[94] A significant example of it is the monastery of Pannonhalma, founded in Hungary in 996, dedicated to Saint Martin;[95] similar importance could be ascribed to Břevnov near Prague, Tyniec near Cracow, and Mogilno near Gniezno.[96] A few monasteries of Slavonic or Greek observance were also founded in this region (Sázava in Bohemia, Veszprémvölgy, Visegràd, and Szávaszentdemeter in Hungary).[97] As for Scandinavia, Anglo-Saxon monasticism was dominant. Anglo-Saxon monks founded one of the first important monastic centres in Denmark, the monastery of St Alban in Odense.[98]

In the eleventh century a very important role was played by Cluny,[99] the great monastic centre of the age. Abbot Odilo accompanied Emperor Otto III to the famous meeting in Gniezno[100] and corresponded with Saint Stephen, the king of Hungary.[101] The Cistercian monastic reformers

---

and Authority in the Western Church (Oxford: Oxford University Press, 1948), 99-101; André Vauchez, *La sainteté en Occident aux derniers siècles du moyen âge. D'après les procès de canonisation et les documents hagiographiques* (Rome: École française de Rome, 1981), 29-30.

[94] Tore Nyberg, *Monasticism in North-Western Europe, 800-1200* (Aldershot: Ashgate, 2000); Beatrix F. Romhányi, *Kolostorok és társaskáptalanok a középkori Magyarországon: katalógus*. (Monasteries and collegiate chapters in medieval Hungary) (Budapest: Pytheas, 2000).

[95] *Mons sacer, 996-1996: Pannonhalma 1000 éve.* (Sacred mountain, 996-1996: thousand years of Pannonhalma), I-III. ed. by Imre Takács, (Pannonhalma: Pannonhalmi Főapátság, 1996); *Paradisum plantavit: Bencés monostorok a középkori Magyarországon* (Paradisum plantavit: Benedictine monasteries in medieval Hungary), ed. by Imre Takács (Pannonhalma: Pannonhalmi Bencés Főapátság, 2001).

[96] Kłoczowski, *A History of Polish Christianity*, 15.

[97] Květa Reichertová, *Sázava ve světle archeologie a stavebních dějin. Sázava Monastery and its Relations to the Slavonic Past* (Prague: Památky stredoceskéno kraje, 1977); Györffy, "A szávaszentdemeteri görög monostor".

[98] Nyberg, *Monasticism in North-Western Europe*, 54-63.

[99] Marcel Pacaut, *L'Ordre de Cluny* (Paris: Fayard, 1986); Pierre David, *Les bénédictins et l'Ordre de Cluny dans la Pologne médiévale* (Paris: Belles Lettres, 1939).

[100] Wolfgang Huschner, "Abt Odilo von Cluny und Kaiser Otto III. in Italien und in Gnesen (998-1001)", in Borgolte, *Polen und Deutschland*, 111-62.

[101] Dezső Pais, "Les rapports franco-hongrois sous les règne des Árpád, 1., Relations politico-dynastiques et ecclésiastiques", *Revue des Études Hongroises et Finno-Ougriennes* 1.1-2 (1923), 15-26; Ferenc Galla, *A clunyi reform hatása Magyarországon* (The influence of the Cluniac reform in Hungary) (Pécs: Dunántúl Pécsi Egyetemi Könyvkiadó, 1931); György Székely, "Ungarns Stellung zwischen Kaiser, Papst und Byzanz zur Zeit der Kluniazenserreform", in *Spiritualità cluniacense*, ed. by Giuseppe Ermini (Todi: Accademia Tudertina, 1960), 312-25.

dedicated special attention to conquering uninhabited territories; which also explains their interest in making new foundations at the peripheries of Western Christendom. The marked presence of this well-organized order became one of the important influences in bringing homogeneity to all-European Christianity.[102] The mendicant orders, founded in the thirteenth century, continued the Cluniac and Cistercian attention to the borderlands[103]—for them it became a new mission among the "pagans": the Cumans, the Frisians, the Prussians, and the Lithuanians.[104] An interesting consequence of their effort to extend the network of monastic and mendicant foundations to the recently Christianized northern and eastern territories was that these orders acquired a particularly marked influence on the ruling dynasties of these countries, and relied upon them for the realization of their religious goals.

The model of royal "*Eigenkloster*" was, to be sure, compatible with the abbey foundations in the Holy Roman Empire of the Ottonians[105] and actually reflected their direct impact. The close royal or princely patronage, however, produced considerable mutations in the religious character of Cluniac, Cistercian, Premonstratensian, Dominican and Franciscan communities. These reform orders were originally keen on their independence from local secular or ecclesiastical authorities, and claimed to be subordinate only to the Holy See, but in the "border kingdoms" they had to rely on their personal contacts with the court.

---

[102] Marcel Pacaut, *Les moines blancs: histoire de l'ordre de Cîteaux* (Paris: Fayard, 1993); Brian Patrick McGuire, *The Cistercians in Denmark: Their Attitudes, Roles and Functions in Medieval Society* (Kalamazoo, Mich.: Cistercian Publications, 1982); James France, *The Cistercians in Scandinavia* (Kalamazoo, Mich.: Cistercian Publications, 1992); Ferenc Levente Hervay, *Repertorium historicum ordinis Cisterciensis in Hungaria* (Roma: Editiones Cistercienses, 1984); Beatrix Romhányi, "The role of the Cistercians in Medieval Hungary: Political activity or internal colonization?", *Annual of Medieval Studies at the CEU, 1993-1994* (Budapest, 1995), 180-204.

[103] Clifford Hugh Lawrence, *The Friars: The Impact of the Early Mendicant Movement on Western Society.* (London: Longman, 1994); Jerzy Kłoczowski, "Les ordres mendiants en Europe de Centre-Est et du Nord", in *L'Église et le peuple chrétien*, 187-200; idem, "Dominicans of the Polish Province in the Middle Ages", in idem (ed.), *The Christian Community of Medieval Poland. Anthologies* (Wrocław-Warsaw, 1981), 73-118; Miklós Pfeiffer, *Die ungarische Dominikanerprovinz von ihrer Gründung bis zur Tatarenwüstung 1241-1242* (Zürich, 1913).

[104] Simon Tugwell, *Notes on the life of St. Dominic*, in *Archivum Fratrum Praedicatorum*, 68 (1998), 98-110; Jean Richard, *La papauté et les missions d'Orient au moyen âge, XIIIe-XVe siècle* (Rome: École française de Rome, 1977); E. R. Daniel, *The Franciscan Concept of Mission in the High Middle Ages* (Lexington: University Press of Kentucky, 1975); J. R. S. Phillips, *The Medieval Expansion of Europe* (Oxford: Clarendon Press, 1998, 2d ed.).

[105] John W. Bernhardt, *Itinerant Kingship & Royal Monasteries in Early Medieval Germany c. 936-1075* (Cambridge: Cambridge University Press, 1993).

As for the Dominican and Franciscan mendicant orders, the courtly patronage was in striking contrast to their original urban nature, and it made the friars transform themselves from urban reformers, glamorous university theologians, or fear-inspiring inquisitors to become the spiritual advisors of pious saintly princesses.[106]

Dynastic Cults

The cult of the saints related to ruling royal or princely dynasties illustrates how closely Christianization was tied to secular power in these two regions. The model of royal and dynastic saints, a distinct medieval type within the pantheon of holy men and women venerated in Christianity,[107] seems to have been especially popular on the peripheries of Latin Christendom.[108] This phenomenon has frequently been attributed to the survival of pre-Christian beliefs about "sacral kingship".[109] The concept of "charismatic" kingship, drawing upon analogous interpretations of Germanic and Anglo-Saxon mythology,[110] was severely criticized by František Graus. He convincingly demonstrated that there was no continuity between the pagan sacrality of the rulers and the emerging Christian dynastic sainthood. There was, rather, a long-standing early medieval resistance of the Church to the idea of the sanctity of

---

[106] Erik Fügedi, "La formation des villes et les ordres mendiants en Hongrie", *Annales E.S.C.* 25 (1970), 966-87; Gábor Klaniczay, "I modelli di santità femminile tra i secoli XIII e XIV in Europa centrale e in Italia", in *Spiritualità e lettere nella cultura ungherese del basso medioevo* ed. by Sante Graciotti and Cesare Vasoli, (Florence: Olschki, 1995), 75-110.

[107] Robert Folz, *Les saints rois du Moyen Age en Occident (VIᵉ-XIIIᵉ siècles)*, Subsidia Hagiographica n° 68 (Brussels: Société des Bollandistes, 1984); idem, *Les saintes reines du Moyen Age en Occident (VIᵉ-XIIIᵉ siècles)*, Subsidia Hagiographica n° 76 (Brussels: Société des Bollandistes, 1992).

[108] Karol Górski, "La naissance des États et le 'roi-saint'. Problème de l'idéologie féodale", in Alexander Gieysztor and Tadeusz Manteuffel (eds.), *L'Europe aux IXᵉ-XIᵉ siècles. Aux origines des États nationaux* (Warsaw, 1968); idem, "Le roi saint. Un problème d'idéologie féodale", *Annales E.S.C.* 24 (1969), 370-6.

[109] Deér, *Heidnisches und christliches in der altungarischen Monarchie*; Walter Baetke, *Yngvi und die Ynglinger. Eine quellenkritische Untersuchung über das nordische "Sakralkönigtum"*, Sitzungsberichte der Sächsischen Akademie der Wissenschaften zu Leipzig, Ph.-hist. Kl. Bd. 109/3 (Berlin: Akademie, 1964).

[110] Otto Höfler, *Germanisches Sakralkönigtum, I. Der Runestein von Rök und die Germanische Individualweihe* (Tübingen/Münster/Cologne, 1952); Jan De Vries, "Das Königtum bei den Germanen", *Saeculum* 7 (1956), 289-309; William A. Chaney, *The Cult of Kingship in Anglo-Saxon England. The Transition from Paganism to Christianity* (Manchester: Manchester University Press, 1970).

the rulers, which vanished only in the course of an evolution lasting several centuries.[111]

How are we to interpret then the multiplication of successful royal and dynastic cults in the recently converted northern and eastern regions? The beginning of an answer seems to lie in the post-conversion situation: in the necessity to foster a close alliance between the ruling dynasty of the new Christian kingdom and the local church that was emerging with its support. The help given in Christianization was rewarded by conferring the halo of sanctity on some exemplary figures (martyrs or pious widows and princesses) of these dynasties. The first "breakthrough" of this model is exemplified by the cult of royal saints in eighth and ninth century Anglo-Saxon England.[112] In a similar historical situation in eleventh and twelfth century Scandinavia, the Anglo-Saxon model was directly influential in shaping the cults of royal saints like Olaf (†1030) in Norway, Knut (†1086) in Denmark, and Eric (†1160) in Sweden.[113] These cults, which typically started during the strife surrounding the succession, were instrumental in securing the ascendance of the dynasties relying on them, and they became touchstones of the identity of these new kingdoms and their ecclesiastical partners. In a subsequent phase, in the later Middle Ages, some surviving elements of pre-Christian mythologies were attached to these cults, adding to their ethnic flavor.[114]

As for Central and Eastern Europe, the dominance of this same type of saint cult among the Czechs, the Hungarians and even in the orthodox Kievan Rus supports the general validity of the model outlined above.[115] The cult of the pious, martyred Czech prince, St. Wenceslas (†929 or 935), revered a ruler whose sainthood resided in renouncing the dignity and the tasks of rulership, but his veneration quickly devel-

---

[111] František Graus, *Volk, Herrscher und Heiliger im Reich der Merowinger. Studien zur Hagiographie der Merowingerzeit* (Prague: Nakladatelstvi Ceskoslovenské akademie ved, 1965); idem, "Mittelalterliche Vorbehalte gegen die Sakralisierung der Königsmacht", in Atsma and Burguière, *Marc Bloch aujourd'hui*, 115-24.

[112] Susan Janet Ridyard, *The Royal Saints of Anglo-Saxon England. A study of West Saxon and East Anglian cults* (Cambridge: Cambridge University Press, 1988).

[113] Erich Hoffmann, *Die heiligen Könige bei den Angelsachsen und den skandinavischen Völkern. Königssheiliger und Königshaus* (Neumünster: Wachholtz, 1975).

[114] Tore Nyberg, "Autour de la Sacralité Royale en Scandinavie", *Annuarium historiae conciliorum*, 27-28 (1995-1996), 177-92.

[115] This is the subject of my recent book: Gábor Klaniczay, *Holy Rulers and Blessed Princesses. Dynastic Cults in Medieval Central Europe* (Cambridge: Cambridge University Press, 2002).

oped into saintly patronage of the whole Czech nation.[116] The model of St. Wenceslas was influential in shaping the cult of the two martyr princes Boris and Gleb (†1015) in eleventh-century Kiev. In the twelfth and thirteenth century it was complemented by the cult of their father, Vladimir, the "apostle" of the Rus, and his grandmother, Olga, both of whom began to be revered as saints.[117] The first group of five Hungarian saints was canonized in 1083, and two of them were members of the ruling Árpád dynasty, King Stephen I and his son, Prince Emeric. Saint Stephen was the first royal saint in the course of the evolution of this cult-type who obtained the halo without having died a martyr, but rather for his merits as a *rex iustus*. This marks a new, important phase in the popularity of royal sainthood in medieval Europe. Besides sealing the alliance between the Church and the royal dynasties as in Scandinavia, these cults were also an important tool in the hands of the ecclesiastics, who imposed the Christian principles of kingship by setting a saintly model for the descendants as the ideal to follow.[118]

The twelfth century saw the further success of these dynastic cults in both the new regions and the "core" territories. As for the latter, the Holy Roman Empire witnessed the elevation of Emperor Henry II and his wife Cunegond to sainthood (1147 and 1200, respectively)[119] and the initiation of a saint cult around Charlemagne (1165).[120] In England, King Henry II obtained the canonization of Edward the Confessor (1163).[121] As for northern and eastern Europe, in Denmark, the martyr prince Knut Laward joined the rank of dynastic saints (1169), and Nicholas of Aarhus (†1180), the murdered son of King Knut Magnusson, was also a future candidate for sainthood; in Sweden the cult of St.

---

[116] František Graus, "St. Wenzel, der heilige Patron des Landes Böhmen" in *Lebendige Vergangenheit. Überlieferung im Mittelalter und in den Vorstellungen vom Mittelalter* (Köln: Böhlau, 1975), 159-81.

[117] N. W. Ingham, "Czech Hagiography in Kiev: The Prisoner Miracles of Boris and Gleb", *Die Welt der Slaven* 10 (1965), 166-82; idem, "The Sovereign as Martyr, East and West", *Slavic and East European Journal* 17 (1983), 1-17; Andrej Poppe, "Politik und Heiligenverehrung in der Kiever Ruś. Der apostelgleiche Herrscher und seine Märtyrer-söhne", in Jürgen Petersohn (ed.), *Politik und Heiligenverehrung im Hochmittelalter*. Vorträge und Forschungen XLII (Sigmaringen: Thorbecke, 1994), 403-22.

[118] More details on his cult are in my *Holy Rulers and Blessed Princesses*, 114-55.

[119] Renate Klauser, *Der Heinrichs- und Kunigundenkult im mittelalterlichen Bistum Bamberg* (Bamberg, 1957).

[120] Robert Folz, *Le souvenir et la légende de Charlemagne dans l'Empire germanique médiéval* (Paris: Belles Lettres, 1950, repr. Genève: Slatkine, 1973).

[121] Bernhardt W. Scholz, "The canonization of Edward the Confessor", *Speculum*, 36 (1961), 38-60.

Eric emerged around the 1160s;[122] in Hungary the initiator of the first series of canonizations, King Ladislas I, was himself canonized in 1192 and was acclaimed as an example of chivalric virtues, an *"Athleta Patriae"*.[123] There is an interesting exception to this phenomenon: Poland did not develop a royal or dynastic cult.[124] The reason for this difference might be the fragmentation of the Polish kingdom into several principalities, to be reunited only in the fourteenth century. Still, the examples of dynastic sainthood started to appear towards the end of the thirteenth century, in the cults of pious princesses such as Saint Hedwig of Silesia (canonized in 1167).[125]

Royal sainthood, popular in these regions, began to pick up adherents all over twelfth-century Christianity. It met, however, increasing opposition from the Papacy. It is not by chance that Pope Alexander III made his claims for the papal monopoly of the canonization of saints only a few years after the canonization of Charlemagne by the antipope Paschal III. More than that, his claim was made in criticizing another emerging royal cult, that of the Swedish St. Eric (for in all probability it was his cult to which the pope alluded in his letter of 1171 or 1172 calling him, with his denigrators, "a man who died while drunk").[126]

The evolution of the model of royal sainthood in the tenth to thirteenth centuries illustrates that the new Christian cultures of the peripheries, far from being passive recipients of a cultural or institutional transfer, developed their own versions of the cults and the ecclesiastical models they received from the various religious centres after their conversion. The emerging autochthonous patterns led to a new differentiation and new dynamics within late medieval Christendom; they could themselves become influential models for others in the "centre" or the in new "peripheries" around the continuously expanding borders of Europe.

Social and Political Implications

Let me now consider very briefly the broad issue of the transfer of social and political categories from the West to Central, Eastern and

---

[122] For these cults see Hoffmann, *Die heiligen Könige.*
[123] Klaniczay, *Holy Rulers and Blessed Princesses,* 161-93.
[124] Górski, "Le roi saint".
[125] Klaniczay, *Holy Rulers and Blessed Princesses,* 195-294.
[126] Erich Hoffmann, "Politische Heilige in Skandinavien und die Entwicklung der drei nordischen Völker", in Petersohn (ed.) *Politik und Heiligenverehrung,* 277-324; see also notes 90-93 above.

Northern Europe. Whereas the conversion and the relatively quick development of ecclesiastical structures and cults achieved a high degree of homogeneity in a few centuries, and the historians' cautious alertness had to concentrate on the recognition of differences and dissimilarities, the field of social and political relations is just the opposite. It took a considerable time for these fundamentally different societies to start showing similar traits. Some historians of these regions continue, for example, research on local variants of "feudalism".[127] Others, swimming in the critical current that has recently questioned the claim of Marc Bloch and his followers to extend this category even to the medieval West,[128] refuse to use the "western model" in the analysis of original local power systems and economic dependencies.[129]

After one or two centuries of autochthonous evolution, however, the thirteenth century brought dramatic change in the social patterns of nobility and peasantry, the urban network, and the organization of political institutions in East Central Europe. With the fall of Byzantium in 1204, and especially with the Mongolian conquest of the Russian half of this region, its Central European (Polish, Czech, Hungarian, Croatian) part was radically pushed toward assimilating itself to *Europa Occidens*.

Let me select the Hungarian example to illustrate this change. The overall *timor tartarorum* and the efforts of reconstruction deployed in Hungary by King Béla IV (1235-1270) resulted in a catalyzing effect similar to the one attributed to Hungarian invasions by Marc Bloch in tenth-century Europe. A large number of fortified stone castles were constructed (which became strongholds of an emerging new noble aristocracy and their kindred).[130] Nascent cities, frequently populated by

---

[127] Makkai, "Les caractères originaux de l'histoire économique et sociale de l'Europe orientale", cf. n. 20; Évelyne Patlagean, "Europe, seigneurie, féodalité. Marc Bloch et les limites orientales d'un espace de comparaison", in Atsma and Burguière, *Marc Bloch aujourd'hui*, 279-98; Stanisław Russocki, "Figuré ou réel: Le 'féodalisme centralisé' dans le centre-est de l'Europe", in *Acta Poloniae Historica* 66 (1992), 31-7; Slawomir Gawlas, "Die Probleme des Lehnswesens und des Feudalismus aus polnischer Sicht", in Borgolte, *Das europäische Mittelalter*, 97-124.

[128] Elizabeth E. Brown, "The Tyranny of a Construct: Feudalism and Historians of Medieval Europe", *American Historical Review* 79 (1974), 1063-88; repr. in Lester K. Little and Barbara H. Rosenwein (eds.), *Debating the Middle Ages: Issues and Readings* (Oxford: Blackwell, 1998). 148-169; Susan Reynolds, *Fiefs and Vassals: The Medieval Evidence Reinterpreted* (Oxford: Oxford University Press, 1994); Dominique Barthélémy, *La mutation de l'an mil a-t-elle eu lieu? Servage et chevalerie dans la France des Xe et XIe siècles* (Paris: Fayard, 1997).

[129] Karol Modzelewski, "The system of the *ius ducale* and the idea of feudalism (Comments on the earliest class society in medieval Poland)", *Questiones Medii Aevi* 1 (1977), 71-99; Engel, *The Realm of St. Stephen*, 66-82.

[130] Erik Fügedi, *Castle and Society in Medieval Hungary (1000-1437)* (Budapest: Akadémiai

German, Wallon, Italian settlers (*hospites*) invited by the kings,[131] were also encircled with walls and provided with royal privileges (two would-be capitals, Buda and Zagreb, were indeed fully new foundations in these decades). The royally promoted "urbanization" was supported by urban liberties that followed principally German models, and soon constituted a network of cities and towns well integrated into the arteries of international trade.[132] The reorganization of the country was actively supported by the mendicant orders and equally supported by the royal court, whose multiplying convents quickly enhanced the urban standing of the new cities.[133]

If the contested term "Westernization" can be applied at all in historical analysis, it would describe fairly well what happened to Hungary in the second half of the thirteenth century. And this radical change brought about, again, a visible resistance: a resurgence of "Orientalism". In the reign of Ladislas IV, surnamed "the Cuman" (1272-1290), this was expressed in various forms: oriental fashions in dress and hairdressing, and "Cuman Laws" providing the Cumans with specific legal status within Hungary.[134] A similar resurgence of the memory of nomadic, oriental origins is expressed in the theory of Hun-Hungarian filiation described in the Chronicle by Master Simon of Kéza.[135]

Kiadó, 1986); idem, *Kings, Bishops, Nobles, and Burghers in Medieval Hungary*, ed. by János M. Bak (London: Variorum, 1986).

[131] György Székely, "Wallons et Italiens en Europe centrale aux XIᵉ-XVIᵉ siècles", *Annales Universitatis Scientiarum Budapestiensis, Sectio historica* 6 (1964), 3-71; on similar phenomena in Bohemia see František Graus, "Die Problematik der deutschen Ostsiedlung aus tschechischer Sicht", in Schlesinger, *Die deutsche Ostsiedlung*, 31-75; on Poland see Jan M. Piskorski, "Die 'Königsfreien' und die mittelalterliche Kolonisation", in Borgolte (ed.), *Das europäische Mittelalter*, 125-33.

[132] Erik Fügedi, "Die Entstehung des Städtewesens in Ungarn", in idem, *Kings, Bishops, Nobles and Burghers*, 101-18; László Gerevich, *Towns in Medieval Hungary* (Boulder, Col.: Social Science Monographs, 1990); András Kubinyi, "Zur Frage der deutschen Siedlungen im mittleren Teil des Königreiches in Ungarn (1200-1541)", in Schlesinger (ed.), *Die deutsche Ostsiedlung*, 527-66; cf. Paul W. Knoll, "The Urban Development of Medieval Poland with Particular Reference to Cracow", in Bariša Krekić (ed.), *Urban Society of Eastern Europe in Premodern Times* (Berkeley: University of California Press, 1987), 63-136.

[133] This process was analysed in detail in the last monograph by Jenő Szűcs, *Az utolsó Árpádok* (The last Arpadians) (Budapest: História, 1993); on urban evolution and mendicant orders see Fügedi, "La formation des villes".

[134] I have discussed this resurgence in my "Everyday life and the elites in the later Middle Ages. The civilised and the barbarian", in Peter Linehan and Janet L. Nelson (eds.), *The Medieval World*, (London-New York: Routledge, 2001), 671-90; A. Pálóczy-Horváth, *Pechenegs, Cumans, Iasians. Steppe Peoples in Medieval Hungary* (Budapest, 1989); cf. also Berend, *At the Gate of Christendom*, 82-5.

[135] Jenő Szűcs, *Theoretical Elements in Master Simon of Kéza's Gesta Hungarorum (1282-1285 a.d.)*, (Budapest: Akadémiai, 1975), repr. in László Veszprémy and Frank Schaer (eds),

This phenomenon is emblematically represented in the fresco series depicting the fight of Saint Ladislas, the holy king, with the Cuman warrior, rescuing a lady abducted by the pagan fighter. Preserved in a passage in the Hungarian Chronicle, continued and augmented since the eleventh century,[136] this germ of a chivalric romance was painted as a fresco cycle in several dozen variations in the territory of medieval Hungary starting around the end of the thirteenth century, and documents record many more that have disappeared.[137] This striking popularity can be explained by its amusingly complex, ambivalent message. Though the Cuman is defeated in this story by Saint Ladislas, the two fighters are virtually equal, and the latter triumphs only with the help of the abducted maiden.

Hungarians in the thirteenth and fourteenth centuries might have identified themselves as much with this pagan warrior as with the saintly Christian knight. The fighting technique of the Cuman was the same by which the Hungarians had obtained their military successes during their plundering raids in ninth- and tenth-century Europe: they pretended flight, and then turning back upon the pursuing enemy, inundated their foes with arrows. This nomadic type of light cavalry survived in the medieval Hungarian army for several more centuries. It was partly provided by Hungarian freemen, partly by "helping troops" recruited from neighbouring Eastern nomadic peoples (such as Cumans) who very much resembled what the Hungarians had been a few centuries earlier. With a metaphoric reading of the fresco cycle, one could say that fighting and defeating the Cuman abductor must have meant for contemporary people not only the protection of the country from the eastern nomadic enemies: with his victory Saint Ladislas also subdued their orientalizing self-image. The fate-deciding victory of the Christian *athleta patriae* sealed the association of the Hungarians to the Christian West. The memory of Eastern, nomadic origins and the conscious adhe-

---

Simonis de Kéza Gesta Hungarorum—Simon of Kéza, The Deeds of the Hungarians. Central European Medieval Texts (Budapest: Central European University Press, 1999).

[136] *Chronici hungarici compositio saeculi XIV*, ed. by Alexander Domanovszky, in *Scriptores Rerum Hungaricarum tempore ducum regumque stirpis Arpadianae gestarum*, (ed.) Emericus Szentpétery (Budapest: Academia Litter. Hungarica, 1938), 368-9; Johannes de Thurocz, *Chronica Hungarorum. II. Commentarii 1. Ab initiis usque ad annum 1301*, Elemér Mályusz and Julius Kristó (Budapest: Akadémiai, 1985), 339-411.

[137] A full documentation is assembled in Gyula László, *A Szent László-legenda középkori falképei* (Medieval murals of the legend of St. Ladislas) (Budapest, 1993).

sion to Western, Christian civilization, became the two contradictory components of Hungarian identity.[138]

The *"caractères originaux"*, the difference and specificity proper to Hungary (and other East-Central and North European states) can be discerned in the scanty documentation we possess. The unusual features of these states should be emphasized. They relied upon a military-economic structure that was labelled "state serfdom" in Poland,[139] which allowed the formation of a western type of semi-dependent peasantry only in the thirteenth century. Two distinct social categories that contributed to the specificity of the medieval West, the knight and the intellectual/cleric,[140] though not altogether absent, did not become decisive elements in the social pattern of these societies until the late Middle Ages. The elite, which developed instead in a quantitatively quite disproportionate manner, comprised both higher and lesser nobility. A number of comparative enquiries target the economic and political consequences of this feature of Hungary and Poland, which could be labelled as *"pays de la noblesse nombreuse"*.[141]

The political evolution of the twelfth and thirteenth centuries was characterized in these countries by fights among the rivalling factions of the mightiest lords and fights among the various pretenders for the throne. This was also the case in Denmark, Sweden, and Norway.[142]

---

[138] Ernő Marosi, "Der heilige Ladislaus als Ungarischer Nationalheiliger. Bemerkungen zu seiner Ikonographie im 14-15. Jh.", *Acta Historiae Artium Hungariae* 33 (1987), 211-56; Klaniczay, *Holy Rulers and Blessed Princesses*, 155-94, 388-94.

[139] Karol Modzelewski, "L'organizzazione dello stato polacco nei secoli X-XIII. La società e le strutture del potere", in *Gli Slavi occidentali e meridionali nell'alto medioevo*. Settimane di Studio 30 (Spoleto, 1983), 557-96; cf. Engel, *The Realm of Saint Stephen*, 25-65.

[140] Their importance is stressed in the comparative reflections by S. N. Eisenstadt, *European Civilization*, and the problem is discussed by Robert Moore in his essay in this volume. As to these two elites, see Maurice Keen, *Chivalry* (New Haven-London: Yale University Press, 1990), and Jacques Le Goff, *Intellectuals in the Middle Ages* (Oxford: Blackwell, 1993).

[141] The term comes from a Hungarian historian, Ferenc Maksay, "Le Pays de la noblesse nombreuse", *Études historiques* (Budapest: Akadémiai, 1980), 167-91; there has been some comparative research on Hungarian and east European nobilities at the Central European University. Cf. János M. Bak (ed.), *Nobilities in Central and Eastern Europe*, thematic issue of *History and Society in Central Europe*, 2 (1994); idem, "Probleme einer vergleichenden Betrachtung mittelalterlichen Eliten in Ostmitteleuropa", in Borgolte (ed.), *Das europäische Mittelalter*, 49-64. As for Poland, see Antoni Gąsiorowski, *The Polish Nobility in the Middle Ages. Anthologies* (Wrocław, 1984); Tomasz Jurek, "Fremde Ritter im mittelalterlichen Polen", *Questiones Medii Aevi Novae* 3 (1998), 19-49.

[142] Erich Hoffmann, *Königserhebung und Thronfolgeordnung in Dänemark bis zum Ausgang des Mittelalters* (Berlin/New York, 1976); idem, *Die heiligen Könige*.

These fights frequently led to a "changing of the guard" each time a new ruler came, and the persistence of these noble factions soon led to elaborate political constructions counterbalancing royal power.

The reign of King Andrew II of Hungary (1205-1235) was, for example, a period of spectacular enrichment for the *barones*. The arrogance of the baronial aristocracy provoked a violent reaction from a class of freemen calling themselves *servientes regis*, whose rebellious gathering in 1222 produced the famous Golden Bull, frequently compared to the English *Magna Carta*.[143] This law guaranteed for this numerous group noble privileges, the liberties allegedly given to them "by the holy king Stephen", among them first and foremost the hereditary possession of their lands (*perpetuo iure*). The Golden Bull codified even a notorious sanction of legitimate resistance by nobles if the king violated the ancient privileges. All this had far-reaching consequences in the evolution of "estates" in Hungarian history, and secured for the lesser nobility legislative power similar to that in Poland.

This preponderance of the lesser nobility was also manifested in the formation of "noble counties" toward the end of the thirteenth century, which gradually took over the territorial administration from the "royal counties".[144] The more and more self-conscious noble kindreds in Hungary formed similar complex interest groups, such as marriage alliances like those in the tenth- and eleventh-century West, though on a smaller scale and with less developed institutions. "Feudal" lord-vassal relations, secured by fiefs and legal codification, could rarely be found. The thirteenth-century developments only led to an intermediate stage of dependence called *familiaritas*, based on the physical sharing of life and residence with the lord in his mansion, castle, curia, or *aula*.[145]

After this glimpse into the possible problems and contradictions related to the *"histoire croisée"* of the medieval West and the evolving states and societies of central and northern Europe, let me conclude with a hint at the new dynamics that emerged from this evolution in the fourteenth century. With the extinction of the dynasty of the Árpádians in 1301, after some years of interregnum and uncertainty, the descendants of the

---

[143] An early example of this comparison: Elemér Hantos, *The Magna Charta of the English and of the Hungarian Constitution. A Comparative View of the Law and Institutions of the Early Middle Ages* (London, 1904); János Bak, *Königtum und Stände in Ungarn* (Wiesbaden: Steiner, 1973).

[144] This evolution is discussed in detail by Jenő Szűcs in "Three Historical Regions" and in *The Last Arpadians*. Cf. Engel, *The Realm of Saint Stephen*, 83-123.

[145] Erik Fügedy, *The Elefánthy: The Hungarian Nobleman and his Kindred* (Budapest: CEU Press, 1998).

Angevins of Naples managed to occupy the Hungarian throne with the active assistance of the Papacy. The reign of Charles Robert I (1308-1342) and Louis I (1342-1382) brought a renewed series of efforts to reorganize the administrative, military, economic, social and cultural structures of the Hungarian kingdom, tying them once again to Western (Italian, German, and French) models.[146] The outcome was impressive: the fourteenth century, generally a period of crisis all over Europe, brought an unprecedented flowering in the Central Europe of the Hungarian Angevins. The same is true of the Czech Kingdom of the Luxemburgs in the time of Charles IV (1346-1378) and the united Poland of the last Piasts, Władisław Łokietek (1320-1333) and Casimir the Great (1333-1370),[147] and similar assertions could be made about Scandinavia of the Kalmar Union.[148] But this chronological period is already beyond our range of comparison.*

---

[146] *Louis the Great. King of Hungary and Poland,* ed. by S. B. Vardy, G. Grosschmid, and L. S. Domokos (Boulder, Col.: East European Monographs/New York: Columbia University Press, 1986); Engel, *The Realm of Saint Stephen,* 124-94; András Kubinyi, *König und Volk im spätmittelalterlichen Ungarn* (Herne, 1998).

[147] This topic is treated by the forthcoming book edited by Marc Löwener, *Die "Blüte" der Staaten des östlichen Europa im 14. Jahrhundert.*

[148] Tore Nyberg, "Frühes und spätes Mittelalter in Skandinavien—ein möglicher Vergleich?" in Borgolte (ed.) *Das europäische Mittelalter,* 197-209.

* I am grateful to Kathleen Much who helped to improve the English of this essay, the final version of which was written during my stay at the Center for Advanced Studies in the Behavioral Sciences, Stanford in 2003/4.

THE TRANSFORMATION OF EUROPE:
THE ROLE OF SCANDINAVIA

SVERRE BAGGE

ABSTRACT

The article examines Scandinavia's role in the transformation of Europe in the Middle Ages. First, an important aspect of this transformation is the great expansion of Western Christendom from the tenth century onwards, which led to the establishment of new political entities rather than to an extension of polities in the "old" Europe. Thus, the expansion meant an important step in the direction of a characteristic European feature, a system of independent polities within a common culture. Second, the article examines the particular form this common culture took in Scandinavia, the introduction of European military technology in at least parts of the area and its consequences, the introduction of Christianity, Latin culture, and Scholasticism, and the introduction of bureaucracy in the service of monarchy and Church, based on the use of writing. However, despite increasing Europeanisation during the period, the Scandinavian countries also show specific features and modifications of European trends.

As pointed out by R. I. Moore in this volume,[1] a new Europe emerged during the eleventh and twelfth centuries through the transition from an economy of plunder to an economy of exploitation, the emergence of a sharp distinction between a secular and a clerical elite through the introduction of aristocratic primogeniture and clerical celibacy, the growth of royal and ecclesiastical government through a standardised education and the emergence of a class of people dependent on their superiors for their careers, and finally through the formation of a common European intellectual culture claiming a monopoly and suppressing rivals by stamping them as heretical.

In his article, Moore mainly focuses on what are usually regarded as the core areas of Latin Christendom, England, France, and Italy, only mentioning in passing the change on the borders through the inclusion of new areas which reduced the possibilities for plunder. However, Western Christendom was greatly extended from the tenth century

---

[1] "The Transformation of Europe as a Eurasian Phenomenon", in this volume; cf. also his *The First European Revolution, c. 970-1215* (Oxford, 2001).

onwards, and this expansion marked the beginning of the European conquest of the rest of the world. Europe, i.e. Western Christendom, expanded in the Mediterranean, Scandinavia, and Central Europe. Like the expansion following the Great Discoveries from the sixteenth century onwards, the conquests were conducted by a number of powers, often in mutual rivalry, rather than by one, great empire. Unlike the early modern expansion, however, the medieval one was not directed at completely unknown peoples and territories. Further, colonies in the real sense played a subordinate part. The conquests mostly consisted in the extension of existing European politics, such as the Spanish kingdoms, the formation of independent, European principalities in the new areas, as in Southern Italy and Sicily and the towns and principalities along the southern shore of Baltic Sea, and, last but not least, the formation of new, indigenous principalities, notably in Scandinavia and Central Europe. Generally, the northern and eastern expansion was to a greater extent religious and cultural than the Mediterranean. Its most characteristic feature was the spread of Christianity, with the book, the Latin language, and a learning and literature derived from Classical Antiquity. But the expansion also had military, economic, and political facets: e.g. the formation of the Hanseatic trade network, the export of military technology (heavy cavalry and castles) and ecclesiastical and royal bureaucracy.

If we regard a multiplicity of centres of political power as an essential feature of Europe, in contrast to e.g. China and the Islamic world during some phases of its history, as is usually done, the expansion becomes equally important as the internal changes. Six new kingdoms of Western Christendom came into existence during this period, i.e. the three Scandinavian kingdoms plus Poland, Bohemia, and Hungary, as well as a number of territorial principalities that later made themselves independent, e.g. Brandenburg, Mecklenburg, and Pomerania. Whereas most of Western Christendom had been united under one ruler in the Carolingian period and a substantial part of it under the Ottonian and Salian emperors, the expansion, combined with the weakening of the central power in Germany, made the territorial principality the normal political organisation of Western Christendom, thus establishing the combination of cultural unity and political division that has characterised Europe until the formation of the European Union in the second half of the twentieth century.

Scandinavian contacts with Europe extend back to the period of the Roman Empire. There is archaeological evidence of trade and cultural contacts from at least the third century onwards. Nevertheless, the period from around 800 is crucial, the age of the first Viking expeditions and—apparently—the first diplomatic contacts between Denmark and the Carolingian Empire. In the following centuries the area was fully included in Western Christendom. In the following I shall discuss (1) the inclusion of Scandinavia into Western Christendom through Christianisation and state formation and (2) the subsequent changes in Scandinavian society and the extent to which they represent an adaptation to conditions in the main areas of Western Christendom.[2]

The Formation of the Scandinavian Kingdoms

The formation of the Scandinavian kingdoms was probably the result of (1) the change from an economy of plunder to an economy of exploitation and (2) the introduction of Christianity, i.e. the reception of Western European models of religion, politics, and administration. Both changes would seem to have been more dramatic than in the older parts of Western Christendom. As for the latter, if the changes in the Western Church in the eleventh and twelfth centuries can be characterised as revolutionary, they were even more so in Scandinavia where Christianity had no basis. As for the former, although the export of slaves was lucrative, the amount of booty to be gained from the northern and eastern parts of Europe would seem to be less than what could be obtained by more efficient exploitation of the rich land resources of Europe between the Alps and the two seas in the north, The North Sea and the Baltic. By contrast, the amount of booty the Scandinavians could gain from plundering Western Europe exceeded what they could gain from their own fairly limited land resources. Thus, the annual tax income of the King of Norway in the High Middle Ages, 3000 marks, was between 2 and 15% of the payments the Vikings received from the king of England in the late tenth and early eleventh century for ending their

---

[2] Most of the facts referred to in the following are to be found in surveys of Scandinavian history, so I do not give detailed references. For recent accounts, see Niels Lund, "Scandinavia c. 700-1066", in Rosamond McKitterick (ed.), *The New Cambridge Medieval History* vol. II (Cambridge, 1995), 202-27; Sverre Bagge, "The Scandinavian Kingdoms", in David Abulafia (ed.), *The New Cambridge Medieval History* vol. V (Cambridge, 1999), 720-42 and "Eleventh Century Norway: The Formation of a Kingdom", in Przemyslaw Urbanczýk (ed.), *The Neighbours of Poland in the 11th Century* (Warszaw, 2002), 29-47; Knut Helle (ed.), *The Cambridge History of Scandinavia* vol. I (Cambridge, 2003). On Sweden, see also Thomas Lindkvist's article in this volume. All these works contain references to earlier literature.

attacks.[3] From an economic point of view, the Viking Age was probably the golden age of Scandinavia, while the inclusion into Christian Europe represented a decline. This means that state formation needs a special explanation and that the relationship between this process and the Viking expeditions needs to be examined.

The Viking expeditions contributed to military specialisation as well as to creating an economic basis for stronger principalities by giving chieftains the gold, silver, and luxury items that could be used for gaining followers. On the other hand, this surplus did not necessarily have to be spent on creating national kingdoms. Many chieftains preferred to establish themselves abroad, in the British Isles, Normandy, or Russia. Moreover, as long as it was easy to gain wealth from Viking expeditions, the principalities that emerged were likely to be unstable: new chieftains with fresh resources might easily expel the old ones. This happened repeatedly in Norway in the tenth and early eleventh century. A consolidated principality might, however, be a platform for further expansion, as when a united Denmark—from the second half of the tenth century—formed the basis of Cnut the Great's North Sea Empire which for a short period of time (1028-35) included Denmark, England, and Norway. In the case of Norway and Sweden, however, the rise of independent kingdoms seems to correspond with the end rather than the beginning of the Viking Age. When the strengthening of feudal Europe in the eleventh century had put an end to the Viking expeditions, the only way for ambitious chieftains to gain wealth and power was within Scandinavia. We then arrive at our next problem, the origins of the present Scandinavian states.

The origin of a country is clearly an important problem in historiography, and much time and effort have been spent in describing how and why the various present-day national states of Europe came into being. This is also the case in Scandinavia. There is a certain national teleology in this concept of "unification". The country has been there from the beginning, is waiting for unification, which is an inevitable process, ending with approximately the present-day borders. Scandinavia was culturally and linguistically homogeneous. Even in the thirteenth century the term "Danish tongue" was used for the language all over

---

[3] Asgaut Steinnes, *Gamal skatteskipnad* vol. I (Oslo 1930), 169 f. The Vikings received £ 10000 in 991, £ 16000 in 994 and £ 36000 in 1006. Finally, Cnut the Great imposed a tax of £ 72000 in 1018, see Peter Sawyer, "The Viking Expansion", in Helle, *Scandinavia*, 118. One mark *brend* (burnt) is c. 50 g. silver, whereas one pound sterling is 320 g.

the area. There were different dialects, but the lines of division between them did not correspond to the later national borders. Religion and customs were also fairly similar, during the pagan as well as the Christian period. Thus, no cultural or linguistic distinctions prevented unification of each country. On the other hand, nor did such distinctions give rise to natural borders between the kingdoms that eventually emerged.

Rather than asking how and why each of the three Scandinavian kingdoms was "unified", we should try to explain the division of the whole area, i.e. why the struggles between the various chieftains trying to carve out principalities for themselves led to the existing result. The process began in Denmark, partly because of its location in the most fertile and densely populated region in the area, partly because of its neighbourhood to imperial Germany. We hear about Danish kings already in the early ninth century, after which there is very little information, until the Jelling dynasty emerged by the mid-tenth century as the main Scandinavian power, while at the same time reaching out towards the Baltic and particularly towards England. The later borders of Denmark clearly show this country to have been the first to consolidate: The Jelling king controlled not only the mainland, Jutland, but also all the surrounding islands, as well as Scania, the southern part of present-day Sweden. In the tenth and early eleventh century, he also controlled, or had some suzerainty over, the coastal regions of south-eastern Norway. The climax was reached under Cnut the Great (1013-35) who conquered England in 1017 and Norway in 1028, thus ruling a North sea Empire during the last years of his reign.

The antecedents of the unification of Norway in the tenth century should most probably be understood as a reaction against the Danish expansion. Starting in the north or the west, local Norwegian chieftains, i.e. the Fairhair dynasty and the earls of Lade, tried to expand their power. Other chieftains in the area were faced with the choice between allying themselves with or submitting to either the Jelling king or these Norwegian chieftains. From a geopolitical point of view, the whole coast of Norway, up to the far north, would seem too large an area to be controlled from a centre in southern Jutland, the more so as the ruler of this centre also tried to conquer England and keep a hand in Baltic affairs. On the other hand, it could easily be controlled from the sea. Most of it was protected by islands and there were plenty of excellent harbours. As most of the population also lived along the coast, Norway was one of the easiest countries to unite under early medieval conditions. Consequently, it is not surprising that a kingdom emerged in this area.[4] Starting with Harald Fairhair (d. c. 932), Norwegian kings seem to have controlled most of the coastal regions with the exception of the south-east. St Olav Haraldsson (1015-30) may possibly have been the first to control most of what later belonged to the kingdom of Norway until he was defeated by King Cnut. After Cnut's death, the North Sea Empire dissolved; Olav's relatives returned to power in Norway and made repeated attempts to conquer Denmark. The death of King Harald Sigurdsson, St Olav's half-brother, in 1066, put an end to these attempts. In the following period the normal situation was two independent kingdoms with relatively stable borders.

The third kingdom, Sweden, was the late-comer in this process. We know very little about early Swedish history, but a unified kingdom does not seem to have emerged until well into the eleventh century. Throughout the Middle Ages, there were more internal struggles in Sweden than in the two other countries. Sweden is naturally divided into two main parts which form the economic and demographic centres of the country, Svealand in the east, around the Mälar valley, where present-day Stockholm is situated, and Götaland in the west. The two regions are linked by a series of lakes and rivers, but their unification clearly took some time, which explains Sweden's late arrival in the Scandinavian competition. Characteristically, the whole western coast of present-day Sweden had been divided between the two other countries before the Swedish kingdom had become sufficiently united to take part in the game. Only in the mid-thirteenth century was Sweden able to gain a tiny corridor out to the sea at the mouth of Göta Älv, near present-day Gothenburg. All that the Swedish king could do in the eleventh century, was to support the weaker power in the Danish-Norwegian struggles in order to prevent the unification of both countries under one king. On the other hand, neither of the two main areas of Sweden was easily accessible for conquest from the other countries. The eastern and to some extent also the western part of the country were separated from the neighbouring countries by wide areas of forest and uninhabited or thinly inhabited land, while a conquest of Sweden from the sea would imply very long lines of communication from the Danish centre in Jutland as well as from the western coast of Norway.

---

[4] Claus Krag, "The Early Unification of Norway", in Helle, *Scandinavia*, 184 f. rightly opposes the deterministic view of the unification of Norway in earlier scholarship. This, however, should not prevent us from considering the geopolitical conditions that make some divisions more likely than others.

In the light of their later history, the Scandinavian kingdoms seem to have been permanently established during the eleventh century. The actual division, however, was probably more the result of temporary exhaustion than a new awareness of national unity. A new series of internal struggles in the twelfth century reduced the possibility for external expansion, although internal divisions in one country often had repercussions in one or both of the others and dynastic unions created alliances over the national borders. Nor was each country's external expansion, insofar as it took place, directed exclusively against its Scandinavian neighbours. Norway, still mainly a sea power, expanded westwards towards the North Sea and Atlantic islands, Denmark towards Northern Germany and the southern shore of the Baltic Sea, and Sweden towards Finland and the northern part of the Baltic region. It was not until the second half of the thirteenth century that a new phase of stronger inter-Scandinavian contact and rivalry began, partly as the result of Norwegian and Swedish interference in inner conflicts in Denmark, partly as the result of dynastic alliances over the national borders, by intermarriage between the royal and eventually also noble families. This led to a series of unions, partly between all three kingdoms, partly between two of them, which from the beginning of the sixteenth century resulted in a union between Norway and Denmark under Danish dominance which lasted until 1814. By contrast, Sweden retained its independence and developed into a great power in the seventeenth century. Nevertheless, the Scandinavian unions were no simple return to the open competition for land and lordship of the tenth and eleventh century, but had their basis in well developed political institutions in each country.

Scandinavia and the European Revolution

The formation of these three kingdoms may to some extent be explained by the contacts with Western Christendom, first by raiding and conquest, and then, when the expansion came to an end, by internal exploitation. What is the relationship between the internal consolidation in Scandinavia and in the rest of Europe? Is there a parallel development or even direct influence, in the form of export of the "European revolution" to Scandinavia?

There has been a tendency in Scandinavian historiography in the nineteenth and twentieth centuries to regard early Scandinavian society as less aristocratic than that of most other European countries, corresponding to contemporary conditions. Recent scholarship has been more inclined to emphasise the aristocratic character of Scandinavian society, even in the early period. Archaeological evidence suggests that powerful men with a large number of clients attached to them must have existed far back in history and that they played a crucial role during the Viking age. However, as long as the aristocracy could profit from external extraction and needed manpower on their plundering expeditions, the distinction between aristocrats and commoners is likely to have been relatively vague. In the same way as in the rest of Europe, a clearer distinction between aristocrats and commoners seems to have emerged with the transition from external to internal exploitation. The end of the Viking age meant an end to or at least a strong reduction of the opportunity to acquire wealth during plundering expeditions abroad. Ordinary warfare plus crusades against the pagans might to some extent compensate for this loss, as might trade in commodities that were abundant in the north, furs and later also fish, but the only really substantial way of compensating would seem to be to increase the internal exploitation.

The clearest evidence of this is the change in military technology. The traditional opinion among historians has been that the military system in the Scandinavian countries from the Viking age onwards was based on the popular levy (No. *leidang*, Da. *leding*, Sw. *ledung*), primarily intended for sea warfare. The whole or parts of each country was divided into districts which were obliged to build and man a ship, according to rules specified in the laws. This organisation is only to be found in the eastern part of Sweden and only in the coastal regions of Norway. As for Denmark, Niels Lund has recently maintained that the oldest military organisation was based on warriors in the service of the magnates and consequently that no *leding* existed until 1170, i.e. that this organisation was introduced as part of the military specialisation in the High Middle Ages.[5] Lund's thesis has met with some opposition, both based on Danish sources earlier than 1170 and on comparison with other countries.[6] Despite the difficulties in tracing the early mili-

---

[5] Niels Lund, *Lid, leding og landeværn. Hær og samfund i Danmark i ældre middelalder* (Roskilde, 1996).

[6] Esben Albrechtsen, [rev. of] Niels Lund, *Lid, leding og landeværn*, *Historisk Tidsskrift [Danish]* 98 (1998), 395-401 and Michael Gelting, "Det comparative perspektiv i dansk højmiddelalderforskning", *Historisk Tidsskrift [Danish]* 99 (1999), 169-81. See also Niels Lund, "Leding, bønder og inerti", *Historisk Tidsskrift [Danish]* 99 (1999), 189-207 and Esben Albrechtsen, "Svar til Niels Lund", *Historisk Tidsskrift [Danish]* 99 (1999), 208-10. A particular problem for Lund's thesis is the reference to the *leding* in King Cnut's priv-

tary organisation in Scandinavia, it therefore seems the likeliest assumption that a popular levy, in some form, existed in all the Scandinavian countries.

By contrast, there were no taxes in the early period. Like in many early societies, not least among the Germanic peoples, the payment of taxes was considered degrading. However, the king and his retainers had the right to be entertained while travelling around in the country. Both these contributions could and did develop into permanent taxes. The Danish king was entitled to great contributions from the people in the form of hospitality. Most probably, such contributions went back to the Viking Age, as is indicated by the king's building activities and his expeditions against England during this period. Thus, the Danish king probably had considerable financial resources from early on. By the middle of the twelfth century, there are indications of a regular tax, which may be a conversion of hospitality. Hospitality was probably important in Norway as well. In addition, there is evidence of great royal confiscations of land, which made the king a far more important landowner in this early period than in the High Middle Ages, when a considerable part of the royal land had been donated to the Church.

As for the military service, the king might issue an order of mobilisation and then take the provisions, while allowing the warriors to go home. Or he might reduce the number of men, but demand better equipment and longer periods of service. Examples of both these procedures are to be found from the twelfth century onwards. During the internal struggles in Norway (1130-1240), the contributions from the people were clearly developing into a regular tax, while the kings built up armies of retainers. Heavy cavalry according to the European model was introduced from the first half of the twelfth century in Denmark; the first known example of its use is the battle of Fodevig 1134. The *leding* provisions from 1170 give the first evidence of a military elite exempted from taxes in return for serving the king in the field. The military reform introduced in Denmark around 1170 reduced the number of ships but demanded longer service from the ones that remained. In addition, land warfare became relatively more important, and cavalry was used from the first half of the twelfth century in this country, somewhat later in Sweden. The process continued during the following

ilege for the cathedral chapter of Lund from 1085. Here the chapter is given the jurisdiction over the land donated by the king, with three exceptions, including failure to participate in the *leding*: "Si expedicionem neglexerit. erga regem emendet", Sten Skansjö and Hans Sundström, eds *Gåvobrevet 1085* (Lund, 1988), 15.

period. In Denmark the peasant levy disappeared to be substituted by full-time warriors, who were exempt from taxes in return for their service, while the tax burden on the rest of the population increased. The formal expression of the new order in Sweden came in *Alsnö stadga* (the statute of Alsnö), probably in 1280, which is usually regarded as a kind of "constitution" for the Swedish aristocracy, confirming the principle of specialised military service in return for privileges. The closest Norwegian equivalent to *Alsnö stadga* are the decisions from two meetings between the king and his men in 1273, entered in the Law of the King's retainers (*Hirdskrå*) shortly afterwards. Here the royal bailiffs agree to maintain a specified number of men on the incomes from their districts, to serve the king in war. Scholars have discussed whether this force ever came into existence in practice. In any case, it is clear that it was not intended as a substitute but rather as a supplement to the peasant levy.

The last step in this transition was the introduction of castles, the first of which were built in the twelfth century. In the 1240s, the king of Denmark had twenty of them, while ten belonged to the Duke of Southern Jutland. The great expansion took place in the following period, as the consequence of the more intense internal struggles from 1286 and during Erik Menved's wars in the early fourteenth century. After a rebellion in Jutland, which was put down in 1313, the king built a number of castles in this region, while until then most of the castles had been in the border regions and along strategic sea passages. In Sweden, small and simple castles were built in the twelfth century, while the really large and elaborate constructions date from the thirteenth century, particularly from its second half. These new castles could serve as residences for the king and his representatives as well as fortifications. The oldest Norwegian castles date from the internal struggles in the late twelfth century. During the thirteenth and early fourteenth century, castles were built in the king's main residential cities and in some border areas.

The castles not only improved the king's military capacity, they also led to far-reaching administrative and social changes. They were expensive both to build and maintain but enabled the king to exploit the people more efficiently, a small number of armed men in a castle being able to suppress a wide area. Thus, in reducing the number of armed men the king needed, and increasing the cost of keeping them, they furthered the transition from the populary levy to a limited number of royal retainers, financed by taxes from the majority of the population. Both for strategic reasons and because of the cost and labour necessary to built and keep the castles, they also turned into administrative centres. The older royal administration consisted in the combination of stewards of the king's estates, who fulfilled various functions on behalf of their master, and allies among the local magnates. Basically, this system was retained in Denmark and Sweden, but transformed through the development of castles, their commanders becoming the governors of the surrounding area.

From an economic point of view, the new system probably, like in the rest of Europe, created greater gross surplus, in the sense that the number of agricultural labourers rose and that each of them paid a larger percentage of the family's earnings to the king or the landowner. It is more questionable to what extent it also created a greater net surplus. Some calculations—admittedly based on very fragmentary material from the later Middle Ages—indicate that most of what was paid in taxes by the peasants went to support the lord of the castle and his household and garrison. Even if this is correct, however, it does not diminish the effects of the military change. It did serve to create a military elite which might even have a centralising effect, at least as long as the king was able to control the appointments of castle commanders.

However, this military specialisation did not take place all over Scandinavia. The central agricultural areas of Sweden underwent much the same transition as Denmark, while freeholders dominated in the less fertile areas, and continued to perform military service in person. In Norway the king managed to make the peasants pay an annual tax, which in the 1270s was fixed at half the amount of the provisions due at an actual mobilisation. This was far less than the taxes in the two other countries. The total annual income of the King of Denmark by the mid-thirteenth century was around 40 000 marks (= 7500 kg.) silver. Much of this consisted of rents from landed estates but the tax incomes were also far higher than the Norwegian ones. The total annual income of the Norwegian king—taxes, fines, land rent etc.—is estimated at about 8000 marks, i.e. 1500 kg. silver. The Swedish incomes are more difficult to estimate, but the level of taxation is closer to the Danish than to the Norwegian one. But then the Norwegian peasants still served in person. The principal reason for this was the importance of the fleet.

Norway has an extremely long coast, along which most of the population lived, then as now. A strong fleet was therefore essential to control the country. With the naval technology that prevailed until the early fourteenth century, superior skill and training were less able to compensate for numerical inferiority in warfare at sea than at land, because of the large number of rowers needed and the fact that it was much more difficult to defeat a numerically superior enemy by surprise attacks or tactical maneuvering. Consequently, the peasant levy could not be replaced by a small force of royal retainers, and the state depended more than in most other countries on the people's cooperation. The lack of military specialisation and the small tax incomes of the Norwegian king also explain that fewer castles were erected in this country than in Denmark and Sweden. The local administration therefore developed in a different way from that of the neighbouring countries. From the second half of the twelfth century a new official, a bailiff (*syslumaðr*), a parallel to the English and continental officials of the same period, was introduced, and from the first half of the thirteenth century the country was divided into fixed districts, around forty in all, each headed by a bailiff, who often had no connection with the district in which he served. He might also be replaced and moved from one district to another. Norway thus developed a local administration more directly under the king's control, while at the same time the Norwegian aristocracy became an administrative more than a military class.

In this way, Denmark largely came to conform to the normal European pattern, whereas the changes in Sweden and particularly Norway went more slowly and were less far-reaching. There is much to suggest that this development was the result of the introduction of European military technology, first to Denmark and from there gradually to the other countries. To the Danes this technology represented a clear advantage in their wars against their neighbours in Northern Germany and to the Swedes in wars against Denmark. Nevertheless, the introduction of heavy cavalry and castles was not simply the introduction of a superior military technology, but also the expression of a change from sea to land warfare. This probably, in turn, reflected the increased importance of the inland regions, a more intense exploitation of the land, and from point of view of foreign policy, from conquests directed towards the islands in the west to inland neighbours, the Danish expansion in Northern Germany and the inter-Scandinavian conflicts in border region between the three kingdoms in or near Scania.

There are, however, alternative explanations to the military one, in Scandinavia as well as in the rest of Europe. Considerable importance has traditionally been attached to demographic growth in Scandinavian, notably Norwegian scholarship. According to "the Marxist-Malthusian school" in Norway, the great transformation in this country took place in the eleventh and twelfth centuries, as a direct result of demographic growth: The population increased until it reached the limits of what the available land could support with the existing technology. This made the peasants dependent on the great lords, who took over their farms, and out of the surplus of their production were able to build up an organised Church and state. In a similar way, there has been a tradition in Swedish and particularly Danish historiography for imagining a society mainly consisting of peasant owners in the Early Middle Ages, which was then transformed in an aristocratic direction during the following period. In Denmark this change is said to have taken place particularly during the "age of unrest" 1241-1340, when most of the peasants became tenants under the great landowners in order to escape the increasingly heavy taxation.[7] The evidence of place names and to some extent archaeology suggests a considerable extension and intensification of cultivated land, which again means demographic growth, in all countries during the period, particularly in Norway and Denmark. The main agricultural areas of Sweden, the plains of Östergötland, Västergötland and the Mälar Valley, were also fairly densely populated towards the end of our period. By the mid-fourteenth century the population of Denmark has been estimated at one million people, while the suggestions for Norway vary between 300 000 and 500 000. The Swedish number must be somewhere in between that of Denmark and Norway.

However, while the demographic growth can hardly be doubted, this fact does not necessarily mean that the pattern of land ownership or the social structure in general in the thirteenth and fourteenth centuries was the result of a Malthusian situation. First, we cannot be sure that the Scandinavian countries were overpopulated by the mid-fourteenth century and even less that they were a hundred years before. Second, other factors may have contributed equally much or more to the social changes during the High Middle Ages. As for Denmark, scholars have pointed out that taxes were already very high in the twelfth century, while the land rent was low.[8] This is an argument in favour of the military rather than the demographic explanation of the social structure of the High Middle Ages, which actually seems to be the explanation favoured by the majority of Danish and Swedish scholars. The opposite situation in Norway, with low taxes and high land rent, may, however,

---

[7] For a survey of these discussions, see Eljas Orrman, "Rural Conditions", in Helle, *Scandinavia*, 297-306.

[8] Erik Ulsig, "Landboer, bryder, skat og landgilde. De danske fæstebønder og ders avgifter I det 12. og 13. århundre", in *Middelalder, metode og medier. Festskrift til N. Skyum-Nielsen* (Copenhagen, 1981), 159.

suggests the opposite explanation, as may the situation following the Black Death, when land rents dropped to around 20% of the level before 1350, far more than in Sweden and Denmark, and also remaining low for much longer. The most likely explanation of this is that the level of land rent in Norway was the result of the relationship between the number of people and the amount of arable land, not of political-administrative pressure.

The Cultural Europeanisation: The Church and Christianity

There seems to be a close temporal connection between Christianisation and the formation of kingdoms, but the causal relationship between the two processes is less clear. Theoretically as well as practically, there are indications of the causal process going both ways. A unified kingdom made the introduction of Christianity easier, while at the same time, Christianity could serve the purpose of political unification. Denmark forms a clear example of unification coming first, whereas Norway and Sweden are more ambiguous.

Christianity could be an effective instrument of colonisation, in the Middle Ages as well as in more recent periods. The crusades in the Baltic area from the mid-twelfth century resulted in the creation of a number of cities and principalities dominated by burghers and aristocrats from the west, who exploited the original population. The Christianisation of Scandinavia was different partly because it occurred at an earlier time, before the Europeans had gained military and technological supe-riority, and partly because the mission to a considerable extent originated in Anglo-Saxon England which was a weak power rather than in Germany which was strong. Only Denmark was close enough to Germany to fear the power of this country, and the conversion of Denmark around 965 may to some extent be the result of German political pressure. However, Denmark was a strong power in the late tenth and early eleventh centuries, and it was also at some distance from the German border until the mid-twelfth century, when the Germans expanded across the Elbe and conquered and Christianised the Slav peoples there. Thus, the Christianisation of Scandinavia was to a considerable extent carried out by Scandinavian kings and nobles, although evidently with the help of ecclesiastics from Germany, England, and other countries.

The Scandinavian churches seem in the beginning to have been dom-inated by kings and magnates. However, the Gregorian reform move-ment spread to Scandinavia during the twelfth century and led to similar conflicts between the Church and secular powers as elsewhere, conflicts that have played an important part in the predominantly Protestant historiography of the Scandinavian countries. Nor is there any reason to deny the problems these conflicts created for the monarchies. However, in accordance with Moore's view as well as some more recent tendencies in Scandinavian scholarship, I shall in this context focus on the positive aspect, the importance of the Church and Christianity for Europeanisation, social change, and state formation.

To what extent did Scandinavia really become integrated into Western Christendom? The question has several different aspects, three of which shall be discussed in the following: (1) the ecclesiastical organisation, (2) the importance of Christianity for popular culture and belief, and (3) the reception of the scholasticism and the intellectual elite culture of Western Christendom in Scandinavia. As for the first point, it took some time for the ecclesiastical organisation to become fully developed, probably longer than in the Central European kingdoms Christianised at the same time. However, after the establishment of the three Scandinavian church provinces (Denmark 1104, Norway 1152/53, and Sweden 1164) and particularly from the thirteenth century, the Scandinavian churches do not seem very different from those of the rest of Western Christendom, with dioceses, parishes, cathedral chapters, and monasteries. New orders, such as the Cistercians and the Mendicants, were introduced not long after their original foundation. Ecclesiastical wealth was also considerable. Just before the reformation, the Norwegian Church possessed 48% of the land incomes of the country. The wealth of the churches in Denmark and Sweden was apparently relatively less, but still substantial.

The rise of an ecclesiastical aristocracy was obviously a result of European influence through Christianisation; what is open to discussion is to what extent it led to a more aristocratic society by increasing the amount of land belonging to great landowners and to what extent the land given to this class came from the king and the secular aristocracy. There is evidence that a large amount of land came from the great landowners, but it is nevertheless difficult to avoid the conclusion that the introduction of Christianity did contribute to the expansion of a landed aristocracy. It probably also contributed to far-reaching changes in the government of society, in the continued existence of a united kingdom and above all in the character of the state that was formed during the Middle Ages. It is important to distinguish between unification and permanent unity. It is a normal phenomenon that political units formed by conquest dissolve again, so normal that the real question about state formation is not why the unit in question was formed but why it continued to exist. For continued existence, institutionalisation and ideology are probably more important than direct physical power. Moreover, medieval military technology did not favour large units. The combination of castles and heavy cavalry that was imported to Scandinavia from the twelfth century onwards favoured relatively small units. It was possible for a magnate controlling a castle and a small elite cavalry to dominate a local region and defend it against a central authority; at least, it was possible for many such units to do so. Admittedly, the Norwegian military technology, based on the popular levy, diminished the risk that the country would fragment. However, both military organisation and technology were simple, thus giving the central government no particular advantage and not necessitating any strong government, in contrast to the situation in the Early Modern Period, with artillery, elaborate fortifications, trained and organised professional soldiers, and large and expensive warships, all so complicated and expensive that only strong and wealthy governments could run them.

In the absence of such advantages, medieval government had to depend on "civilian" means, including Church and religion. A comparison between Christianity and the ancient Nordic religion indicates that the former had a greater potential in this direction than the latter. From a materialistic point of view, the conversion meant that a cheap and unbureaucratic religion was replaced by an expensive and bureaucratic one. Admittedly, we do not know exactly how expensive the pagan religion was. How costly and time-consuming were the sacrifices? Were there special cult buildings and religious specialists, and how numerous and expensive were the latter? Burials were no doubt elaborate and expensive, as is documented by the famous Oseberg burial from the early ninth century, as well as other finds. The most widespread opinion today is that the old religion lacked particular cult buildings as well as religious specialists and that religious ceremonies and expenses were closely linked to other social functions and reflected existing power structures. Although some recent excavations have questioned this view, it is likely that special cult buildings were the exception rather than the rule. The priests were local magnates and the religious ceremonies the expression of their wealth and power. Moreover, the food and drink collected for the sacrifices were mostly consumed by the participants themselves, only a minor part being left to the gods, in the same way as in the ancient Greek and Roman religion.

By contrast, Christianity meant that the faithful had to support a numerous and wealthy class of religious specialists. The clergy in medieval Norway around 1300—admittedly long after the missionary period—is estimated at around 2000 people, i.e. one per 175-225 inhabitants (depending on the size of the population which is very uncertain), compared to one per 3800 in 1970. Further, this class received a tax of one tenth of the agricultural production and may have owned around 40% of the land rent in the country. No doubt, the wealth of the Church was not only the result of the conversion, but also of demographic and economic change, which favoured secular landowners as well. Nor did this wealth exclusively benefit the clergy; parts of it were returned to broader strata of the population in the form of hospitals, alms, and numerous opportunities for laymen to make a career in the service of the ecclesiastical aristocracy. Nevertheless, the main benefit the laity received from the Church was of a spiritual nature: by sacrificing material wealth, they gained the spiritual treasures the Church could offer which gave them protection against the dangers facing them in this life as well as in the life to come.

From a materialistic point of view, the clergy might well be regarded as a parasitic class, and even believers might think that they gave little in return for the wealth they received. Nevertheless, they were not purely parasitic, they constituted an organised bureaucracy with a well-defined purpose—admittedly only partly conforming to the Weberian ideal—in which office-holders were appointed and certain skills were necessary for appointment. The establishment and expansion of the ecclesiastical bureaucracy thus formed a major step in the direction of organised government. It is doubtful whether it would have been possible to bureaucratise any other purpose than religion to the same extent under contemporary conditions.

Concerning the functions of this bureaucracy, Moore points to the inquisition as a particularly instructive example, enabling the ecclesiastical authorities to intervene in the minutest detail of local life, as illustrated for instance by the material from Montaillou and the studies which have been made of the inquisition as the expression of elite power. There was no inquisition in Scandinavia and very few examples of heresy. There was, however, a well developed and apparently effective ecclesiastical jurisdiction which interfered in a number of matters in local society that had earlier been of no concern to the central power: fasts and rest from labour on holidays, marriage and sexual life, testaments, the protection of clerics against laymen, etc. This jurisdiction and its procedures also formed an important model for the development of the royal courts. As for the inquisition, Moore hints that it was not only a reaction to the growth of heresy, but also an expression of the ecclesiastical hierarchy's wish to expand its own power by suppressing the common people.[9] If so, the authorities would probably have found ample opportunity to institute parallel procedures in Scandinavia, given the recent Christianisation of this area and the likely existence of magic or rituals of pagan or quasi-pagan origin. There are also prohibitions of such practices in the laws. However, the Church seems in practice to have had a fairly relaxed attitude to them, regarding them as less dangerous than the movements directly challenging its own doctrine and authority. Thus, the inquisition seems to have been a reaction against a perceived danger rather than an offensive measure.

In light of the later conflicts between the monarchy and the Church, the rise of the ecclesiastical bureaucracy may seem to have been a mixed blessing for the institution we tend to regard as the forerunner of the modern state, i.e. the monarchy. Nevertheless, the Church continued to be an important state-building power, partly by the introduction of writing as an administrative tool and by offering the king educated personnel, an ideological legitimation of public power, and a legal system, partly by carrying out public functions on its own. There is thus a close connection between Christianity and state formation. How close the connection is, should be discussed further by comparing Western Christendom to other religious traditions, such as Eastern Christendom and Islam, and not least, the apparent exceptions to this rule, notably Ireland which was Christianised already in the fifth century but never developed a united state, and Lithuania which remained pagan until 1386 but did develop a strong state. As for Ireland, a possible explanation may be that the church in this country was dominated by monasteries rather than the normal hierarchy of bishops and priests, so that the main administrative elements of the Church were lacking or weakly developed. As for Lithuania, there is much to suggest that the religious as well as the secular administration was developed according to models taken from Christian Europe. Moreover, the correlation between Christianity and state formation should, like most historical "laws", be regarded as probabilistic rather than deterministic.

Given the wealth of the Church and its strong position in Scandinavian society, it would seem a reasonable assumption that religious life in

---

[9] Moore, *Revolution*, 169 ff.

Scandinavia was not fundamentally different from the rest of Europe.[10] There has, however, been a fairly widespread opinion, particularly among Norwegian scholars in the nineteenth and early twentieth century, that Scandinavians did not "really" become Christians in the Middle Ages. This probably has to do with the romantic notion of an original, Germanic culture with its centre in Scandinavia which to some extent was able to resist the ecstatic, superstitious, and "unhealthy" aspects of European Catholicism: the belief in miracles, extreme asceticism and the rejection of sexuality and the body, and the unquestioned acceptance of ecclesiastical authority. In this respect, romanticism was reinforced by Protestantism; without directly favouring paganism, Protestants could approve of some "healthy" resistance to the more questionable aspects of Catholicism.

The evidence that have been adduced in favour of this interpretation includes non-Christian elements in popular cult, failure to respect Christian morality, for instance by taking revenge for insults and killings or disregard for the Church's strict sexual norms, and the existence in Norway and Iceland of a secular literature with norms and values different from or even contrary to those of the Church. All this can be found in the rest of Europe as well. There is therefore no particular reason to regard the Scandinavians as less Christian than other Europeans, although it must be admitted that the evidence for popular religious attitudes is fairly limited. As far as "official" religion is concerned, Scandinavia seems to conform to the rest of Europe. This includes liturgy, holidays, and religious practices in daily life, as well as the official norms regarding marriage and sexuality, which, likely enough given the late Christianisation of Scandinavia, were introduced somewhat later than in the old countries of Christian Europe. Divorce was banned, and the prohibitions against marriage in forbidden degrees were made official law, controlled by the Church. The woman's consent now became a necessary precondition for a lawful marriage. Although the clerics were not particularly eager to enforce this provision, there are examples in the sources of marriages being annulled because of the lack of such consent. Until the twelfth and thirteenth century, we have evidence of concubinage being practiced publicly and officially, as a regular kind of relationship, normally in cases where the woman's social status was somewhat below that of the man. Thus, most Norwegian kings had such relationships,

---

[10] For the following, see Eljas Orrman, "Church and Society", in Helle, *Scandinavia*, 455-62 and Sverre Bagge, "Ideologies and Mentalities", ibid., 476-85.

normally before marriage, and these unions often resulted in children who would later hold a prominent position. From the thirteenth century onward, concubinage gradually came to be regarded as an unofficial and even illegal union, and the sources tell far less about the offspring from such unions. This does not necessarily mean that such relationships became less common, but certainly that their legal status changed. As for clerical celibacy, the Church succeeded insofar as the clerics did not officially marry and could not be succeeded by their sons, at least not without papal dispensation, but not in the sense that they stopped having sexual relationships with women. As far the sources allow us to draw any conclusion, they seem to have lived in regular concubinage, as was probably to a considerable extent the case in the rest of Europe as well.

On the other hand, Scandinavia hardly belonged to the most advanced regions of Europe regarding Christian faith and practice. In his great book on medieval sainthood, André Vauchez distinguishes between "hot" and "cold" regions, according to their ability to produce saints.[11] Scandinavia as a whole must be considered relatively "cold". Most of the saints venerated in the region during the Middle Ages were the common saints of western Christendom as they appear in the Roman calendar. However, some local saints emerged from fairly early on, and a few of them were even venerated outside Scandinavia. Most Scandinavian saints belong to Vauchez's northern type, i.e. they are people holding high office, who are mainly venerated for their miracles after death. Their official lives are usually very impersonal and stereotype, as well as fairly brief, while the main focus is on their miracles. By contrast, the southern type is a charismatic figure, whose reputation for sanctity is largely based on a remarkable life—St. Francis is the most well known example of this kind of saint. The only real example of this kind of saint in Scandinavia is St. Birgitta of Vadstena in Sweden (1303-1373).

While there can hardly be any doubt that the Church succeeded in introducing its doctrine and rituals in Scandinavia in the Middle Ages, there is less evidence of the newer trends towards a more personal religion, which in the late Middle Ages were expressed for instance in the *devotio moderna*. This may be due to the nature of the sources; after all, the external aspect of religion is more likely to leave traces than the

---

[11] André Vauchez, *La sainteté en Occident aux derniers siècles du Moyen Âge d'après le procès de canonisation et les documents hagiographiques* (Rome, 1980), 121-29, 154-62.

internal one, and the new, Lutheran Church was not interested in preserving Catholic devotional literature. We should also beware of the "Protestant" tendency to draw conclusions from the presence of external piety to the absence of an internal one. Nevertheless, the extant sermons, as far as they have been analysed, the number and type of saints, as well as the religious art mainly seem to point in the "traditional" direction. So does also the fact that there was no heresy in Scandinavia. Rather than forming evidence of the Scandinavians' faithful adherence to the Catholic Church, this absence seems to indicate that the personal religion was weaker, that religious customs and rituals were well integrated into daily life, but that few people were personally moved by the message of the Gospel.

If we turn to the heresy that eventually did occur in Scandinavia and in short time abolished the Catholic Church, the Protestant Reformation, we may notice a significant difference between Denmark and Sweden on the one hand and Norway and Iceland on the other. The former countries had a real Reformation movement and even, to some extent, a Counter-Reformation, while in Norway, and to a lesser extent Iceland, the Reformation was introduced from above, with little preparation. Consequently, the new trends in the pre-Reformation Church are more likely to be found in the former countries than in the latter. This impression is also confirmed by the fact that the Mendicants were stronger in Sweden and particularly Denmark than in Norway. In addition to the Franciscans and the Dominicans, the Carmelites were introduced in the fifteenth century, founded a number of houses, and were engaged in the reform of the Church. The most prominent example of religious renewal is, however, the Birgittine movement, which also influenced the laity, particularly the social elite.

The most important aspect of Christianity in Moore's "revolutionary" perspective is the development of an increasingly sophisticated but also conformist religious doctrine, an intellectual revolution, leading to a new reading of ancient authorities and a systematic attempt to reconcile them with Christianity which greatly stimulated thought and creativity, combined with increasingly systematic suppression of religious opinions regarded as heretical. The apparent paradox in this combination is partly solved by the observation that the Church's persecution was above all directed against heretical *movements*, i.e. that it was in practice more likely to hit ordinary, unlearned people who openly opposed the Church. Although professional intellectuals might also be condemned and even executed, orthodoxy was not so strict as to suppress discussion and innovation. Until the mid-fourteenth century, the centres of this intellectual culture, the universities, were all situated in Europe west of the Rhine, i.e. in England, France, Italy, and the Spanish kingdoms. However, the universities attracted students as well as scholars from all over Europe, including Scandinavia. We know of a considerable number of Scandinavians, mostly Danes and Swedes, studying in Paris in the first half of the fourteenth century, some also in Bologna, and no doubt there were others at other universities of whom we have no record. With the foundation of universities east of the Rhine, the first of which was Prague (founded 1347/48), the majority of Scandinavians seem to have moved to Germany or Central Europe. The foundation of a number of universities in Germany and Central Europe in the following period made it easier for Scandinavians to study abroad, and most Scandinavian students in the Later Middle Ages went to German universities, notably Rostock (founded 1419) and Greifswald (founded 1456). The earliest Scandinavian universities date from 1477 (Uppsala) and 1479 (Copenhagen), but both had very few students in the beginning.[12]

Corresponding to the more extensive contacts with the European universities, the literature of Denmark and Sweden shows greater influence from European scholasticism than the Norwegian and Icelandic one.[13] The literary use of the Latin language corresponds to the administrative one. It was used all over Scandinavia, but there is a marked difference between Denmark and Sweden on the one hand and Norway and Iceland on the other, in administrative as well as literary use. Hardly anything is preserved in the Danish language before 1300, except for the laws, whereas the Latin literature is fairly extensive. The great breakthrough for Danish as a literary language comes in the period after 1450. Most of what is extant of medieval literature from Sweden dates from after 1300, but here the vernacular is relatively more important than in Denmark. In this respect, these countries conform to the pattern of the "new" countries of Central Europe, Poland, Hungary, and Bohemia, where the use of the vernacular in writing came very late, in the case of Bohemia admittedly with a great output from around 1400.

---

[12] Sverre Bagge, "Nordic Students at Foreign Universities", *Scandinavian Journal of History*, 14 (1984), 5-13.

[13] For the following, see most recently Lars Lönnroth, Vésteinn Ólason and Anders Pilz, "Literature", in Helle, *Scandinavia*, 515-19 and Sverre Bagge, "On the Far Edge of the Dry Land: Scandinavian and European Culture in the Middle Ages", in Jonathan Adams and Katherine Holman (eds.), *Scandinavia and Europe 800-1350* (Tournhout, 2004), 355-69.

From the late thirteenth and early fourteenth century onwards, the reception of scholasticism becomes another great divide within Scandinavia. In the late thirteenth century, Boetius de Dacia, probably a Dane, was a leading representative of Averroism in Paris; the Swedish Dominican Petrus de Dacia was a theologian as well as devotional writer and a spokesman for the mystic Christina of Stommeln. In the fourteenth century, the Swedish Master Mattias, Birgitta's confessor, was an important theological as well as a devotional writer.

By contrast, there is no evidence of scholasticism in Norway. A large religious literature is preserved in Old Norse, mostly in Icelandic manuscripts, but most of it must be characterised as devotional rather than theological. Further, there is a substantial secular literature from the thirteenth century in the form of narratives ("sagas") about kings and great men, most of it written by Icelanders but at least the kings' sagas clearly known in Norway, some of them even commissioned by Norwegian rulers. This, however, is not specific to these countries; an increasing amount of secular works in the vernacular was produced in most countries of Western Europe at the time, corresponding to spread of literacy to the secular aristocracy and to more refined manners and ideals within this class. To some extent, Norway and Iceland conform to the pattern of the old Christian countries of Western Europe, like England, France, Germany, Italy, and the Spanish kingdoms, where the vernacular was increasingly used as a literary language from the twelfth and particularly the thirteenth century. What was characteristic of Norway and Iceland, however, was that it was used, not only for poetry and heroic or romantic narrative, the normal genres in the rest of Europe, but also for learned literature, such as *The King's Mirror* and grammatical, astronomical, and theological treatises. The translation of devotional literature is less remarkable, as this was done all over Europe as the result of the Church's increasing emphasis on the piety of the laity in the High and Later Middle Ages.

The clearest expression of the spread of the common ecclesiastical elite culture to Scandinavia is canon law. This was one of the most popular studies at medieval universities, as it was very useful for making a career in the Church as well as in the royal administration, and we know of a number of Scandinavians with degrees in this discipline. Moreover the central texts of canon law, from Burchard of Worms' *Decretum* (c. 1020) via Gratian to the great papal collections from the thirteenth and early fourteenth century were all known in Scandinavia and to some extent influenced local legislation. The knowledge of canon law can also be studied through the great number of legal documents from various ecclesiastical institutions, which has only been done to a limited extent. Canon law is important, not only as an example of a common learned culture but also as an intellectual system with a clear and strict method for analysing a number of other questions, thus probably contributing to the great scientific discoveries made in Europe in the Early Modern Period.[14] It also had important practical consequences in the development of ecclesiastical as well as secular justice and legislation.

In sum, Christianity as well as the scholastic culture did find their way into Scandinavia during the Middle Ages, although the region was not one of the great centres of this culture. The stronger position of the vernacular and secular culture in Norway and particularly Iceland is less unique that it is often thought to be, notably by Scandinavian scholars, and should rather be regarded as a warning against exaggerating the importance of the ecclesiastical culture in Europe in general.

The King and the Royal Government

Finally, we come to the most immediate precursor of the modern state, the king and the royal government. How does Scandinavia relate to the "main countries" of Western Europe which usually serve as the examples of European state formation, i.e. England, France and the Spanish kingdoms? The expansion of Europe in the tenth and eleventh century exported the Carolingian model of state formation to the new countries, i.e. on the one hand a direct connection between the king and the majority of the people, expressed in a broad military mobilisation, on the other a considerable amount of informal links of patronage between the king and prominent men. The king's power to intervene directly in local society and to reward and punish even the mightiest magnates is well illustrated in Otto of Freising's description of Hungarian society from the mid-twelfth century, stressing the king's arbitrary power in contrast to what Otto regards as the balanced, feudal constitution of Germany.[15] The formal limits to what the king could do were appar-

---

[14] Toby E. Huff, *The Rise of Early Modern Science* (Cambridge, 1993), 119-48, 160-9, cf. also Harold Berman, *Law and Revolution: The Formation of the Western Legal Tradition* (Cambridge, Mass., 1983).

[15] *Ottonis et Rahewini Gesta Frederici I. Imperatoris*, eds G. Waitz and B. von Simson, MGH Scriptores ... in usum scholarum, vol. 46 (Hannover etc., 1912) I.33, cf. Sverre Bagge, "Ideas and Narrative in Otto of Freising's *Gesta Frederici*", *Journal of Medieval History* 22.4, (1996), 359 f.

ently few or non-existent in Central Europe as well as in Scandinavia at the time, but this should not make us overlook the considerable limits to the king's power in the form of an undeveloped administrative apparatus.

The development in the following period shows some similarity to the feudal dissolution in the west in the post-Carolingian period. A powerful secular and ecclesiastical aristocracy emerged between the king and the people, setting limits to the king's arbitrary power and demanding privileges as well as a share in the king's power. On the other hand, a more professional administration emerged through the introduction of writing and professional, often university educated personnel, while at the same time a clearer distinction between the elite and the people resulted in the centralisation of government. Which of the two processes was the more important varies from country to country. The aristo-cratisation of Central Europe seems in the long run to have weakened the power of the state and contributed to these countries succumbing to the empires that developed in the Later Middle Ages and the Early Modern Period, Hungary to Turkey in the sixteenth century, Bohemia to the Hapsburg Empire in the early seventeenth century, and Poland to Russia in the eighteenth century. As for Scandinavia, both Denmark and Sweden developed in a similar way and went through periods of chaotic struggles between pretenders and aristocratic factions, Denmark in the early fourteenth century and Sweden for parts of the period c. 1350-1523. Both would probably have succumbed to mightier neigh-bours if any such had existed, but having the advantage of a protected geographical position, they managed to overcome the crises. After its fourteenth century crisis, Denmark regained its position as the great power of Scandinavia through a mostly harmonious cooperation between the king and the aristocracy, the latter having substantial privileges and strong local power as well as sharing the central power with the king through the council of the realm, but usually supporting the king's expansionist policy against sharing its rewards. The internal divisions in Sweden created ample opportunities for the Danish king to intervene in this country, but he was never strong enough to control it effectively for a longer period, and the final result was a united Sweden in oppo-sition to Denmark, which, through massive militarisation in the early seventeenth century, became a European great power. The only Scandinavian country to succumb to mightier neighbours was the least feudalised, Norway, which in the thirteenth century had modernised the Carolingian model by introducing contemporary European administrative

reforms. However, the lack of a strong aristocracy, largely as a consequence of the demographic and economic disaster caused by the Black
Death, fatally weakened its military power and made the country an
easy prey to Denmark in the early sixteenth century.

Despite periods of crisis, the Scandinavian kingdoms were to a considerable extent able to develop state-like features according to Western
European models. The ideology of the king as a *rex iustus* and God's
representative on earth was introduced from the twelfth century onwards
and expressed in charters, narrative and didactic texts, and the ceremony of unction and coronation. The latter was introduced for the first
time in Norway in 1163/64, in Denmark in 1170, and in Sweden in
1210 and became permanent from the thirteenth century in all countries.
An earlier tendency in the same direction was the cult of royal saints,
St Olav (d. 1030) in Norway, St Cnut (d. 1086) in Denmark, and St
Erik (d. 1160) in Sweden. The gradual development of a royal dynasty
from the eleventh century onwards and of the idea of sole succession
created a clearer difference between the king and other great men.
Rules for the succession to the throne were formulated and even to
some extent codified from the twelfth century onwards. In Norway the
law of succession of 1260 established hereditary succession, whereas
Denmark and Sweden became elective monarchies from the beginning
of the fourteenth century, although in such a way that the king's eldest
son was elected to succeed his father, but, from the fifteenth century,
had to issue a detailed list of promises after negotiations with his elec-
tors (*håndfestning*).

The more practical aspects of government also developed along
European lines. As in the rest of Europe, the monarchy's most important function apart from the military was the legal one. There was a
development in all three countries from conflicts being solved either by
local assemblies, mediation or negotiation or even open fighting, to regular courts of law with authority from the king. Formally, the whole
judicial system—apart from the ecclesiastical courts—seems to have come
under royal control in Norway from the second half of the thirteenth
century, and the Norwegian king was also able to ban feuds and private revenge. By contrast, the Danish and Swedish kings had to share
their judicial power with the aristocracy and be content with more modest claims in the direction of public justice. Royal legislation developed
parallel to this. The early, regional laws from the twelfth century in
Norway and the thirteenth in Denmark and Sweden were apparently
issued by the local assemblies themselves or were understood as collec-

tions of rules or provisions for the local community, although in practice they were probably influenced by the king. Explicit royal legislation started in the second half of the twelfth century, first with statutes on particular matters, then with royal law codes. Norway was one of the first countries in Europe to have such a code for the whole country (1274-77). Sweden followed in 1350, whereas Denmark had to wait until 1683. In addition to local customs this legislation was to a great extent influenced by Roman and canon law. The early development of Norway is clearly connected to the relative strength of the king compared to the aristocracy, which in contemporary terminology might justify the term *regimen regale* about this country, whereas Denmark and Sweden would rather seem to correspond to the model of *regimen politicum*.

In the judicial as well as other fields, the royal administration became increasingly based on writing. There is a sharp increase in the number of royal—as well as other—charters from the very modest beginnings in the late twelfth century to the end of the thirteenth, when the use of written documents seems to have become normal routine. This implies a more professional royal administration, able to issue and handle documents and with knowledge of Latin and of Roman and canon law. As for language, Latin was the normal administrative language in Denmark and Sweden until the late fourteenth or early fifteenth century, whereas Norwegian royal charters were normally written in the vernacular, except when addressed to the Church or foreign powers.

We then arrive at one of Moore's crucial characteristics of the European development, the royal bureaucracy.[16] How were the Scandinavian bureaucrats recruited? Were they men who depended solely on the king for their careers, thus making the monarchy an independent political force? There are examples in Scandinavia of low-born royal servants getting powerful positions and ending their careers as bishops or archbishops, notably under strong and autocratic rulers, such as in Denmark under Margrete and Erik of Pomerania in the late fourteenth and early fifteenth century and Hans and Christian II in the late fifteenth and early sixteenth century. However, this was the exception rather than the rule, not only in the highly aristocratic kingdoms of Denmark and Sweden, but even in Norway. Attempts have been made to distinguish between magnates and prelates on the one hand and "professionals" of

---

[16] Moore, "Transformation", see also his "The Eleventh Century in Eurasian History: A Comparative Approach to the Convergence and Divergence of Medieval Civilizations", *Journal of Medieval and Early Modern Studies* 33 (2003), 1-21.

lower rank on the other in the late thirteenth and early fourteenth century, when the Norwegian royal administration was at its peak, before
the period of unions with the neighbouring countries.[17] Within the clergy,
it is possible to identify a group of specifically royal clerks, attached to
the royal chapels, but the king also made use of ordinary canons and
regular clergy, notably the Mendicants. Among the king's lay servants,
however, it is very difficult to distinguish between genuine aristocrats
and low-born people. As far as we can know, the latter category seems
rare or non-existent among high-ranking royal servants, at least after
the period of King Sverre (1177-1202), who promoted some low-born
men in return for their merits in the intense internal struggles at the
time. Later in the thirteenth century, high-ranking royal officials seem
normally to have had an aristocratic background, although not necessarily a very prominent one, which means that the king was able to
choose his officials fairly freely. Further, local officials only rarely held
office in their home regions. However, there is certainly no correspondence between low rank and professionalism. On the contrary, some of
the best educated royal servants belonged to the top aristocracy. In this
respect, Norway and probably Scandinavia as a whole seem to conform
to the eastern rather than the western pattern of contemporary Europe.
At least until the mid-fourteenth century, university education was more
common in Western than in Central Europe and consequently, it was
easier for people without aristocratic rank to advance in the royal and
ecclesiastical administration.[18] Scandinavia belongs to the East in this
respect; Scandinavian bishops and a large part of the higher clergy in
the later Middle Ages seem normally to have university education, but
to a considerable extent, these clerics were recruited from the aristocracy and several of them had probably also had their education paid
by their families. Thus, education served to strengthen the established
aristocracy rather than to further social mobility. This picture may possibly have been modified towards the end of the Middle Ages with the
foundation of new universities in Northern Germany.

With some differences over time and from country to country, there
hardly existed a class of professional bureaucrats in Scandinavia who
depended solely on the king for their careers, or, insofar as it did, such
men did not rise to really powerful positions. Instead, members of the

---

[17] Knut Helle, *Konge og gode menn i norsk riksstyring ca. 1150-1319* (Bergen, 1972), 565 f.,
576-602 and *passim*.
[18] Moore, *Revolution, 132-4.*

aristocracy played a prominent part in the royal administration. On the other hand, Scandinavian aristocrats generally had less local power and depended more on the king for their power and wealth than their counterparts in most of continental Europe. This applies particularly to Norway but also to some extent to Denmark and Sweden. Formally, aristocratic rank was conferred by the king through knighthood, which means that there was no hereditary nobility. In practice, however, knighthood tended to be reserved for members of certain families. With a few exceptions, mainly members of the royal family, fiefs did not become hereditary, and the distinction between public office and private property was not blurred in the way it was at least in some parts of feudal Europe. This may possibly be the reason why primogeniture and sole succession to aristocratic property were not introduced in Scandinavia. As there were two sources of wealth and power, not only the family's estate, but also incomes from the service of the king, it was less necessary for the family's survival to leave the whole to only one member.

Thus, the line of division between monarchy and aristocracy seems to have been blurred in Scandinavia in a way that seems archaic compared to Moore's picture of contemporary Europe after the "medieval revolution". On this point, however, Moore's picture is highly controversial. No doubt, schools and universities, together with mercenary companies, opened up new possibilities of social mobility for younger sons of aristocratic families, and people of the bourgeoisie, petty nobility, or even the peasantry. There are also some well-known examples of men of a humble background rising to the top in the royal service, for instance in France under Philip IV (1285-1314). The French kings normally avoided people who had their origin in the district when appointing local officials, and they certainly tried to create a counterbalance to their many and powerful vassals. On the other hand, they could not rule without a reasonably good relationship to those vassals. As for England, the most centralised kingdom at the time and the model of successful state building in the Middle Ages, a close cooperation between the king and the aristocracy was essential. From the thirteenth century onwards, the king's local power was largely delegated to local aristocrats, just the opposite was the case in France. And the king's most trusted counsellors were to a large extent bishops or high-ranking magnates. A king who ran into conflict with the top aristocracy risked deposition or murder, as can be illustrated by the fate of Edward II (1307-27) and Richard II (1377-99).

Thus, the royal administration became professionalised in the High

Middle Ages, in Scandinavia as well as in the rest of Europe, which
gave kings a certain independence in relations to other powerful men.
However, the low-born royal servant "who can be promoted without
creating envy and destroyed without fear of revenge", is an Eastern
more than a European figure, characteristic of the Muslim kingdoms
or empires, to some extent also Byzantium, whereas the characteristic
feature of Europe is the kings' need for support from powerful groups
in society. The point is well expressed in Machiavelli's comparison
between the Turkish Empire and France: the former is difficult to conquer but easy to hold, whereas the opposite applies to the latter.[19] This
is to say that the highly centralised and absolutist Turkish Empire can
mobilise a formidable army against a conqueror, but once conquered,
it will obey the conqueror as it has obeyed its former master. By contrast, France can always be conquered through an alliance with some
internal opposition, but the French will be as unwilling to obey their
new master as their old one. Or perhaps more correctly: the new master will have to prove himself more able to satisfy the people than the
old one. This logic does not only apply to the Middle Ages when the
royal power was relatively weak, but also to the period of absolutism.
Even if we do not go as far as Perry Anderson[20] and regard absolutism
as essentially a regime serving the interests of the nobility, the king had
to buy his suppression of the constitutional assemblies with considerable
privileges to the nobles. In this comparison, Scandinavia belongs in the
same category as France. Despite some differences in social structure
and the level of education, the Scandinavian countries developed in the
same direction as the rest of Europe after their entrance into Western
Christendom.

Scandinavia, the Medieval Revolution, and the Uniqueness of Europe

To some extent, Moore's "first European revolution" in the Middle
Ages is intended to explain the later European uniqueness compared to
other civilisations that led to Europe's superiority over the rest of the
world. This uniqueness can be summarised in three points: (1) capitalism
and industrialisation, (2) modern science, and (3) a strong, bureaucratic
state, combined with a high degree of political participation by the
inhabitants. On the other hand, this first revolution led to the foundation

---

[19] Niccolò Machiavelli, *Il principe*, ed. Sergio Bertelli (Milan, 1960) ch. 4.
[20] Perry Anderson, *Lineages of the Absolutist State* (London, 1979).

of "the old regime" which was replaced by a truly modern Europe only from the French revolution onwards. Therefore, an explanation of the emergence of this Europe cannot directly be sought in the Middle Ages; we rather have to look for features that either survived this second revolution or can serve to explain the specific form it took. The medieval revolution did not create a capitalistic society and even less an industrial revolution, nor the modern science, nor Weberian bureaucracy or anything approaching modern democracy. However, the features dealt with in the preceding pages may all in some way or another contribute to the formation of a civilisation with unique features compared to what can be regarded as a "normal" pre-industrial society and may even serve to explain that the second revolution took place in Europe rather than in any other part of the world.

The social and economic revolution described by Moore did lead to more intensive agriculture as well as to urbanisation and growth in trade but hardly set Europe on a unique path compared to the rest of the world. It was rather a question of bringing Europe up to the same level as the great civilisations of the South and East. One feature may nevertheless serve to explain the later development: Europe was not only urbanised, but the cities became organised communities with considerable independence from kings and princes, which enabled them to act politically to defend their commercial interests. Although the majority of these self-governed cities became parts of larger principalities in the post-medieval period, they had by then become sufficiently important to influence the politics of these principalities. The main examples of this are England and the Dutch Republic, the centres of early modern capitalism, the former also the country where the first phase of the industrial revolution took place. Further, European ecology may have contributed to the later development in another way. As Europe was situated wholly in the temperate zone and further north than the other great civilisations, its agriculture was less intensive than in the typical river civilisations. On the other hand, it had a large amount of arable land, ideally suited for food production but less so for spices and various luxury products. As for other resources, there was still quite a lot of forest, even after the great expansion of agriculture. Iron was relatively readily available—although far more expensive than in later ages—but a there was a lack of precious metals like gold and silver. Thus, Europe had the resources for sustaining a large and growing population, and for the production of ships, castles, monumental buildings, armour, and various kinds of arms, but also a need for additional resources which was an incentive for expansion abroad, including the expeditions during the Age of Discovery. Secondly, the extensive but—compared to Asian conditions—relatively thinly populated arable land may also form part of the explanation for the political division. There was no parallel to the fertile and densely populated river areas of the other civilisations, like the Nile area, Mesopotamia, or the lands along Ganges and the great Chinese rivers, which might form the core areas of great empires.

The relationship between medieval culture and the scientific revolution from the sixteenth and above all the seventeenth century onwards may form a parallel to the agricultural expansion. To what extent the output of the first revolution led to a European superiority already in the Middle Ages, is open to discussion.[21] Two basic structures of great future importance were, however, laid down already in the Middle Ages, i.e. independent institutions for the transmission and preservation of learning and a rigorous scholarly method for achieving and evaluating knowledge, most clearly expressed in scholastic philosophy and theology and in canon law. Both factors have been regarded as fundamental for the later scientific revolution, and both are specifically European, not to be found in other civilisations.

As for the third aspect, there is nothing specifically democratic about the society that was the result of the first European revolution, nor does the contemporary bureaucracy have much in common with the rational, impartial civil service corresponding to the Weberian ideal. The most important point in the present context, however, is to what extent it differed from other, contemporary bureaucracies. Moore clearly believes that it did, that it was more ruthless, efficient, and interfering than other bureaucracies, and that it lead to greater centralisation, strengthening the two central powers, the monarchy—including the great princes—and the Church, while marginalising the common people and eventually also the military aristocracy. As we have seen, this may be open to discussion, and we probably need more detailed and exact comparisons between European and other bureaucracies to reach a definite conclusion. However, Moore is probably right on some specific points. One is the importance of the bureaucratisation of religion. It is a normal phenomenon that religion has an important place in the great,

---

[21] Joseph Needham regards China as superior until around 1400 or possibly even 1600, see e.g. *Science and Civilisation in China*, vols I-VII (Cambridge, 1954-), vol. V/2, xxii and *The Grand Titration* (London, 1969), 16, whereas Huff, *The Rise*, 32-40, 119-40 concludes that Europe was superior already in the Middle Ages.

preindustrial civilisations, notably in those based on a "religion of the book", but the strictly organised religion of Western Christendom is unique. Moreover, the degree of organisation increased markedly in our period, as did also the functions of the religious bureaucracy, notably through the development of the inquisition.

The royal bureaucracy, to which it is easier to find non-European parallels, may also have had its specific features. Moore points to the contrast between the Chinese bureaucracy, which largely left the village communities and their lords to themselves, and the European one, notably the English, which interfered in the minutest details.[22] Why this difference? The most likely explanation seems to be the difference in size. European political entities in the Middle Ages as well as later were relatively small and in intense competition with other, similar ones. The Chinese emperor could manage well without interfering too much in village life; the king of England could not. Within Europe, the most efficient polities, England and the kingdom of Sicily, were both relatively small, as were also, in the Early Modern Period, Sweden and Prussia which could only compete by compensating for their small size and poverty by being extremely efficient. By contrast, larger and wealthier polities like France, Austria, Spain, and Russia, could afford a greater amount of inefficiency. However, efficiency in this context does not only mean brutal force and manipulation but the ability to mobilise the support of the wealthy and influential part of the population. Here England is once more the main example. The Magna Carta was a defeat for King John personally, but in the long run a victory for the English monarchy by attaching the nobility, the gentry, and the burghers more firmly to the royal government, which meant that the reduced personal power of the king was more than compensated by the increased power of his government. Admittedly, the Magna Carta is in no direct sense an anticipation of modern democratic principles—Margaret Thatcher was wrong when she tried to reduce the importance of the French declaration of human rights in 1789 by pointing to Magna Carta. The principles of the former are not only different but to some extent directly the opposite of those of Magna Carta, which is essentially a defence of the class or estate privileges that the French revolution wanted to abolish. However, the small size and relative stability of the European polities, as well as the intense competition between them not only made them more burdensome and interfering but also gave them a broader

---

[22] Moore, *Revolution*, 193 f., cf. also. "Transformation".

basis than the empires of other civilisations, which serves to explain that the old regime was eventually replaced by constitutions based on the ideas of the Enlightenment and the French Revolution.

The extent to which the different parts of Europe contributed to the evolution in these fields varies from country to country and between the different aspects. As for demography, there seems to be a difference between west and east, the former being relatively densely populated and with considerable pressure to take up new land, the latter apparently thinly populated throughout the Middle Ages, to the extent that its nobility and rulers encouraged immigration from the west. Scandinavia, with the possible exception of parts of Sweden, notably present-day Finland, clearly belongs to the west in this respect. Scandinavia was also integrated in the European trade network, exporting fish and iron, in addition to luxury commodities like furs, to Western Europe. Most of this export was in the hands of German merchants organised in the Hanseatic League. Only from the end of the Middle Ages and in the Early Modern Period were they replaced by a national bourgeoisie. As for the development of universities and intellectual life, England, France, and Italy were no doubt the leading countries in the first phase, but the Western universities attracted students and scholars from all over Europe. In the second phase, after c. 1350, the gap between East and West was reduced, although there was probably still a difference in the amount of social mobility made possible by university education. The position of the Church most probably corresponds to that of the rest of Europe, with the exception of the inquisition, which had little importance in the Scandinavian countries.

Finally, there is the question of state formation. Here Moore's bureaucratisation probably went less far than in the West, although the local as well as the central administration shows considerable parallels. Despite several crises and conflicts, the King, in fashion similar to that of the English King, managed to integrate the most powerful men in the realm in the government. Medieval England was certainly "a much governed country", more so than the Scandinavian countries. It may nevertheless be valuable to examine the extent to which the alliances between king and aristocracy in the latter may have had similar effects on local government as the rise of a class of professional bureaucrats in countries like England and France. After the Middle Ages, the two remaining independent kingdoms, Denmark and Sweden, developed in different ways, the former resembling France, the latter England. After a long period of division of power between the king and the aristocratic council of the realm, a crisis enabled the king to gain absolute power in 1660, making Denmark-Norway the most absolutist country of Europe, even having a constitution enabling the king to do exactly what he liked, except (1) give up the Lutheran faith and (2) give up his absolute power. By contrast, Sweden, despite a period of more or less absolute rule by the king in the late seventeenth and early eighteenth century, maintained the political institutions developed during the Middle Ages, i.e. the aristocratic council of the realm and the General Estates, representing the nobles, the clergy, the burghers, and the peasants. The latter institution, which probably did not emerge in fully developed form until 1527, but had forerunners in the preceding centuries, continued to exist until it was replaced by a more modern national assembly in 1866. Generally, there seem to be greater differences within Western Christendom in the field of state formation and the development of the modern national and democratic state than in the cultural and intellectual fields. Nevertheless, students of this development should not confine themselves to England, France, and the Netherlands, but should also consider the Scandinavian countries. Denmark, Sweden, and Norway fairly easily and harmoniously made the transition from either absolutism or the medieval estates to modern parliamentary democracy. The medieval background to this transition and its relationship to the first medieval revolution still remain to be considered.

THE MAKING OF A EUROPEAN SOCIETY. THE EXAMPLE OF SWEDEN

THOMAS LINDKVIST

ABSTRACT

In this article the transformations in Sweden during the period 1000-1300 are discussed as forms of Europeanization. The transformation was carried out and promoted by indigenous elites and entailed the establishment of a Christian monarchy. Christianization meant gradual assimilation to the wider cultural context The clergy and the ecclesiastical organizations introduced new economic and cultural institutions as well as new concepts. All this took place in tandem with a transition from an economy based partly on plunder and external appropriation to a feudal economy. The changes to social and economic structures, such as the establishment of a manorial economy and the disappearance of slavery, were Swedish variants of a general European change. The particular role of the Cistercians in Sweden is noted. Due to the later development of Church and Christian monarchy , in comparison with the other two Scandinavian monarchies., administrative and cultural literacy was mainly introduced by this order.

The making of a European society in Sweden is certainly, as elsewhere, a matter of definition. The label "Europeanization" has been attributed to several historical phenomena and transformations. During the period 1000-1300 CE Sweden emerged as a political unit, with economic, social and cultural structures similar to those of Western Europe. The formation of a Christian kingdom, and the introduction of other European-style institutions, however, occurred later in Sweden than in Denmark and Norway. Europe itself emerged and was defined during this period, with the *first European revolution*, as defined and delineated by R. I. Moore, occurring during the first centuries of the second millennium. The period has also been characterised, from a slightly different perspective, by Robert Bartlett as *the making of Europe*. The Western form of Christendom became the common denominator, with more or less homogeneous classes of knighthood and clergy emerging throughout this nascent European community. The development of the aristocracy and the Christian monarchies played an integrative role in this culture, alongside the Church, the clergy and especially the monastic orders. The formation of this European elite, which was relatively homogeneous across the community, was part of a new political and intellectual culture, which was itself increasingly homogenized. The geographical boundaries of this new world were also being defined; as *one* European unity was formulated, it excluded the Eastern Church, Russia, the remains of the Byzantine Empire and other kingdoms. The relatively late integration of Sweden and the Baltic Sea area in this new culturally defined Europe entailed a redefinition of the frontiers.[1]

These historical transformations were social and economic, as well as cultural and political. These processes are often referred to as "Christianization", the unification of a kingdom, or the "making of" a Sweden, Norway or Denmark. The change in religion and the emergence of a Christian, if fragile, monarchy has been generally understood as a crucial turning point in history. Especially as concerns the later Scandinavian kingdoms, this turn has been commonly identified as the origin of the modern nation state.[2] But it must also be recognized that this transformation cannot be adequately understood through a perspective that reduces it to a nodal point in the later development of the nation state. It must be understood as part of a more general restructuring process with many regional and local variations.

The transformation has, from another perspective, been described as a "feudal revolution". Georges Duby formulated this idea to explain the changes that occurred around the year 1000 in Western Europe, or more particularly, in Northern France. This transition has also been discussed by Guy Bois, who focused especially on transformations in the relations of production. Social and economic relationships were totally restructured, and new forms of lordship arose. The new "feudal" and "European" lords formed a new social elite whose positions were based upon their systematic appropriation of agrarian production. The age of plunder and predation was gradually replaced by a system in which lordship was based upon control over people and, eventually, land. Slavery was replaced by a manorial and feudal system, based on a dependent peasantry. Countless variants of the manorial and seigniorial

---

[1] Robert Bartlett, *The Making of Europe: Conquest, Colonization and Cultural Change 950-1350*, London: Allan Lane 1993; R. I. Moore, *The First European Revolution c. 970-1215*, Oxford: Blackwell 2000. Concerning the frontier perspective, see also Eric Christiansen, *The Northern Crusades: The Baltic and the Catholic Frontier 1100-1525*, London: Macmillan 1980.

[2] Cf. Patrick J. Geary, *The Myth of Nations: The Medieval Origins of Europe*, Princeton University Press 2002.

system emerged in Europe during this period. And yet it is necessary to stress the frequently made observation that the "classical" manor was far from dominant and all-pervasive. The small-scale agrarian production that came to typify medieval Europe emerged and the peasantry was increasingly subject to exploitation. As social power moved from the warrior lords to the landlords, the structures of inheritance and marriage were also substantially transformed, at least for the aristocracy.[3]

Economic and Cultural Transitions

A new economic system began to be formed, with substantial variants, in central parts of what is today Sweden in the twelfth and thirteenth centuries. The socio-economic structures of the pre-medieval (or late Iron Age) Sweden had been far from egalitarian, as has been emphasized by recent research. The large farms of the social elite of the Viking Age had been sustained with slave labour. Slave owning remained legal in Sweden until the early fourteenth century, but by then had become insignificant and gradually faded away.[4] But the new economic system soon instituted new forms of appropriation and exploitation.

The Viking Age of Scandinavia, ca. 750-1000 CE, has often been identified as a sort of prototype of this type of systematic appropriation, But it might be more accurately understood as an economy of external appropriation. The material position of the elite depended to a great extent on their capacity to control the means of appropriating wealth from outside their own society. While those means clearly included plunder and pillage, it also included the regular demand of tribute. But controlling the means of external appropriation also required controlling the exchange of precious products and the emporia where such exchanges were conducted. These emporia (ports of trade) were situated all over Northern Europe: Birka on Björkö in Lake Mälaren, Hedeby in Southern Jutland and Kaupang/Skiringsal in Vestfold in Norway are perhaps the

---

[3] Georges Duby, *Les trois ordres ou l'imaginaire du féodalisme*, Paris: Gallimard 1978 pp. 183-205; See also Guy Bois, *La mutation de l'an Mil: Lournand, village mâconnais de l'antiquité au féodalisme*, Paris: Fayard 1989. Concerning the politics and economics of plunder, see also Timothy Reuter, 'Plunder and Tribute in the Carolingian Empire', *Transactions of the Royal Historical Society*, vol. 35, 1985.

[4] Clara Nevéus, *Trälarna i Landskapslagarnas Samhälle: Danmark och Sverige*, (Studia Historica Upsaliensia, 58) Uppsala 1974 pp. 139-165; Tore Iversen, *Trelldomen. Norsk Slaveri i Middelalderen*, Bergen: Historisk Institutt, Universitetet i Bergen 1997; Thomas Lindkvist & Janken Myrdal (eds), *Trälar. Ofria i Agrarsamhället från Vikingatid till Medeltid*, (Skrifter om Skogs- och Lantbrukshistoria, 17) Stockholm: Nordiska Museet 2003.

best known and researched in Scandinavia. They constituted the northernmost reaches of an exchange network that stretched from the Black and Caspian Seas via the Russian waterways and the Baltic Sea region to the North Sea and the kingdoms of Western Europe. Controlling the exchange and distribution of certain products over these trade-routes was vital for various local elites to maintain their social positions and status.[5] But at the same time, the economy of plunder remained important throughout the (late) pre-medieval period in some parts of Sweden—the Lake Mälaren region, for example—to maintain and reproduce social positions of domination.[6]

The Danish were later somewhat more successful at running an economy of plunder. Expeditions of pillage, colonization, tribute taking and finally conquest travelled west towards the wealthy societies of the Frankish empires and the British Isles, with profound organizational implications for the Danish homeland. Organizing such expeditions demanded greater internal control, and centralizing power, and thus laid the foundations for an emergent kingdom. Thus, what began as raids under more or less local chieftains in the eighth century had, by the early eleventh century, become great expeditions organized by kings with more or less absolute control over Denmark and much of England. With its many islands and waterways, Denmark was easier to control than the region that would become Sweden.

The feudal revolution, then, was a gradual transition from a society based on an economy of plunder, in which slavery played a functionally important role, to one in which the subjugation of a dependent peasantry sustained the hierarchy of the social elites.[7] This new estate system, a modified version of the continental feudal system, was in part introduced by monastic and other ecclesiastical institutions, and it entailed new concepts of ownership. Thus through the late thirteenth and early

---

[5] Sture Bolin, 'Mohammed, Charlemagne and Ruric', *Scandinavian Economic History Review*, vol. 1, 1953, pp. 5-39; Richard Hodges & David Whitehouse, *Mohammed, Charlemagne and the Origins of Europe: Archaeology and the Pirenne Thesis*, London: Duckworth 1983.

[6] Erik Lönnroth, *Scandinavians*, Göteborg 1977 pp. 7-16; Peter Sawyer, *Kings and Vikings. Scandinavia and Europe AD 700-1100*, London: Methuen 1982 pp. 113-143; Thomas Lindkvist, *Plundring, Skatter och den Feodala Statens Framväxt: Organisatoriska Tendenser i Sverige under Övergången från Vikingatid till Tidig Medeltid*, (Opuscula Historica Upsaliensia, 1) Uppsala 1990 pp. 38-55.

[7] See e.g. Thomas Lindkvist, *Landborna i Norden under Äldre Medeltid*, (Studia Historica Upsaliensia, 110) Uppsala 1979 pp. 128-149; Sigurd Rahmqvist, *Sätesgård och Gods. De medeltida Frälsegodsens Framväxt mot Bakgrund av Upplands Bebyggelsehistoria*, (Upplands Fornminnesförenings Tidskrift, 53) Stockholm 1996 pp. 296-302.

fourteenth centuries we find the introduction of extensive and detailed regulations concerning agrarian production in the provincial law codes in Sweden. The village or hamlet, consisting of several farmsteads, became the normal unit of production in the plains of Sweden. It was also evident that the division of land within the village between aristocratic and ecclesiastical landowners as well as a land-owning peasantry was widespread. The origins of the hamlets and villages were partly the redistribution of land owned controlled by the chiefs of the Viking Age, partly privatisation of commonly owned land. The regulations of the provincial law codes mainly served the interests of the aristocratic and institutional landowners. The development of the village or hamlet system was marked by regional and local variation, but its origins are generally traced to the High Middle Ages, after 1000 CE, when the large Viking Age farms were broken up. A more feudal mode of production emerged. New concepts and instruments for controlling agrarian production were introduced, in no small part through the mediations of the ecclesiastical institutions.

Forested districts were substantially colonized during this period, sometimes on the initiative of peasant communities. Swedish peasants also colonized coastal areas of Finland, generally without any sort of centralized planning.[8] In other areas a monastery, such as the Cistercians at Nydala in Småland, promoted the extensive reclamation of land.[9] Other Cistercian houses initiated less colonization and the major part of its lands were cultivated by peasants in old cultivated areas. The Cistercians of Sweden were in general less colonizers of new land than introducers of a manorial system.

The greatest cultural change of this period was, of course, the transition from paganism to Christianity,[10] which was more or less concluded by the beginning of the twelfth century. An ecclesiastical organization was in the making, as churches were built, parishes formed, tithes paid, and

---

[8] See the discussion in Anne-Marie Ivars & Lena Huldén (eds), *När Kom Svenskarna till Finland?*, (Skrifter Utgivna av Svenska Litteratursällskapet i Finland, 646) Helsingfors 2002.

[9] Clas Tollin, *Rågångar, Gränshallar och Ägoområden: Rekonstruktion av Fastighetsstruktur och Bebyggelseutveckling i Mellersta Småland under Äldre Medeltid*, (Meddelanden från Kulturgeografiska Institutionen vid Stockholms Universitet, 101) Stockholm 1999, pp. 185-207.

[10] Concerning the Christianization of Sweden, see esp. Sven Ulric Palme, *Kristendomens Genombrott i Sverige*, Stockholm: Bonniers 1959; Carl F. Hallencreutz, *När Sverige blev Europeiskt: Till Frågan om Sveriges Kristnande*, Stockholm: Natur och Kultur 1993; Jan Arvid Hellström, *Vägar till Sveriges Kristnande*, Stockholm: Atlantis 1996; Bertil Nilsson (ed.), *Kristnandet i Sverige: Gamla Källor och nya Perspektiv*, (Projektet Sveriges kristnande. Publikationer, 5) Uppsala: Lunne 1996.

a clerical hierarchy began to take shape. This conversion was from a dynamic and variable system of thoughts and rituals to a relatively dogmatic confessional religion, with an elaborate organization and a specialised clergy who maintained monopoly control over ritual performances. The two systems of faith and cult were radically different in many respects. "Paganism" was non-doctrinal and relatively more flexible. "Paganism" is relatively inclusive, and Christianity more exclusive. There was no Scandinavian (Norse) word for religion *per se*. Cultural traditions and customs, especially the customary performance of rites, was the essence of pre-Christian "religious" practices. The cult itself was of central importance, and paganism was deeply embedded in broader political and social structures. There is also evidence to suggest that great transformations took place within paganism during pre-historic times, esp. during the Iron Age. From a cult of the lakes and moors it gradually became a cult of the halls of an emerging group of chieftains. That is, the cult changed to reflect the local society's increasing stratification and hierarchization. In the process, the mythology became more martial, and the leadership of the cult was increasingly associated with the political elite.[11]

In the Christianization of the Nordic world we must differentiate between a rapid shift in political ideology and a more gradual transformation of the cultural belief system. Both dimensions involved an internal transformation of beliefs and ideology. But the conversion from above was part of the political history, a result of deliberate political decisions aimed at centralizing control over men and, later, territories. The conversion of beliefs and values, "below" so to speak; was a much more complex and prolonged process.

Christianization occurred later in Sweden than in the other Scandinavian kingdoms. In the Norse and Danish literature the Swedes are described as pagans, or as hesitant and reluctant to accept the new creed. There is some evidence of "pagan reactions", for example, in the beginning of the twelfth century. Some of the local saints, according to legend, were martyred during uprisings in the Lake Mälaren area. But it is important to recognize that the term "paganism" soon lost its cultic

---

[11] Charlotte Fabech, 'Samfundsorganisation, Religiøse Ceremonier og Regional Variation', in Charlotte Fabech & Jytte Ringtved (eds), *Samfundsvariation og Regional Variation: Norden i Romersk Jernalder*, Højbjerg: Jysk arkæologisk selskab 1991; Lotte Hedeager, *Skygger af en Anden Virkelighed: Oldnordiske Myter*, København. Samleren 1998.

specificity to become a more general term for othering one's political and religious enemies and adversaries.[12]

The kings and other lords who strove to increase their control over society were among the earliest converts to the new religion. Pre-Christian paganism, as far as can be deduced from the sparse records, was readily adaptable to a variety of existing social organizations, and provided no basis from which to challenge or transform the existing social order. In contrast, Christianity, with its elaborately hierarchical cosmology and clergy provided both an ideological justification and a concrete model for establishing and legitimizing a new social hierarchy.

Building churches and creating parishes was one way to demonstrate and reinforce local or regional power. The many Romanesque stone churches in southern Scandinavia—in Sweden, most notably in Väster-götland and Östergötland—were originally initiated as private enter-prises by the local aristocracy. These projects may well have been seen as a new way to extract payments from the surrounding peasantry, as tithes were initially a means of appropriating the agrarian product, and of augmenting social control and prestige.[13] But church building was also a potent means for political aspirants to demonstrate their fealty to the Church, which in turn legitimized their political status as lords, etc.[14]

The ecclesiastical organization in Sweden was initially established in the Götaland provinces. The first permanent bishoprics were Skara and Linköping, with the former established in the first half of the eleventh century and the latter at the beginning of the twelfth century.[15] While

---

[12] Peter Foote, 'Icelandic Historians and the Swedish Image: Comments on Snorri and his Precursors', in Göran Dahlbäck (ed.), *Snorre Sturlasson och de Isländska Källorna till Sveriges Historia*, (Runica et Mediævalia, 1) Stockholm 1993, pp. 9-42.

[13] Stefan Brink, 'Sockenbildningen i Sverige', in Olle Ferm (ed.), *Kyrka och Socken i Medeltidens Sverige*, (Studier till Det medeltida Sverige, 5) Stockholm: Riksantikvarieämbetet 1991, pp. 113-142.

[14] Husaby in Västergötland and Örberga in Östergötland are two churches with mas-sive West towers with galleries for ceremonial purposes. The prototypes are Westphalian and they have been interpreted as royal churches. They are dated to the beginning of the twelfth century. They are, nevertheless, from a politically chaotic period, when king-ship was disputed and contested. But the fragile power could be demonstrated and uphold in this way, through an ecclesiastical legitimization. Palme, op. cit. 1959 pp. 115-119.

[15] Herman Schück, *Ecclesia Lincopensis. Studier om Linköpingskyrkan under Medeltiden och Gustav Vasa*, (Stockholm Studies in History, 4) Stockholm 1959, pp. 43-59; Jan Arvid Hellström, *Biskop och Landskapssamhälle i Tidig Svensk Medeltid*, (Rättshistoriskt bibliotek, 16) Stockholm 1971, pp. 44-53.

Uppland is often referred to as a centre of persistent paganism, there is good evidence to suggest, however, that Christianity was already well established there in the eleventh century, but without any connection to a centralized ecclesiastical organization such as those that were established under the patronage of the kings in the Götaland provinces. In other words, there were different ways of organizing a new church in the nascent Sweden, reflecting diverse regional social and political structures.

The Lake Mälaren region followed a rather conservative path to Christianity, where there was hostility towards, or reluctance to accept the new social structures associated with the European or feudal society. One reason can perhaps be found in the external appropriation economy, in which a fairly dynamic and powerful group of chieftains were occasionally able to conduct large scale expeditions. It was not uncommon for the magnates and chiefs in the district to refuse to recognize the man who claimed to be the king of the *Svear*, who usually resided in the Götaland provinces. Uppland, and especially Uppsala, was an ancient centre of political power, which the Norse *Ynglingasaga* attributes to a partly mythical kingship. According to the Icelandic *Hervararsaga*, there was a pagan uprising there in the 1080s, in which the Christian king Inge I (d. ca. 1100), usually associated with the province of Östergötland, was deposed after he refused to perform the established pagan cult at Uppsala. According to the saga, the pagan usurper Sven ruled the area for the next three years. Adam Bremensis contrasted the pagan Uppsala with the Christian Sigtuna in his chronicle from the 1080s. The city of Sigtuna was a planned city of the late tenth century, founded as a centre for the kings and a Christian stronghold. There may be some exaggeration in representing Uppsala as a pagan centre in the late eleventh century, but it clearly remained a centre of opposition and resistance to the ideals advanced by the bishoprics of Linköping, Lund, Bremen and Rome.[16]

State Formation and Dynastic Conflict

The changes in the social and political structures of Sweden during the early middle ages are often described in terms that anticipate the cre-

---

[16] See the contributions in Anders Hultgård (ed.), *Uppsala och Adam av Bremen*, Nora: Nya Doxa 1997; Olof Sundqvist, *Freyr's Offspring. Rulers and Religion in Ancient Svea Society*, (Acta Universitatis Upsaliensis. Historia Religionum, 21) Uppsala 2002.

ation of a kingdom or a realm. From this perspective, the "making of Sweden" typically means that the two main parts, *Götar* and the *Svear*, were united under the rule of a single recognized king. Previously kingship had been contested, or a king was recognized only in one or the other of the two regions, and thus, exercising uniform control over the vast territories of the Sweden to come was impossible. It was rare for the king to be recognized simultaneously in the two main provinces, and sometimes there were co-regents. Thus the lists of "historical" kings found in various sources are typically the products of later compilations whose aims were to represent Sweden as a naturally unified kingdom.

It was not until the archbishopric of Uppsala was founded in 1164, inaugurating a Swedish ecclesiastical province, that the King, Karl Sverkersson, was addressed for the first time as *rex Sweorum et Gothorum*, "king of the *Svear* and *Götar*". In other words, the kingdom of Sweden only came into being when a Swedish ecclesiastical province was established within the greater community of Christendom. The identification of the kingdom as a territory was thus a construction of the Church.[17] Sweden was established as an ecclesiastical province more than a decade later than Norway by the cardinal Nicholas Breakespeare, who considered the political situation in Sweden to be far too delicate and uncertain for an archbishopric.

Europeanization implied a new political culture, in which new forms of lordship emerged, legitimized by the church. But the making of a kingdom and the creation of a state are two quite distinct processes. The making of a kingdom can be understood as the founding of a more or less permanent territorial lordship. That process was accomplished in Sweden—more or less—by the end of the twelfth century. The creation of a state, i.e. the formation of permanent and settled political institutions with recognized functions, is a much more complicated and prolonged process. In Sweden at least, state-building also entailed the introduction of the rigidly hierarchical social system typical of Western Christendom.

The fragile Christian kingdom that established itself in Sweden in the eleventh century was frequently contested. Mighty local lords sometimes proclaimed themselves as kings and were sometimes elected. They were occasionally recognized by other magnates or the bishop. Sometimes legitimacy was sought through intermarriage with other powerful families.

---

[17] Peter Sawyer, *The Making of Sweden*, (Occasional Papers on Medieval Topics, 3) Alingsås: Viktoria 1988.

The second half of the twelfth and the beginning of the thirteenth centuries are characterised by the rivalry between two dynasties, referred to in modern terms as the Sverkerians and the Erikians, after their progenitors: Sverker I (ca. 1130-1156) and Saint Erik or Erik Jedvardsson (?—ca. 1160). The Sverkerians in the province of Östergötland had good relations with the bishops of Linköping. The diocese of Linköping played an important role in promoting the Christian kingdom and the formation of a new political order. Saint Erik is associated, by martyrdom and cult, to Uppsala and Uppland, but his ancestral estates were in Västergötland. The rivalry between the two dynasties has been credited to their different allegiances: Sverker and his faction subscribed to the Gregorian ideal of the Papal Church, while Erik advocated a more national and conservative church ideal. This sharp dichotomy was outlined by Knut B. Westman. Thus their strategies for creating a more European society and for implementing the hierarchic political and social structures of a new, feudal or European monarchy differed in important ways.

The political and ideological importance of royal saints for the establishment of the Christian monarchies has often been noted. This role has been studied in-depth, including most recently by Gábor Klaniczay. Royal saints serve to legitimize emergent Christian monarchies, and sometimes certain dynasties. There were great differences between the Scandinavian kingdoms in this regard. Norway's Saint Olaf was by far the most successful; the cult of his martyrdom spread rapidly and widely, and different traditions emerged, recorded in both Latin and the vernacular. He became the patron of the dynasty, the monarchy, and eventually the entire Norwegian ecclesiastical province. He also came to signify the just king. As the iconic symbol of the good king, the popular cult of Saint Olaf spread across Northern Europe, including parts of Sweden. King Cnut of Denmark, martyred in the church of St Albans in Odense in 1086 during an uprising of the aristocracy, likewise became the patron saint of his dynasty and his cult was widely promoted by the Church.

Erik of Sweden was a later saint, martyred by assassination around 1160 at Uppsala during a dynastic conflict. Saint Erik was initially viewed with suspicion by the Papal Church. When Pope Alexander III complained that less worthy persons were venerated as saints in Sweden, he was probably referring to Saint Erik. Erik was totally ignored by the otherwise well informed Saxo Grammaticus in *Gesta Danorum*. But there were other obstacles to Erik's recognition as a royal saint, too. His cult was long confined to the province of Uppland and thus his importance remained limited to the dynastic and provincial levels. It was only much later that he was elevated to the role of national saint and patron. He became a "national" patron during a revolt against the union king Erik of Pomerania in the 1430s. But Saint Erik could not, due to the dynastic conflicts of his lifetime, become a unifying symbol for the kingdom or symbolize the good and Christian king. He did not play the important ideological and political role of his celebrated Norwegian counterpart, Saint Olaf.[18]

The making of the kingdom of Sweden and the later emergence of a state society came about through a very complicated melding of different forms of political leadership and structures. Monetary systems, the extent of a monetarized economy, taxation, systems of measurement and land valuation all differed from region to region. Older traditions and organizations had to be more or less transformed before they could be incorporated into the new, "European" framework.

A firm and more concrete political structure was established during the regency of the earl (*jarl*) Birger Magnusson (d. 1266), who united the two dynasties by marriage. The dynastic principle of the kingdom was thus settled; although internal conflicts continued between vying brothers. Rival factions of magnates, the so-called *folkungs*, who enjoyed substantial support in Uppland, were crushed after a series of rebellions and revolts.[19] From the mid thirteenth century the king's representatives had a firm grip on the Lake Mälaren area, and the locus of political power was finally settled. During the second half of the thirteenth century the transformation of political institutions was intense, especially during the reign of *jarl* Birger's son Magnus Ladulås (1275-1290). The privileges of the aristocracy and the secular clergy were confirmed around 1280, based upon European models, thus consolidating a feudal society of prayers, warriors and labourers. The European and feudal order of society definitively replaced the old social values. During Magnus' reign the administrative apparatus became more or less settled, as new written law codes affirmed and legitimized the new social and economic relations.

In June 1319 the infant Magnus Eriksson, was, after a dynastic conflict, elected king of Sweden at Mora outside Uppsala. The election charter issued on that occasion has been widely recognized as the first constitutional document in Swedish history. It recognized and definitively

[18] Gábor Klaniczay, *Holy Rulers and Blessed Princesses: Dynastic Cults in Medieval Europe*, Cambridge University Press 2002; Bengt Thordeman (ed.) *Erik den Helige: Historia, Kult, Rreliker*, Stockholm: Nordisk Rotogravyr 1954.

[19] Erik Lönnroth, *Från Svensk Medeltid*, Stockholm: Bonniers 1959 pp. 13-29.

settled the unity of the kingdom; the various political institutions were also defined and their jurisdictions more or less established. The kingdom was defined not by the person of the king alone, but also a powerful council with formal rights and duties. In some respects the charter of 1319 can be regarded, at least symbolically, as the definitive end of the process through which Sweden became a state. From this point forward, political elections were conducted in accordance with the dictates of the charter. Any suggestion that the charter merely enshrined ancient custom, however, appears to be an invention of tradition. The election charter was an aristocratic document, created by leading members of the aristocracy, including the bishops, on behalf of the kingdom. But they also acted, perhaps foremost, as representatives of the different provinces. That is, although Sweden was now irrevocably united as a single kingdom, with the aristocracy and bishops acting on its behalf, the kingdom still consisted of different provinces with, for example, their own legal traditions.

The Regional Context

These political transformations fundamentally changed the nature of the relationships around the Baltic Sea area. For a long period leading up to this political transformation, contacts were characterized by efforts to control the exchange of precious products, to carry out pillaging and plundering expeditions, and to levy tributes. Records of the *Svear* demanding tribute in Curland for example, can be found as early as the ninth century.

There is evidence that warlike contacts continued across the Baltic during the following centuries. In many respects the seaborne martial enterprises until the thirteenth century seem to be essentially a continuation of the Viking expeditions of plundering and demanding tribute. As late as 1197, according to the Chronicle of Henry of Livonia, a Swedish duke—probably the *jarl* Birger brosa—was more interested in demanding tribute in Vironia than in Christianizing the pagan inhabitants. An expedition of 1142, according to the Chronicle of Novgorod, aimed to plunder merchants, led by a Swedish "prince" and a bishop. There are few indications of wars begun for territorial conquests during this period.

The nascent kingdom of Sweden nevertheless expanded its territory during the early Middle Ages. Peripheral areas were integrated with the political centre. The control exercised by the church and king increased. For example, Finland became part of the ecclesiastical province of Uppsala, with Åbo (Turku) as bishopric, well before Finland became part of the Swedish political kingdom. The details of Saint Erik's legendary crusade to Finland in the 1150s are unclear, but it was probably a plundering expedition.[20]

The efforts to acquire additional territories by force did not begin until the reign of King Johan Sverkersson (1216-1222) and his followers, Bishop Karl of Linköping and the *jarl* Karl the deaf, in 1219. For a short while they maintained a Swedish stronghold at Leal in Western Estonia.

When *jarl* Birger Magnusson led a war expedition in the late 1230s against the Häme (the Tavastians) and, consequently, the Novgorodians, the aim was to establish control over the Neva estuary. The campaign was unsuccessful. The wars at the end of the thirteenth and beginning of the fourteenth centuries, carried out in the name of the crusades, were clearly aimed at achieving territorial control. With the construction of a fortress at Viborg in 1295, the kingdom of Sweden acquired a firm stronghold in the Eastern part of the Finnish Gulf. It also controlled the Neva estuary for some period, and maintained a stronghold at Keksholm, on the shore of Lake Ladoga, but only fleetingly.

Military enterprises before the end of the thirteenth century were most likely conducted by aristocrats, kings, bishops, and their seaborne retinues. There is no reason to believe that the maritime naval organization known as the *ledung* existed yet in Sweden during this period. Niels Lund has recently observed that the *ledung*, the naval war organization, was introduced in Denmark rather late compared to Norway. The *ledung* is described in laws dating from the mid thirteenth century, but originated as an organization to defend against the pillaging activities of the Wends ca. 1170.[21]

The Swedish *ledung* has similar origins. One plausible date for its foundation is in the late twelfth century, when eastern Sweden was attacked by pirates from across the Baltic Sea. This perhaps coincides with the sacking of Sigtuna recorded in 1187. Defensive constructions along the eastern shore of the Baltic Sea have been dated to that period.

---

[20] Per Olof Sjöstrand, 'Den Svenska Tidigmedeltida Statsbildningsprocessen och den Östra Rikshalvan', *Historisk Tidskrift för Finland*, vol. 79, 1994, pp. 530-573.

[21] Niels Lund, *Lið, Leding og Landeværn*, Roskilde: Vikingeskibshallen 1996 pp. 245-284.

Sometime in the late thirteenth century, the *ledung* was formally instituted via the tax codes. That is, according to the provincial laws, the *ledung* was established as an organization to which the peasantry was obliged to contribute men, ships and victuals to the king's fleet. In this sense, it was perhaps more of a fiscal construction than a military institution.[22]

As mentioned, the raids and wars in the early Middle Ages were mainly conducted as "private" enterprises. In this respect, the nature of Swedish military activities changed significantly in the late thirteenth century. The so-called third crusade of 1295 and the later wars and skirmishes in Carelia, according to the Chronicle of Erik, indicate substantial maritime expeditions. The Chronicle of Erik describes it as the greatest fleet ever seen in that area. The finances for these wars were probably raised through something similar to the *ledung*. These were perhaps the first wars to be carried out in the name of the Swedish crown, i.e. by a Swedish state.

The transition to a feudal economy also meant that trade became increasingly important. The economic and social system that accompanied it—largely modelled on the ecclesiastical organizations—led to increased appropriation of domestic agrarian production, as products circulated in greater quantities. The expansion of internal trade was a consequence of the social appropriation of wealth through taxes, feudal rents and other duties levied by the diverse ecclesiastical institutions and the kingdom. The emergence of towns in the medieval sense, i.e. towns that served an economic function for the inhabitants of the immediate hinterland, especially in eastern Sweden from the second half of the thirteenth century, is indicative of this economic revolution.[23] The increased circulation of agrarian products and the monetary economy promoted the expansion of specialised handicraft production. The urban culture was, like the market oriented monetary economy, vital to the making of a European society.

The Europeanised Swedish society became integrated in the international trade system of the Baltic, dominated by the expanding German *Hansa*, which consequently changed the relations with the rest of the Baltic area. The third crusade and the following skirmishes with Novgorod, more or less settled at Orekhov (Nöteborg) in 1323, were triggered by

---

[22] Lindkvist 1990 pp. 56-64.
[23] Hans Andersson, 'Städer i öst och väst—Regional Stadsutveckling under Medeltiden', *Bebyggelsehistorisk Tidskrift*, vol. 3, 1982, pp. 55-67.

the aspirations of the Swedish kingdom to control increasingly important trade routes.

Until the second half of the thirteenth century, the Christian monarchy was primarily associated with the provinces of Västergötland and Östergötland. Especially during the last quarter of the thirteenth century, though, the political centre shifted to the area around Lake Mälaren. During this period, the production of iron and copper ore in the Bergslagen hinterland expanded and became fundamental to the economy. The exports contributed to making the Lake Mälaren region the most economically dynamic area in Sweden, as well as the most intensely urbanized.

The transformation and the adaptation of European institutions and ideas was favoured by an endogenous elite of aristocrats and kings. One important force of this cultural import was the Cistercian Order. Their introduction to Swedish society, which made it much more European in many respects, occurred under the auspices, patronage, and close collaboration of the Sverkerian dynasty and the bishopric of Linköping. The two first monasteries, Alvastra in Östergötland and Nydala in Småland, were founded, respectively, by King Sverker and his queen, and Bishop Gisle of Linköping in 1143.

The Erikian dynasty initially had a quite complicated relationship with the Cistercians. Erik's queen had been involved in a conflict with the Cistercian monastery at Varnhem. Later, however, the Erikian dynasty acted on the Cistercian behalf, and received their support in return. The difficulties in elevating Erik to the status of national patron saint might nevertheless be explained, at least in part, by the Cistercian resistance.

The importance of the Cistercians is not limited to their devotional or cultural activities. There is reason to believe that they may have introduced the manorial/feudal estate system; at the very least, it is clear that they favoured this mode of production.

The connection between the Cistercians and the crusading ideology has also been noted. The Cistercians were not a military order, far from it in fact. The leading Cistercian Bernhard of Clairvaux, however, was very active in propagating a crusading ideology and the second crusade was proclaimed by Pope Eugene III, a Cistercian, in 1147. Bernhard promoted the idea that a crusade could be conducted against any enemy of Christendom, not only those in the Levant. The connection between the Wendish crusades of the Danish bishops and kings and the crusading ideology is obvious. Founding Cistercian monasteries, such as those at Dargun (later moved to Eldena) and Kolbatz, was one of the means used to establish a political presence in new frontier regions.[24]

This is not to suggest that such wars can be adequately explained on exclusively ideological grounds. But the Cistercian crusading ideology offered further legitimation for warfare and plundering. The activities of Swedish kings, *jarls*, bishops and other powerful men are far too obscure to say anything conclusive about their intentions or motivations. It is, however, striking that in 1142, the year before the Cistercians arrived and settled in Sweden, an unsuccessful expedition was launched under the leadership of a Swedish prince or king with a bishop in the retinue (according to a Russian chronicle). Sweden was then a far too primitive kingdom to be able to carry out large scale expeditions and to establish monasteries in foreign areas. The Cistercians provided administrative skills and a legitimizing ideology to the kingdom and the emerging state.

In the late eleventh century, all of Scandinavia was incorporated into the archbishopric of Hamburg and Bremen. The first wholly Scandinavian archbishopric was established in Danish Lund in 1103. It was later divided when the Norwegian ecclesiastical province was founded in 1153 with Nidaros (Trondheim) as the See, and again in 1164, when the Swedish ecclesiastical province was established at Uppsala. The first archbishop of Sweden was Stephen, one of the founders of the Cistercian monastery at Alvastra. An early chapter of the new archbishopric was probably of the Cistercian order, which was a rather unique arrangement. The Cistercian influence on the early archbishopric appears to be echoed in the liturgical tradition. The Cistercians introduced a Latin administrative literacy, and an incipient royal chancery dates from the latter half of the twelfth century. The Latin culture of literacy arrived in Sweden later than in Denmark, for example, and Sweden became more integrated into European culture when the Reformed Church was established in the sixteenth century. Medieval Sweden had no significant culture of writing history, and thus there was no construction of the "nation's" past to parallel the Latin Saxo Grammaticus in Denmark or the vernacular historiographical tradition of Norway. The meagre and rudimentary historical writing that did exist was confined to a regional perspective, such as the *Gutasaga* of Götaland.

Contrary to what happened across the Baltic Sea, Sweden was not Europeanized by conquest and by external force and violence. This

---

[24] Christensen 1980 pp. 48-69.

transformation entailed the introduction of new and more effective modes of appropriation. This delivered increased and more systematic control over the people and material resources, and resulted in a particular variant of the political and social culture of Western Christendom.

BYZANTIUM TRANSFORMED, c. 950-1200

PAUL STEPHENSON

ABSTRACT

Two phenomena were paramount in the transformation, and ultimate collapse, of the Byzantine imperial system in the period c. 950-1204: sustained economic and demographic growth, which the state failed fully to direct or exploit; and the emergence of a powerful, self-conscious aristocracy, willing to exploit resources to the detriment of the state. During the tenth and eleventh centuries imperial policies were devised which aimed to bolster existing political and fiscal structures, prop up the state economy, and delimit the power of aristocrats. These measures failed. Twelfth-century efforts took another tack, seeking to harness the interests and wealth of the aristocracy, anchored in the land, to those of the state. These provided no lasting solution, but instead led to greater political fragmentation, internecine conflict, social unrest, and ultimately to the collapse of the state system in the last years of the twelfth century.

The Byzantine Empire, like its European and Mediterranean neighbours, experienced sustained demographic and economic growth through the later tenth, eleventh and twelfth centuries. But while the civilizations which lay directly to the west and east succeeded in developing new institutions to control and exploit growth, those developed by the Byzantines failed. Moreover, expansionary neighbours to the west and east were able to exploit Byzantine weaknesses. Two obvious episodes may be cited in the first instance: the Seljuk victory at the battle of Manzikert in 1071, and consequent Turkish and Turkoman settlement of Anatolia; and the sack of Constantinople by the forces of the Fourth Crusade in 1204, which saw the end of Byzantium as an imperial power. Both episodes were symptoms rather than causes of Byzantine political decline or transformation.[1]

---

[1] The dominant interpretation during the twentieth century was that of G. Ostrogorsky, *History of the Byzantine State*, 2nd English edn, tr. J. Hussey (Oxford, 1968). Significant portions of this brief paper do not follow Ostrogorsky. Nevertheless, much may appear to echo the following: "From Romanus I to Basil II the central authority had tried to erect a barrier against the great magnates' urge to acquire land, and this had now broken down. The free small-holdings rapidly disappeared without a protest, and the wealthy landlords absorbed the property of peasant and soldier, turning the former owners into

An inability to harness economic expansion in the interests of the state was the root of Byzantium's decline as a centralised political power, and the trajectory of that decline is most readily traced in two areas: the loss of state control of gold, the medium for taxation and payments to holders of public office; and the growth of an aristocracy, which was increasingly self-aware and cohesive, and possessed interests opposed to those of the state. Known in contemporary legislation as the "powerful," these aristocrats placed private concerns above those of the state, even as they held public office. Dispersal of resources which hitherto had accrued to the state—largely in the form of taxes and levies on land— and of rights which had hitherto been the preserve of the state—again, principally concerned with taxation of landed interests, but also there- fore over those who worked the land—led to political fragmentation and the emergence of new socio-economic hierarchies. During the tenth and eleventh centuries policies were devised which aimed to bolster existing political and fiscal structures, prop up the state economy, and delimit the power of aristocrats. These measures failed. Twelfth-century efforts to harness the interests and wealth of the aristocracy, anchored in the land, to those of the state provided no lasting solution, but instead led to greater political fragmentation, inter-necine conflict, social unrest, and ultimately to the collapse of the state system in the last years of the twelfth century.

The Eleventh Century: c. 950-1081

It is now clear, contrary to interpretations which prevailed through most of the twentieth century, that the economy of the Byzantine Empire expanded rapidly between 950 and 1200.[2] It is also clear that in this

---

peasants. Thus the very foundations on which Byzantium had been built ever since its revival in the seventh century were swept away, with the result that the strength of the armed forces and of the revenue declined, and the consequent impoverishment weak- ened the military power of the state still further. There is not, however, any justification for regarding the rulers of this period as responsible for initiating this process. The change in policy which appeared to originate with them was in reality due to a devel- opment which it was no longer possible to control. They were merely the exponents of vigorous and irresistible social and economic forces." My interpretation diverges from Ostrogorsky on the nature of these forces, for he was writing at a time when it was universally believed that Byzantium experienced economic decline and stagnation in this period, and its institutions were corrupted under the influence of "feudal" practices imported from Latin Christendom.

[2] The essay by Michael Hendy, "Byzantium, 1081-1204: an economic reappraisal," *TRHS* 5th series, 20 (1970), 31-52, swiftly received almost universal acceptance. The

same period an aristocracy emerged which was integral to the state system, but whose power did not rest exclusively on access to offices of state. While public office remained prestigious and potentially lucrative throughout the period under consideration, to paraphrase Michael Psellos, the great Byzantine polymath of the eleventh century, many preferred to "belch forth their family's great name."[3] These belchers included the Phokades, Doukai and Komnenoi, each in turn an imperial family, but whose members were committed in the first instance to the promotion of the family and its interests at the expense of the state. The emergence of a self-aware aristocracy can be traced in histories, chronicles and saints' lives, where by 1200, 80% of individuals bear a second name, in contrast to 20% in c. 800.[4] The emergence of aristocratic self-consciousness is even more marked on the lead seals which were used to secure and guarantee official correspondence. There has survived from before 900 not a single seal which bears a family name, but dozens from the last quarter of the tenth century, and hundreds (perhaps thousands) from the eleventh century bear surnames. The typical seal bears a forename followed by the title and rank held by the individual in the state hierarchy, and ends with the surname.[5] These individuals, representatives both of the state and of their families, may have felt conflicted loyalties, but a wealth of evidence suggests that few felt any compunction to place the interests of the state above those of kin.

---

new orthodoxy has been enshrined in the recent and monumental *The Economic History of Byzantium: From the Seventh Through the Fifteenth Century*, ed. A. Laiou, 3 vols (Washington, DC, 2002), henceforth *EHB*.

[3] Michael Psellos, *Mesaionikê vivliothêkê*, ed. K. Sathas (Paris, 1874), IV, 430-1, quoted in fuller translation by M. Angold, *The Byzantine empire. A political history, 1025-1204*, 2nd edn (London & New York, 1997), 67. There have been, in recent years, extensive studies of the aristocracy and its ethos. To start, see the papers collected in M. Angold, ed., *The Byzantine Aristocracy* (Oxford, 1984), especially P. Magdalino, "Byzantine snobbery," 58-78.

[4] E. Patlagean, "Les débuts d'une aristocratie byzantine et le témoignage de l'historiographie: système des noms et liens de parenté aux IXe et Xe siècles," in Angold, ed., *The Byzantine aristocracy*, 23-43; A. Kazhdan, "The formation of Byzantine family names in the ninth and tenth centuries," *Byzantinoslavica* 58 (1997), 90-110.

[5] P. Stephenson, "A development in nomenclature on the seals of the Byzantine provincial aristocracy in the late tenth century," *Revue des études byzantines* 52 (1994), 187-211; with corrections offered by W. Seibt, "Beinamen, 'Spitznamen', Herkunftsnamen, Familiennamen bis ins 10. Jahrhundert: die Beitrag der Sigillographie zu einem prosopographischen Problem," in W. Seibt, ed., *Studies in Byzantine Sigillography* 7 (Washington, DC, 2002), 119-36. See also W. Seibt, "Probleme mit mittelbyzantinischen Namen (besonders Familiennamen) auf Siegeln," in J.-C. Cheynet and C. Sode, eds, *Studies in Byzantine Sigillography* 8 (Munich, 2003), 1-7.

The best researched body of evidence for this conflict between the state and the aristocrats is the land legislation issued by emperors of the tenth century, principally Romanos I (920-44), Constantine VII (913/944-59), and Basil II (963/976-1025). Each of these emperors issued laws, known as "novels" (*nearai*), directed against the so-called "powerful" (*dynatoi*), seeking to curtail encroachments upon lands pertaining to the "poor" (*penêtes, ptochoi*). The rhetoric of "powerful" and "poor" masked an underlying reality which had little to do with the well-being of the humble subject or peasant farmer: the state was losing taxable land to wealthy families who were better placed to offer protection or assert patronage, and to resist taxation.[6] Land acquisition might follow crop failure, famine or drought, as the earliest legislation suggests. However, the "powerful" were increasingly able to assert dominance in good years, thanks to population growth and a fairly vigorous land market. Having acquired land, by fair means or foul, the "powerful" could resist demands for taxes more easily than the "poor," whether by barring access to tax collectors and their armed retinues, by seeking exemptions from the emperor, or indeed by gaining responsibility for the fiscal administration of a particular district.[7] Consequently, emperors began to demonstrate a keen desire to ensure the fiscal integrity of the village (*chorion*), which also happened to be the corporate entity responsible for the payment of land taxes. The fact that, in 996, Basil II issued stronger legislation to enforce this policy suggests, of course, that it was not working. But by now, emperors had devised alternative methods to compete with the aristocrats: to act as the "powerful" were, but to back this with the coercive force of the state.[8]

Romanos I, author of the first novels against the "powerful" (*dynatoi*) was also the first emperor to incorporate newly-conquered land into the imperial domain as an estate (*kouratoria*). However, it remained the case that abandoned land (*klasma*), for example that abandoned in the face

---

[6] The division of society into the powerful and the poor had been articulated in late antiquity, and no new vocabulary had been introduced to better describe the medieval situation. See E. Patlagean, *Pauvrété économique et pauvrété sociale à Byzance 4-7ᵉ siècles* (Paris, 1977), 11-35.

[7] N. Oikonomides, "The role of the Byzantine state in the economy," in *EHB*, 1005, "... the difficulty of preventing encroachment on state land was largely the result of the inherent weaknesses of an administrative mechanism staffed by aristocrats [who] were called upon to take action against aristocrats."

[8] The texts of all relevant novels are collected with commentary in N. Svoronos and P. Gounaridis, eds, *Les novelles des empereurs Macédoniens concernant la terre et les stratiotes* (Athens, 1984).

of threat, invasion or crop failure, was to remain within the *chorion*. Basil II reversed this policy, acquiring *klasma* for the state, and adding to it further conquered territories, upon which were settled dependent peasant farmers (*paroikoi*) who paid rents. Basil also instituted a new government department, the *Sekreton tôn oikeiakôn*, which was responsible for the control of state land, including the collection of rents from dependents. By the turn of the twelfth century this department had become the principal body responsible for taxation in the provinces. This change in policy had a significant social impact, especially when placed alongside the continuing growth in landed interests of the "powerful." Nicolas Oikonomides summarised it thus: ". . . there was undoubtedly an increase in the assets of the state, [and consequently] the composition of society in rural areas changed substantially as the number of dependent villagers (*paroikoi*) rose. In other words, there was a tendency for the economic benefits of the state to be maximized to the detriment of the social structure of the provinces, as the state turned to implementation of the same policy as that which the *dynatoi* . . . were also applying."[9]

One might temper this negative characterisation with the information, provided by Psellos, that emperors sought also to improve productivity through land reclamation and innovations in estate management and farming techniques. Thus, "the acumen [of Constantine IX] was proved by the profits he made; by the clever ways in which he saved labour; the successful yet economical basis on which he ran his estates . . . by the way he forestalled the seasons in the development of crops; by the ingenious inventions which enabled him to dispense with farmworkers; by the miracles of improvisation, so wonderful that most people could not believe their own eyes when they saw a field today where yesterday they had seen a flat plain and two days ago a hill."[10] Monasteries were also active in cultivating new land and improving estate management. The founder of the Great Lavra on Mt Athos, St Athanasios, is said to have reclaimed land and provided irrigation to a barren rocky headland.[11] Athanasios benefited from a large donation by the future emperor Nikephoros Phokas which financed the initial construction. Thereafter, the Lavra was as acquisitive and competitive as any of the

---

[9] Oikonomides, "The role of the Byzantine state in the economy," 1006.

[10] Michael Psellos, *Chronographia*, VI, 175; *The History of Psellus*, ed. C. Sathas (London, 1899), 168; *Michael Psellus, Fourteen Byzantine Rulers*, tr. E. R. A. Sewter (Harmondsworth, 1966), 247.

[11] *Life of Athanasios of Athos*, Vita B, 24: *Vita duae antiquae sancti Athanasii Athonitae*, ed. J. Noret, (Turnhout, 1982), 150-1.

"powerful," at the forefront of those whose ability to coerce and patronise created a class of *paroikoi* from previously free peasant farmers.
Indeed, it is redundant to distinguish between the activities of secular
aristocrats and monasteries, for in a society which knew no religious
orders, members of the secular aristocracy were able and anxious to
establish private religious foundations, for the salvation of their souls
and those of family members. To ensure the continuity of such foundations, exemptions (*exkousseia*) were secured from additional land taxes
and corvées.[12] Every emperor but Michael V (who died within a year
of taking office in 1041) is known to have granted extensive privileges
to leading monasteries, particularly those on Athos. As the monasteries
acquired greater wealth, increasingly they were not obliged to send gold
back to Constantinople.

Basil II evidently inspired fear in his "powerful" subjects sufficiently
that he could enforce his legislation, even obliging the wealthy to pay
tax arrears owed by the "poor." That is, he shifted the corporate responsibility for taxes (*allêlengyon*) owed by peasants who had defaulted or disappeared from the village (*chorion*) to the powerful (*dynatoi*).[13] The *Peira*,
a collection of case law, derived largely from the career of one judge,
Eustathios Rhomaios who flourished under Basil, "not surprisingly reflects
the extreme fiscalism of Basil's reign. There is a whole section . . . on
'The fisc and its privileges.' Eustathios rigorously applied Basil's land
legislation."[14] Besides simple acts of state coercion or confiscation, the
"poor" were encouraged to make claims against the "powerful" in private actions which resulted in compensation for the disadvantaged peasant and the acquisition of the land for the state. Basil also added
substantially to the landed interests of the state, and to the treasury, by
conquest and seizure of property and treasure. He was, therefore and
notoriously, able to leave 200,000 talents (*talanta*) of gold. A talent (*talanton*) in this period was a pound of gold, or 72 gold coins (*nomismata*),
hence Basil left approximately 14,400,000 *nomismata* in the treasury at
his death.[15]

---

[12] See in general R. Morris, *Monks and Laymen in Byzantium, 843-1118* (Cambridge,
1995).

[13] For a careful explanation see P. Lemerle, *The Agrarian History of Byzantium from the
Origins to the Twelfth Century* (Galway, 1979), 78-80. On the fear Basil inspired, see now
P. Stephenson, *The Legend of Basil the Bulgar-Slayer* (Cambridge, 2003).

[14] P. Magdalino, "Justice and finance in the Byzantine state, ninth to twelfth centuries," in A. Laiou and D. Simon, eds, *Law and Society in Byzantium, Ninth-Twelfth Centuries*
(Washington, DC, 1994), 93-115, at 105.

[15] Psellos, *Chronographia*, I, 31; ed. Sathas, 16; tr. Sewter, 45. See Oikonomides, "Role

Keeping such a sum out of circulation would have had deflationary effects, for the Byzantine state economy operated with an extremely inelastic supply of precious metals with which to mint and circulate gold and silver coins. The expanding economy had produced a demand for coinage that the state system could not easily nor willingly meet. Here it is worth quoting Michael Hendy: "Coinage [in Byzantium] was essentially a fiscal phenomenon: produced and distributed, that is, in order to provide the state with a standard medium in which to collect public revenue and distribute public expenditure. It would be absurd to suggest that it did not circulate freely and perform the function of mediating private exchange; but this was not its primary function, only its secondary."[16] Public expenditure in the tenth and eleventh centuries was primarily annual payments in gold (*rogai*, pl., *roga*, sing.) to state functionaries, military, ecclesiastical and civilian, Constantinopolitan and (partially) provincial.[17] One distribution ceremony was observed, famously, by Liudprand of Cremona on Palm Sunday, 24th March 950.[18] This gold was then expected to trickle down to lower levels, through payments by the elites to their subordinates, by commercial exchanges or via professional money changers, for all were obliged in September to

of the Byzantine state in the economy," 1017. The *talanton* had earlier signified a *kentenarion*, or 100 pounds of gold. This confused Angold, *Byzantine Empire*, 31, who offered an estimate of the value in modern terms: $128 billion, based on a price of gold of $400 per ounce. However, see C. Morrisson, "Byzantine money: its production and circulation," in *EHB*, 908-66, at 920, for clarification. The price per ounce of gold today, 5th March 2004, is again $400, up from $350 at the time of the Uppsala symposium (June 2003), giving an approximate equivalent figure of between $1 billion and $1.3 billion.

[16] M. Hendy, "Introduction," *The Economy, Fiscal Administration and Coinage of Byzantium* (Northampton, 1989), xi-xii. Cf. Oikonomides, "Role of the Byzantine state in the economy," 978.

[17] Certain provincial functionaries were entitled, indeed obliged to draw their salaries as levies or "donations" (*synetheiai*) from their localities. One can imagine that this blurring of the distinction between the exercise of public authority and private power would lead to greater tension in the periphery, and also would exacerbate the principal phenomenon here described, namely the growth of private aristocratic wealth and power at the expense of the state. It is important in this context to note that the principal functionaries who drew no state *roga* and were obliged to draw all resources from the lands where they were based included all the military governors (*strategoi*) of lands west of the river Strymon, being the Balkan lands conquered by Basil II. See N. Oikonomides, "Title and income at the Byzantine court," in H. Maguire, ed., *Byzantine Court Culture from 829 to 1204* (Washington, DC, 1997), 199-215; Oikonomides, "Role of the Byzantine state in the economy," 999, 1009-11.

[18] Liudprand, *Antapodosis*, VI, 10; tr. F. Wright, *The Works of Liudprand of Cremona* (London, 1930), 211-12.

pay their taxes in gold if the amount owed was valued at over 2/3 *nomisma*. Change (*antistrophê*) would be given in copper coins.[19]

Following Basil II's death, less stringent fiscal policies were introduced and the treasury reserve was rapidly depleted. Without the fear engendered by Basil, it was no longer possible to extract the *allêlengyon* from the "powerful," and this stipulation of Basil's novel was rescinded by Romanos III (1028-34).[20] Within a decade there are signs that gold coins were in short supply once again in Constantinople, and measures were taken then, and throughout the eleventh century, which suggest a sustained thirst for gold to service the state economy.[21] The failure of these attempts left the state bankrupt in the 1070s, following a rapid debasement of the coinage. An early sign of this state thirst for gold is the demand, in the late 1030s, that taxes in the lands of Bulgaria be paid in gold coin. Basil II had annexed Bulgaria to the empire in 1018 and, recognising the low level of monetization in the region, demanded only taxes in kind. This policy made sense when the Byzantines maintained a large army of occupation in the annexed lands. Over time, however, the standing army was disbanded, and taxes were demanded according to the same rules that applied elsewhere in the empire. This combination sparked a series of rebellions in the western Balkans between 1040 and 1042.[22] Although the rebellions were suppressed, the policy of disbanding local forces continued, largely as a measure to draw taxes in precious metals to the centre. This policy is widely referred to as the fiscalization of the *strateia*, meaning the policy whereby those who formerly owed military service (*strateia*) to the state were able, indeed often were obliged, to commute this to a cash payment. The most notorious failure associated with this policy is attributed to Constantine IX Monomachos (1042-55), who determined to disband the armies of

---

[19] Oikonomides, "The role of the Byzantine state in the economy," 995-6.

[20] *Ioannis Scylitzes Synopsis historion*, ed. J. Thurn, CFHB 5 (Berlin & New York, 1973), 375; Lemerle, *Agrarian History*, 79-80, 202.

[21] After Basil II's accumulation of booty, the Byzantine state appears to have been able to import only limited additional gold supplies. Thus, Cécile Morrisson has discerned no appreciable increase in the gold supply available to Byzantine mints beyond that necessary to counteract natural wastage. This has been reckoned at various levels, from an unsustainable 2%—which would result in 90% of the coinage disappearing from circulation in a century—to a more sensible 0.2-1.0%. See Morrisson, "Byzantine money: its production and circulation," 939.

[22] P. Stephenson, *Byzantium's Balkan Frontier. A Political Study of the Northern Balkans, 900-1204* (Cambridge, 2000), 130-5, where it is argued further that coinage was needed to facilitate a trading policy on the lower Danube, aimed at preventing raids by steppe nomads, first Pechenegs and later Cumans.

Caucasian Iberia, which was promptly overrun by the Seljuk Turks. It has been argued that the large peasant armies were ill prepared to resist bands of fast-moving nomads, and that commuting payments to cash allowed the purchase of services of mercenary forces far better suited to the task at hand.[23] However, it is hard to escape the conclusion that Monomachos' decision was less strategic than financial, and represents another example of a thirst for gold within the state economy as it struggled in the wake of general economic expansion and the siphoning off of gold reserves for private purposes.[24] Thesaurisation (*thesaurizein*)—i.e. stashing money away in (underground) hoards—had always been popular, and thus legislated against by a state anxious to keep gold in circulation.[25] In the 1030s massive private fortunes were amassed, only a few of which the state was empowered to confiscate. For example, two senior clerics, Patriarch Alexios Stoudios (d. 1043) and Theophanes, metropolitan of Salonika (d. 1038) were deprived of gold stores of, respectively, 2500 and 3300 talents (a total of 417,600 *nomismata*).[26] This amount of gold held by just two of the "powerful" was the equivalent of perhaps 10% of the annual state budget, which has been estimated at 4-5 million *nomismata*; and is probably more than the number of new *nomismata* minted in any given year (c. 250,000-350,000).[27]

The same minister of state who demanded taxes in gold from the Bulgarians, John the *Orphanotrophos*, introduced tax farming on a grand scale throughout Byzantine lands, presumably as a device to extract large sums of gold quickly from the wealthy as supplies in state coffers dried up. This policy continued throughout the eleventh century, with

---

[23] Stephenson, *Byzantium's Balkan Frontier*, 91-2; J. Shepard, "The uses of the Franks in eleventh-century Byzantium," *Anglo-Norman Studies* 15 (1993), 275-305.

[24] *Pace* Ostrogorsky, *History of the Byzantine State*, 331-2: "The civilian government so hated the military aristocracy that it had systematically reduced the strength of the armed forces and in its attempts to discover fresh sources of revenue had converted the peasant-soldiers into taxpayers . . . the undermining of the organization of the themes meant nothing less than the disintegration of the system of government on which Byzantine greatness had been built during the preceding centuries."

[25] Morrisson, "Byzantine money: its production and circulation," 939, 950, estimates that at any given time 1/3 of all gold coins would be hoarded, and thus out of circulation. Angold, *Byzantine Empire*, 85, translates a short poem of the mid-eleventh century, by Christopher of Mytilene: "Having gazed on money, much as a polecat does on fat / You accumulate gold just to bury it in a vat / What good does it do you underground / When that is where you are bound?" See E. Kurtz, ed., *Die Gedichte des Christophoros Mitylenaios* (Leipzig, 1903), no. 134.

[26] Angold, *Byzantine Empire*, 85; Oikonomides, "Role of the Byzantine state in the economy," 1018.

[27] Morrisson, "Byzantine money: its production and circulation," 937, 941.

serious social consequences. In the first instance, selling taxation rights to the "powerful" was at the expense of the "poor"—these tenth-century legal categories persisted through the eleventh century. The "poor" were immediately subject to a massive increase in extraordinary levies and corvées, and if they could not pay were obliged to sell up and enter the service of the "powerful."[28] Ultimately, therefore, the policy was at the expense of the state, which experienced greater social unrest, and enjoyed a diminished capacity to control its own agents. Moreover, since the "powerful" had no inclination to levy taxes on their own lands, less taxation revenue reached the imperial treasury even as more of the excess wealth was siphoned off into private hands.

The demand for gold also led to a rise in interest rates in Constantinople. According to the aforementioned case law collection, the *Peira*, which was compiled before 1045, there was a corresponding reduction in the yield of annual stipends (*rogai*) on honorific titles in the Byzantine administration.[29] Offices of state were, for the most part, purchased for a non-refundable cash payment. This represented an investment in and over a bureaucratic career, since the annual *roga* payment represented a return of 2.5-3.5% on junior titles, and 5.5-8.3% for more senior (e.g. senatorial) titles.[30] By 1045, most *roga* payments, which were fixed, represented a poor investment when compared with lending money at interest on the open market. However, offices of state carried great prestige, and as such proved extremely attractive to the *nouveaux riches*. Psellos wrote disparagingly of Constantine IX for having "thrown open the doors of the senate" to different social groups, principally administrative employees formerly ineligible for such promotion.[31] Constantine did so not to diversify the social basis of the elite—even if this was one of the consequences—nor indeed to promote the interests of the "civilian" over the "military" aristocracy, as Ostrogorsky once argued.[32] The most obvious reason to offer offices of state more widely was the desire

---

[28] The total tax burden, the *arithmion*, usually amounted to 23-30% of income on farmed land. Exemptions from payments of additional levies could be granted, most often to monasteries and the "powerful." At the other end of the spectrum, additional corvées could be imposed upon the "poor" by unscrupulous tax farmers (i.e. agents of the "powerful"), significantly increasing their total tax burden. See Oikonomides, "Role of the Byzantine state in the economy," 995-6.

[29] Oikonomides, "Role of the Byzantine state in the economy," 1020.

[30] Oikonomides, "Role of the Byzantine state in the economy," 1009.

[31] Psellos, *Chronographia*, VI, 29; ed. Sathas, 105; tr. Sewter, 170. It is likely that all those promoted were not "rascally vagabonds of the market."

[32] Ostrogorsky, *History of the Byzantine State*, 342. On this generally see Angold, *Byzantine Empire*, 16-17: "The old notion . . . that the eleventh century crisis received political

to receive large payments in gold from those with social aspirations.[33] Even more obvious, therefore, was the determination by Constantine X Doukas (1059-67) to make merchants and manufacturers in the capital eligible for membership of the senate. According to Michael Attaleiates, Constantine X "desired above all else the increase of public finance and the hearing of private lawsuits" to raise money though fines.[34] A complementary policy was the sale of senatorial status, to the extent of devaluing the prestige which attached to it.[35] If the tenth-century price of the rank of *protospatharios*—the entry level rank for a senator—remained the same, each new senator provided a lump sum payment in gold of 60 talents (4320 *nomismata*) to the treasury, redirecting money from the booming markets of Constantinople back into the state economy.

The most obvious way for an emperor, or indeed empress, to retain gold was to scorn traditional distribution ceremonies. We know that upon her accession to sole rule, following the death of her husband Constantine IX in 1055, Theodora refused to make the distributions to state functionaries expected of any new monarch. She did so by claiming that this was not her first accession, having ruled with her sister Zoe before her marriage to Constantine in 1042. Isaac I Komnenos, who acceded in 1057, had no such excuse, but went further still, rescinding donations made by his ephemeral predecessor Michael VI (1056-7). He earned the wrath of the Church by "cutting off the greater part of the monies set aside for their sacred buildings and, having transferred these funds to the public funds, estimated the bare necessities for the clergy."[36] Without Basil II's iron-grip on power, Isaac's actions brought his ouster in 1059.

---

expression in the shape of a struggle between the civil and military aristocracy ... has been quietly shelved."

[33] This runs contrary to Psellos' assertion that "Constantine's idea was to exhaust the treasury of its money." Elsewhere Psellos attributes the poor state of public finances to the building projects of various emperors (generally imperial church or monastic foundations) and to the extravagance of the empresses Zoe and Theodora, who "confused the trifles of the harem (*gynaikonitis*) with important matters of state." See Psellos, *Chronographia*, VI, 5; ed. Sathas, 95; tr. Sewter, 157. Angold, *Byzantine Empire*, 83, follows this line of reasoning.

[34] Michael Attaleiates, *Historia* (Bonn, 1853), 76; quoted in fuller translation by Magdalino, "Justice and finance in the Byzantine state," 94.

[35] Psellos, *Chronographia*, VI, 30; ed. Sathas, 105, tr. Sewter, 171: "Gradually the error of the policy became apparent when privileges, much coveted in the old days, were now distributed with a generous abandon that knew no limits, with the consequence that the recipients lost distinction." See John Zonaras, *Epitomae historiarum*, eds M. Pinder & T. Büttner-Wobst (Bonn, 1897), III, 676, for further information on the sale of offices.

[36] Psellos, *Chronographia*, VII, 60; ed. Sathas, 218; tr. Sewter, 312.

Still these measures were not sufficient to prevent the debasement of the coinage, gradually to the end of the 1060s, and rapidly as the state went bankrupt in the 1070s. Emperors from Michael IV (1034-41) to Romanos IV (1068-71) reduced the gold content of the full-weight *nomisma* from 22 to 18 carats. In the 1070s this slumped to 16, to 10, and then to 8 carats. There was a correspondingly rapid debasement of the silver coinage, since much of the limited silver supply was being added to the gold coinage.[37] According to Morrison, the gradual debasement of the period c. 1040-70 was deliberate for the purposes of development, given that the volume of trade had increased much more rapidly than the quantity of gold available to service its demands. Although the entire gold coinage was not melted down and restruck by each emperor, if it had been the number of gold coins in circulation would have increased by 5% each year. A more realistic figure, Morrisson suggests, is 1% per year, or an increase of one-third in the number of gold coins circulating over the period 1040-70. Still, this was not enough to meet ever increasing demands, triggering the crisis debasements of the 1070s, and the collapse of the entire fiscal and tax systems.[38]

What sparked the crisis debasement, and thus served as a catalyst for the collapse of the state economy? In 1071 the Empire suffered assaults by the Seljuk Turks and Turkoman nomads, and by a range of peoples in the Balkans and beyond the Balkan frontier. It has long been argued that the battle of Manzikert, which the Byzantines lost to the Seljuks on 26th August 1071, was not a major military reversal for the Empire. However, it was symptomatic of factionalism within the capital between competing aristocratic families: Emperor Romanos IV Diogenes lost the support of the Doukas family, who betrayed him on the battlefield and afterwards.[39] Nor did the extended aftermath of the battle, where bands of Turkoman nomads gradually settled the interior plateau of Anatolia, deprive the Empire of essential, productive lands. The region was occupied primarily by huge ranches owned by a few aristocratic families, and the loss of these was of far less consequence than the preservation of control over the fertile coastal lands of Asia Minor. It has even been suggested that the loss of the central plateau, if not to the benefit of the state in geo-political terms, was to the benefit

[37] Morrisson, "Byzantine money: its production and circulation," 930-2; C. Morrisson, "La dévaluation de la monnaie byzantine au XI siècle: essai d'interprétation," *Travaux et mémoires* 6 (1976), 3-48.

[38] Oikonomides, "Role of the Byzantine state in the economy," 1020.

[39] Angold, *Byzantine Empire*, 44-8.

of the new imperial dynasty, the Komnenoi, who demonstrated no urgent desire to drive the Turks and Turkmen out. Ultimately the empire paid a high price, but it was not primarily economic.[40]

The Balkan and Italian lands of the Empire were no more stable at this time than Anatolia. In 1071 again, Bari, the last Byzantine stronghold in southern Italy, fell to the Normans. In the same year, the Danube frontier came under attack from the Hungarians, at Belgrade, and the Pechenegs who crossed the lower Danube and plundered throughout Thrace and Macedonia. Consequently "the Slavic people threw off the Roman yoke and laid waste Bulgaria taking plunder and leaving scorched earth. Skopje and Nish were sacked, and all the towns along the river Sava and beside the Danube between Sirmium and Vidin suffered greatly. Furthermore, the Croats and Dukljans throughout the whole of Dalmatia rose in rebellion."[41] Skylitzes Continuatus considered the reason for the rebellions to be the "insatiate greed" (aplêstia) of the state treasurer Nikephoritzes, who was desperate to recoup coinage. One might assume he needed cash to mount a decent defence, but Skylitzes Continuatus was far from sympathetic, comparing Nikephoritzes' actions to those of the money-grubbing John the Orphanotrophos, whom we met earlier. Whereas the rebellions of 1040-2 were put down with few immediate consequences, the instability of the 1070s saw tax revenues shrink and large sums of gold lost to the system. Crisis debasement ensued, but recovery did not. It fell to Alexios I Komnenos and his—aristocratic—family, first to restore order, which took until 1091; and then to devise structures and institutions that reflected, developed and exploited new realities in the twelfth century.

The Twelfth Century: 1081-1183

The coup which brought Alexios I to the throne in 1081 was a family affair, and the regime that he established placed family—his own relatives

---

[40] M. Hendy, "'Byzantium, 1081-1204': the economy revisited twenty years on," in Hendy, *The Economy, Fiscal Administration and Coinage of Byzantium*, III, 1-48, at 3-9, esp. 9: ". . . there can be little doubt that it was the disruption and/or loss of its main (i.e. Anatolian) territorial base that provided one of the main factors sealing the fate of the old military aristocracy and permitting the formation—indeed the deliberate construction—of a new one involving the virtually complete Comnenian dynastic appropriation of the pre-existing state apparatus."

[41] *Nicéphore Bryennios Histoire*, ed. P. Gautier, CFHB 9 (Brussels, 1979), p. 211. See also Skylitzes Continuatus, *Ê synecheia tês chronografias tou Ioannou Skylitze*, ed. E. T. Tsolakês (Thessaloniki, 1968), 162-3; Stephenson, *Byzantium's Balkan Frontier*, 141-4.

by blood or marriage—at the centre of government. For this reason the rise of the house of Komnenos has been considered proof of the triumph of the military aristocracy. We might better consider it the culmination of a number of tendencies which, coming to the fore over the previous century, had seen power and wealth decentralized and central government—not "the civilian aristocracy"—starved of gold. It was the great achievement of the Komnenoi that they brought the state back from bankruptcy even as they restored the geographical integrity of the Empire, driving waves of invaders back and reaching accommodations with new settlers. However, the methods by which this recovery was achieved saw the Empire of earlier centuries transformed.

Alexios, like his imperial uncle Isaac I, made an early enemy of the institutional Church through his attempts to finance recovery. Soon after his accession he seized holy vessels from churches and monasteries and melted them down to strike coin, much of which he used to pay his troops. Anna Komnene's *apologia* for her father's behaviour suggests that criticism was fierce, although this was certainly not the first time such an action had been taken.[42] While Alexios was engaged in warfare against Normans, Pechenegs and Turks, he placed his mother in charge of domestic administration, with an offical known as the *logothetês* of the *sekreta* to act on her behalf as head of the civil service.[43] At the same time, the traditional system of honours was radically altered: honorary ranks and titles were not abolished, but they were left to wither on the vine with the removal of associated stipends (*rogai*). Initially left unpaid as a response to the bankruptcy of the state, Alexios determined simply not to restore the *rogai*.[44] Moreover, rather than pack the existing hierarchy with his appointees, Alexios instituted an entirely new tier of court titles over and above those which existed, based on the rank of *sebastos*. The term—an imperial epithet deriving from the Greek translation of Augustus—was reserved for members of the emperor's extended family, by blood or marriage (and some high foreign dignitaries). "Alexios created a sizeable group of *sebastoi*, some of whom were distinguished by

---

[42] Indeed, Oikonomides, "The role of the Byzantine state in the economy," 1017, suggests we might view this as standard procedure: excess wealth was hoarded in this form, a symbol of imperial generosity in good times, to be cashed in periods of crisis. See *Alexiad*, V, 1-2; tr. E. R. A. Sewter, *The Alexiad of Anna Comnena* (Harmondsworth, 1969), 156-60.

[43] On this official, see P. Magdalino, "Innovations in government," in M. Mullett and D. Smythe, eds, *Alexios I Komnenos, I: Papers* (Belfast, 1996), 146-66 at 153-5; Magdalino, "Justice and finance," 110-11.

[44] Oikonomides, "The role of the Byzantine state in the economy," 1021.

the addition of prefixes to the basic title: thus the Emperor designated his brothers Adrian and Nikephoros *protosebastos* and *pansebastos* respectively, while another brother-in-law, Michael Taronites, eventually rose to the rank of *panhypersebastos* . . . At the same time, Alexios devised for his favourite brother Isaac a rank . . . by combining the title *sebastos* with an element of the exclusive imperial title *autokrator*, to form the title *sebastokrator*."[45]

The historian John Zonaras criticized Alexios for acting not as an emperor, but as the head of an aristocratic house, running the government for the benefit of his family. Indeed, "he thought of and called the imperial palace his own house."[46] Alexios did not pay his relatives in gold, but rather in privileges relating to land, and more specifically to the taxation of land. Examples are numerous, of which a couple may be cited: "[I]n 1084 the *protosebastos* Adrian Komnenos was entitled to collect all the taxes of the Kassandra peninsula, directly and for his own benefit. The land did not belong to him; the state had conceded to him its revenue."[47] Similarly, but more extensively, in 1094, the *sebastokrator* Isaac received the revenues of lands of Thessalonika, at the time the Empire's second city.[48] Besides his family, Alexios rewarded his commanders. Gregory Pakourianos, commander-in-chief of the army, controlled extensive lands in and around Bachkovo (in present day Bulgaria), where he founded the Petritzos monastery for his own retirement, and those of his loyal retinue of Armenians and Georgians. Pakourianos died before he could be tonsured, riding his horse headlong into a tree while fighting the Pechenegs, but his monastic foundation document (*typikon*) reveals that his estates were all granted to him by the Emperor; that these had previously been state lands; and that he was to collect all state revenue connected with these lands as his own.[49] On a smaller scale, the general Leo Kephalas received, in 1084, a public estate (*proasteion*) which had previously been granted to other military men. There

---

[45] P. Magdalino, *The Empire of Manuel I Komnenos, 1143-1180* (Cambridge, 1993), 181. See also Magdalino, "Innovations in government," 147-8, for fuller references to research on "the family regime."

[46] Zonaras, *Epitomae historiarum*, III, 766.

[47] Oikonomides, "The role of the Byzantine state in the economy," 1040. See *Actes de Lavra*, I, eds P. Lemerle et al., Archives de l'Athos, V (Paris, 1970), no. 46.

[48] Oikonomides, "The role of the Byzantine state in the economy," 1041; *Actes de Lavra*, I, no. 151.

[49] P. Gautier, "Le typikon du sébaste Grégoire Pakourianos," *Revue des études byzantines* 42 (1984), 5-146; P. Lemerle, *Cinq études sur le XIᵉ siècle byzantine* (Paris, 1977), 113-91.

is no indication that this was a grant of taxation revenue, and it must be imagined therefore that Leo received the land in order to extract the profits from the dependent peasantry, while still paying taxes, and with the obligation to return the land to the state upon request or at his death. By contrast, in 1086, after his heroic defence of the city of Larissa in Thessaly, Leo received the village (*chorion*) of Chostiani, with exemption from all taxes and the right to bequeath the property. Ultimately, these lands came into the possession of the Great Lavra monastery on Athos.[50]

Clearly, relatives of the Emperor or his loyal commanders received income directly from taxpayers, who became their dependents (*paroikoi*). This obviated the need for the state to collect revenue itself, and thus circumvented, to some extent, the need to recoup gold and mint ever larger numbers of coins to service the state economy. Oikonomides summarised the state of affairs which came into being under Alexios I thus: "Simplification and decentralization [occurred, which] can be explained by a change in the state economy: the state, which had previously been the motive power and had imposed the circulation of money, now partially withdrew from circulation and turned to the granting of privileges. A significant portion of the state economy thus functioned on the form of entries on paper, without any real money changing hands."[51]

Still, money continued to change hands, and did so with ever increasing currency. It was a further achievement of this emperor to introduce an entirely new coinage in or shortly after 1092, based on the *hyperperon nomisma*, a cupped or "scyphate" gold coin of 21 carats. The electrum *nomisma* (or *aspron trachy*), valued at 1/3 *hyperperon* and containing 7 carats of gold, replaced the silver *miliaresion*; a billon *aspron trachy* followed, worth 1/48 *hyperperon*; finally two copper coins, the *tetarteron* and half *tetarteron* were circulated, with values of 1/864 and 1/1728 *hyperperon*. The *follis*, the traditional copper coin, was maintained only as a unit of account, between the billon *trachy* and *tetarteron*, being 1/288 *hyperperon* (i.e. 3 *tetartera*).[52] The fractions of the *hyperperon* represented a range of values not known since the sixth century, surely reflecting the fact that coinage was no longer minted merely to service the state econ-

---

[50] Oikonomides, "The role of the Byzantine state in the economy," 1041; *Actes de Lavra*, I, no. 44, 45, 48, 49, 60.

[51] Oikonomides, "The role of the Byzantine state in the economy," 995.

[52] Morrisson, "Byzantine money: its production and circulation," 924, 932-3. The identification of the reformed coinage was the achievement of M. Hendy, *Coinage and Money in the Byzantine Empire, 1081-1261* (Washington, DC, 1969).

omy, but with the needs of the market in mind. Recent calculations, while confirming that the economy remained fundamentally agrarian, have estimated that the non-agricultural sector grew to represent 25% of the total economy by the mid-twelfth century. The same calculations, advanced by Laiou and Morrisson, suggest that while the agricultural sector was 35% monetized—still a large percentage in medieval terms— the non-agricultural sector was 80% monetized. The Komnenian coinage system both reflected and encouraged these new realities.[53] The reformed currency also allowed for, indeed required a radical revision of the taxation system.[54]

The foundation of the new system, which achieved its final form in 1109, was the collection of land taxes in the new electrum *aspra trachea*. Fractions of the *trachea* were collected in copper *folleis*, for as long as they remained in circulation, and later in *tetartera* (three to a *follis*). The pure gold *hyperperon* was not used for taxation, which, as a complement to the decline of the *roga*, diminished massively the function of gold within the state economy. Moreover, as we have already seen, much of the taxation revenue accrued not to the state, but to those granted privileges by the emperor. Details of the transition from the old to the new system are contained in two remarkable documents known as the *Palaia Logarikê* and *Nea Logarikê*, "the old and new accounting."[55] Here we may discern recognition of the shift which had taken place from a system predicated on the existence of a largely free peasantry, organised into fiscal units known as villages (*choria*), to one where large estates predominated, and efficiency demanded assessment of disparate, non-contiguous holdings pertaining to "powerful" families or institutions. "The archaic term *epibol[ê]* was used to refer to the new fiscal practice that amounted to the first step toward the simplified taxation on land for centuries to come and that was easier to apply to large holdings of agricultural land."[56] Unlike the old system, it took no account of the quality of land to be taxed, so while a simplification, it cannot be regarded as an improvement. In parallel with the *epibolê*, the compilation of *praktika* came to replace the onerous system of maintaining land registers recording the fluctuating holdings of each village throughout the empire.

---

[53] A. Laiou, "The Byzantine economy: an overview," in *EHB*, 1153-6.

[54] A. Harvey, *Economic Expansion in the Byzantine Empire, 900-1200* (Cambridge, 1989), 80-119.

[55] Oikonomides, "The role of the Byzantine state in the economy," 976, 1030.

[56] Oikonomides, "The role of the Byzantine state in the economy," 1031.

Instead, taxpayers who owned land in more than one tax unit (*chorion*) could request that all their obligations be grouped in one document, the *praktikon*, which could more easily be updated as an individual or institution gained more land or secured greater privileges. Naturally, this was accompanied by a thorough fiscal survey of, at least, the empire's core European provinces.

Such a drastic overhaul of the fiscal and taxation systems required a similar restructuring of the fiscal administration. The *Sekreton tôn oikeiakôn*, which was initially responsible for the control of state land, became the principal bureau in all matters relating to provincial taxation, preparing the way for an institution we shall examine shortly: *pronoia*.[57] Furthermore, Alexios swept away many obsolete departments in creating two new accounting bureaux (*logariastika sekreta*), each presided over by a *logariastês*: the *megas logariastês tôn sekretôn*, "grand accountant of the departments," who audited all fiscal services; and the very similarly named *megas logariastês tôn euagôn sekretôn*, who was concerned with "charitable departments," but primarily audited imperial property.[58] The title "grand accountant of charitable departments" reflects the fact that the emperor placed philanthropy *qua* social welfare at the centre of his financial reforms. As a pious autocrat, he did so in a manner intended to glorify his own reputation and family name, and to patronise the urban poor: he founded, or more correctly re-founded, a massive charitable enterprise known as the *Orphanotropheion*, or "Orphanage."[59]

Alexios I's reign, therefore, was punctuated by measures aimed at refining and reforming aspects of the eleventh-century situation he had inherited. Early measures smacked of crisis management, cobbled together as they were in the face of state bankruptcy, foreign invasion and a cumbersome bureaucracy. Later measures exploited the political capital won by averting the total collapse of the state to construct a system which suited and benefited a small, inter-married, aristocratic elite. It will perhaps suffice, in place of a lengthy survey of the Komnenian system under Alexios' son and grandson, John II (1118-43) and Manuel I (1143-80), to offer observations on the evolution and ramifications of two Alexian measures, one an example of crisis management, the other

[57] N. Oikonomides, "L'évolution de l'organisation administrative de l'empire byzantin au XIᵉ siècle," *Travaux et mémoires* 6 (1976), 125-52 at 136-7.

[58] Oikonomides, "L'évolution de l'organisation administrative," 140-1; Oikonomides, "The role of the Byzantine state in the economy," 994-5.

[59] See now T. Miller, *The orphans of Byzantium* (Washington, DC, 2003).

rooted in aristocratic exploitation of the land: trade privileges granted to Italian merchants; and *pronoia.*

In 1082, needing a navy to support his vain early campaigns against the Normans who had invaded the empire's western provinces, Alexios I offered to the doge of Venice extensive incentives to support the imperial cause. At this time—or possibly later: the exact date of the privileges has long been disputed—the Venetians secured the right to trade throughout the empire (with the exception of Cyprus, Crete, and the Black Sea) free of the obligation to pay harbour tolls or customs duty of 10% (*kommerkion*) on their merchandise. Moreover, in Constantinople they were granted quays along the Golden Horn with much property, and the doge received the title *protosebastos*, bringing him within the imperial family as one of the more senior *sebastoi.*[60] It is highly unlikely that Alexios considered the lasting economic impact of his concessions to the Venetians, any more than he did in 1111 when, bowing to pressure from the Pisan fleet, he allowed Pisans to pay a reduced *kommerkion* of 4%. Efforts by Alexios' son, John, to rescind these privileges failed dismally, and in 1155, John's own son Manuel extended privileges to the Genoese, once again with little regard for economic policy.[61] It was once maintained that these privileges depressed "native" Byzantine trade, giving the Italians a stranglehold on mercantile activity in the empire and undermining its economy.[62] Now one may choose between two upbeat interpretations. The first maintains that the benefits of an open market and increased Italian activity stimulated the economy such that the benefits outweighed any losses to the fisc. Taxing the Pisans and Genoese at 4% in a vigorous market was more lucrative than 10% of a weak market; and the Venetians, who paid no tax, were the greatest stimulant to that market. Thus, Oikonomides observed that "In the twelfth century the state's revenue from the revitalized trade economy seems to have been substantial, and certainly much greater than it had been in the tenth. Perhaps this may explain why . . . the state of the Komnenoi appears wealthy for its time; it possessed large sums in cash and experienced no particular difficulty in financing a costly foreign policy and maintaining an even more expensive army of mercenaries."[63]

[60] *Alexiad*, VI, 5; tr. Sewter, 191.

[61] Magdalino, *Empire of Manuel I*, 142-50.

[62] Hendy, "'Byzantium, 1081-1204': the economy revisited," 21-2: 'It would be exceedingly tedious and indeed invidious to document the point.'

[63] Oikonomides, "Role of the Byzantine state in the economy," 1052.

That is to say, gold coin, which in the tenth century was largely recouped by the state in land taxes, and which had been bleeding from the state economy to service the trade economy, was now pumped into the trade economy in the knowledge that much would be recouped. The alternative explanation holds that the mercantile economy was insufficiently large, when compared to the agrarian economy, to have any substantial effect; and the Italian portion of the mercantile economy was still paltry when compared to "native" investment. Hendy has argued that "The entire Latin investment will very probably have amounted to less than the fortunes of half a dozen members of the Byzantine higher court aristocracy. The tax revenues forfeited by the state will have been a shade less than the annual revenues possibly thought appropriate to a single [*sebastokrator*] (40,000 *hyperpera*) . . ."[64]

Neither explanation, however, is in itself sufficient, since the most consequential effect of the privileges was not on the economy, but on the political and social life of the empire, particularly in Constantinople. The ever increasing presence of Latins, most notably the resident merchants, provoked resentment which was not restricted to frustrated competitors. Spontaneous acts of aggression were not unknown, but the worst clashes accompanied political initiatives. On 12th March 1171, the emperor Manuel I engineered the general arrest of Venetian merchants throughout the empire and the seizure of their property. Exactly why he did so remains an open question: it appears to have been inspired by strained relations between the Venetians and their commercial competitors, particularly the Genoese, whose quarter in Constantinople the Venetians attacked in 1170. But Manuel's own relations with the Venetians had soured as he pursued an aggressive policy towards Dalmatia, northern Italy and Sicily, largely in competition with the German emperor Frederick Barbarossa. The suspicion and mutual hostility which followed the arrest of 1171 demonstrated the error of the undertaking. Worse still, however, was the massacre of Latins in Constantinople which was ordered in 1182 by the usurper Andronikos Komnenos. Regarding the Latins as supporters of the regime he intended to oust, but also aware of the political capital to be made by such an action—which might be expected to garner the support of the urban populace, as well as bureaucrats and churchmen opposed to rapprochement with the West—Andronikos unleashed the resentment of his troops and the mob. Merchants' quarter was burned and plundered;

---

[64] Hendy, "'Byzantium, 1081-1204': the economy revisited," 26.

the hospital of the Knights of St John was sacked; and a Roman cardinal who happened to be in the city was murdered, among hundreds of others. Many have seen the events of 1204 as inspired, at least in part, by those of 1171 and 1182.

The spectacular growth in international trade, in which phenomenon the Italian merchants were a most visible and loathed agent, stretched far beyond Byzantium. But the importance of Byzantine ports and cities in this trade was certainly enhanced by Komnenian policies. Trade privileges were supported, as we have seen, by an entirely novel coinage, and gold was released from the state economy to circulate in the market economy by the massive expansion in grants of land-based tax privileges. These grants—some examples of which we have explored above—may even have bolstered local market economies, where the new masters of lands "encouraged" dependent peasants (*paroikoi*) to expand production. Whereas the state collected taxes in cash, those granted the right to taxation revenues most likely collected taxes and rent in kind, and sold the surplus to pay off obligations to the state (if they were not granted complete exemption). While such grants of land and tax privileges had a long history, and had grown significantly in the eleventh century, particularly in the realm of grants to monastic foundations, Alexios Komnenos was the first to use them systematically to reward his family and military. Thereafter, "in the twelfth century, the special donation ceased to be a mere fiscal instrument and became a fully developed system for the financing of state officials and officers. It was based on a change that made little practical difference to the beneficiary but was of colossal significance to the state: the donation was for life only and could not be inherited."[65] In this way, state land was not permanently alienated, and could be regranted. This system came to be known by well established terms for imperial "dispensation" or "foresight": *oikonomia* or *pronoia*.

There are a few references to state land being granted to soldiers, and subsequently regranted to other soldiers during Alexios' reign, for example in Macedonia.[66] However, examples become numerous during the reign of Manuel I, and the historian Niketas Choniates provides a clear explanation of the practice. Soldiers, some of whom were "barbarians" Choniates notes, collected from the peasants what they would

---

[65] Oikonomides, "Role of the Byzantine state in the economy," 1042.

[66] *Actes de Lavra*, I, nos. 56, 64; Oikonomides, "Role of the Byzantine state in the economy," 1043.

otherwise have paid to the state, and the emperor ceased to pay the soldiers from the treasury. This was no longer restricted to soldiers of exceptional merit—for example Gregory Pakourianos or Leo Kephalas—but was applied write large.[67] The de-centralization and de-monetization of the Byzantine taxation system had significant social consequences. Many peasant farmers now enjoyed the regular presence of a military "lord" who will have treated them as his dependents, although technically they remained state *paroikoi*. This may also, of course, have entailed benefits: an interested overseer willing to provide capital investment and protection for his benefice. But any such "patronage" was a significant departure from the days of peasant corporate responsibility through the village (*chorion*).[68]

Collapse, 1183-1204

Three key features of the mature Komnenian system, therefore, were an increased reliance on land and taxation privileges; an increased role of westerners, particularly Italian merchants, in the life of the empire and its capital; and the consolidation of the power and influence of a group of aristocrats related to the Komnenoi by blood or marriage. Each proved problematic in the last decades of the twelfth century; in combination they proved cataclysmic for the empire, provoking a series of invasions and rebellions which could not be resisted. Niketas Choniates offers the following explanation for the rapid decline in imperial fortunes: "It was the Komnenos family that was the major cause of the destruction of the empire. Because of their ambitions and their rebellions, she suffered the subjugation of provinces and cities and finally fell to her knees. These Komnenoi, who sojourned among barbarian peoples hostile to the Byzantines were the utter ruin of their empire, and whenever they attempted to seize and hold sway over public affairs, they were the most inept, unfit, and stupid of men."[69]

Here Choniates highlights the major problem with the Komnenian system: reliance on kinship ties led, over time, to internecine competition between powerful rivals with equally acceptable claims to rule. Very

---

[67] *Nicetae Choniatae historiae*, ed. J.-L. Van Dieten, CFHB 11/1 (Berlin, 1975), 208-9; Lemerle, *Agrarian History*, 230-6.

[68] Magdalino, *Empire of Manuel I*, 172, 175-7: "Manuel made a significant, positive and conscious contribution to the development of local, 'grass roots' feudalism."

[69] Choniates, ed. Van Dieten, 529.

early in his reign, Manuel I had survived at least three challenges to his authority by *sebastoi*.[70] The most notorious threats to have been reported were that of his confidant Alexios Axouch in 1167, and those of his cousin Andronikos in the 1150s and 1160s. Andronikos finally succeeded, in 1182-3, removing Manuel's young son Alexios II. Andronikos had a powerbase within the upper echelons of the aristocracy, favouring alternative members of Manuel's, and therefore his own, extended kin group. Ultimately, his regime, which commenced with the massacre of Latins, proved too cruel to secure widespead support, and too brief to implement substantial reforms. Just two years after his accession, Andronikos was deposed by one of the many cousins in his extended kingroup, Isaac Angelos, the great grandson of Alexios I. But Isaac, who had represented the interests of a group aristocractic families opposed to Andronikos fell victim to factionalism himself. He endured numerous coups during his ten-year reign before, in 1195, he was himself over-thrown. He was replaced by his own brother, Alexios III Angelos, who also suffered a series of coups. An attempt which nearly succeeded was engineered in 1200 by a certain John Komnenos "the Fat," who was the grandson of John II by his daughter Maria. His father was the sedi-tious confidant of Manuel I, the *sebastos* Alexios Axouch.

As the *sebastoi* competed for control of the centre, the periphery of the Empire slipped from their grasp. According to Angold, "there were now important local interests to protect. Their defence was increasingly in the hands of local ascendancies, often referred to as *archontes*. There was always a tendency at times of weak government or political crisis for each town to come under the control of a dynast or city boss, who was normally a representative of local interests."[71] Now *archontes* were in receipt of local taxation revenues, and increasingly reluctant to re-cognise ineffectual and ephemeral rulers in Constantinople. Several, in regions with no history of independent rule, claimed autonomy from Constantinople. Notable examples are Theodore Mangaphas in Philadelphia (near Sardis in Asia Minor) and Isaac Komnenos on Cyprus.[72] Others, with dormant traditions of independent rule, began to look elsewhere for patrons or symbols of power and prestige. Thus

---

[70] Magdalino, *Empire of Manuel Komnenos*, 217-20, suggests that we have probably under-estimated the prevalence of factionalism among the *sebastoi* during Manuel's reign. For documentation and analysis see J.-C. Cheynet, *Pouvoir et contestations à Byzance* (Paris, 1990), 106-10, 413-25.

[71] Angold, *Byzantine Empire*, 177.

[72] Angold, *Byzantine Empire*, 307-10.

in 1189 the rulers of Serbia and Bulgaria sought an alliance with the German emperor Frederick Barbarossa. They intended not merely to defend their own interests, as had several pretenders to the Hungarian throne during Manuel's reign, but to launch an attack on Constantinople itself. And in 1203-4, Kalojan (Ioannitsa), the ruler of the Bulgarian realm, rejected an offer by the Byzantine emperor, Alexios III, to recognise his imperial title and grant Bulgaria a patriarch. He preferred to negotiate with Pope Innocent III, and to receive his insignia of regnal and archiepiscopal—not imperial and patriarchal—office from Rome.[73]

In the same year, 1203-4, the Venetian fleet that ferried the forces of the Fourth Crusade to Constantinople carried the blinded Isaac II and his son Alexios. We know from western sources that Alexios offered the Venetians full payment of the sum specified in their contract with the leaders of the Fourth Crusade. Therefore, instead of ferrying the Latins directly to the Holy Land, the fleet sailed via Zadar to Constantinople in order to install Alexios on the imperial throne. Alexios IV was the archetypal Komnenian princeling, so loathed by Choniates: nurtured among barbarians, an inept and stupid man who brought utter ruin to the empire. With the sack of the city the imperial system collapsed, never fully to be reconstituted.

Provisional Reflections on Byzantium in a Broader Context

The foregoing analysis suggests that two phenomena were paramount in the transformation and collapse of the Byzantine imperial system: sustained economic and demographic growth, which the state failed fully to direct or to exploit; and the emergence of a powerful, self-conscious aristocracy, willing to exploit resources to the detriment of the state. This formulation proved to be fruitful in the context of a workshop exploring contemporary Eurasian civilizations, where similar phenomena were frequently evident, expressed as interactions between "state" and "elite." The natures of the "state" and "elite" vary and require close definition in each case. In the Byzantine case definitions are fairly straightforward. The Byzantine Greek term *politeia*, which might suitably be translated as "state," was an abstract concept which implied a developed system of public law and taxation. It was nearly identical with the *basileia*, or imperial authority, centred on the emperor, who "personified the state and was the repository of political and judicial authority [and]

---

[73] Stephenson, *Byzantium's Balkan Frontier*, 279-81, 305-12.

was also the source of all grace and responsible for the implementation of the law" and the collection of taxes.[74] The Byzantine "elite" was evidently the aristocracy, known to us through legislation as the "powerful," and to each other by family names and ties of blood and marriage. We no longer seek to distinguish between "civilian" and "military" aristocracies, for it is clear that these were two elements of the same "elite." The aristocrats were officers of the state, but operated also, and increasingly, in their own interests. The culmination of this process was the establishment of imperial government by and for the Komnenos family.

At this point, a further formulation suggested by R.I. Moore is useful. The interest of the "elite" was to undermine the state sufficiently to benefit from its weakness; but not to weaken it so substantially that it collapsed in the face of internal and external pressures. In the Byzantine case, the internal pressures were applied by those deprived of access to resources (in Moore's formulation, the poor), but also by aristocrats seeking greater benefits in competition with each other. External pressures were applied by neighbouring powers, which, when applied concurrently, provoked periods of crisis. Two periods of crisis, therefore, can be discerned: the first began in 1071 and ended in 1091-2, when aristocrats competed for the throne even as the state faced invasions from both east and west; the second period commenced in 1183-6, and ended in 1204, when once again competition for control of the throne provoked provincial rebellions in the north and east, and foreign invasions from the west. The Byzantine state recovered from the first period only through extensive reforms of the imperial system. The consequences of these reforms were to render the state unable to recover from the second period of crisis, when it succumbed to the confluence of internal and external pressures.

The analysis presented here is impoverished in a number of respects, focusing exclusively on "interlinked transformations in socio-economic and political practices," and paying scant regard to "profound change[s] in the nature of discursive practices."[75] Unfortunately, it is not feasible

---

[74] D. Jacoby, "The encounter of two societies: western conquerors and Byzantines in the Peloponnesos after the Fourth Crusade," *American Historical Review* 18 (1973), 875; quoted by M. Angold, "The Byzantine state on the eve of the battle of Manzikert," *Byzantinische Forschungen* 16 (1991), 9-34 at 9-10. See now G. Dagron, *Emperor and Priest. The Imperial Office in Byzantium* (Cambridge, 2003).

[75] B. Wittrock, "Cultural crystallization and conceptual change: modernity, axiality and meaning in history," in *Zeit, Geschichte und Politik. Zum achtzigsten Geburtstag von Reinhard Koselleck*, ed. E. Konttinen et al. (Jyväskylä, 2003), 105-34 at 106.

in this short paper to "search for more sensitive modes of representation that highlight cultural and institutional legacies," and hence "go beyond a mere amassing of interesting insights."[76] I trust, however, that the analysis offered here facilitates further speculation by historical sociologists, to augment preliminary investigations by Arnason.[77] Can Byzantium be said to have shared in an ecumenical renaissance, as per Wittrock's definition?[78] That is, did it share in a set of transformations occurring between the ninth and thirteenth centuries CE which led to "intense patterns of intellectual reflexivity"?[79] One might certainly argue for such a scenario in the empire of the ninth and early tenth centuries. However, from the later tenth century Byzantium took a different path. If it participated in such an ecumenical renaissance in the eleventh and twelfth centuries, it did so as the principal casualty of the emergence of Europe and resurgent Islam.

---

[76] Wittrock, "Cultural crystallization," 119; B. Wittrock, "Social theory and global history: the three cultural crystallizations," *Thesis Eleven* 65 (May 2001), 27-50 at 32.

[77] J. Arnason, "Approaching Byzantium: identity, predicament and afterlife," *Thesis Eleven* 62 (August, 2000), 39-69; See also Wittrock, "Social theory and global history," 39-40, which demonstrates a willingness to incorporate Byzantium into a broader analysis.

[78] Wittrock, "Social theory and global history," 37-40.

[79] Wittrock, "Social theory and global history," 38.

III. CIVILIZATIONS,
TRANSFORMATIONS, ENCOUNTERS

TRANSFORMATION OF THE ISLAMICATE CIVILIZATION: A TURNING-POINT IN THE THIRTEENTH CENTURY?

SAID AMIR ARJOMAND

ABSTRACT

The possibility of a Eurasian ecumenical renaissance is examined in relation to the transformation of the Islamicate civilization in the East in the thirteenth and four-teenth centuries. The focus of the analysis is on the possibilities and limits for self-government and role of civic associations. The long-term effects and transformative potential of the urban and constitutional reforms of the late ʿAbbasid Caliph al-Nāsir at the beginning of the thirteenth century are assessed in the context of instances of city government during the half century following the disintegration of the Il-Khanid Empire in the latter part of 1330s. The final section of the essay on urban politics in fourteenth-century Iran highlights the hindrances on the Islamicate path to political modernity.

Until recently, the dominant paradigm for comparative civilizational analysis had sought to explain the distinctiveness of the Western pat-tern of development (capitalism and democracy) in terms of the *absence* of certain preconditions. Perhaps the most compelling argument along these lines was put forward by Benjamin Nelson, who highlighted the parting of the paths of development in the High Middle Ages.[1] One unsolved problem in this approach is due to the fact that no system-atic distinction is made between the contingent historical factors in Western development and what could plausibly be considered non-con-tingent and necessary. A novel approach to comparative civilizational analysis is put forward by Pollock[2] and by Wittrock, who has provoca-tively suggested the possibility of an ecumenical renaissance in the thir-teenth century.[3] The new approach focuses on *common patterns* of

---

[1] B. Nelson, *On the Road to Modernity* (Totowa, NJ: Rowman & Littlefield, 1981).
[2] S. Pollock, "India in the Vernacular Millennium: Literary Culture and Polity, 1000-1500," *Daedalus*, 127.3 (1998), 41-74.
[3] B. Wittrock, "Social Theory and Global History. The Periods of Cultural Crystal-lization," *Thesis Eleven*, 65 (2001), 27-50.

development across Eurasian civilizations. The search for common patterns turns to highlighting inter-civilizational encounters as an easy way of explaining commonalities. However, other kinds of explanations are also necessary for this approach. Conversely, the approach focusing on divergent paths is not inconsistent with recognition of the impact of inter-civilizational contacts. In fact, Nelson emphasized the importance of such contacts with the Islamicate civilization as triggers setting the West on the road to modernity.

In fact, as the dichotomy of the uniquely dynamic West versus the stagnant rest is generally discarded, I hope we can all agree that there are common features and some or many differences in the developmental trajectories of different civilizations and take dialogical positions by assigning different weights to commonalities and differences. Accordingly, I propose a systematic comparison of the contrasting directions of Islamicate and Western developmental paths. The Western developmental path should itself be analyzed as "a changing constellation of different and sometimes rival rationalities," as should the Islamicate trajectory.[4] Furthermore, directionality of social change can only be meaningfully assessed in terms of cultural significance. Here, value-relevance will inevitably be among our regulative principles of research and determine the choice of problematics. The regulative values in my enquiry should be evident as those associated with modernity which I take to have universal cultural significance and therefore relevance for our generation.

Among the students of Islam, Marshall Hodgson sought to accommodate both unity and diversity by setting the trajectory of the Islamicate civilization in the context of the ancient urban civilization of western Eurasia. He should be credited for emphasizing multiple tensions among various components of the latter, which can be read as clashes among Islamicate rationalities. Hodgson's ideal-type of Islamic "contractualism," in contrast to Western "corporatism," couples the "individualism" of the Islamic law, regulating socio-economic and hypothetically also the political relations on the basis of contracts among individuals, and its "moralism."[5] The latter characteristic impedes the formal rationalization of law which is necessary for modern socio-economic and political organiza-

---

[4] J. P. Arnason, "East and West: From Invidious Dichotomy to Incomplete Deconstruction" in G. Delanhy, E. Isin and M. Somers, eds, *Handbook of Historical Sociology* (London: Sage, 2003).

[5] M. G. S. Hodgson, *The Venture of Islam* (Chicago: University of Chicago Press, 1974), 2:329-68.

tion. According to Hodgson, therefore, Islamic law facilitated great social mobility but not institutional development. The Shariʿa ignored public law and state action, and left too little room for initiative to the Caliph in theory. Consequently, social activism tended to take the form of revivalist movements outside the framework of the state and of governmental institutions.

It should be noted that this ideal-typical contrast between Islam and Christianity contrasting Islam and Christianity in ahistorical terms is included in the medieval section of Hodgson's posthumously edited *Venture of Islam,* and is somewhat at odds with his fully historicized picture of the Islamicate civilization, comprising different configurations in "the age of Caliphal absolutism," "the Shiʿite Century," "the military-patronage system" of the Turko-Mongolian period and the era of "the gun-powder empires," and so on. I suspect that it was only intended for the medieval era and not as a general, trans-historical model. Be that as it may, Hodgson's model of the invariant contractualism of Islam shares the ahistorical characteristic of Schluchter's holistic view of rationalism as the atemporal property of entire civilizations,[6] both being similarly inspired by Max Weber's holistic characterization of "Western rationalism" in the introduction to his collected works on the world religions in 1920. Building on Hodgson, Eisenstadt has also offered an interesting model of the dynamics of the relationship between the public sphere, the state and religio-political movements in Muslim societies.[7] The problem with all these broad ideal-types of entire civilizations is their lack of historicity. To be assessed empirically, these models must be historicized.

In Hodgson, however, we also find a theoretically more challenging implicit argument that the Islamicate civilization was on the verge of a breakthrough to modernity, albeit of its own kind, at the time of the Mongol invasion—i.e. in the same period Nelson places the (divergent) inception of modernity in the West. (And he implies the Mongol

[6] W. Schluchter, "The Paradox of Rationalization: On the Relation of Ethics and World," in G. Roth and W. Schluchter, *Max Weber's Vision of History. Ethics and Methods.* (Berkeley & Los Angeles: University of California Press, 1979), and *The Rise of Western Rationalism. Max Weber's Developmental History,* Translated by G. Roth (Berkeley & Los Angeles: University of California Press, 1981).

[7] S. N. Eisenstadt, "Concluding Remarks: Public Sphere, Civil Society, and Political Dynamics in Islamic Societies," in M. Hoexter, S. N. Eisenstadt and N. Levtzion, eds, *The Public Sphere in Muslim Societies* (Albany: State University of New York Press, 2002), 139-61.

devastation spoiled it!) This analysis of the long reign of the late 'Abbasid Caliph, al-Nāsir [li-Din Allah] (1180-1225), *is* historicized. It combines this "contractualism" with an emphasis on the urban and mercantile character of medieval Islamicate civilization and the development of guilds, on the one hand, and the integrative political and religious policies of the Caliphate as its symbolic center. To assess Hodgson's thesis, I will examine al-Nasir's reign in the perspective of institutional developments in the twelfth to fourteenth centuries as a period of crystallization and pose the counterfactual question: what if his policies had succeeded? As the continuities in institutional development outweigh the change brought about by the Mongol invasion, I will propose an alternative framework (to Hodgson's) for comparing the directionality of institutional change in the Western and Islamicate civilizations.

Civic Agency and its Legal Framework

It was Max Weber who identified the cultural significance of the medieval European cities by highlighting their contribution to the Western developmental trajectory, his regulative value-ideas being capitalism and democracy. In a 1917 address, Weber added democratic legitimacy to his three types, and identified as its specific social career the *"sociological formation of the Occidental city."*[8] This is evident in the key contrasts between Occidental and Oriental cities, the foremost being that only in the West the bourgeoisie with a distinct social status develops.[9] Weber distinguished three meanings of citizenship which, in an uncharacteristically anti-comparative manner, he attributed exclusively to the Western developmental pattern. Leaving aside the political sense of membership in the modern nation-state, citizen can mean the burgher as the member of a unitary urban community in possession of "its own law and court and of an autonomous administration of whatever extent" who participates

---

[8] Cited in italics by W. Schluchter, "Hindrances to Modernity: Max Weber on Islam," in T. E. Huff & W. Schluchter, eds, *Max Weber and Islam* (New Brunswick: Transaction Publishers, 1999), 136 n. 192.

[9] "Den "Bürger" im ständischen Sinn gab es schon vor der Entwincklung des spezifisch abendländischen Kapitalismus. Aber freilich: nur im Abendlande." (Cited in H. Bruhns, "La ville bourgeoise et l'émergence du capitalisme moderne. Max Weber: Die Stadt (1913/14-1921)," in B. Lepetit & C. Topalov, eds, *La ville des sciences socials* [Paris: Belin, 2001], 60-61) The second distinctive feature is the absence in the Oriental city of "the specific political character (politischer Sondercharakter)." The Ancient and the Oriental cities do have politically defined characteristics, but those are other than the specific ones of the Occidental city.

in choice of administrative officials." Or, it can mean the bourgeois as a status group of "persons of property and culture" enjoying certain social prestige.[10] The second sense only had one dimension, but the first has at least two dimensions which must be unpacked for comparative purposes.

Let us take the issue of urban community first. Inspired by Weber and drawing his evidence from the pattern of strife in medieval Mamluk cities, Ira Lapidus has put forward the influential thesis that "the Islamic city" lacked a sense of urban community and consisted of an agglomeration of mutually hostile city-quarters.[11] We do have evidence of factional strife in the cities of medieval Iran.[12] During the decade after al-Nāsir's death, Isfahan was torn by internal strife between the Hanafis and the Shāfi'is, and the latter in fact delivered the city to the Mongols in the hope of their rival's destruction.[13] For that matter, Lane argues persuasively that the initial destruction and plundering of Baghdad before its fall to the Mongol conqueror, Hülegü, in 1258 was the result of sectarian strife between the Shi'ites and the Sunnis.[14] But we are still entitled to ask if there is also an overarching sense of urban community? It is not a bad idea to take philology as a starting point. The word *hamshahri* (fellow-burgher/city-dweller) is found in the oldest Persian texts and remains a very common word in Persian and Turkish. Nor can there be any doubt that the major cities had a strong historical memory, recorded in local histories, biographies of their learned men and surveys of their colleges, mosques and charitable foundations since the medieval period. Furthermore, the Kadi, the market police and the official preacher at the congregational mosques, as well as the mayor (*ra'is*) in the East, though appointed by the government, were men of the city and shared in its local pride.[15] But it was otherwise with the existence of elected city officials and municipal self-government. Cities in the Islamicate world had no elected officials and no political autonomy.

---

[10] M. Weber, *General Economic History* (New Brunswick: Transaction Books, 1981 [1927]), 315, 318.

[11] I. M. Lapidus, "Muslim Urban Society in Mamluk Syria," in A. H. Hourani and S. M. Stern, eds, *The Islamic City* (Philadelphia: University of Pennsylvania Press, 1970), 195-205.

[12] C. Cahen, *Mouvements populaires et autonomisme urbain dans l'Asie musulmane du moyen âge* (Leiden: E. J. Brill, 1959), 27-29.

[13] J. E. Woods, "A Notes on the Mongol Capture of Isfahan," *Journal of Near Eastern Studies*, 36.1 (197), 50.

[14] G. Lane, *Early Mongol Rule in Thirteenth Century Iran. A Persian renaissance* (London: Routledge Curzon, 2003), 31-34.

[15] Cahen, *Mouvements populaires*, 54, 76-79.

The influential Oxford symposium on *The Islamic City* (1970) proposed a monocausal explanation for arrested development of urban life—indeed for the failure of Islam to develop modernity—that has lingered on:[16] the individualism of Islamic law, which can conceive no intermediate legal personality between the individual and the *umma* (universal community of believers).[17] The Shari'a is accordingly said to withhold recognition to the most crucial such intermediary, the city. Although I consider the character of Islamic law very important, I think this alleged individualism misses its crucial feature. According to this theory, the individual freedom of action, contractual obligations, notably commercial partnerships and transactions in private property are legally protected by the Shari'a, but free and autonomous civic and public action is severely restricted because no intermediaries between the individual and the universal *umma* are recognized in the Islamic law.

I have argued against this view elsewhere, maintaining instead that a sphere of autonomy and universality along the lines of Hegel's conceptual definition of civil society was in fact constituted and protected by the Shari'a, in particular by the law of endowments (*waqf*).[18] The (civil) law of *waqf* served as the basis for the creation of a vast sphere of educational and charitable activity; and the same civil law granted the ruler, the royal family and the highest office-holders an instrument of public policy which they could activate as individual agents.[19] I should add that I also treated the strength of that civil society to be historically variable, as protection by the law is one factor among many, and in fact showed that it was overwhelmed by a contrary development or trend in nomadic state formation after the eleventh century.

The assertion of the absence of intermediaries between the individual and the *umma* has also been vigorously refuted with reference to the Ottoman guilds by Haim Gerber, who states that "the guild system

---

[16] T. Kuran, "Islamic Influences on the Ottoman Guilds," in K. Çiçek, ed., *The Great Ottoman-Turkish Civilization*, vol. 2: *Economy and Society*, (Ankara: Yeni Turkiye, 2000).

[17] A. H. Hourani, "Introduction," and S. M. Stern, "The Constitution of the Islamic City," in A. H. Hourani and S. M. Stern, eds, *The Islamic City* (Philadelphia: University of Pennsylvania Press, 1970).

[18] S. A. Arjomand, "The Law, Agency and Policy in Medieval Islamic Society: Development of the Institutions of Learning from the Tenth to the Fifteenth Century," *Comparative Studies in Society and History*, 41.2 (1999), 263-93.

[19] A very important implication of this Islamic legal system is that the private/public distinction of the Roman Law applies very imperfectly, and the line between the two spheres must be drawn very differently.

enjoyed a wide measure of autonomy and . . . its legal basis was customary law."[20] Gerber is absolutely right that guilds were covered by customary law, which was in turn recognized by the Shari'a. The agency of guilds was made licit as custom and thus granted autonomy by the legal order in principle. The legal position of the city is, however, more complicated.

There was no independent municipal law, but the Islamic law did contain regulations for urban life. These have been examined by Brunschvig, who shows certain strong rights (including the right of preemption among the Hanafis) of neighbors, which could only have encouraged urban solidarity. On the other hand, he points out that the question of roads was always approached from the viewpoint of private property, and was not linked to public law.[21] Johansen (1981-82) demonstrates that the city was a legal entity and presents several competing definitions of the "comprehensive city" (al-misr al-jāmi'), centered on its congregational mosque and defining its limits.[22] It is interesting to note that the legal argument that there should be a single Friday mosque for each city to preserve its communal unity, which still persisted in one 12th-century jurists' restriction of the number to two, no longer corresponded to reality as several Friday mosques appeared in the city quarters.[23] The city was also under a unified jurisdiction of a single Kadi.[24] In short, the allegation of the complete lack of recognition of the city as a legal entity and indifference toward it in Islamic law must be rejected. The provisions of the Shari'a concerning the city, however, fall far short of the contemporary municipal constitutions of Western Europe as a legacy of Roman Law.

To demonstrate this, let me move to the furthermost western frontier of the Islamicate world. A revealing encounter between the politico-legal traditions of the two civilizations took place with the reconquests of Portugal and Castile (Andalusia) in the latter part of the twelfth and

---

[20] H. Gerber, *State, Society and Law in Islam. Ottoman Law in Comparative Perspective* (Albany: State University of New York Press, 1994), 119.

[21] R. Brunschvig, "Urbanisme médiéval et droit musulman," in *Études d'Islamologie* (Paris: Maisonneuve et Larose, 1976), 2:7-35, especially at 11.

[22] B. Johansen, "The All-Embracing Town and its Mosques," *Revue de l'Occident Musulman et de lal Méditerranée*, 32 (1981-82), 139-61.

[23] Johansen, "All-Embracing Town," 150.

[24] With the expansion of the imperial city of Baghdad in the late eighth and early ninth century and the appearance of additional congregational mosques, we also find the creation of a second and a third Kadiship (Duri 1980:56).

through the thirteenth centuries,[25] and of Aragon under James I (1213-76). This encounter brought certain *mudéjar* (Spanish Muslim) communities into a relationship of vassalage with the Christian rulers who extended the Iberian municipal law (*fueros*) to them. James I, for example, granted his Muslim subject communities the *fuero* of Cuenca, incorporating the Muslim offices.[26] He thus created self-governing communities with a legal constitution. Within the feudal world in which they lived, *mudéjar* individuals and communities won for themselves a political niche of considerable autonomy. Each *aljama* (community) chose its own officials, notably the *qadi* (*alcalde*, Span., judge), the *sahib al-madina* (*zalmedina*, Span.), who served as the *aljama*'s principal peace officer, and the *muhtasib* (*almutazaf*, Span., market police).[27] When we compare this situation, which lasted for decades, with the roughly contemporary cases of municipal self-rule on the other side of the Mediterranean as described by Ibn Khaldun, the latter prove to be de facto, transitional and by default.

Ibn Khaldun consistently explains them as resulting from the disintegration of the central authority of the ruling dynasty, which necessitated an ad hoc resort to local councils (*shurā*).[28] He applies his model of the disintegration of central authority which followed the temporary emergence of Shurā to the establishment of the first dynasty of feudal lords/kings (*muluk al-tawā'ef* or *reyes de taifas*) by Ibn 'Abbād, the Kadi of Seville, after the disintegration of the Caliphate of Cordova in early eleventh century. The Kadi was also, like his father, the vizier of Seville and his assumption of power follows the widespread usurpation of authority by the chamberlains and other office-holders of the Caliphate of Cordova. After a series of intercity alliances and warfare, the 'Abbadid house gained control of the city Cordova which itself came to domi-

---

[25] J. F. O'Callaghan, "The Mudejars of Castile and Portugal in the Twelfth and Thirteenth Centuries," in J. M. Powell, ed., *Muslims under Latin Rule, 1100-1300*, Princeton University Press, 1990), 20-30.

[26] *The Code of Cuenca. Municipal Law on the Twelfth-Century Castilian Frontier*, J. F. Powers, tr. with an Introduction (Philadelphia: University of Pennsylvania Press, 2000).

[27] J. D. Kagay, "The Essential Enemy: The Image of the Muslim as Adversary and Vassal in the Law and Literature of the Medieval Crown of Aragon," in Frassetto M. & Blanks, D. R., eds, *Western views of Islam in Medieval and Early Modern Europe*, London: Macmillan, 1999), 126.

[28] 'Abd al-Rahmān Ibn Khaldun, *Tārikh (Kitāb al-ʿibar)* (Beirut: Dār al-kutub ʿIlmiyya, 1992), 6:370, 490-500, 506-7, 510-39; French tr. by Baron de Slane, *Histoire des Berbères* (Paris: Librarie Orientaliste Paul Geuthner, 1999 [1840]), 2:352, 3:91-113, 119-22, 124-76.

nate Western Andalusia under the Kadi's son, who assumed the title of al-Mu'tadid (1042-70/433-461). Lack of legitimacy, however, forced al-Mu'tadid to make the improbable claim that he had found the deceased last Cordova Caliph, Hishām, and was ruling on his behalf,[29] and the 'Abbādid government could in no way be conceived as municipal self-rule. Ibn Khaldun, however, uses the term *shurā* for the brief period at the beginning (1013/414) when the Kadi ousted the governor of Seville and shared power with two other officials "until he became autocratic (*istabadda*) over them, organized an army but did not resign his Kadiship."[30] As Stern correctly points out, earlier historians do not use the term.[31] The Moroccan Muhammad b. Ibrāhim (d. 1169/564), to take a different example from those cited by Stern, speaks of the period of the triumvirate as "partnership in rule" until Ibn 'Abbād gathered money and troops and began to exercise his autocracy. Then he "pounced on the two men, thus breaking with his partners."[32]

In his history of the Maghreb, Ibn Khaldun mentions three or four patrician families for a handful of cities but the council is typically dominated by one or two members of one patrician family at the time, in alliance with the Hafsid ruler of Tunis or one of the rival Sultans or with a nomadic tribal leader of the region.[33] Much of Ibn Khaldun's information is contemporary, covering the three decades marked by the disintegration of central authority following the death of the Hafsid Sultan Abu Bakr of Tunis in 1346/747.[34] Reference to the people of the city in Ibn Khaldun are very rare. In one instance, the populace of Righ is mobilized, in alliance the nomadic tribes, by a call to the Sunna (Tradition of the Prophet) in an unsuccessful siege of the city of Biskra. In another, a member of the leading patrician family associates with the plebeians to gain control of the city of Tawzar.[35] In yet a third

---

[29] E. Lévi-Provençal, "'Abbādids," *Encyclopedia of Islam*, new ed. (E. J. Brill, 1960), 1:6.

[30] Ibn Khaldun, *Tārikh*, 4:187.

[31] Stern, "Constitution," 33 n. 16.

[32] R. P. A. Dozy, *Scriptorum Arabum loci deAbbadidis* (Hildesheim: Georg Olms Verlag, 1992 [1846]), 4.

[33] Ibn Khaldun, *Tārikh*, 6, 519-22, 526-27, 530; French tr., 3:141-45, 154-55, 158-60.

[34] This includes the history of the patrician families of the cities of Jarid and Zab from the latter part of the thirteenth and throughout the fourteenth century down to the time of his writing in the early 1380s. (Ibn Khaldun, *Tārikh*, 6:510-39; French tr. 3:124-76).

[35] Ibn Khaldun, *Tārikh*, 6:516-21; French tr. 3:135-43.

instance, Ibn Khaldun describe the following of two patrician brothers in a rebellion suppressed around 1380, not long before the time of his writing, as "the lowly ruffians and rabble" and "the riff-raff."[36]

As Stern remarks, the term *shurā* is used both in the abstract—[as central authority disintegrated,] "it became a matter of consultation"— and to refer to the municipal council. In the latter sense, a more informal term, *mashyakha* (elderly notables), is often substituted for it.[37] *Shurā* may thus be taken as Ibn Khaldun's conceptual term for collective rule and does not connote a constitutional structure. The councils, when and if constituted, lacked a formal character and did not put down their resolutions in writing. Nor is there any evidence of political action by guilds or other urban corporations. The nomadic tribes of the region, by contrast, are frequently drawn into strife within and between cities. Temporary patrician rule in the cities collapses with the reassertion of central authority without any constitutional development of municipal autonomy.

The Decisive Counterfactual: Caliph al-Nāsir and Civic Associations

Under the interpenetrating influences of Weber and Elias, the importance of "state-formation" for intra-civilizational and other long-term developmental processes has been generally recognized.[38] We need to broaden our notion by thinking of changes in the structure of authority— i.e. hierocracy/church formation alongside that of the state. In fact, the main change in authority structure in Western Europe begins with Gregory VII and the investiture contest and the proclamation of papal monarchy, with the incipient state formation becoming the dominant trend only in the subsequent period. And by all accounts, it was the contest between empire and papacy that made possible the growth of independent cities and contributed to the legal development of feudalism. The reign of the Caliphate al-Nāsir begins in a situation of unusual fragmentation of authority at the center of the Islamic world which did not reoccur and which approximates, despite obvious differences, the contemporary Western church-state dualism. His policy of reviving the

---

[36] Ibn Khaldun, *Tārikh*, 6:493, 526.
[37] Stern, "Constitution", 33-36.
[38] E. Ikegami, *The Taming of the Samurai. Honorific Individualism and the Making of Modern Japan* (Cambridge, MA: Harvard University Press, 1995); and Arnason, "Eurasian Transformations" in this volume.

Caliphate and extending its authority to the political realm in Baghdad can fruitfully be compared to the pursuit of papal monarchy in Rome. But as the relation between religious and political authority in Islam is riddled with misconceptions, I must begin with a sketch of the structure of authority in the late twelfth century. It will then be followed by an examination of al-Nāsir's urban policy in the light of the Weberian thesis on the centrality of medieval urban autonomy to the Western developmental trajectory.

An irreversible bifurcation of supreme authority into Caliphate and Sultanate (monarchy) began with the Buyid (Arabized as Buwayhid) seizure of power in Baghdad in the mid-tenth century CE, and lasted for a little over three centuries to the mid-thirteenth Century (1258, to be precise). The Caliphate and monarchy were different concepts and drew on two different political theories. Monarchy was the older Near Eastern concept, and the imperial (post-Medina) conception of the Caliphate was elaborated with increasing reference to it. I have argued that a "theory of the two powers" had been in the making since the 'Abbasid revolution: the ethico-legal order grew around the idea of the Shari'a, independently and at the same time as the conception of the political order as monarchy.[39] After the mid-tenth century bifurcation of supreme authority into Caliphate and Sultanate, attempts were made to synthesize the two sets of political ideas and theories. The pair of well-known mid-eleventh century revisions of the theory of Caliphate under the identical title of al-Ahkām al-Sultāniyya, integrated monarchy into it as "authority (emirate) by seizure."

The condition of dual sovereignty in Baghdad had continued unchanged, with the Seljuk Sultans displacing the Buyids in 1055. By the second half of the twelfth century, the differentiation of the two powers had become much clearer, and the Seljuks forcefully maintained that the function of the Caliph as the Imam of the community of believers (umma) was restricted to the religious sphere.[40] Al-Nasir tried to reverse this well-entrenched trend through an innovative and long sustained policy of invigorating and controlling urban associations as an institutional mechanism for mobilizing support for the Caliphate throughout the Muslim world. His attempt to end the condition of dual sovereignty

---

[39] S. A. Arjomand, "Medieval Persianate Political Thought," *Studies on Persiante Societies*, 1 (2003), 5-34.

[40] A. Hartmann, "al-Nāsir li-Din Allāh," *Encyclopedia of Islam* (Leiden: E. J. Brill, 1993), 7:109.

was initially successful. He demolished the Seljuk palace in Baghdad in
1187, and had the last main-line Seljuk Sultan, Togril III, defeated and
killed at the age of 25 in 1193. But trouble began immediately with
the rival dynasty of Khwārazm-shāhs from Central Asia, whom al-Nāsir
had used as an ally to destroy the Seljuks. The Khwārazm-shāh Tekish
soon filled the place of the Seljuk Sultan and insisted on the right of
the Sultan to exercise secular power. After his death in 1200, his son,
Mohammad II, went even further and broke with the ʿAbbasid Caliphate
altogether, setting up a puppet Caliph, who was a descendant of ʿAli
and whose name was put on the coins and in the Friday sermon instead
of al-Nāsir.[41]

What al-Nāsir's called "the rightly-guided mission" (al-daʿwa al-hādiya)
and I would call his constitutional policy had two important aspects:
one legal, the other sociological. On the legal front, he sought to
strengthen autocracy by bringing the Sunni theory of the Caliphate
closer to the Shiʿite doctrine of the Imamate. At the sociological level,
his goal was the wedding of Sufi orders and the Futuwwa associations
of the men and youths of the city-quarters, including the artisans. Both
these policies also promoted the integration of the Shiʿite sectarians to
the Sunni body politic, especially as the Futuwwa culture idealized the
first Shiʿite Imam, ʿAli. Although the Caliph himself was the architect
of this integrated constitutional policy, a critical role in the formulation
of its ideology was played by his counselor and spiritual master, Shaykh
ʿOmar Sohravardi.

As opposed to the traditional Sunni idea of the Caliph as the defender
of the Shariʿa, Sohravardi's theory of the Caliphate primarily presented
the Caliph as the Imam who was the intermediary between God and
the community of believers and an inspired interpreter of His Law (as
in the Shiʿite doctrine);[42] and secondarily considered the Caliph selected
by God for [spiritual] perfection (kamāl), and constructed his relationship to the subjects on the model of a spiritual master and his disciples (as in Sufism). The traditional reference to the consensus of the
community (ijmāʿ) was dropped altogether in this theory.[43] Consequently,

---

[41] Hartmann, "al-Nāsir," 997.

[42] To make good this claim as the heir to "the heritage of Prophecy" (mirāth al-
nubuwwa), Caliph al-Nāsir published and widely disseminated a collection of the Prophetic
Traditions he considered authentic. See A. Hartmann, an-Nāsir li-Din Allāh (1180-1225).
Poltik, Religion, Kultur in der späten ʿAbbāsidenzeit, (Berlin: Walter de Gruyter, 1975), 216-32.

[43] Hartmann, an-Nāsir li-Din Allāh, 111-21, 226.

the autocracy of the Caliph was enhanced in a charismatic and anti-legalistic direction.

The centerpiece of al-Nāsir's innovative urban policy, on the other hand, was the wedding of Sufism and the Futuwwa, associations of the men and youths of the city-quarters, including the artisans. He sought to reorganize sports, hunting of birds with bows and pigeon-raising, of which he was an active practitioner, within an ethical framework of the promotion of Futuwwa virtues. The latter were in turn integrated with Sufism. Gibb highlighted an irreconcilable conflict and tension between the legalistic approach of the ulema, which made of Islam "a religion of the mind" that left the masses cold, and the emotional approach of the Sufis, which created a popular "religion of the heart."[44] Al-Nāsir, whose authority as the head of the hierarchy of ulema and kadis was undisputed, sought to turn Sufism into an official organization of popular Islam under the control of the Caliph. At the same time, he attempted to tie urban organizations to Sohravardi's Sufi order.

It will be recalled that the Franciscan and Dominican orders which built their convents in the cities of Western Europe served the Papacy as a remarkable instrument to control popular religion and stem the sectarian tide until the Reformation. Al-Nāsir studied Islamic law and had himself certified as a doctor (*mujtahid*) in all the four Sunni (ortho-dox) schools of law. Nor did he neglect supporting the colleges (*madrasas*) and orthodox learning, but added public meetings and debates at Sufi convents to the repertoire of activities in the public sphere. This inge-nious meeting point of the college and the convent could have had tremendous consequences for the trajectory of Islamicate development. He even brought the radical Shi'ite Ismā'ili sectarians back to the fold of an official, Caliphal Islam, reinforced by Sufism, and made a major attempt to reconcile the moderate, Twelver Shi'a, and the Sunnis, and appointed many Twelvers viziers. Last but not least, he recruited the artisans and urban youths into the Futuwwa, constituted as an order of chivalry with ranks and elaborate ceremonies, into which he recruited the princes of the Islamicate world according to his international pol-icy of reassertion of Caliphal suzerainty over the entire community of believers. Al-Nāsir himself had been initiated early in his reign, and in 1207 he unified all Futuwwa orders as "the purified Futuwwa," and declared himself its supreme head (*qibla*) and pole (*qutb*), appropriating

---

[44] H. A. R. Gibb, *Mohammedanism* (Oxford University Press, 1948).

these terms from Sufism. Hunting of birds and other sports were also brought under the Caliph's supervision, and he established his monopoly over raising pigeons, to be used both for communication and for gifts to new nobility who were ranked according to the kind of pigeon they formally received from the Caliph. Members of the unified Futuwwa order called each other "comrade" (*rafiq*), the term being appropriated from the Ismaʿilis. Leaders of the guilds and city-quarters were invested with the Futuwwa trousers (*shalwār*) and admitted to different ranks. Missionaries (another idea taken from the Ismaʿilis) were sent out to spread the Caliph's "rightly-guided mission" and promote his new integrated order. The trousers and paraphernalia of investiture were sent to Muslim princes from northern India to Egypt, and the entire subjects of the prince were admitted to the Futuwwa order upon his investiture! The one group he wished to exclude from the unified community was the philosophers, whose libraries in Baghdad were burned.[45]

Differences notwithstanding, all this surely amounts to a remarkable and totally independently conceived analogue to the Papal policies of alliances with the cities, support for the Dominican and Franciscan Orders and the promotion of Papal monarchy. It was an ambitious attempt "to translate civilizational unity into an integrative power structure," and it failed even more clearly and faster than the two parallel Western attempts, namely the Holy Roman Empire and papal monarchy.[46]

The only official corporate bodies under the ʿAbbasid Caliphate were the two estates of nobility (*ashrāf*), the ʿAbbasids and the ʿAlids (Tālibids), whose members received pensions and were supervised by an alderman (*naqib*). The aldermen were among the most prominent members of the ruling elite in Baghdad.[47] Futuwwa (chivalry) referred to organizations of young men and was most probably of Iranian origin, akin to if not identical with groupings such as the *ʿayyārān* in Iran and *ahdāth* in Syria. Already in the eleventh century, there was a special Kadi in charge of *ʿayyārān* (also called *fityān*, from the same roots as *futuwwa*) in Baghdad, and we hear him criticized for his toleration of pederasty.[48] The *ahdāth*

---

[45] Hartmann, *an-Nāsir li-Din Allāh*, ch. 2; M. J. Mahjub, "Introduction" to Vaez-e Kāshefi, Mollā Hosayn, *Fotovvatnāma-ye Soltāni* (Tehran: Bonyād-e Farhang-e Irān, 1971/1350), 52-59.

[46] See Arnason, "Eurasian Transformations" in this volume.

[47] A. A. Duri, "Governmental Institutions," in R. B. Serjeant, ed., *The Islamic City* (Paris: Unesco, 1980), 62-63.

[48] Mahjub, "Introduction," 20-21, 60.

in Syria and Palestine appear to have been even better organized and enjoyed some official recognition, with their chief (ra'is) collecting a protection tax (himāyāt) on their behalf in eleventh and twelfth century Damascus, Aleppo and Jerusalem. The 'ayyārān played an important role in the power struggle between the 'Abbasid Caliph and the Seljuk Sultan in Baghdad during the decades preceding al-Nasir's accession to Caliphate.[49] Cahen is right is asserting that a family resemblance between these urban groups and the militias of the European cities in the eleventh century cannot be denied.[50]

In support of al-Nāsir's policy of integrating civic associations and Sufism, Shaykh 'Omar Sohravardi wrote two tracts on Futuwwa (fotov-vat-nāma), significantly in the Persian vernacular.[51] In these, he made a fundamental contribution to endowing the urban associations with cosmic significance. His shorter tract, accordingly, begins with sacred history, claiming that Adam, as God's lieutenant (khalifa) on earth, taught all of mankind industry (san'at) and craftsmanship (herfat), except for Seth, who was given responsibility for the "world of the souls," and learned to till the land and to weave in order to make the Sufi cloak. Adam instituted the Law (shari'at) and Seth the Path (tariqat) "for the people of Futuwwa and virtue, as being a Muslim [one who submits to God] cannot be attained except through moral practice." Futuwwa was in due course inherited by Abraham and transmitted through his son, Ishmael, to Muhammad. Sohravardi extends the Sufi notion of a chain (selsela) of gnostic/initiatic authority, linking the present master to the Prophet, to the Futuwwa. He also delineates the ethics of the Futuwwa, which can be characterized as an authoritarian system of patriarchal and "exemplary" authority:[52] the novice to be educated (tarbiya) is the son and the disciple of the master (sāheb).[53] Furthermore, the emphasis on the chain of authority of the masters extending back to the Prophet makes this ethics firmly "traditional" (as opposed to rational).[54]

---

[49] Cahen, Mouvements populaires, 15-22, 42-3, 86.

[50] Cahen, Mouvements populaires, 84.

[51] A Kitāb al-Futuwwa by Ibn al-Mi'mār (d. 1244) appeared in Arabic as the manual grounding the new policy.

[52] In the sense of Max Weber's 'exemplary prophecy'.

[53] H. Corbin, Rasā'el-e Javānmardān (Traités des Compagnons-Chevaliers) (Tehran: L'Institut Franco-Iranien, 1971), 93-94, 122-26.

[54] This latter aspect is clearly illustrated in a fourteenth century tract, which subordinates reason ('aql) to tradition (naql), just as in Islamic jurisprudence:

> Likewise, in the Path of Poverty (i.e., Sufism) and Futuwwa, a hundred years of endeavor will have no validity until a man serves a master, who is linked to the Prophet through investiture and tradition (naql) . . ., and who can rectify his rela-

One of the terms mentioned by Sohravardi for the members of the Futuwwa, alongside "comrade," is *akhi* (brother). The Futuwwa associations and Akhi organizations spread in Western Iran and Anatolia. In fact, in the fourteenth century, Akhi appears as the main term of designation for members of such associations, which are explicitly so defined in a tract by the famous Sufi master of the Kobravi order, Mir Sayyed 'Ali Hamadāni (d. 1384 0r 85/786).[55] Somewhat earlier in the fourteenth century, the famous traveler, Ibn Batuta, was entertained by an Akhi/Futuwwa organization (al-akhiyyat al-fityan) consisting of (a) artisans and (b) young celibate men of the city neighborhoods. Their number is put at about 200.[56] They elected their leader and congregated in a convent every night to share their earnings.[57] We shall see several Akhis taking part in the politics of Iranian cities in the fourteenth century. Another term synonymously used for the Akhi leaders in Iran is Kolu. According to Ibn Batuta's report on Isfahan (1: 399), it designated the heads of craft associations and those of the city quarters and/or their youth confraternities. The leading members of the city quarter youth confraternities are also identifiable by their title of Pahlavān (sports champion).

This low level of differentiation between the professional guild and the confraternity is very interesting, and is reflected in all subsequent manuals on Futuwwa ethics and ceremonies. Even as late as about 1500, Vāez Kāshefi still combines the ethics of the Sufi orders and their general duties toward the community, as well as the specific functions of Sufi convents, with the ethics of the notional Futuwwa, on the one hand, and with professional rituals and ethics of some real guilds as well as fictive professions, on the other. The one thing all these manuals do is give dignity and cosmic significance to the professions, thereby serving as an obvious source of professional pride.[58] Many such manu-

---

tion to the Prophet through the chain (*selsela-ye nesbat*) of Futuwwa and of the Path. (Mir Sayyed 'Ali Hamadāni, "Resāla-ye Fotovvatiyya," in M. Riaz, ed., *Ahvāl va Āthār-e mir Sayyed 'Ali Hamadāni* (Islamabad: Markaz-e Tahqiqāt-e Fārsi-ye Irān va Pākestān, 1985), 344-45.

[55] Hamadāni, "Resāla," 343, 354, 362.

[56] Ibn Battûta, *Voyages* (Paris: Découverte, 1990). 2:139-42.

[57] The Akhi organizations developed and took part in the Ottoman conquest of Bursa in the fourteenth century, but Sultan Mehmed the Conqueror began to limit their activities, confiscated some of their endowments and seized many of their convents. See K. C. Topal, "Ahî Zaviyes in the Ottoman Empire," in K. Çiçek, ed., *The Great Ottoman-Turkish Civilization*, vol. 2: *Economy and Society* (Ankara: Yeni Turkiye, 2000).

[58] M. Afshāri, & M. Madāyeni, eds., *Chahārdah Resāla dar bāb-e Fotovvat va Asnāf* (Tehran: Nashr-e Chashma, 2002), 180-81, 254-55.

als or tracts also have a section extolling the virtues of earning a living (*kasb*) through a craft. Even the profession of porters is endowed with such significance and subjected to ethical and ritual regulation.[59] But the mix ultimately did not take, and Futuwwa either dissolved into Sufism (Bektāshiyya in the Ottoman empire and the Khāksārs in Iran), or was fragmented into guilds (especially in the Ottoman empire but also in Iran); alternatively, it survived among the young men of the city neighborhoods.[60] It is important to see how the trajectory bearing on different aspects of al-Nāsir's policies actually developed in the subsequent course of Islamic history. There were short-term difficulties, including fighting among different Futuwwa groups of different city-quarters in al-Nāsir's own time.[61] But the long-term failures were more consequential: Sufism was never integrated into the state, as al-Nāsir had hoped, and spread independently of it. Shi'ism was never integrated into the Sunni orthodoxy. The Futuwwa policy, by contrast, was continued by al-Nāsir's grandson, al-Mustansir, as was the recognition of the four Sunni schools of law in the grand college he founded in Baghdad. But the insurmountable problem was the overthrow of the Caliphate itself by the Mongols in 1258.

Westwards, in the Mamluk kingdom in Egypt and Syria, a shadow 'Abbasid caliphate was installed, and even the Futuwwa policy of al-Nāsir and his successors was followed for a time.[62] Futuwwa and Akhi organizations spread further east, and may have been introduced to Kashmir and northern India by Mir Sayyed 'Ali Hamadāni in the second half of the fourteenth century. But the Caliphate was dead for all intents and purposes until it was officially absorbed into the Sultanate after the Ottoman conquest of Egypt in 1517. Eastwards in Iran, a dualistic system of political and religious authority emerged. This was entirely different from the one projected by al-Nasir, and could indeed be viewed as a resumption of the pattern that had developed with the revival of Zoroastrianism before the Muslim conquest—i.e., from the third to the sixth centuries, CE.[63]

---

[59] Mollā Hosayn Vaez-e Kāshefi, *Fotovvatnāma-ye Soltāni*, M. J. Mahjub, ed. (Tehran: Bonyād-e Farhang-e Irān, 1971/1350), 222-25.

[60] J. Baldick, "The Iranian Origins of the *futuwwa*," *Annalli del'Istituto Universitario Orientale di Napoli*, 50.4 (1990), 328.

[61] Hartmann, *an-Nāsir li-Din Allāh*, 100-101.

[62] Mahjub, "Introduction," 70-73.

[63] S. A. Arjomand, "Rationalization, the Constitution of Meaning and Institutional Development," in C. Camic & H. Joas, eds, *The Post-Disciplinary History of Modern Academic Disciplines*, (Lanham: Rowman & Littlefield, 2004), 265-69.

As for the guilds, although they maintained their religious legitimation and rituals, no systematic link between them and the Sufi orders
developed. They became professional associations of craftsmen. Both in
the Ottoman empire, as we have seen, and in Safavid Iran, the agency
of guilds was made licit as custom and thus granted autonomy by the
legal order in principle. Guild law was administered by the secular
courts under the *divān-begi* in Iran, but by the Kadi courts in the unified
Ottoman judiciary system. For the Ottoman Empire, we have a valuable source in the Kadi court records[64] in which appeals were always
made to the old custom of the guilds, and often to the (unanimous)
agreements of the guild members.[65]

The extent of this autonomy, however, may have been overstated by
Gerber. At any rate, it is much more limited in Safavid Iran. Its autonomy is, again, undeniable. Gerber's most decisive proof of this (and
refutation of despotism) is a decree issued by the Sultan in 1697-98
which voids the appointment of a warden by central authorities: "The
one who has been chosen among the guild themselves, [is] to be the
kethuda (warden) with the help of law courts; even if the letter of appointment [to the contrary] has been issued by the government, it should
not be acted upon."[66] The Ottoman crafts guilds jealously guarded their
narrowly specialized monopolies and were imbued with a strong sense
of equality, using the Kadi courts frequently to restrain unreasonable
profit-making by their members. This must have perpetuated the low
social status of the guildsmen. We should also guard against the notion
of a guild democracy, and a 1732 decree of appointment of warden of
the guild of haberdashers in Istanbul, shows that wardenship had become
a personal property transferred by sale.[67] The Iranian guilds seem to
have enjoyed greater autonomy in punishing offenders within the guild,
but this may have been due to the less developed legal system in Iran.
Nevertheless, the fiscal responsibility of the warden and the collective
liability of certain guilds for unpaid provision of services to the state is
very clear. The control of the guilds by the Safavid state appears much
tighter than the Ottoman one (according to Gerber at any rate). But

---

[64] We have none for Iran.
[65] Cited in Gerber, *State, Society and Law*, 113-29.
[66] Gerber, *State, Society and Law*, 120.
[67] Cited in S. A. Arjomand, "Coffeehouses, Guilds & Oriental Despotism: Government
& Civil Society in late-17th-early 18th Century Istanbul and Isphahan, and as seen from
Paris & London," *Archives européennes de sociologie*, 45.1 (2004).

some of the Ottoman guilds also had fiscal and liturgical obligations, which may have become lighter with the development of tax-farming in the eighteenth century. Furthermore, offending guild members were subject to harsh and humiliating public punishments by the police in Safavid Iran. This brings us to the status dimension, which is unexpectedly revealing in terms of the weakness of the Ottoman and Iranian urban strata and their civic associations vis-á-vis their respective governments. The low socio-economic status of the Ottoman craftsmen, scrupulously enforced by their egalitarian ethos and at times by recourse to the law courts, and the similarly low socio-economic status of the Persian artisans, reinforced by the state through their cruel and humiliating public punishment, make it very unlikely that they would acquire the self-esteem of the guild masters of the Dutch republic, and their sense of entitlement to participate in government as a bourgeoisie. State power over municipal civil society was oppressive and unlikely to encourage it to extend its agency beyond the legally protected economic activities.[68]

Urban Associations and City Politics in the Century following al-Nāsir's Reforms

Perhaps the decisive counterfactual conditional test for the validity of Hodgson's hypothesis on the opening of the path to an Islamic modernity by al-Nāsir's reforms consists in an examination of municipal politics. We have seen through Ibn Khaldun that there was no urban autonomy in the Maghreb and civic associations were absent. Was the situation different after al-Nāsir's reforms in the Eastern Islamic lands which fell under Turko-Mongolian domination?

During the period between the disintegration of the Il-Khānid (Iranian Mongol) Empire in 1335/735 and the establishment of a new empire by Timur (Tamerlane) in the 1380s, we find a pattern of fragmentation of authority and usurpation of power that broadly follows Ibn Khaldun's model for the Maghreb. By contrast, however, there is also considerable evidence of the involvement of a few overlapping urban groupings—the craftsmen and members of the Akhi, Futuwwa organizations and Sufi orders. Despite the scarcity of specific information on the social background of individuals, it is possible to determine the social status of many by their titles, more specifically, 'Amir' and 'Khwāja' for the members of the 'patrician' class and 'Akhi' or 'Kolu' for the

---

[68] Arjomand, "Coffeehouses".

'plebeian' leaders.[69] On this basis, I will offer a typological examination of three important cases of the involvement of urban patrician and plebeian classes in city politics.

The untimely death of the Il-Khānid Sultan Abu Saʿid in 1335/736 without an heir shattered the century-old empire in less than a decade. The powerful vizier, Ghiyāth al-Din Mohammad, managed to hold the fiscal bureaucracy together until his execution, alongside the prince he had put on the throne, in 1336/736, and the struggle for succession and disintegration of the empire accelerated. The populous cities of Transoxania and northern Iran had been completely destroyed by the Mongol invasion in the early thirteenth century. But the cities of the petty Seljuk (Atābek) successor states in central and southern Iran who had submitted to Mongol rule by treaties were spared devastation, and kept their civic institutions—colleges and *waqf* charitable foundations—under an urban patrician class of old families.[70] While the rest of the Il-Khānid empire witnessed a violent power struggle among the Turko-Mongolian tribal princes backing rival contenders for the throne, the patricians of Shiraz and Yazd attempted to create new independent dynasties. The Inju family in Shiraz failed to consolidate its rule in Shiraz and Isfahan but the Mozaffarids of Yazd succeeded in creating an independent state that absorbed the short-lived Inju kingdom as well as Kerman.

The Rule of Patrician Dynasties in Shiraz, Yazd, Kerman and Isfahan, 1343-1387

The sons of Mahmud-shāh Inju, the official in charge of the crown lands (*inju*) of Fars under Sultan Abu Saʿid, had joined opposite Ilkānid (or Jalāyerid) and Chubānid tribal factions in the succession struggles after his death and governed Shiraz for them. After two of them were unceremoniously killed by their respective Turco-Mongolian overlords in 1340/740 and 1343/743, Shaykh Abu Eshāq Inju (d. 1357/758), who had narrowly escaped the same fate himself, proclaimed himself

---

[69] Needless to say, the term is used in analogy to the Roman classes. Unlike Rome, however, the division was not legal, and there was considerable overlap between the two classes, with the *raʾis* and the *kādi* and perhaps other individuals belonging to the upper class but representing the lower.

[70] S. A. Arjomand, "Philanthropy, the Law and Public Policy in the Islamic World before the Modern Era," in W. Ilchman, S. N. Katz & E. L. Queen, eds, *Philanthropy in the World's Traditions* (University of Indiana Press, 1998), 118-25.

the independent king of Fars, struck coins in his own name and later began building the replica of the famous Sasanian palace on the Tigris river, Ivān-e Madā'en. However, his reign of over a decade was troubled and he did not succeed in consolidating his power. As his protégé, the great poet Hāfez of Shiraz, put it,

> Verily did the signet of Bu Eshāqi turquoise
> Shine brightly; but it was a fast-passing turn in power[71]

Abu Eshāq Inju fled Shiraz when it was conquered in November 1353/Shawwāl 754 by his obstinate rival, Amir Mobārez al-Din (d. 1364/765), a patrician of Meybod, near Yazd, and Abu Sa'id's governor of the latter city who had added Kerman to his dominion in 1341/741. Isfahan was held by the Injus for only a few more years. Amir Mobārez al-Din Mozaffar, on the other hand, did succeed in establishing a new dynasty, and his sons and grandsons ruled central and southern Iran until 1387.

The patricians performed their usual functions as viziers and kadis under the Inju and Mozaffarid dynasties, but there is no evidence of their being treated any differently than by the Turco-Mongolian rulers. The Mozaffarids certainly did not treat the patricians serving them as colleagues, but were just as imperious and ruthless toward their viziers as other rulers. Presumably to overcome his lack of legitimacy, Amir Mobārez al-Din, within two years of conquering Shiraz, gratuitously acknowledged the sovereignty of the 'Abbasid shadow-Caliph in Cairo and struck coins in the latter's name. His son, Shāh Shojā' (1359-1384), the most important of the Mozaffarid rulers, continued to keep the shadow Caliph's name on his coins.[72] Otherwise, he behaved just like any other king and upheld the ethos of Persianate monarchy.[73] Nor were the Mozaffarids militarily independent of the Turco-Mongolian nomadic tribes in the region. Indeed, Shāh Shojā' had a Turkish mother, as did his father, and exploited his ties to the tribal leaders in his campaigns. Nevertheless, the plebeian urban class played an important role in the Mozaffarid regime and in the politics of the post-Ilkhānid era generally.

---

[71] *Dīvān-e Hāfez*, P. Nātel-Khānlari, ed., (Tehran Khwārazmi, 1980/1359), 422; my translation.

[72] Q. Ghani, *Bahth dar Āthār va afkār va ahvāl-e Hāfez* (Tehran: Zavvār, 1990/1369 [1943/1322]), 1:177-80, 247.

[73] Arjomand, "Medieval Persianate Political Ethic".

In 1340/740, the inhabitants of Shiraz rebelled against their first Chubānid governor, Amir Pir Hosayn, when he brusquely killed his Inju lieutenant and ordered the rest of the Inju family to leave the city. The rebellion probably began when the Inju dowager, Shaykh Abu Eshāq and the victim's mother, appeared in the marketplace without a veil as was her custom and appealed to the people of Shiraz for help. A carpenter, Pahlavān Mahmud, rose and said "I will not allow any-one to expel this woman!"[74] The eldest Inju brother, who had married the daughter of the late vizier Ghiyāth al-Din Mohammad and been appointed to his office by the Jalāyerid (Ilkānid) faction at one time, returned to the city and ruled Shiraz until he, too, was killed by the resident Jalāyerid governor, Yāghi Bāsti, three years later. According to Hāfez-e Abru, the people of Shiraz were divided after his murder. A considerable number of Kolus (five are named) in fact sided with the Turco-Mongolian governor and against the murdered patrician's brother, Shaykh Abu Ishāq, who, nevertheless, gained control of Shiraz and began to rule independently.[75] Perhaps because of this, Abu Eshāq did not trust the Shirazis and tried to disarm them (presumably the mili-tia), while recruiting men from Isfahan and the Turco-Mongolian tribes of the region into his army.[76] During the critical siege of Shiraz by Amir Mobārez al-Din in 1353, Abu Eshāq made the fateful mistake of killing two leaders of two city quarters. The *ra'is* Nāser al-Din 'Omar, the Kolu of the Murdastān quarter and the chief of Kolus of the city who feared the same fate opened the White (*bayzā'*) Gate in his quar-ter to the Mozaffarid forces. Kolu Nāser al-Din 'Omar and Amir Mobārez al-Din swore mutual loyalty in a holy shrine, and the latter killed the Kolu of Darbandān quarter. Amir Mobārez al-Din then sent *ra'is* Tāj al-Din and Kolu Fakhr al-Din of the neighborhood of the Gate of Kazerun to Kerman with his son, Shāh Shojā', with the order, duly carried out, that they be killed. Two years later, after the inhabitants of Shiraz briefly delivered the city back to Shaykh Abu Eshāq who failed to hold it, Kolu Nāser al-Din 'Omar, with the Mozaffarid troops at his disposal, completely devastated the neighborhood of the Kāzerun Gate, which remained uninhabited for over a year.[77] In short, the Kolus

---

[74] Ibn Batuta, *Voyages*, 1:412; Ghani, *Bahth*, 1:41.
[75] Hāfez-e Abru, *Dhayl-e Jāmeʿ al-Tavārikh-e Rashidi*, Kh. Bayani, ed. (Tehran: Anjoman-e Āthār-e Melli, 1971/1350), 215.
[76] Ibn Batuta, *Voyages*, 1:411.
[77] Ghani, *Bahth*, 1:103-107.

of the city of Shiraz, and the confraternities and associations they controlled, were divided, as they had been ten years earlier over the murder
of the eldest Inju patrician by the Jalāyerid governor. And there certainly is no evidence of formal deliberation and unified decisions in any
councils.

Be that as it may, the plebeian urban leaders played a notable part
in the Mozaffarid regime. In 1365/766, the patricians and plebeians of
Shiraz sent a certain Kolu Hasan to Shāh Shojāʿ, who had been in
Kerman for more than a year, to complain about his disobedient brother's
misrule and to beg him to return to the city. When he returned with
his army, all the Kolus of Shiraz confirmed their loyalty to him and
opened the gates of the city.[78] The Pahlavāns are even more conspicuous. Already in the Inju/Mozaffarid fight over Kerman in early
1340s/740s, we find Pahlavān Tāj ʿAli-shāh in Amir Mobārez al-Din's
army and hear that the Pahlavān of the Inju army was killed.[79] In the
coup d'etat that made him king in 1359/760, Shāh Shojāʿ used Pahlavān
Mosāfer Audāji and six strong men to arrest his father.[80] Later, Pahlavān
Khorram served Shāh Shojāʿ in his campaigns, as did other Pahlavāns,
and was appointed the governor of Isfahan in the last years of his reign.
When Khorram died, another Pahlavān was appointed governor of
Isfahan in his place.[81] Shāh Shojāʿ also appointed Pahlavān Mohadhdhab
governor of Abarghuh.[82] Pahlavān Zayn al-Din of Shar-e Bābak and
Pahlavān Amir Kāshi commanded Mozaffarid armies at different times
under Shāh Shojāʿ's son, Sultan Zayn al-ʿĀbedin (1384-87) in Shiraz,
and Pahlavān ʿAli Qurji commanded the Mozaffarid army in Kerman.[83]

Of particular interest is another Pahlavān, Asad Khorāsāni, whom
Shāh Shojāʿ had appointed governor of Kerman in 1365/766, and who
rebelled against him in 1372/773 and held Kerman for some two years.
The starting point of the rebellion, a wrestling match between a com-
patriot of Pahlavān Asad from Khorasan and the Kermani champion,
does not point to a struggle for municipal independence but rather to
inter-city rivalries. The mother of Shāh Shojāʿ, who was a descendant
of the previous Turco-Mongolian local rulers of Kerman and resided

[78] Ghani, *Bahth*, 1:230, 240-42.
[79] Ghani, *Bahth*, 1:89-109.
[80] Ghani, *Bahth*, 1:157.
[81] Ghani, *Bahth*, 1:305.
[82] Ghani, *Bahth*, 1:366-67.
[83] Ghani, *Bahth*, 1:378, 408.

in that city, rooted for the Kermani wrestler, together with the inhabitants, while the governor took the side of his fellow Khorasani. The queen mother left the city in a huff, and Pahlavān Asad arrested and tortured her companions and confiscated their property. He recruited men for his armed retinue from Khorasan, and rebelled against Shāh Shojā' in alliance with the latter's nephew and rival, Shāh Yahyā, who ruled in the original Mozaffarid capital, Yazd, and sent one hundred men to Kerman to help the rebel. Upon Shāh Yahyā's request, the Sarbadār ruler of Khorasan, Khwāja 'Ali Mo'ayyad, also sent a few men led by Pahlavān Ghiyāth of Tun to Kerman for the same purpose.

Shāh Shojā' sent an army led by Pahlavān Khorram to quell the rebellion. Pahlavān Khorram was seconded by Palavān 'Ali-shāh Mazināni, who conducted the peace negotiations with Pahlavān Asad, stipulating, among other things, that the latter's son, Pahlavān Toghān-shāh be sent back with them to Shiraz as a hostage. Asad agreed, and was allowed to continue his oppressive rule in Kerman. Before long, however, his wife, who had been enticed by Palavān 'Ali-shāh Mazināni with the secret promise of marriage to Shāh Shojā' himself, poisoned the commander of Asad's army, Pahlavān 'Ali the Red (sorkh), and arranged her husband's murder. Pahlavān Asad's widow was assailed by her conspirators and then cut to pieces by the people of Kerman in February 1374/Ramadān 775; and the pieces were sold by a butcher who was said to have made a total of 200 dinārs![84] Pahlavān Asad and his Khorasani troops were evidently resented by the citizens of Kerman, and his rule is unlikely to have helped the cause of municipal solidarity and self-government.

Nor were the Mozaffarids the only rulers to be served by urbanite Akhis and Pahlavāns in a military or administrative capacity in this period. The commander of the fortress of Bam was Akhi Shojā' al-din Khorāsāni until it was captured and he was killed by Amir Mobārez al-Din in the early 1340s.[85] Akhi Shāh-Malek, for instance, served the Chubaind ruler of Tabriz in a diplomatic mission in 1346/747;[86] Pahlavān Haji Kharbandeh was a commander in the Jalāyerid army in 1375/777;[87] and Akhi Irān-shāh Sanjari held the fortress of Soltaniyya for

---

[84] Ghani, *Bahth*, 1:279-86.
[85] Ghani, *Bahth*, 1:79.
[86] Hāfez-e Abru, *Dhayl*, 225.
[87] Ghani, *Bahth*, 1:296.

Timur until 1386/788.[88] It thus appears that the Akhis and Pahlavāns, trained as sportsmen in the urban youth associations and confraternities, would enter the service of local rulers as *condottiere*, and typically be posted outside of their own cities. Municipal loyalties do not appear to have affected their motivation.

The Mozaffarids submitted to Timur in the 1380s: the ruler of Kerman before he had set out from Samarkand, and that of Isfahan upon his arrival with a massive army in 1387. The people of Isfahan rebelled, however, during the collection of the heavy tribute imposed on them and killed some of the collection agents while Timur was in his camp outside the city. Timur ordered a massacre, and at least 70,000 heads were collected and used to build several minarets. The news of the minarets of severed heads preceded Timur and his army to Shiraz. When he reached the vicinity of that city in December 1387/Dhi'l-Hijja 789, all the dignitaries, city-quarter wardens and Kolus of Shiraz welcomed him, kissed the ground before his feet and offered a tribute heavy enough to be acceptable. In the following month, the Mozaffarid governor of Abarguh, Pahlavān Mohadhdhab, delivered that city likewise. Timur returned to Samarkand, taking a number of artisans with him but leaving Sultān Zayn al-ʿĀbedin and some of the other Mozaffarids as his governors. The self-destruction of the dynasty through internecine warfare among the princes began as soon as he left, however, and had gone far when he returned to Fars to repossess Shiraz I 1393/795. This time, he ordered the forced migration of (all) the craftsmen of Fars to Samarkand and had all the Mozaffarid princes put to death, except for Sultān Zayn al-ʿĀbedin who had in the meantime been blinded by his cousin, Shāh Mansur.[89]

"The Sarbedār Republic" in Khorasan, 1338-1381

The most famous case of some four decades of municipal self-government in the city of Sabzavār, whose dominion was intermittently extended over much of Khorasan, is also our most theoretically instructive case. Hailed as the Sarbedār "Republic" by many modern historians, and as the uprising of the "popular mass" of peasants, urban poor and artisans against the Turco-Mongolian nomadic aristocracy by the great Marxist

---

[88] Hāfez-e Abru, *Dhayl*, 289, 295.
[89] Ghani, *Bahth*, 1:397-419, 440.

historian, I. P. Petrushevskii, in 1956.[90] It is in fact a complicated case of intermixture of three things: a failed attempt to establish a patrician dynasty like the Mozaffarids, a trans-municipal Mahdist or millenarian movement in popular Sufism, and municipal self-government. Elsewhere, I have presented its Mahdist aspects alongside a number of similar contemporary Sufi millenarian movements in the region.[91] Here, I will examine it in terms of urban politics in Sabzavār and Nishāpur.

There is evidence that the vizier of Khorasan, Khwāja ʿAlā al-Din Mohammad, held the fiscal bureaucracy together through a few more years of internecine warfare from the execution in 1336/376 of the last great Il-Khānid vizier, Ghiyāth al-Din Mohammad, until the end of the decade. The tax burden on Khorasan appears to have become heavier as a result of the latter's fiscal reforms, and increased even further because of the military campaigns on behalf of the new ruler, Toghā-Timur, in the 1337-39 period.[92] With the support of the new ruler, Khwāja ʿAlāʾ al-Din Mohammad in fact persuaded the Turko-Mongolian elite that it was in their interest to pay taxes on their estates and lighten the tax burden of the subjects until stability returned to the empire.[93] He ran into local trouble, however, with at least one patrician from the small city of Bāshtin who killed his tax collector. Amir ʿAbd al-Razzāq, the eldest son of an important local notable, whose prowess as a sportsman apparently extended beyond the youth association of Bāshtin and had won him a lucrative tax-farm in Kerman,[94] became an outlaw after killing the district tax-collector in 1337/737, and engaged in banditry with a growing band of young men who protested against fiscal oppression and pledged their loyalty until their heads (sar) were upon the gallows (be-dār).[95] The number of Sarbedārs grew into the hundreds, as their loot increased in value, and they conquered the nearby city of Sabzavār

---

[90] As cited in J. M. Smith, *The History of the Sarbadār Dynasty 1336-1381 A.D. and Its Sources* (The Hague & Paris: Mouton, 1970), 105. My patricians appear in Petrushevskii's account as "Iranian small feudalists" who manipulated the mass uprising.

[91] S. A. Arjomand, *The Shadow of God and the Hidden Imam: Religion, Political Organization and Societal Change in Shiʿite Iran from the Beginning to 1890* (The University of Chicago Press, 1984), ch. 3.

[92] Smith, *History*, 95, 101.

[93] Hāfez-e Abru, *Dhayl*, 205-6.

[94] Mir Mohammad b. Borhān al-Din Mir-Khwānd, *Tārikh-e Rawzat al-Safā*, (Tehran: Khayyām, 1950/1339), 5:600-601.

[95] Smith's argument for rejecting the alternative account of the origins of the Sarbedār rebellion in the killing of an official by two brothers in Bāshtin. The stereotypical naming of the bothers Hasan and Hosayn as victims of oppression does suggest populist Shiʿite propaganda by the official historian of the Sarbedār state.

within the year. In 1338/738, Amir ʿAbd al-Razzāq was murdered by his brother, Amir Vajih al-Din Masʿud, who took over Sabzavār, a city where there had been a lot of movement recently. A dervish who had won a large following among the Shiʿite inhabitants of the city for his Sufi order had been found hanged in the mosque in 1335/736 shortly after the Sunni ulema had failed to obtain an order for his execution from Sultan Abu Saʿid. His successor as the leader of the Sufi order, Shaykh Hasan Juri, left Sabzavār and traveled widely in Khorasan and Transoxania, recruiting a militia clandestinely and telling the initiates to get armed and be ready for the advent of the Hidden Imam as the Mahdi.[96] According to our best source, the followers of Shaykh Hasan were predominantly craftsmen, as were the members of his order seven decades later.[97] Shaykh Hasan's presence in Mashhad made the Sunni ulema restive, and they induced the Turco-Mongolian governor to order his imprisonment in a castle.

While acknowledging the sovereignty of Toghā-Timur for some time, Masʿud expanded the band of bandits into an army which eventually numbered 12,000.[98] To secure independence from Toghā-Timur, Amir Masʿud took seventy men from Sabzavār with him, rescued Shaykh Hasan Juri from the castle in 1340/741 and made him his partner in rule in the city of Sabzavār. The registered members of the Shaykh's dervish militia were called to that city and joined the Sarbedar army. Nishāpur was taken by them in the same year. In the following year, Toghā-Timur sent an army against the Sarbedārs. That army was defeated and the vizier ʿAlā' al-Din Mohammad who was accompanying it was killed in 1342/742.[99] Thus, a dual polity under Amir Masʿud and Shykh Hasan Juri, whose followers were respectively called the *sarbedārān* and the *shaykhiyān*, came into being and lasted for three years, until Shaykh Hasan was killed at the instigation of Amir Masʿud in a campaign in 1343/744. Amir Masʿud continued his ambitious plans for extending his dominion, but was defeated in a battle in 1344/745 and delivered to the son of ʿAlā' al-Din Mohammad for execution in revenge for his father.[100] His lieutenant, Āytimur, who had been born to a slave in his family, took over the Sarbedar state until he was

---

[96] Hāfez-e Abru, *Cinq Opuscules de Hafiz-I Abru concernant l'histoire de l'Iran au temps de Tamerlan*, F. Tauer, ed., Supplements to the *Archiv Orientální*, 5 (1959), 16.

[97] Hāfez-e Abru, *Cinq Opuscules*, "Commentaire," 10 n. 50 & n. 55.

[98] Smith, *History*, 109.

[99] Smith, *History*, 115.

[100] Mir-Khwānd, *Rawzat al-Safā*, 615.

deposed by the patricians, led by Khwāja Shams a-Din ʿAli, and killed by Kolu Esfandyār in the summer of 1346/747.

Kolu Esfandyār, the master of an Akhi-Futuwwa organization, became the first plebeian ruler of Sabzavār.[101] Khwāja Shams a-Din ʿAli, a patrician close to the dervishes and the guilds, had recommended him on grounds of his good relations with the dervish order, which had fallen out of favor with Amir Masʿud and Āytimur. Within three months, however, Kolu Esfandyār was killed by an artisan and another man in a brawl. The Sarbedār elite then considered the family of the late Amir Masʿud, and as his son was too young, turned to his brother, Amir Shams al-Din, who ruled for some seven moths and then abdicated in favor of his advisor, Khwāja Shams a-Din ʿAli, in 1347/748. Khwāja Shams a-Din ʿAli ruled the Sarbedār state effectively for over four years. He favored the dervish order in Sabzavār and appointed a certain Darvish Hendavi Mashhadi his governor in Dāmghān. The latter rebelled, however, but was suppressed.[102] Khwāja Shams al-Din ʿAli threw the prostitutes of Sabzavār down into a well and strove for a Shiʿite republic of virtue in the city. Indeed, he fell victim to his moral rigor and financial scruples and was killed by Haydar the Butcher (*qassāb*) in 1351/752. Shams al-Din ʿAli was succeeded by another patricians, Khwāja Yahyā Karāvi, who proved an equally effective ruler and expanded the Sarbadar state considerably after returning to the vassalage of Toghā-Timur only to kill him in his tent, with the Koran cantor (*hāfez*) Shaqāni and another Sarbedār man in December 1353/Dhu'l-Qaʿda 754. Khwāja Yahyā Karāvi was also assassinated by his brother-in-law in 1355/756.[103] He was succeeded by his nephew or brother, Zahir al-Din, who was, however, a figurehead for Haydar the Butcher and abdicated in the latter's favor after forty days. Haydar the Butcher was assassinated by another plebeian, Pahlavān Hasan Dāmghāni after ruling briefly for four months. Pahlavān Hasan put the scion of the Bāshtini patrician family who had been his pupil, Amir Lotfollāh, on the throne and kept him as a figurehead for some two years. But this last chance for the establishment of a patrician dynasty in Khorasan

---

[101] As Smith rightly notes (*History*, 58), Kolu Esfandiar is described by Hāfez-e Abru (*Cinq Opuscules*, 16) as an Akhi. But the word that decisively establishes him as the master of the Futuwwa association comes in the following phrase which states that the co-conspirators who helped him kill Āytimur were a few young men who were his disciples (*tarbiya*).

[102] Mir-Khwānd, *Rawzat al-Safā*, 618.

[103] Smith, *History*, 139.

lapsed when Pahlavān Hasan Dāmghāni deposed and killed Amir Loftollāh and ruled on his own for four more years.[104] In 1362/763, this third and last plebeian ruler of the Sarbedār state was decapitated outside Sabzavār by the Sabzavāri citizens whose families were held hostage in the city by Khwāja ʿAli Moʾayyad, a patrician who had rebelled against Pahlavān Hasan a few years earlier.[105]

ʿAli Moʿayyad had already decided to revive the dual polity of Amir Masʿud and Shaykh Hasan Juri as a means to realize his ambitions when he had rebelled in Dāmghān by calling an exiled leader of the latter's order, Darvish ʿAziz, to join him. Perhaps not having learnt the lesson of the last dual polity, Darvish ʿAziz, responded favorably and proceeded after a stay of some length in Dāmghān, to march on to Tus and set up a millenarian government there, striking the only coin we have that proclaimed the actual sovereignty of the Hidden Imam as "Sultan Mohammad, the Mahdi"![106] Pahlavān Hasan, however, had managed to repossess Tus, and Darvish ʿAziz joined Khwāja ʿAli Moʿayyad in 1362/763, to reconstitute a dual Dervish-Amir polity in Sabzavār that lasted nine or ten months. Presumably to appropriate the millennial yearning without Darvish ʿAziz's mediation, ʿAli Moʿayyad began the practice, also attested to elsewhere, of sending a caparisoned horse to the gate of the city every day at dawn in anticipation of the advent of the Mahdi, but without putting the latter's name on the coins as the actual ruler of the Sarbedār state.[107] By 1363/764, however, ʿAli Moʿayyad had repeated the liquidation of the dual polity by killing Darvish ʿAziz and some seventy disciples, and put his former partner's head on display in the marketplace of Sabzavār.[108] Thereafter, he "engaged in ruling for a long time with independence and autocracy (estebdād)."[109]

After ruling effectively as an autocrat for some fifteen years, Khwāja ʿAli Moʿayyad was dislodged in 1377/778 by a new alliance between a dervish, Rokn al-Din, who had fled from his persecution to the Mozaffarid Shāh Shojāʿ with three hundred men of the dervish militia,

---

[104] Smith, *History*, 141.

[105] Smith, *History*, 145-46. Curiously, ʿAli Moʿayyad had rebelled in Pahlavān Hasan's native city of Dāmghān, probably as early as 1358/159 (Smith, *History*, 76-77).

[106] Smith, *History*, 144, 198.

[107] Smith, *History*, 146.

[108] Mir-Khwānd, *Rawzat al-Safā*, 623.

[109] Mir-Khwānd, *Rawzat al-Safā*, 624-25. Remarkably, Mir-Khwānd uses the same term as Ibn Khaldun for the transition from collective to autocratic rule.

and a young Amir, Eskandar Chelāvi, who had lost his local kingdom in Mazandaran to another popular Sufi movement and was free floating as a condottiere for hire! This last period of Amir-Dervish joint rule in the cities of Sabzavār and Nishāpur is the most obscure, perhaps because it occurred after the "official history" of the Sarbedārs had been written for ʿAli Moʿayyad.[110] Nevertheless, this third and final Sarbedār dual polity lasted at least two years, and possibly longer than any other.[111] It appears, however, to have been a period of ascendancy of the millenarian dervishes who settled scores with ʿAli Moʿayyad's supporters. ʿAli Moʿayyad had taken refuge with his former enemy, Amir Vali, the local ruler of Astarabad, and was restored by him to Sabzavār in 1379/780 or later after the destruction of the city and termination of dual rule of Darvish Rokn al-Din and Amir Eskandar. ʿAli Moʿayyad even foreswore Shiʿism, the distinctive cement of his now broken state, in order to serve Timur as a governor in 1381. The Sarbedār state thus came to an end and was absorbed into the Timurid Empire, as was soon to be the fate of the Mozaffarid state further south.

Leaving aside the six or seven inconclusive years of dual power, we have less than five years of plebeian rule in the 43 years of recorded Sarbedār history. The period of collective rule between the death of Āytimur and the autocracy of ʿAli Moʿayyad, however, amounted to a decade and a half. The plebeian leaders such as Haydar the Butcher and Pahlavā Hasan, as well as the dervish militia, were integrated into the patrician rule of Shams al-Din ʿAli and Yahyā Karāvi. Similarly, plebeian rulers deferred to the patricians. Shams al-Din ʿAli was influential with Kolu Esfandyār, and Pahlavān Hasan appointed another patrician, Khwāja Yusof Semnāni, as his vizier.[112] The internal violence in collective rule was another matter. There are only two instances of peaceful transfer of power, and those by two figurehead patricians who stepped down in seven months and forty days respectively. All other rulers were murdered by their colleagues or other citizens. A lasting legal development was initiated by the Sarbadārs when they commissioned the foremost Twelver Shiʿite jurist of Syria to write a manual of religious law

---

[110] The *Tārikh-e Aarbedārān* is no longer extant, but it was used by most of the other sources.

[111] About four years, if we follow the chronology of Hāfez-e Abru, who placed the reconquest of Sabzavār in 1381-82/782 (Smith, *History*, 153).

[112] Mir-Khwānd, *Rawzat al-Safā*, 623.

for their use that turned out to be a classic,[113] but it had little to do with constitutional law and norms of government. There was no change in the political ethic of patrimonial monarchy and the norms of state-craft, which goes far to explain the failed attempt to set up a Bāshtini patrician dynasty, the praise of the historians for the Sarbedār patricians who followed those norms and the effective return to autocracy by 'Ali Mo'ayyad in 1363/764.

The Year of Akhi Juq in Tabriz, 1358-59/759-60

The disintegration of the Il-Khānid Empire left the native Sarbedārs and the Kart dynasty in control of Khorasan, the native Mozaffarids in southern and central Iran, the Turco-Mongolian Jalāyerid in Iraq and Western Iran, and the rival Turco-Mongolian Chubābids in the north. Our final case is the rebellion of the city of Tabriz against the Chubānid Malek Ashraf's oppressive rule in the mid-fourteenth century. The patricians of Tabriz were not able to alleviate the ill effects of the continuous nomadic depredation of the city, and appealed to other local powers for help. One notable patrician, Kadi Mohy al-Din Bardā'i, became a political activist in exile and we find him preaching at the court of the ruler of the Golden Horde in 1357-58/758 in order to persuade him to attack Malek Ashraf and liberate Tabriz from the oppressive Chubānid rule.[114] His host was persuaded and the Golden Horde invaded Azerbaijan. At that point, a Futuwwa member, Akhi Juq, who was serving the Chubānid Malek Ashraf and had recruited "2,000 men, mostly mule grooms and [crafts] apprentices" for him,[115] defected to the invaders and joined them in conquering Tabriz. Malek Ashraf was killed upon the advice of Kadi Mohy al-Din, and his head was hanged in the mosque of the (quarter of) the natives of Marāghah. There is an obscure reference to the "*jemri* folks," who may have included some craftsmen and were presumably the remnants of the uprising of a dervish who had claimed the Seljuk Sultanate in Anatolia a century earlier.[116]

---

[113] S. A. Arjomand, "Conceptions of Authority and the Transition of Shi'ism from Sectarian to National Religion in Iran," in F. Daftary & J. W. Meri, eds, *Culture and Memory in Medieval Islam*, (London: I. B. Tauris, 2003), 391-93.

[114] Hāfez-e Abru, *Dhayl*, 235.

[115] Hāfez-e Abru, *Dhayl*, 236.

[116] Hāfez-e Abru, *Dhayl*, 234-35; F. M. Köprülü, *The Seljuks of Anatolia. Their History and Culture According to Local Muslim Sources*, G. Leiser, ed. & tr. (Salt Lake City: University of Utah Press, 1992 [1943]), 56-57.

When the Golden Horde prince left Tabriz, Akhi Juq formed an alliance with the Chubānid military elite and took control of the city in the spring of 1358/759, appointing two patricians, Khwāja 'Ali-shāh Jilāni and Khwāja Mahmud Kermāni to the vizierate of the city. However, the Jalāyerid Sultan Oveis marched on Tabriz. Akhi Juq fled but Sultan Oveis executed forty-seven of the Chubānid military officers. However, Sultan Oveis returned to Baghdad two months later. 'Ali Piltan, a sportsman who can be assumed to belong to a Futuwwa youth association, invited Akhi Juq to return to the city. Akhi Juq returned with the surviving Chubānid military officers, but only to be defeated by the Mozaffarid Amir Mobārez al-Din in the spring of 1359/760. The latter, however, did not capitalize on his victory and left because of an astrological prediction that he would be killed by a handsome Turk. Sultan Oveis, whom he presumed to be the predicted Turk, occupied Tabriz once more. Akhi Juq and 'Ali Piltan were captured and executed, and the turbulent year of self-government in Tabriz came to an end.[117]

Conclusion

Our survey enables us to confirm that Caliph al-Nāsir's civic reforms did have a lasting effect in the eastern Islamic lands, and that the growth of Akhi/Futuwwa confraternities made for a conspicuous presence of plebeian urban groups not known in the Maghreb as surveyed by Ibn Khaldun. Nevertheless, this development did not constitute an irreversible stride on the path to modernity. Self-government remained a matter of default and soon gave way to autocracy and/or the establishment of a new dynasty. In none of the three cases analyzed above do we find a development of a new theory of government or any normative justification of self-rule and consolidation of the practice of municipal self-government. The situation of absence of municipal self-government did not change in the early modern Muslim empires. The Safavid capital, Isfahan, had no mayor. Instead, there was a Vizier of Isfahan, and a Vizier of Endowments, the police chief (*dārugha*) and the *kalāntar*, an official in charge of city affairs who appointed the wardens (*kadkhodā*) of the city quarters with the Vizier of Isfahan. Similarly, there was no mayor of Istanbul, and the endowments were centrally supervised. With the unprecedented development and centralization of the judiciary orga-

---

[117] Hāfez-e Abru, *Dhayl*, 236-38.

nization of the Ottoman Empire, the kadis in effect became the chief municipal officials of the provincial cities. There is, however, a significant difference between this Ottoman and the Safavid pattern. Although appointed by the Sultan, the kadis applied a law that did not emanate from him but was superior to him, and which normatively protected the agency and autonomy of civil society. The Ottoman kadis, therefore, did check the power of provincial governors, unlike their Safavid counterparts. Still, we did not have municipal self-government.

THE TRANSFORMATION OF CULTURE-POWER IN INDO-EUROPE, 1000-1300

SHELDON POLLOCK*

ABSTRACT

While it is no easy matter to identify convincing and coherent Eurasia-wide transformations during the early centuries of the second millennium (section 1), it is possible to demonstrate unequivocally that much of South Asia and Western Europe
underwent comparable changes in culture and power, with vernacular replacing
cosmopolitan forms of language and literature in many areas of cultural production,
and regional forms of polity replacing empire (this are briefly exemplified here by
the cases of Hoysala Karnataka and Alfonsine Castile, section 2). Far more difficult
is it to account for the peculiar structure and synchrony of these transformations.
Any monocausal explanation for so complex a transformation is inherently improbable.
A range of factors that may have contributed include the dynamic expansion of
world trade and agriculture, the rise of the nomadic empires, and the spread of
Islam on its western and eastern frontiers. Yet none of these factors is obviously
causal, nor even as an ensemble do they fully explain why the culture-power complex changed the way it did only in South Asia and Europe (sections 3-4).

1. *Eurasian Transformations?*

If one thing is certain in scholarship it's that we usually find what we
are looking for. If we set out to hear global harmonies amidst the
cacophony of history we probably will. Large-scale world-historical generalizations, such as the postulation of an Axial age around mid-first
millennium BCE, seem especially susceptible to such wishful thinking.
Correlatively, we also tend to think something is new because we don't
always know enough to know how old it may in fact be. The world
system (or world-system) of the early second millennium CE, for example,
as Janet Abu-Lughod conceives of it, has a tensility—or so it seems in

---

* I am grateful to the participants in the Workshop on Eurasian Transformations,
especially Johann Arnason, Björn Wittrock, and Robert Moore, for their comments. All
Indic diacritics have been eliminated from this version of my essay.

the hands of Andre Gunder Frank—enabling it to be stretched back six millennia earlier.[1]

What is less certain than finding what we are looking for is explaining why we are looking for what we look for in the first place. It seems unlikely that only those such as I who are not professional historians feel haunted by the question of why we want historical knowledge at all any more, let alone world-historical knowledge, let alone world-historical knowledge of supposedly discrete ages where things are thought to have changed simultaneously and everywhere once and for all. No purpose is served even trying to address here the first part of this question, but surely the disfavor into which historical thinking has fallen should give us pause, as should the extravagant and unapologetic presentism of the social sciences today (in particular the meltdown of historical sociology in the United States), the repeated philosophical and especially hermeneutical assaults on the possibility of historiographical truth, the demonstrable irrelevance of knowledge of the past to practices of the future—except for those who like me continue to ascribe, vaguely and usually tacitly, a certain emancipatory value to the sheer awareness of the contingency, openness and alternative possibilities of cultural and political life as demonstrated in history.

Even assuming some acceptable response to the first part of the question, the two latter seem equally troubling. Global history is, I suppose, politically correct history for those who, again like me, see themselves as post-national, world citizens, since such history serves to facilitate—or at least William McNeil thinks so—"a tolerable future for humanity as a whole."[2] But why do we find it a compelling project to try to connect the whole world in a unified set of processes? There is no obvious reason to believe that anything that happens somewhere happens everywhere, and the point of attempting to prove otherwise is not entirely self-evident. Is it the impulse to find one of Hemple's covering laws in history, or Kant's "universal history according to a natural plan directed to achieving the civic union of the human race" (this despite what he calls the "idiotic course of things human"), or a residue of Vico's stage

---

[1] Janet Abu-Lughod, *Before European Hegemony: The World System A.D. 1250-1350* (New York: Oxford U. Press, 1989); *The World System: Five Hundred Years or Five Thousand* ed. Andre Gunder Frank and Barry K. Gills (London and New York: Routledge, 1993); Andre Gunder Frank, "Immanuel and Me with-out Hyphen," *Journal of World-Systems Research* 6,2 (2000), 216-231. For some thoughts on Axial-age theory, see my "Axialism and Empire," *Axial Civilizations and World History*, ed. Johann Arnason et al. (Leiden: E. J. Brill: 2004).

[2] In *World History: Ideologies, Structures and Identities*, ed. Philip Pomper et al. (Malden, Mass. and Oxford: Blackwell, 1998), 40.

theory of economic or cultural development, or the relic of an evolutionary Marxism, or some other species of conceptual totalization?

Consider only the methodological delusions that threaten the Indianist who, inspired by conceptions of a twelfth century renaissance in Europe or Sung China, attempts to find South Asian homologies with an Aquinas and Averroës, or with the Neo-Confucians from Chou Tun-I to Chu Hsi. If, in accordance with some earlier reflections on this problematic,[3] we were to examine Indian intellectual history in the domains of reflexivity, agency, historicity, textuality, or any other component of an Axial-like conceptual transformation, a number of apparently strong candidates do readily present themselves. Yet historical scrutiny shows how hard it is to argue for any sharp discontinuity and true innovation. This can be briefly illustrated by exploring several such candidates: philosophical redefinitions of *atman* (the self); *bhakti* (devotionalism); religious conversion and monasticism; and textualizations of Hindu life ways and their apparent transformation.

The time-space of my case study below—the region comprised in today's union state of Karnataka in south-western India over some three or four centuries beginning around 1000—was marked by what to all appearances was indeed astonishing intellectual ferment every bit as momentous as that of the twelfth-century renaissance in Europe. One notable component of this ferment was the attempt at fundamental reconceptualization of the self and its identities, which were variously deconstructed, rendered contingent, or reconstructed. In the centuries around the beginning of our period a radical monism was systematized and elaborated, especially by intellectuals at the Srngeri monastery in the far west of the region, achieving a certain finality with the scholar-abbot Vidyaranya (known before his renunciation as Madhava, d. 1386). With new discursive rigor this system argued for a radical metaphysical erasure of all difference and all contingent identities, and a fundamental unity of being (or at least at the theoretical level it argued such; in practice, social distinctions of caste were vigorously reasserted). In the period 1100-1300 two major variations on this *advaita* (non-dual) conception were developed. The first was the "qualified monism" of the Srivaisnavas, a sect of monastic and lay devotees of the god Visnu and his interceding consort Sri that had originated in Tamil country but was strongly present in the southern Karnataka region. Theologically, Srivaisnavas maintained a kind of personal individuality, with the

---

[3] Björn Wittrock, "Social Theory and Global History: The Three Cultural Crystallizations," *Thesis Eleven*, 65 (2001), 27-50.

individualized souls constituting the body of God. Sociologically, they seem to have extrapolated the Advaitins' highly abstract monism toward a kind of social equality; reforms associated with the theologian Ramanuja (d. 1137?), the principal theoretician of the movement, may even have sought to establish Shudras, the lowest of the caste groups, as temple functionaries (eventually this egalitarian aspect, assuming it actually existed, was lost and the community eventually reverted to caste orthodoxy). The second major variation was a dualistic revision formulated by Madhva (d. 1317) in coastal Karnataka, which restored real selves ontologically different from God, real identities, new doctrines of predestination and election, and, for some of its history at least, a re-assertion of caste privilege. Yet what may appear in all this ferment to be new forms of philosophical or religious thought are in fact intimately linked to earlier breakthroughs without which they cannot be explained or understood: Vidyaranya in the fourteenth century to Sankara in the eighth to Gaudapada in the seventh and even to the synthesis of the core text itself of Advaita, the *Vedantasutras*, many centuries earlier. Similarly, one can trace the apparent innovations of Ramanuja in the twelfth century back to Nathamuni at the beginning of the tenth, the Alvars at the beginning the seventh, Bodhayana's third-century (?) commentary on the *Vedantasutras*, and so on. Worth stressing, too, is that in Sanskrit intellectual history, generally speaking, recovery was a far more dominant ideologeme than innovation, so much so that, within the interpretive horizon of the subjects of this history, "transformation" as such would probably have been denied, or have even been unintelligible as an explanation of what they were doing.

A similar argument could be made with respect to the congeries of phenomena too often and too misleadingly grouped under the heading of bhakti. The (vernacular) poets of *saguna* bhakti (devotion to a personalized god) in sixteenth-century north India (the followers of Vallabhacarya, for example, as well as poets like Surdas) were closely linked to (Sanskrit) south Indian Vaisnavism in the tenth century (the doctrines of the *Bhagavata Purana* preeminently) and indeed to the *Bhagavad Gita* itself from seven or eight centuries earlier, where the "path of devotion" is first clearly spelled out. Not as prominent an object of historical inquiry as bhakti, though it certainly should be, is what seems to have been the upsurge in conversion that occurred in our period. The conversion of Brahmans to Jainism appears especially prominent, but conversion from Jainism to other forms of theistic Hinduism is noticeable, too. For example, the king of the Hoysala dynasty of Karnataka, Bittideva (afterwards known as Visnuvardhana, "Promoter of Visnu"), is thought to have been converted to the Srivaisnava order around 1100 at the hands of Ramanuja himself.[4] But we have in fact no way at present to know whether this "upsurge" is anything more than an artifact of our data; one could easily point to an increase of conversion to Buddhism— if "conversion" is the appropriate category here—in the seventh century, or indeed in the last centuries BCE.[5]

One might likewise be inclined to find a resurgence of monasticism paralleling what was occurring in Europe (especially the dramatic expansion of monastic power and prestige emanating from Cluny). The Vedanta reforms mentioned above were accompanied by the founding or strengthening of *matha*s, or monastic institutions, across the region. Srngeri has already been mentioned; it was complemented by other so-called Dasanami institutions founded (at uncertain dates) at the cardinal points of the compass of South Asia: Dvaraka in today's Gujarat in the west, Bhadrinath-Kedarnath in Gharwal in the north, Puri in Orissa in the east. Similarly, other Vedanta reformers established new monastic institutions, including Madhva in Udupi, and Ramanuja in Tamil country. Yet it is entirely unclear how well-organized, let alone how powerful these institutions were. To be sure, Srngeri had demonstrably close ties to the rulers of the early Vijayanagara empire (founded 1365), but it is hard to believe, from the evidence available, that they were anywhere near as socially or politically significant as the Cluny network in Europe, which around 1100 controlled some 1500 monasteries across Europe organized into what some have called a shadow empire, or even as the Lingayat mathas in present-day Karnataka. Moreover, like the religio-intellectual reforms themselves, the twelfth century monastic movement (if it was such) in Karnataka was again linked in a chain of movements reaching back in time, from radical Saiva and Pancaratra Vaisnava sects to far older Jaina and Bauddha institutions of the late centuries BCE.

---

[4] Pampa, the great pioneer poet in Kannada (fl. 950), the Ganga minister and general Camundaraya (975), and Nagavarma II (1040), a poetician and grammarian at the Kalyana Calukya court, were all either themselves converts to Jainism or sons of families that recently were. The phenomenon is known elsewhere, too (e.g., the family of Dhanapala, the celebrated Jaina court poet of the Paramara kings). On the conversion of Bittideva see B. R. Gopal, *Sri Ramanuja in Karnataka* (Delhi: Sundeep Prakashan 1983), 14-17, but the matter needs more study. Another celebrated royal conversion, outside Karnataka, was that of King Kumarapala of Gujarat by the Jaina scholar Hemacandra around 1170.

[5] On the concept of conversion in connection with early Buddhism see the cautions in Pollock, "Axialism and Empire," n. 15. Any future study would want to address the history and character of the process by which conversion—among Jainas, Srivaisnavas, and Madhvas—simply ceased and these communities closed themselves to outsiders.

A final component is what appears to be a new wave of textualization of core cultural material as witnessed by the invention of the *dhar-
manibandha*s, encyclopedias of Hindu life ways, along with what might
be thought to have been a transformation of social practices. I once
argued that it was during this period, indeed, just in advance of the
temporal and spatial progress of the Khalji Sultanate (1290), that these
enormous compendia achieved "perhaps their first and certainly their
most grandiose expression. Totalizing conceptualizations of the society,
one can argue, became possible only by juxtaposition with alternative
life-worlds; they became necessary only at the moment when the total
form of the society was for the first time believed, by the professional
theorists of society, to be threatened."[6] But the continuity of the dhar-
manibandha genre with earlier commentarial literature is unmistakable,
so that, once again, talk of a truly radical break seems misplaced.

So, too, with respect to the more specific components of this literature. In what would be a striking parallel with contemporaneous Europe,
the question of inheritance appears to have been raised anew and
answered in what, retrospectively at least, became its quintessential textual formulations in Hindu law: Vijnanesvara's *Mitaksara* (The Breviloquent),
composed at the Kalyana Calukya court between 1100-1120, and
Jimutavahana's *Dayabhaga* (Division of Inheritance), written sometime
between 1090-1130 (if not produced in Bengal, it eventually became
restricted to Bengal). To reduce a complicated matter to a phrase, for
the *Mitaksara*, a son becomes an owner of the paternal estate by (and
presumably at) birth; for the *Dayabhaga*, he becomes so only after the
father has died (or is otherwise disqualified to own property). Yet it is
not in the least clear how new this distinction was: earlier commenta-
tors than Vijnanesvara accepted inheritance by birth.[7] And in any case
the real-world implications of these textual innovations, if there were
such, are exceedingly difficult to determine. The *Mitaksara*'s guidelines
affects who inherits, and when, and to what extent family property may

---

[6] Sheldon Pollock, "Ramayana and Political Imagination in India," *Journal of Asian
Studies* 52,3 (1993), 286.

[7] Such as Visvarupa and Medatithi. Contra Ludo Rocher and Rosane Rocher,
"Ownership by Birth: The Mitaksara Stand," *Journal of Indian Philosophy* 29 (2001), 241-
255, see Gautama cited on p. 249 and cf. P. V. Kane, *History of Dharmasastra*, vol. 3
(Pune: BORI, 1993), 557. The second major work of the period is now available in
Ludo Rocher, *Jimutavahana's Dayabhaga: The Hindu Law of Inheritance in Bengal* (Oxford:
Oxford U. Press, 2002). I am grateful to my student Ethan Kroll for helping me think
through and formulating some of the key issues involved here.

be disposed of during the lifetime of the father, even whether a son can seek to divide the property against his father's wishes (something that could never happen under *Dayabhaga* doctrine). In principal, all this should have had some social resonance. Yet we have no data whatever to determine if this was ever so or if the new formulations marked a change in practices. At all events, there seems no reason to suspect that innovations occurred in India that were remotely comparable to the major social consequences of the introduction of primogeniture in Europe.[8]

It is of course easy to throw this kind of dust in the eyes of any historian who wants to extrapolate from particular known cases to other unknown cases in order to frame higher-order generalizations—as any non-trivial history seeks to do. But how does one proceed without falling victim to the thought-fathering wish, without starting to perceive meaningful figures in a meaningless carpet? And how does one avoid the pitfall of mistaken novelty without being prepared, as few of us are prepared either professionally or temperamentally, to hunt down a fugitive innovation by following its track back in time, hypothetically ad infinitum? No doubt the questions of generalization and beginnings have to be addressed, and can be successfully addressed, in any historical work. But they seem especially debilitating when the problematics themselves are generated, not from within the local historical stuff itself, but imported from outside.

Those who want to write a world history of the period 1000-1300 might instead proceed by expecting at the very start of the inquiry to find more dissimilarities across areas than similarities, fewer similarities across fewer areas, and more continuities with the past within each area than true discontinuities. To be sure, there is a use in what, to the world historian, might appear to be an adversity: it is precisely in its extensive set of differences from processes elsewhere, its few commonalities, and its forms of stability in the face of episodes of rupture in other parts of the world, that the specificity of each region may be located. (A good example here from a later period would be the absence in South Asia of the supposedly global "seventeenth century crisis.")[9] The history of South Asia during the early centuries of the second millennium illustrates these postulates rather well. It would not be very interesting to show, though it could be shown, that, for example,

---

[8] Robert Moore, this volume.

[9] John Richards, "The Seventeenth-century Crisis in South Asia," *Modern Asian Studies* 24,4 (1990), 625-38.

urbanization during this period evinces stronger continuities than in other places.[10] I prefer instead to concentrate here on what I believe to have been the critical transformations, those emerging out of the primary materials of specific local history. But these turn out to be by no means *Eurasia-wide* transformations: they bring South (and parts of Southeast) Asia into close, indeed astonishingly close, comparison with western Europe, but at the same time they mark off these two cases sharply from western and eastern Asia. In previous studies I have referred to these transformation processes collectively as the *vernacularization* of culture and power.[11] Included here are a number of innovations in the practice and theory of both literature and polity that become manifest around the end of the first millennium, and that by the middle of the second had achieved full development more or less everywhere in the two areas. Through these processes transregional modes of cultural communication (that is, Sanskrit and Latin) and transregional ideologies of rule (that is, empire) were replaced by newly regionalized forms: recently invented vernacular styles of expressive writing and rescaled conceptualizations of the nature of polity.

In a recent contribution to discussions on the Axial age I explored the components of the imperial culture-power complex in Eurasia in the first millennium BCE (Achaemenid, Maurya, Roman, Gupta). Here I want to sketch out what the vernacular culture-power transformation looked like in southern Asia, concentrating on one particular region in southern India. The comparable transformations in Europe during this period will be far more familiar to readers, so I need provide only a very brief account of an exemplary instance, Alfonsine Castile, by way of preface to the Indian case with which it was contemporaneous. I

---

[10] A case could be made for a powerful new phase of urbanization *after* our period, from 1400-1600, see David Ludden, *An Agrarian History of South Asia* (Cambridge, England: Cambridge U. Press, 1999), 120, as well as for a demographic explosion. The population of South Asia nearly doubled between 1400 and 1650, increasing from some 46 million to 80 million; cities like Agra, Delhi, and Lahore had over 500,000 inhabitants, many others had 200,000, and some 15% of the population lived in urbanized areas of over 5000, see Andre Gunder Frank, *ReOrient: Global Economy in the Asian Age* (Berkeley: U. of California Press, 1998), 168.

[11] The lineaments of this are sketched in Sheldon Pollock, "The Sanskrit Cosmopolis, A.D. 300-1300: Transculturation, Vernacularization, and the Question of Ideology," in *Ideology and Status of Sanskrit: Contributions to the History of the Sanskrit Language*, ed. J. E. M. Houben (Leiden: E. J. Brill), 197-247; "India in the Vernacular Millennium: Literary Culture and Polity, 1000-1500," *Daedalus* 127,3 (1998), 41-74; "The Cosmopolitan Vernacular," *Journal of Asian Studies* 57,1 (1998), 6-37; "Cosmopolitan and Vernacular in History," in *Cosmopolitanism*, ed. Carol Breckenridge et al. (Durham: Duke U. Press, 2002).

then go on in greater detail to ask what historical explanations are available to account for these homologous and synchronous changes in western Europe and South Asia, and what these might tell us about the larger problematic of "Eurasian transformations."[12]

2. *The Paradigm of Culture-Power Transformation in South Asia: Hoysala Nadu, 1100-1300*

An actualization of the ideal-typical process of the vernacularization of culture and power in Europe—showing the trends that had been underway at the Anglo-Saxon court in the ninth to tenth centuries, at the Anglo-Norman court in the eleventh, at the Capetian court in the eleventh to twelfth, at the Occitanian and Sicilian courts of the same period—is found in thirteenth century Castile. Its basic components can be delineated in the broadest strokes: literization (*Verschriftlichung*), or the initial inscription of the vernacular in a documentary mode; literarization, or adjustment toward the norms of a superposed literary culture; and the transformation of polity into an order of power that takes seriously both the vernacularization of culture—the court was almost everywhere the prime mover in this process—and its new limits, its regionality.

It has recently been demonstrated with great precision that the vernacular documentary state in Castile had its birth at the start of the thirteenth century, when court functionaries for the first time began to write intentionally in the vernacular for political purposes. The inaugural instance, a treaty between Castile and Leon, is actually extant and can be dated exactly to Palm Sunday, 1206. Drawn up in the Castile chancery, the document would have appeared, in that context, to be a revolutionary if not heretical act: The archbishop was in charge of the chancery *ex officio*, Romance was still largely denied validity in its written form, and any reform of spelling (in the service of vernacularization) bordered on sin.[13] From that point on, however, despite periodic interruptions in the first decades, vernacular political culture

---

[12] The material that follows is adapted from my forthcoming book *Language of the Gods in the World of Men: Culture and Power in Premodern India* (Berkeley: U. of California Press).

[13] Fundamental is Roger Wright, "Latin and Romance in the Castilian Chancery (1180-1230)," *Bulletin of Hispanic Studies* (Liverpool) 73 (1996), 115-28, on the struggle between Latin and Castilian proponents in the chancery, and the simultaneous development of political and literary texts; for the treaty itself, Roger Wright *El Trabado de Cabreros (1206): Estudio sociofilológico de una reforma ortográfica* (London: Queen Mary and Westfield College), 2000. A decree of 1214 (read 1254) mandates the use of Castilian

and, closely dependent on it, vernacular literary culture developed with
an extraordinary intensity. A telling example is offered in the year
following the treaty document, when the sole surviving manuscript of
the *Cid* was prepared. Central to the consolidation of this process were
the innovations at the court of Alfonso X el Sabio ("the Learned,"
r. 1252-82).

The meaning and memory of the historic break that Alfonso's reign
signaled—and "break" is much more appropriate than the usual descrip-
tor "renaissance," since textual vernacularity was being generated, not
regenerated—are recorded two centuries later when Antonio Nebrija
remarked in the celebrated preface to his grammar of Castilian (1492)
that it was at Alfonso's court that Castilian first "began to show its
powers." Again this was what I have called a cosmopolitan-vernacular
idiom, but one shaped as much by Arabic culture, which was now being
translated into Castilian rather than as earlier into Latin, as by Latin
(in particular Roman jurisprudence) and Romance (the works constituting the models of literarization for the author of the *Cid* included
the French *chanson de geste*, *Roland* in particular, and, to some degree,
classical rhetoric); and it was cultivated across the full spectrum of textual production, both political and literary. Vernacularization in both
areas was clearly seen as related and mutually supportive, and the
chancery and the scriptorium have rightly been viewed as united. The
use of the vernacular for all state documents (except international diplomacy) was now becoming a matter of royal policy. Well-known is the
remarkable Castilian redaction of the laws of the realm, the *Siete par-
tidas* (Seven Divisions [of Law]), which aimed to extend royal control
over all judicial and legislative activities. Of a piece with the vernacularization of law is the invention of a Castilian-language historiography,
which sought to narrate the past of both the local geopolitical space,
in the *Estoria de Espanna* (The Chronicle of Spain) and the world
as a whole, in the *General Estoria* (The Chronicle). Although the vernacularization of political communication commenced under Alfonso
VII (d. 1214), these grand prose works had no predecessors; the history of Spain commissioned by Alfonso VII's father, for example, had
been produced in Latin (written by the archbishop of Toledo). Instead,
they were born, as one scholar puts it, in a trope figuring forth the
astonishment of the sudden invention—and not the "evolution"—of the

---

in royal communications, see Colin Smith, "The Vernacular," in *The New Cambridge
Medieval History*, v. 5, ed. David Abulafia (Cambridge, Eng.: Cambridge U. Press, 2000).

literary vernacular here as, say, in Anglo-Norman England, "full-fledged like Minerva, with Alfonso assuming the role of Jupiter." The impetus given to the creation of unified culture in both the literary and the political domain was unprecedented and irreversible. And it maps closely against Alfonso X's peninsular political aspirations. His desire to unify all forms of knowledge and the Castilian language finds its analogy in his quest for the political centralization of Castile: "dominating everything, centralizing everything around himself," very much as in Alfred's England four centuries earlier, or the France of François I two centuries later.[14]

The Hoysala kingdom, which once ruled much of what is today's union state of Karnataka in southern India, constitutes an exemplary case of the new culture-power order of South Asia. The two defining transformations become visible here in all their details: At the level of culture, a powerful stimulus was provided by the court for the creation of political and literary works in the Kannada language (rather than as previously in Sanskrit), along with a wide range of other texts to complete the corpus of a cosmopolitan vernacular (grammars, prosodies, dictionaries, poetry anthologies, and the like). At the level of power we can observe the creation of a new and very self-aware regionalized territorialization of the political domain, finding expression in the public poems commissioned by the Hoysala kings and inscribed on copper plate land-grants and dressed stone plaques in temple precincts.

It is the latter dimension of the practice of power that I concentrate on here since it constitutes the most prominent of the *differentia specifica* distinguishing vernacular polity from the earlier world of empire. The development of a vernacular political discourse, literature, and philology at the Hoysala court in this period requires only the broadest outline, since I have discussed similar material elsewhere.[15] Unlike the literati of thirteenth century Castile, the Hoysala poets and scholars were not the actual inventors of a vernacular tradition—this was already some three centuries old, having commenced at the court of the Rastrakuta

---

[14] See especially Socarras cited in *Emperor of Culture: Alfonso X the Learned of Castile and his Thirteenth-century Renaissance*, ed. Robert I. Burns (Philadelphia: U. of Pennsylvania Press, 1990), 11. On Alfonso see Smith, "The Vernacular," and Burns, *Emperor of Culture*, especially 1-18, 90-108 (chancery-scriptorium), 141-58 (historiography), 183-4 (law); the citation on the origins of Alfonsine prose is from p. 38. For Nebrija's quote see Antonio de Nebrija, *Gramatica Castellana* (Madrid: Edición de la Junta del Centenario, 1946), 8. On Anglo-Norman literary beginnings see David Howlett cited in Pollock, "Cosmopolitan and Vernacular in History," 32.

[15] See especially Pollock, "Cosmopolitan Vernacular".

dynasty of northeast Karnataka in the early ninth century, pursued with
ever-increasing vigor by their successors, the Calukyas of Kalyana and
by the Gangas of southern Karnataka. But they were the proud inheritors
and conscious consolidators of what should still be seen as a nascent
tradition. The three paradigmatic features of cultural vernacularization
are dramatically present here: the dominance of a vernacular (as opposed
to a Sanskrit) political discourse; the intensified production of belles-
lettres in the vernacular, and the perfection of vernacular philological
theory. These components may be illustrated by cursory reference to a
few representative texts and persons, all kinsmen or close associates and
all members of the royal court.

The percentage of vernacular to Sanskrit political texts—those records
issued by the court that typically commence with a historical account
of the dynasty and the achievements of the ruling lord (the *prasasti*, or
praise-poem), and the conditions of the benefice that the text was produced to record—underwent a complete inversion from the time of the
early Rastrakutas (c. 800) to the Hoysalas. Most of the great prasastis
of the Hoysalas are in Kannada, and many were the work of the foremost court poets of the day. Preeminent among these is Cidananda
Mallikarjuna, who wrote the grand eulogy of the dynasty carved onto
the walls of a temple in the town of Basaralu (dated 1234 and 1237).
The same poet also prepared for the Hoysala king Virasomesvara (r.
1234-54) the *Sukti-sudha-arnava* (Nectar Ocean of Poetry), the foremost
anthology of early Kannada literature, and perhaps the first anthology
of vernacular literature in India (outside the Tamil tradition). What is
above all remarkable about this work is its completely *laukika*, or this-
worldly, character (its dominant organizational principle is derived from
the eighteen *katha-vastus*, or thematics, of Sanskrit court poetry). Massive
evidence could easily be added to this one small datum to prove that
for most of South Asia, and contrary to every account available in scholarship to date, it was not demotic religious insurgency against a sup-
posed Sanskrit spiritual hegemony that propelled the transformation of
literary culture in South Asia, but the aspirations of a vernacular aesthetic state. Even works like *Yasodhara-carita* of Janna, court poet to
Viraballala (1173-1220), while a story of Jaina inspiration, has little of
the religious about it. The kinds of cultural issues of importance to
Janna are made fully manifest in the prelude to his *Anantanathapuranam*
(1230). Here, in his praise of poets past, the criteria of literary judgment and standards of taste include clever language (*jannudi*, in reference to the poet Gunavarma), sweetness (*impu*, Pampa) quality of thought
(*bage*, Ponna), erudition (*bahujnate*, Nagavarma), formal and affective bril-

liance (*kanti*, Ranna), registers of feeling and emotion (*rasa-bhavam*, Nagacandra), excellence of tropes (*vakrate*, Aggala), the aesthetic of Place (*dese*, Nemi), and mellifluence of style (*mrdhubandham*, Puspabana). Janna was a student of this last poet (also known as Sumanobana), who had been a *kataka-acarya*, or "teacher of the royal camp," of the Hoysala rulers. His nephew (and son of the poet Mallikarjuna) was Kesiraja, a kataka-acarya as well. More important, he was the author of the *Sabda-mani-darpana* (Jeweled Mirror of Language, 1260), one of the supreme achievements of vernacular grammatical science in the premodern world. This work embodies the radically new paradigm of philological knowledge that differentiated the vernacular from Sanskrit: here the poet-grammarian and ultimately the patron king are the legislators of language correctness, and not, according to the Sanskrit episteme, the eternal grammar itself, which was thought to pre-exist and regulate all usage.[16] Political eulogy, literature, and philology completed the toolbox of vernacular courtly culture. There were no histories as such of the dynastic realm, nor codification of laws in the Hoysala or anywhere else in the medieval Indic world, on the model of contemporaneous Castile (or earlier Britain or later France). Neither the quest of origins of a people (*Ursprungsparadigmen* or *mytho-moteurs*) nor the standardization of administrative practices of the nascent absolutist state could have found place in the conceptual scheme of premodern Indian polities.[17]

More important for our present purposes than the history of the transformation of culture—crucial though that is in itself and indissociable from the transformation of power—is the political self-identification of the Hoysala dynasty and the regional dimension of their political frame of reference. From the time the Hoysala dynasty decisively entered the historical record at the end of the eleventh century, with the royal inscriptions of Vinayaditya, until the disappearance of the lineage as a political power in the mid-fourteenth century (according to what seems nearly a law of political entropy in old India), the limits of their geopolitical sphere are articulated clearly, consistently, and even insistently in their public records. It is in fact immaterial whether these limits were actualized—as they most certainly were not always; the point is that

---

[16] On Kesiraja's philology, see my "A New Philology: From Norm-bound Practice to Practice-bound Norm in Kannada Intellectual History," in *Festschrift François Gros*, ed. Jean-Luc Chevillard (Pondichery: Institut Français d'Indologie, 2004), 399-417. Janna's *Anantanathapuranam* 1.35 is cited in K. V. Puttappa, ed., *Kannada Kaipidi* (Mysore: U. of Mysore Press, 1988), 90. The Basaralu prasastis are found in *Epigraphia Carnatika* (*EC*) 7:211 ff. nos. 29 and 30.

[17] See Pollock, "India in the Vernacular Millennium," 62-65.

limits were set. From his base in Sasakapura (in today's Kadur district) Vinayaditya is represented as ruling all the lands "bounded by the Konkan, Alvakheda, Bayala Nadu, Talakad, and Savimale," boundaries repeated in the inscriptions of his grandson Ballala (1101). The identification of several of these toponyms is uncertain, but some are clarified in the inscriptions of Ballala's brother and successor, the great Visnuvardhana. In 1117 he described the extent of his domain as follows:

> By relying on the strength of his arms he guarded the earth bounded on the east by the lower ghat of Nangali, on the south by Kongu, Ceram, and Anamale, on the west by the Barakanur and other ghats of Konkana, on the north by Savimale.

In 1140 near the end of his reign Visnuvardhana provided a list of the provinces "united under the single umbrella" of his rule. These include the Gangavadi Ninety-six Thousand, the Banavase Twelve Thousand, the Palasige Twelve Thousand, and the "two [that make] Six Hundreds" (i.e., Belvola 300 and Puligere 300). This corresponds to the area extending from the southern Mysore plateau, north as far as present-day Belgaum, and eastward as far as Hampi between the Krishna and Tungabhadra rivers. In later records, such as those of Visnuvardhana's son Narasimha in 1143 and Narasimha II in 1228, although the urban core has shifted to Dvarasamudra, these boundaries reappear with only slight variations: Nangali in the east, Vikramesvara in the south, Alvarakheda in the west, the Heddore (or Perddore) river in the north. When we combine all this information, the zone that manifests itself is bounded by present-day Kolar district in the east (where Nangali is to be located), Coimbatore/Salem districts in the south (Kongu), Konkan and the ghats in the west, and the Krishna river in the north. Lastly, in a record of 1237 from the reign of Virasomesvara (the prasasti of Mallikarjuna referred to earlier), the king, "emperor of the south" (*daksi-nacakravarti*), is said to have gotten "incorporated in the book of accounts" a dominion whose limits were Kanci in the east, Velapura in the west, the Krishna in the north, and Bayala Nadu in the south. The north-south limits remain the same, as apparently does the west, but the Hoysala power-sphere is now represented as having stretched further eastward.[18]

---

[18] See Lewis Rice in *EC* 5.1, xii-xiii and note (Vikramesvara probably means Ramesvara;

Several aspects of the new political order are unequivocally manifested in these documents. First, over the course of some three centuries the Hoysalas represented their political power as contained within boundaries. Not only was this representation remarkably stable over the entire period, but the boundaries themselves and the conception of political territoriality they constituted had nothing whatever fuzzy about them. What will be less immediately obvious to most readers is that the demarcated zone conforms largely to a Kannada-culture region, one that was produced and continuously reproduced by the concrete distribution and discursive messages of the representations themselves. There was no longer any aspiration to extend political rule far beyond the Krishna northwestward into Marathi-speaking areas, or northeastward into Telugu land, nor beyond Kolar into Tamil country (the southern zone, to some degree, excepted), nor beyond the ghats into Kerala. Looting expeditions, so frequent in this world, would continue to be undertaken against polities considerably beyond this region. Thus the attack on Dhara in Madhya Pradesh by Vinayaditya's son Ereganga around 1095, which was described in one inscription as "the first deep draught in his feast of the lands of his enemies during his conquest of the north." Visnuvardhana in the 1130s could continue to claim to have defeated an epic array of capitals and kingdoms across the Sanskrit cosmopolis (Anga, Kuntala, Kanci, Madhura, Malava, Cera, Kerala, Nolamba, Kadamba, Kalinga, Vanga, Bangala, Varala, Cola, Khasa, Barbbara, Oddaha, Kach, Sinhala, Nepala). And in 1173 Narasimha could still be described—according to the ancient patriarchal trope that equated political dominion with sexual domination—as

> a great swan sporting in the lake of the women of Andhra, a sun to the lotus faces of the women of Sinhala, a golden belt to the waists of Karnata women, a musk ornament on the cheeks of the women of Lata (Gujarat), saffron paste on the goblet-like breasts of Cola (Tamil) women, a moon to the waterlily eyes of Gauda (west Bengal) women, a wave on the [river] that is the beauty of the girls of Bangala (east Bengal), a bee to the lotus faces of the women of Malava (Malwa).[19]

---

the unknown Savimale is to be located somewhere around the Krishna). The epigraphs referred to in this paragraph are, in order: *EC* 4: Ng 32; *EC* 5: Bl. 199; *EC* 5: Bl. 58; *EC* 5: 270 (Ak. 18); *EC* 5: Ak. 55; *EC* 5: Cn. 204; *EC* 7: 215. 7-9. "Hundreds" and "thousands" refer to village administrative units that are still poorly understood.

[19] For the citations see *EC* 5: xiv n., and p. 128; xix.

Yet by the thirteenth century this had become an entirely symbolic discourse, one deriving its power from the nostalgic and still-cultivated cultural memory of quasi-universalist power in cosmopolitan space, of which the most apposite communicative correlate is the magnificent Kannada inscriptional form in which it is promulgated—itself a supreme example of the cosmopolitan vernacular style, illustrated in the extended "garland of metaphors" in the above citation. Real political power now acknowledged new and narrower constraints, of a geocultural sort, in a way that previously had never, or never so insistently, been the case. And this is a limited domain that is fully aware of its place in the world. The Hoysala Nadu, or the Culture-land of Hoysala power, "a land that milks out every wish," is placed, in the kind of telescopic or nested representation familiar from this period, within Kuntala-desa, which is within the land of the descendents of Bharata, Bharata-varsa itself being found to the south of Meru in the midst of Jambudvipa, hemmed in by the ocean.[20] Power, like language and literary culture, was now no longer quasi-universal as it had been for the whole previous millennium, but de-fined and firmly em-placed.

It should be unnecessary to insist that these newly crystallizing vernacular places must not be thought of as the bounded territories of nation-states *avant la lettre*. Before modernity, boundaries both of power and language, and, for the latter, both real and conceptual, were not knife-edged but broad, porous and not policed. Ruling lineages themselves were in some instances also far more mobile than this model of territorialization implies.[21] Yet by the beginning of the second millennium, vernacular areas of the sort found in the Hoysala sphere—generated through a complex dialectical process with language-practices in general and literary-cultural practices in particular—had begun to constitute something like a limit of political enterprise, becoming perceptibly operationalized as such in royal communication, as the find-spot

---

[20] *EC* 5: 475 (Cn. 197 of 1233). For visions of Indian imperial space see Pollock, "Axialism and Empire".

[21] About forty ruling lineages are estimated to have existed in the subcontinent at the beginning of the second millennium. Whereas some of these were not necessarily tied to given territories (for example, Karnata kings migrated to rule in Mithila from around 1000 until ousted by the Tughluqs in the fourteenth century), Chattopadhyaya is right to speak in other cases of "lineage areas" e.g., Gangavadi, as being "integrated as administrative units to form supralocal power" (in *The State in India: 1000-1700*, ed. Hermann Kulke [Delhi: Oxford U. Press, 1995], 217-20).

maps of local-language inscriptions demonstrate, corroborating the royal representations themselves.[22]

Whatever other interpretations such data may bear, they suffice to refute, for southern Asia at least, the broad scholarly consensus that only the modern map could have brought such geo-bodies to life in the political imagination and made discourse about them sensible; or that concepts of "country (des) and realm (rajatva)" are recent colonial imports; or, more grandly, that belief in the premodern existence of regionality as such constitutes "a curious misreading," since "a sense of region and nation emerged together through parallel self-definitions—and this point is essential to any understanding of the distinctive, layered character of Indianness." On the contrary, the layered character of Indianness cannot be understood without an understanding of the long-term production of its multiple spatial components, of which the Hoysala records are an eloquent example.[23] Precisely the same is true in western Europe, and in both areas the rise of vernacular power, and the culture that underwrote that power and was underwritten by it in turn, are the signal transformation of the early second millennium.

3. Making Historical Sense of Vernacularization

Is it possible to conceive of the gradual abandonment of transregional in favor of regional languages for the creation of literary and political texts, along with the transformations in political space that this choice both reflects and reproduces, as a connected Eurasian historical phenomenon? Can we identify any credible existing account, or provide any new ones, that might explain such transformations as a unified spatiotemporal process connecting Karnataka (and even Java) to England from the beginning of the second millennium and intensifying over the following three or four centuries, by which time the lineaments of vernacular literary cultures were set? This would be a very tall order in

---

[22] Note that from the time the Hoysalas took firm control of the region from Kolar to Mysore, they issued records in the area in Tamil (far more in fact than the Colas), thus reinforcing the image and fact of language boundaries.

[23] Thongchai Winichakul, "Maps and the Form of the Geobody of Siam," in Asian Forms of the Nation, ed. Stein Tønnesson and Hans Antlöv (London: Curzon, 1996), 76 (cf. Michael Biggs, "Putting the State on the Map: Cartography, Territory, and European State Formation," Comparative Studies in Society and History, 41,2 [1999], 374-411); Partha Chatterjee, The Nation and Its Fragments (Princeton: Princeton U. Press, 1993), 95 ff.; Sunil Khilnani, The Idea of India (New York: Farrar, Straus, Giroux, 2000), 153.

itself. But no less difficult are the theoretical questions such an account would have first to have answered, concerning among other things the relationship between culture and power, or whether very distinctive out-comes—the highly differential character of the emergent political orders, from vernacular polities in some places to national states in others—can be brought under a single historical explanation.

In my recent essay on the world that vernacularization replaced, no attempt was made to account for the consolidation of the empire-form of polity and culture across this same space during the first millennium (beginning with the Mauryas c. 250 BCE, and around the same period the Romans).[24] This, so it seemed, was the way things were. The end of the old empire era, on the other hand, and the consolidation of new, more localized cultural-political formations seem to demand some kind of explanation, both for what, relatively speaking, is the near simul-taneity of these events, and for the many homologies across cases that can be perceived in everything from lexical choice between cosmopolitan and vernacular registers and ideologies of philologization to the pro-duction in literary texts of newly regionalized political landscapes and the growth of vernacular documentary states. There is far too much evidence of human choice and agency—made visible in the often sub-stantial time-lag between inaugural inscription and the commencement of literary vernacularization, for example, or in the anxiety so many vernacular intellectuals experienced before deciding to write locally—to ascribe vernacularization to simple evolution (the very proposition that culture "evolves" is itself dubious). But how else do we explain it?

Even granting that all the multifarious instances I have adduced in earlier work as examples of vernacularization do represent related phe-nomena and a coherent and unified conceptual object, the very idea that one grand historical account can tie them all together must strike us as preposterous, notwithstanding the genre of popular world history that discovers monocausal explanations in ecology, technology, or what-ever. The understandable antipathy of the scholarly age, except among some cultural and linguistic biologists, for such unified theories and total-izing explanations undoubtedly places constraints on us, as does abiding theoretical uncertainty about the very mechanisms of cultural change, once simplistic materialist models are questioned. More serious problems, again, are raised by the substantial lack of clarity about key develop-ments in the historical period itself, especially in southern Asia from

---

[24] Pollock, "Axialism and Empire".

about 900-1200, or even up to 1500. Most of our most significant positive data for this period are in fact supplied by the vernacularization process, and clearly that cannot be called upon to explain itself. But even here few hypotheses are on offer, beyond the now-discredited premise of religious reaction. Structures of economy and polity have been much less studied; admittedly the evidence for doing so is very thin (which may explain if not justify the fact that two major new scholarly projects have effectively written the most important centuries of the vernacular epoch out of the story of what counts in Indian history).[25] If, by contrast, European historiography shows fewer areas of darkness, the relationship of literary culture to social and political power has been largely ignored in all the grand syntheses. We have learned a great deal about the lineage of the absolutist state and the history of the civilizing process, but rarely in the impressive body of scholarship of which these thematics are representative are the language and literary medium of the political and social changes described or analyzed.[26] In view of these obstacles, it seems sensible here to attempt no more than a survey of some trends and tendencies that may have created conditions under which the new vernacular choices in culture and polity made better sense than the cosmopolitan choices that for so long had been the single option.

The first of several striking temporal conjunctures between the commencement and intensification of vernacularization in the first three centuries of the second millennium and Eurasia-wide developments relates to the global integration of trade and commerce. Originating in the eighth century and continuously developing through the eleventh, a new world system came into being that linked westernmost Europe, the Near East, and southern and eastern Asia in a network of material exchange on a vaster scale than anything previously known. This international trade economy reached its climax by 1350, and began to disintegrate after 1400 under a series of major disruptions, both socio-political and environmental, that produced world-wide recession (most significant among the former was the Ming Rebellion and China's ensuing isolation

---

[25] The *Cambridge Economic History of India* commences in 1200; the *New Cambridge History of India* begins almost two centuries later with Vijayanagara.
[26] I allude to Perry Anderson, *Lineages of the Absolutist State* (London: Verso, 1974), and Norbert Elias, *The Civilizing Process* (Oxford: Blackwell, 1994), in both of whom the silence on the vernacular revolution is deafening. The same can be said of such recent attempts at synthesis of late-medieval Asian societies as K. N. Chaudhuri, *Asia Before Europe* (Cambridge, Eng.: Cambridge U. Press, 1990).

from Central Asia; among the latter, the Black Death, which however spared southern Asia). The Indian subcontinent was fully integrated into both the Near Eastern and East Asian circuits. It profited greatly from the export of spices and finished cloth—with a balance of trade that would remain in its favor throughout the period and beyond—and like the rest of the system experienced at its height a powerful resurgence of urbanization, with more stable political cores.[27]

Trade may not have played quite the same direct role for the agrarian communities of the central Deccan, where vernacularization was most intense during these centuries, that it did for southern Gujarat, Kerala, or the Coromandel coast, although the rise to power of the Rastrakutas in central Karnataka may be connected with the expansion of west-coast trade following the Arab conquest of Sindh in the eighth century, which marked the start of the new world system in the Indian ocean. We can point to the growing importance of overseas merchant guilds from this region. One such association from Karnataka, the Five Hundred Masters of the Ayyavole, was established about the time the vernacular transformation began and lasted until the fourteenth century, and with increasing reach throughout this period it participated in the huge inter-national trading circuit mentioned above. Through its periodic meetings (called the gathering of "the Great Nadu") it seems to have constituted a vernacular social formation of a regionally coherent kind, and, what is equally important, it announced its culture and its power in a set of remarkable inscriptions in courtly literary Kannada.[28]

Yet trade had more indirect consequences for the new vernacularizing

---

[27] Much of this paragraph derives from the work of Abu-Lughod, *Before European Hegemony* (especially 268 ff.) and "The World System in the Thirteenth Century: Dead-End or Precursor?" in *Islamic and European Expansion: The Forging of a Global Order*, ed. Michael Adas (Philadelphia: Temple U. Press, 1993), 75-102; see also Andre Gunder Frank, "The Thirteenth Century World System: A Review Essay," *Journal of World History* 1,2 (1990), 249-56. Kulke refers to "the resurgence of trade and urbanism around A.D. 1000," and as the title of his book shows, he makes this a key point of periodization. Yet the year's significance is scarcely discussed (1995: 13; cf. 226 n.), and it seems to have a largely numerological quality. According to Frank, the vitality of southern Asia continued into the sixteenth-seventeenth centuries, see *ReOrient*, 234.

[28] Meera Abraham, *Two Medieval Merchant Guilds of South India* (Delhi: Manohar, 1988), especially 45 ff. An epigraph in *Karntak Inscriptions* (*KI*) 1:38 ff. reports that in 1186, a *maha nadu* meeting took place in a small town in the northwest of present-day Karnataka, consisting mostly of members from what is today's Dharwar and Belgaum, but attended also by chief merchants from Lata (Gujarat) and Maleyala (Kerala) who were settled in Karnataka. Their extraordinary executive powers may be gauged in another inscription in *KI* 4: 118 ff.

regions, since linked with the new material abundance it generated was the expansion of agrarian territories all across Eurasia, and especially in India. Indeed, according to a recent authoritative account, the five centuries up to 1300 constitute "the crucial formative period for agrarian history in the subcontinent," when the "interactive expansion of agricultural and dynastic territories produced the basis for all the major agrarian regions of modern South Asia."[29]

There is no reason to doubt, then, that this world system of trade and its consequences for agricultural production were real and new. What may be doubted is whether some necessary connection, in Karnataka or Castile, links the new wealth from trade and agriculture and the urbanization they may have stimulated to self-expression in the vernacular, whether in literary or in political texts, especially when this expression was not itself especially mercantile in character (indeed, the works of Pampa and the poet of the *Cid* are far more concerned with the old military aristocracy). Scholars who have theorized the precapitalist world system are completely silent about cultural change, and few cogent hypotheses are available even for Europe. One recent study, while correctly locating the key developments in the differentiation of the Romance languages in the period 1000-1300, is unable to offer any persuasive argument linking economic growth or political regionalization and centralization with developments in literary culture. Instead, vernacularization is seen as a functional response to a new need "to keep in touch throughout large regions," while the terminological identification of the new vernaculars, especially those that were "culturally and politically important," is vaguely ascribed to the changes in the "fabric of society."[30] The view of some historians of southern Asia that the expanding world system had an impact on the formation of states and regional cultures that constitutes a "second, medieval revolution," bumps up against the fact that regionalization and vernacularization began in earnest in many places, such as the Midlands, well after the fourteenth century, when this system is said to have weakened—or elsewhere, such as Karnataka, by the tenth century, before it had become strong.[31] The place of the flourishing new world system of

---

[29] Ludden, *An Agrarian History*, especially 77 ff. and 106 ff.
[30] Tore Janson, "Language Change and Metalinguistic Change: Latin to Romance and Other Cases," in *Latin and the Romance Languages in the Early Middle Ages*, ed. Roger Wright and Rosamund McKitterick (London: Routledge, 1991), 23.
[31] David Ludden, "History Outside Civilization and the Mobility of South Asia," *South Asia* 17,1 (1994), 9-10.

trade in the origin and crystallization of vernacularization may therefore be one of concomitance rather than causality.

What is considerably more important, a functionalist theory of cultural change based on the late-medieval world system certainly cannot
accommodate the very different developments of literary culture in East
Asia. While the region was a crucial component of that system, with
the sole exception of Japan there is complete absence of vernacularization as I define the phenomenon. In Vietnam in the fourteenth or
fifteenth century, a demotic script was indeed developed (*chu' nom*, an
adaptation of Chinese characters for the writing of Vietnamese sounds)
by means of which Vietnamese literature was able to present itself in
a non-Chinese form for the first time. But this innovation died on the
vine as far as inaugurating a new cultural politics is concerned, and the
breakthrough to vernacularization is absent elsewhere in the Chinese
world. As for China itself, the full maturation of a written "vernacular
Sinitic" does not occur until the May Fourth Movement of 1919, whereas
"the amount of unadulterated writing in the other vernacular Sinitic
topolects and languages is so pathetically small as to be virtually nonex-
istent."[32] The full vernacularization of Vietnam (like that of Korea,
despite a similar development of demotic writing system in the mid-
fifteenth century) seems similarly to be derivative project of Western
modernity. All this may arguably be ascribed to the very different character of imperial language and polity present in the Chinese sphere. At
any event, the new world system of trade can hardly be counted as
consequential to vernacularization if its consequences were so uneven.

The period 1000-1400 is not only the age of a great precapitalist
world system, but also a time of emergence of new nomadic empires
based in and radiating out from Central Asia. It would be unwarranted
to define the entire epoch by these political formations, as a recent contribution to the periodization of Eurasian history invites us to do. They
had little direct impact on any of the vernacularizing regions dealt with
here; and unlike what occurred in Iran there was no "renomadization"

---

[32] Victor H. Mair, "Buddhism and the Rise of the Written Vernacular in East Asia:
The Making of National Languages," *Journal of Asian Studies* 53 (1994), 707, 725, 730
(his argument regarding Buddhist missionizing and vernacularization, see especially
p. 722, is, however, false for many language realms in southern Asia, as is that regarding the perpetually "positive attitude" toward the languages of Place in India, p. 724).
For Vietnam, see O. W. Wolters, *Two Essay on Dai-Viet in the Fourteenth Century* (New
Haven: Council on Southeast Asia Studies,1988), 27, vii, 31-32, and Nguyen The Anh,
"Le Vietnam," in *Initiation à la Peninsule indochinoise*, ed. P. B. Lafont (Paris: L'Harmattan,
1996), 113-39.

of either South Asia or Western Europe. Yet the very existence of these empires may have had repercussions in Western Europe and South Asia. One of course was to secure the new world trading system itself. But the historic role of nomadic peoples was not limited to the mediation of international trade. The new spatial identities of western Europe and southern Asia may have owed something to the Eurasia-wide migrations of the nomadic peoples. Some scholars have spoken recently of a new "parcelization of space" in South Asia as a result of the nomadic migrations, producing new and mutually exclusive units of territory governed by ever more uniform political orders.[33]

But of course the two regions differed completely in their ability to deal with the nomadic migrations: Western Europe succeeded in excluding them, precisely at the moment when South Asia became most open to their advances, which culminated in the establishment of a powerful new conquest state in the north of the subcontinent, the Delhi Sultanate. And if the analysis of literary and political vernacularization given here is even remotely correct, Europe and India would have to have reacted in similar ways in the face of these two very different kinds of stimuli, developing literary cultures that unified the language of the region through unprecedented works of imaginative power, and, so to speak, textualized the region of the language through new representations of territorial coherence. The outcomes are comparable, but the proximate causal factors—nomadic defeat on the one hand, and success on the other—are diametrically opposed.

Also left unaccounted for in an explanatory model based on trade, agricultural expansion, or the growth of the nomadic empires is the vernacularization of Southeast Asia. No direct role can be ascribed to the migrations of the nomadic peoples in the vernacular transformation of tenth century Java or fourteenth century Thailand. Moreover, while southeast Asia in general participated in the world system of trade from 1000-1400, recent studies now see in the period beginning in the fifteenth century developments in commerce, urbanization, political absolutism,

---

[33] Jos Gommans, "The Eurasian Frontier After the First Millennium A. D.: Reflections Along the Fringe of Time and Space," *Medieval History Journal* 1,1 (1998), especially 132-3, and for the new periodization based on nomadic empires, J. H. Bentley, "Cross-Cultural Interaction and Periodization in World History," *American Historical Review* 101,3 (1996), 766-8. The "post-cosmic" polities of eastern Java (Kadiri, Singhasari, Majapahit), for their part, seem to show a different and new kind of economic organization—mixed agricultural-maritime—but I have not yet been able to find a good account of what other kinds of social or political transformations may have taken place in the so-called post-*pralaya* period, when the central plains were abandoned for the east.

and religious orthodoxy without earlier precedent.[34] Yet another objection to this model is the highly variable pace of vernacularization: While this whole set of factors—the expansion of trade, the development of agrarian regions, heightened urbanization, the consolidation and increasing centralization of dynastic realms—is in evidence across the entire Indian subcontinent during these five centuries, virtually no courtly vernacular literature is to be found in the Gangetic plain before the mid-fifteenth century at the earliest.

4. Islam on its Eastern and Western Frontiers

To speak of the world system in the early centuries of the second millennium or the rise of nomadic empires as these impinge on South Asia is eventually to speak of the expansion of Islam as a factor in global change during this period. Scholars have long recognized that the first three or four centuries of the second millennium constitute a major watershed in southern Asian history, but this has typically been conceptualized in religious terms, as "the rise of Muslim power"; the new system of trade and the expansion and consolidation of agrarian regions have only recently come to be appreciated as shaping forces operating entirely outside the confines of religion. For other intellectual and political reasons there is a palpable reluctance among contemporary scholars to regard Islam as itself a substantialized agent of historical change (rather than particular trader groups or nomadic peoples who happen to be Muslim), to think of its advent as defining an age over against the archaizing Hindu and the modernizing colonial, or offering a universal solvent for all tough questions of history in medieval Asia. Undoubtedly the expansion of nomadic empires and the global trading network were fostered as much by non-Muslims (the Mongols) as by the recently converted Turkish tribes (Ghaznavids, Ghorids, Khaljis, and others) who were to transform India. Yet there unarguably did occur an expansive movement of Muslim peoples under the ideology of Islam—a movement, as one scholar has it, consisting of "well-executed military maneuvers

---

[34] Victor Lieberman, "Local Integration and Eurasian Analogies: Structuring Southeast Asian History, *c.* 1350-*c.* 1830," *Modern Asian Studies* 27,3 (1993), 475-572; "The Eurasian Context of the Early Modern History of Mainland South East Asia, 1400-1800," *Modern Asian Studies* 31,3 (1997), 449 ff. and Anthony Reid, "An 'Age of Commerce' in Southeast Asian History," *Modern Asian Studies* 24,1 (1990), 1-30 have argued most strongly for a historical break in mid-fifteenth century southeast Asia that would count as "early modern," after the "classical era," 1000-1350.

directed by a central command," "undertaken for quite rational purposes," and "driven by powerful religious forces"—that to some degree coincided with the vernacular revolution in Western Europe and South Asia.[35] What the expansion of Islam may have contributed to the conditions of vernacular possibility therefore merits consideration here, however brief the narrative must be and however inexpert the narrator.

Interactions with the carriers of Islam actually commenced in the two regions with striking simultaneity—around the year 711, when Arab and Berber armies under the Umayyad dynasty of Baghdad took Gibraltar and, half a world away, Arab forces rode into Sindh. The conquest of the western Mediterranean has been credited with profound and enduring consequences. Perhaps the first scholar to argue this out cogently was Henri Pirenne in the early decades of the last century. His general thesis regarding the economic history of Europe, which, broadly stated, posits a retardation of the Mediterranean economy through what he believed was an obstruction of trade routes by the Arabs, enabling the rise of northern Europe ("Without Mohammed Charlemagne would have been inconceivable"), has recently been reexamined and seriously contested. But Pirenne was also interested in the literary-cultural consequences of these events, and this component of his analysis has been entirely ignored, though it retains considerable interest.

As Pirenne rightly pointed out, previous movements of peoples into Europe, such as those of the Germanic tribes in the fourth and fifth centuries, resulted in their eventual assimilation into the literary culture of "Romania" (by a kind of Romanization I describe elsewhere). In this respect, the eighth century conquest was unprecedented. There was no such assimilation; instead, there occurred a complete redirection of literary culture, "a profound transformation where language was concerned." Much of what Pirenne goes on to argue can, in fact, no longer be accepted. Although it is true, and importantly true, that Arabic eventually replaced Latin in north Africa, Pirenne was wrong to believe that Latin and an educated clergy disappeared from Spain after the

---

[35] The quotation is from Richard Eaton, "Islamic History as Global History," in *Islamic and European Expansion*, 10-11. The discussion on 8 ff. usefully reviews the historiography of Arab conquests. Ludden, "History Outside Civilization" exemplifies the ambivalence about the role of Islam in explaining large-scale political and cultural change in South Asia: on the one had the "second medieval revolution" is clearly shown to be tied up with Muslim power (pp. 9-10 and 15), on the other, it is denied that the "rise of Muslim power" should function as the "one overarching theme" (p. 10).

conquest: ninth century Córdoba knew a vibrant and literate clerical culture, that of the Mozarabs, whose extant writings fill several volumes. Latin did not suddenly "cease to be spoken about the year 800," and people were not "beginning to speak Spanish." In Francia, Latin had long been changing as a spoken language, as all spoken languages change, but it continued to be spoken as "Romance," which for its part would only be conceptually constituted as something different from Latin after the Carolingian spelling reforms of the early ninth century. With respect to the decline of Latin literary culture, this had already been remarked on by Gregory of Tours at the end of the sixth century, long before the Arab conquests, a decline perhaps not unconnected with the decay of city life in the Mediterranean. As for Spanish (or rather Castellano), this would not even be created for another six centuries (and "Español" not until the sixteenth century). If it may largely be true that "By the most curious reversal of affairs, which affords the most striking proof of the rupture effected by Islam, the North in Europe [between the Seine and the Weser] replaced the South both as a literary and as a political centre," traditions of Latin textuality remained strong in the south. And at all events, the Arab conquests in the western Mediterranean were only one aspect of a vast movement of peoples in medieval Europe, including Vikings from the north and Slavs and Magyars from the east, all of whom left in their wake widespread disruption of educational institutions in England, France, and Spain. All that said, Pirenne is pointing toward something significant about these historical events in relation to the course and character of vernacularization. If the actual linguistic processes are more complex than he realized, the emergent Islamic states do appear to have constituted a new and enduring stimulus to language and literary-cultural development.[36]

It seems reasonably clear that, in its initial stages, vernacularization in northern Europe, as in the case of England, developed for reasons that had nothing directly to do with the expansion of Islam on its western frontier. In southern Europe, by contrast, the creation of a continental French literary culture in the twelfth century or a Castilian one

---

[36] Henri Pirenne, *Mohammed and Charlemagne* (London: Allen and Unwin, 1958 [1939], 274-8. No good critique of the Pirenne thesis on literary culture exists, to my knowledge. For the economic thesis, see R. Hodges and D. Whitehouse, *Mohammed, Charlemagne and the Origins of Europe: Archaeology and the Pirenne Thesis* (Ithaca: Cornell U. Press), 1983; *The Pirenne Thesis: Analysis, Criticism, and Revision*, ed. Alfred F. Havighurst rev. ed. (Lexington, MA: Heath, 1976).

in the thirteenth took place within an environment that to an important degree had been marked by interactions with Arabic cultural-political
formations in both the western and the eastern Mediterranean, most
powerfully during the Crusades. Some scholars have pointed to the general upsurge in vernacular textualization at just this period. And of
course the *chansons de geste* themselves, while addressing a range of local
issues such as family prosperity and honor, explicitly thematize the
Christian wars against the Saracens. Many of the songs in the important
cycle *La geste du roi* (twelfth century) have to do with Charlemagne's battles against the infidel, which again have been said to embody the ideal
of the Crusades;[37] the composition of the Oxford version of the *Chanson
de Roland* itself is now generally dated to about 1100 (though admittedly
it looks back imaginatively three centuries), and is closely connected
with the spirit of the First Crusade (1095-99), strong echoes of which
may be heard in the text (recall only the line *Paien [Sarrazins] unt tort /
e chrestiens unt dreit*, "The pagans [Saracens] are wrong, and the Christians
are right," l. 1014).

In Spain the Reconquista, which ended around 1250, conditioned
the environment within which the kings of Castile, and especially Alfonso
X, created Spanish as a language of culture and polity. The inaugural
vernacular literary text, *Poema de mio Cid*, was shaped by similar forces
as the *chansons de geste*, importantly, again, the Crusades. As one recent
study describes it, "The example of Castile's great command in battle
against the Moors was modernised and held up, very much in the way
that the example of Charlemagne and Roland, campaigners against the
Moslems of Spain, was held up by 'Turoldus' [putative author of the
Chanson de Roland] for the French of about 1100, as the barons and
armies sought recruits to hold Syria and Palestine against the Moslems."
The one extant manuscript of the *Cid* is dated to 1207, a year after a
Papal Bull was issued to encourage Christians to unite against the
Muslims of Spain, and it is arguable that the textualization of the poem
was meant to contribute to the goal of attracting soldiers to the Christian
armies fighting the Muslim south.[38]

Such facts, though the tip of an iceberg, are still only one dimension

---

[37] Michel Zink, *Littérature française du moyen age* (Paris: Presses universitaires de France,
1992), 78, cf. 78-87. On increased textualization, see Denis Hollier, ed. *A New History
of French Literature* (Cambridge, MA: Harvard U. Press, 1989), 20.

[38] Colin Smith, *The Making of the Poema de mio Cid* (Cambridge, Eng.: Cambridge U.
Press, 1983), 96-9.

of a vast and complex picture of political and cultural interaction. Muslims had served among the forces of Christian kings (in Leon, for example), and vice versa; the *Cid* is anything but an anti-Muslim tract; part of the splendor of Alfonso's cultural world resulted from his eagerness to recreate something of the glory of the Córdoba caliphate, and from his appropriation of Islamic learning through translation. (One literary event that suggests this, as well as the structural homologies between European and Indian vernacularization, is the 1251 adaptation from the Arabic into Castilian of *Kalila wa Dimna*, the celebrated mirror for princes, the Sanskrit original of which, the *Pancatantra*, had been adapted into Kannada by Durgasimha in 1031 at the Kalyana Calukya court.) And features of Occitan literary culture, some argue, are unimaginable without literary communication with Arabic poetry.[39] Clearly nothing here (I leave out the Church) suggests an attitude of hostility toward Muslims qua Muslims. But all that it seems possible to assert with any confidence about Islam in relation to western European vernacularization is that it contributed to the creation of a political and communicative context within which speaking literarily from a regional position, a position in Place, so to put it, seems to have made far more sense than speaking from a cosmopolitan location. Something that corroborates this assessment appears at work in a later encounter further east in Europe, where Hungarian literati first produced a vernacular literary culture in response to the consolidation of Ottoman hegemony in the sixteenth century. The new cultural-political realities of the early second millennium seem to have been such as encouraged a multiple and hence vernacular response, rather than a unified and hence Latin one.

In South Asia, too, vernacularization in its inaugural stages developed without any direct connection with the expansion of Islam on its eastern frontier. Like England, Tamil and Kannada country had well-developed literary cultures of Place by the end of the first millennium. Moreover, the effects of the Arab conquest of Sindh seem to have been of a much different order from those in the western Mediterranean. While its economic impact turned out to be substantial, especially in bringing the region into denser networks of exchange than had previously been the case (in particular by mediating the transfer of southern Asian crop species to the West), Arab political power was largely confined to

---

[39] On the last point, see for example, Maria Rosa Menocal, *The Arabic Role in Medieval Literary History: A Forgotten Heritage* (Philadelphia: U. of Pennsylvania Press, 1987).

Sindh and seems at all events to have had little measurable cultural impact. It would be another three centuries before vastly more transformative interactions took place with competitors for power from Central Asia (starting around 1000), leading to the establishment of the Delhi Sultanate in the early 1300s. And the events of these later centuries did have cultural consequences in northern India, at least, that bring them into closer comparison with developments in southern Europe.

To be sure, not all these consequences are related to the problem of vernacularization. In both southern Asia, as to a lesser extent in Europe, the very presence of Islam seems occasionally to have prompted new constructions of transregional identities among cosmopolitan literati (something that stands in some tension to the regionalization of consciousness noted earlier). The term "Hindu," for example, is used for the first time in fourteenth century Sanskrit inscriptions as a (contrastive) self-identification in response to the presence of Turkic power. Similarly, it was in reference to Charles Martel's defeat of the Arabs at Tours and Poitiers in 732 that the term "Europeans" (*Europenses*) was first employed by an anonymous Latin chronicler of Córdoba, "Europe" thereafter coming into frequent use in reference to Charlemagne.[40] The cosmopolitan culture that underwrote the new, and surely very thin, transregional collective identities in southern Asia was undoubtedly eroding in many areas in the north of the subcontinent, though not necessarily as a result of these political events. In Kashmir, for example, the production of most major forms of Sanskrit court poetry ceased after the twelfth century, but this seems to have resulted from internal processes of civic disintegration unrelated to the Central Asian power seekers, whose control over the Valley would not be consolidated until the fifteenth century and who in fact sought thereafter, though unsuccessfully, to revitalize Sanskrit culture.[41]

With the collapse of some important urban sites of cosmopolitan learning in the Midlands such as Kanyakubja at the end of the twelfth century, the center of Sanskrit culture can be said with some justice to have shifted southward to the sphere of the Vijayanagara empire from

[40] Cynthia Talbott, "Inscribing the Self, Inscribing the Other: Hindu-Muslim Identities in Pre-Colonial India," *Comparative Studies in Society and History* 37,4 (1995), 700; Klaus von See, *Neues Handbuch der Literaturwissenschaft.* v. 6: *Europäisches Frühmittelalter* (Wiesbaden: Aula-Verlag, 1985): 42.

[41] See Sheldon Pollock, "The Death of Sanskrit," *Comparative Studies in Society and History* 43,2 (2001), 395-400.

the late fourteenth century on, in a way not unlike the apparent northward shift of Latin culture in the ninth century. Few areas in northern India, outside of what then came newly to be seen as the frontier zone of Mithila on the Nepal border, would show quite the same level of Sanskrit cultural production as had earlier been in evidence until a revival set in during the early Mughal period, and this diminution is hardly surprising given the widespread enfeeblement of the courtly culture required to sustain it. The fate of Sanskrit learning more broadly construed, however, remains for north India a matter of scholarly disagreement and requires far more serious empirical study than it has yet received. There seems little reason to believe that reproduction of *pandita* lineages, the real educational infrastructure of Sanskrit culture, was disrupted during this period to any degree serious enough to create a vacuum for the consolidation of vernacular literary cultures, in a way that would be analogous to the weakening of Latin education in western Europe (assuming for the sake of argument that there was indeed such a weakening). The fact that those who first produced these cultures were trained, and trained seriously, in Sanskrit, suggests that the transmission of Sanskrit knowledge had not diminished in any appreciable sense, as the various renaissances seem to suggest was indeed the case in Latinate Europe.

While the impact of these events on vernacular literary cultures also awaits in-depth research, it may well have been substantial. It is only from the late thirteenth century at the earliest that evidence is found for literary production in any of the north Indian vernaculars (those now named Gujarati, Marathi, Bangla, Brajbhasha and the other varieties of Hindi); what we do not know is exactly how this development relates to the social and political events of the epoch. There are, to be sure, instances of dramatic vernacularization largely contemporaneous with the expansion of Sultanate power, and which actually remark on its presence; just this seems to have occurred in Maharashtra. Reverberations of the rise of the new political powers, quite like that in the *chansons de geste*, may be heard in a wide variety of early vernacular works. These are sometimes very explicit and hostile, as in one of the earliest western Rajasthani texts, the *Kanhadade-prabandha* of Padmanabha (1455), which purports to describe the events of Mahmud of Ghazni's sack of the great temple of Siva at Somnath (Gujarat) four centuries earlier. Sometimes they are very muted, as in the vernacular *Ramayanas*, whose composition around the periphery of the Sultanate—like the creation of the *dharma* encyclopedias mentioned earlier, which sought to totalize an entire way of life—have seemed to me a comment on its expansion.[42] But all these cases may once again mark historical coincidence rather than consequence.

What is likely to have been far more consequential than all this is the example provided by those Muslim literati who themselves, perhaps as actual inaugurators, composed literature in South Asian languages of Place—something unexampled in Western Europe, incidentally, where Muslims did not participate directly in the nascent vernacular literary cultures (there is no premodern French Muslim literature, as there is a premodern Bangla and Hindi and Kannada and Tamil Muslim literature). There are indications that this aesthetic accommodation or convergence might have begun as early as the eleventh century with Mas'ud Sa'd Salman of Lahore; it was certainly part of the oeuvre of Amir Khusrau in the early fourteenth century and of the collection of Baba Farid's texts a little later. At all events, the great Hindavi Sufi works of the late fourteenth and fifteenth centuries (often exemplary instances of the cosmopolitan vernacular style), including Daud's *Candayan* and Jayasi's *Padmavat*, are unlikely to have gone unnoticed by non-Muslim communities of readers and listeners, as adaptations outside Sufi communities suffice to indicate. That said, there is admittedly little evidence of true cross-community literary communication during this epoch in other areas, such as Gujarat or Andhra.[43]

The expansion of Islam on its western and eastern frontiers may accordingly be an additional piece in the complicated puzzle of historicizing the vernacular millennium, though one generating additional puzzles of its own. In some cases the consolidation of vernacular cultural-political orders may have been a consequence of the presence of

---

[42] Here, too, however, alterity may not always be what it seems. The patron of the Bangla Ramayana, for example, is now thought to have been a Muslim, Rukannuddin Barbak Sah, 1459-74, see W. L. Smith, *Ramayana Traditions in Eastern India* (Stockholm: U. of Stockholm, Department of Indology, 1988), 38. The character of the political-military environment of early Marathi vernacularization may be captured by a passage from the *Smrtisthala* translated in A. Feldhaus and S. G. Tulpule, *In the Absence of God: The Early Years of an Indian Sect* (Honolulu: U. of Hawaii Press, 1992), 92 ff.

[43] Intercommunity literary communication is another important and under-researched problem of South Asian literary history. No one seems to have studied the question whether the Gurji poetry of Shaikh Baha ud-Din Bajan (d. 1506) was read outside the Muslim community in Gujarat, or whether Dakani poetry found any resonance among Telugu writers. Certain religious poets such as Qazi Qadan in Sindhi or Bullhe Shah in Punjabi were more amenable to such circulation, as noted by Ali Asani, "At the Crossroads of Indic and Iranian Civilizations: Sindhi Literary Culture," in *Literary Cultures in History: Reconstructions from South Asia*, ed. Sheldon Pollock (Berkeley: U. of California Press, 2003), 639.

the new competitors for power: war may have made vernacular polities as much as the vernacular polities seem to have made war.[44] Other kinds of interactions with Islamicate cultures suggest that more strictly literary processes were at work: emulation of and appropriation from literati who provided fresh forms and themes, as in twelfth century Sicily or Occitania, or who first demonstrated, as in fifteenth century Avadh, the very possibility of vernacular literacy, much as the imitation of the declining imperial formations helped make possible the English and Kannada vernacular worlds beginning in the ninth century.

Summary and Conclusions

The precise weight of the contribution of globalizing Islam cannot, however, be easily calculated because as we have seen it was part of other larger-scale forces at work in the period, above all the new world network of trade that enriched both South Asia and Western Europe and helped make possible the burgeoning development of agricultural regions and urbanization. All these Eurasia-wide factors may well have conditioned, in ways that await adequate clarification, the development of vernacular literary cultures. What is puzzling however is that they did not effect such developments evenly across Eurasia itself, but only in particular regions. How we explain this unevenness is a very difficult problem in its own right, and would require a far more intensive comparative study of civilizational structures, communication practices, cultural presuppositions and the like than we now possess. Puzzling, too, are the conceptual and political variations found in the outcomes of the vernacularization process. Like the imperial political and cultural formations that preceded them and upon whose foundations they were built, these vernacular formations show that people in Europe and India reacted very differently to the various forces in play, and in these differences lie important implications for political and cultural theory.

---

[44] I here adapt a phrase from *The Formation of National States in Western Europe*, ed. Charles Tilly (Princeton: Princeton U. Press, 1975), 42.

EURASIAN TRANSFORMATIONS OF THE TENTH TO THIRTEENTH CENTURIES: THE VIEW FROM SONG CHINA, 960-1279

PAUL JAKOV SMITH

ABSTRACT

This essay addresses the nature of the medieval transformation of Eurasia from the perspective of China during the Song dynasty (960-1279). Out of the many facets of the wholesale metamorphosis of Chinese society that characterized this era, I focus on the development of an increasingly bureaucratic and autocratic state, the emergence of a semi-autonomous local elite, and the impact on both trends of the rise of the great steppe empires that encircled and, under the Mongols ultimately extinguished the Song. The rapid evolution of Inner Asian state formation in the tenth through the thirteenth centuries not only swayed the development of the Chinese state, by putting questions of war and peace at the forefront of the court's attention; it also influenced the evolution of China's socio-political elite, by shaping the context within which elite families forged their sense of coorporate identity and calibrated their commitment to the court. I conclude that intersecting cycles of state-building in China and the steppe during the Eurasian transformation stimulated the rise of a Neo-Confucian ideology that helped the literatus elite transfer its energies away from the unresponsive and autocratic court to more local concerns, allowing it to gain autonomy from the Song state that had conceived it, adapt to life under Mongol rule, and project its influence over Chinese culture well into the late imperial era.

In this essay I address the nature of the medieval transformation of Eurasia from the perspective of China during the Song Dynasty (960-1279). Ever since the work of the Japanese historian Naitô Torajiro (1866-1934), historians have viewed the period encompassed by the Song and its late-Tang and Five Dynasties precursors—that is, roughly the eighth through the thirteenth centuries—as an era of fundamental change in all aspects of Chinese society.[1] The primary engine of this medieval

---

[1] For a precis of Naitô's argument see Hisayuki Miyakawa, "An Outline of the Naitô Hypothesis and its Effects on Japanese Studies of China," *The Far Eastern Quarterly* 14.4 (1955), 533-552. Richard von Glahn puts the Naitô hypothesis in larger perspective in "Imagining Pre-modern China," in *The Song-Yuan-Ming Transition in Chinese History*, eds. Paul Jakov Smith and Richard von Glahn (Cambridge, Mass.: Harvard University Asia Center, 2003), 35-70.

transformation was undoubtedly the shift in the demographic center of gravity from the old political heartland of North China to the lush frontier regions drained by the Yangzi River. The percentage of the entire population residing in South China had increased from roughly 25 percent in the year 605 to 46 percent by the inception of the great transformation in the mid-eighth century, and climbed steadily thereafter to 65 percent in 1080 and 71 percent by 1200. Expansion into South China stimulated advances in rice agriculture, whose robust productivity broke the cycle of agrarian self-sufficiency and freed producers to specialize in market-oriented crops and handicrafts. As landowners and peasants throughout China were drawn into a network of trade in daily necessities as well as luxury goods for the rich, trade itself spilled beyond the confines of regulated urban markets into an articulated hierarchy of periodic rural markets, intermediate towns, and great urban centers of distribution and consumption.[2]

No less important than this economic metamorphosis, however, were the political aspects of the medieval transformation: the collapse of the medieval aristocracy of great clans that had dominated China politically and socially from roughly the fourth through the ninth centuries and the increasing bureaucratization of the Chinese state from the eighth century on.[3] Both trends were shaped by a third factor that had consequences not only for China but for all of Eurasia: the rise of the great steppes polities that began (from a Chinese perspective) with the Tibetan, Turkish, and Uighur states during the Tang; continued with the Khitan Liao (907-1125), Tangut Xi Xia (ca. 990-1227), and Jurchen Jin (1115-1234) empires during the Song; and culminated in the Mongol Empire of the Yuan (1260-1368). The rise of the steppe had a direct influence on the development of the Chinese state, by putting geopolitical imperatives and questions of peace and war at the forefront of any policy agenda. At the same time it indirectly influenced the evolution of the

---

[2] Mark Elvin provides a richly textured description of China's medieval economic revolution in *The Pattern of the Chinese Past* (Stanford: Stanford University Press, 1973). For a more evolutionary interpretation of the agrarian changes from the eighth through the sixteenth centuries see Li Bozhong, "Was There a 'Fourteenth-Century Turning Point'? Population, Land, Technology, and Farm Management," in Smith and von Glahn, *The Song-Yuan-Ming Transition*, 135-175.

[3] On the demise of the medieval aristocracy see David Johnson, *The Medieval Chinese Oligarchy* (Boulder: Westview Press, 1977). On the emergence of specialized bureaucratic agencies during the late Tang see, for example, Denis Twitchett, "The Salt Commissioners after the Rebellion of An Lu-shan," *Asia Major* (new series) 4.1 (1954), 60-89.

socio-political elite, by shaping the context within which elite families forged their sense of corporate identity and calibrated their commitment to the court.

It is precisely these intersecting themes of elite transformation and state-building in China and on the steppe that I focus on in this essay. That perspective requires a somewhat broader chronological scope than the tenth to thirteenth centuries that frame most of the essays in this volume. For especially with respect to the evolution of the Chinese state and its socio-political elite, some historians now envision not one great transformation starting in the Tang and ending in the Song, but rather two identifiable historical eras spanning the eighth to the sixteenth centuries. The first phase constitutes the Tang-Song transformation itself, encompassing at one end the collapse of the medieval aristocracy and the fall of the Tang, and at the other end the reunification of China under an increasingly activist Northern Song state staffed by an exam-mobilized elite dedicated to multigenerational service in government as their principal source of political power and social prestige. The second phase begins with the conquest of North China by the Jurchen in 1127, which drove the remnants of the Song court south to preside over a polity (termed the Southern Song) just two-thirds the size of its northern predecessor, while forcing the descendants of the Northern Song bureaucratic elite to recast their relationship to the central state and reorient their focus from the court and the capital to their home regions and locales.[4] For Song historians of widely different approaches, the move south comprised more than a territorial shift; it also signalled important changes in the structure of the Chinese state and the nature, orientation, and political vision of the Chinese elite. Although largely seen as the final episode in the Tang-Song transformation, some historians have tentatively identified the Southern Song as the beginning of a new historical phase, termed the Song-Yuan-Ming transition. At its

---

[4] The argument for a transformation of both the state and the socio-political elite in the transition from the Northern to Southern Song is developed most fully by Robert M. Hartwell, "Demographic, Political, and Social Transformations of China, 750-1550," *Harvard Journal of Asiatic Studies* 42.2 (1982), 365-442; and Robert P. Hymes, *Statesmen and gentlemen: the elite of Fu-chou, Chiang-hsi, in Northern and Southern Sung* (Cambridge: Cambridge University Press, 1986). The Hartwell—Hymes paradigm is refined by Beverly Bossler in *Powerful Relations: Kinship, Status, and the State in Sung China (960-1279)* (Cambridge, Mass.: Harvard University, Council on East Asian Studies, 1998). James T.C. Liu confirms a sharp change in political orientation from Northern to Southern Song in *China Turning Inward: Intellectual-Political Changes in the Early Twelfth Century* (Cambridge, Mass.: Harvard University, Council on East Asian Studies, 1988).

broadest, the concept of the Song-Yuan-Ming transition seeks to highlight a cluster of geopolitical, economic, social, and cultural trends that
mark the period spanning the Southern Song through the late Ming as
an evolutionary conduit linking the Tang-Song transformation of the
eighth to eleventh centuries with the equally transformative late imperial era of the sixteenth to nineteenth centuries. Although most of my
discussion in this essay focuses on the Song, it is the larger era of the
Song-Yuan-Ming transition that defines the end-point of my perspective.[5]

The picture that I attempt to draw here is very broad, and is based
far more on the work of fellow scholars than on original research of
my own. In the first two sections I trace state-building efforts in China
following the fall of the Tang and the parallel cycle of state formation
on the steppe; in the third section I discuss the impact of Sino-steppe
competition on the activist policies crafted by Wang Anshi for the irredentist Emperor Shenzong and his sons; and in the fourth and final
section, I outline the failure of the activist state and its consequences
for the evolution of the socio-political elite during the Song-Yuan-Ming
transition.

*Coming out of the Tang: Re-building the state in the five dynasties and
early Song*

The collapse of Tang power in the final decades of the ninth century
unleashed massive forces of rebellion, warlordism, and territorial fragmentation, inducing a half-century of social turmoil under the Five
Dynasties (907-960) in the north and Southern Kingdoms of the south
before the reestablishment of unity and order by Zhao Kuangyin and
his new dynasty, the Song (960-1279). Although the social disruptions
of this era of disunity were powerful enough to sweep away the underpinnings of the old Tang order, military hegemons in the north and
outlaw chieftains in the south initiated immediate efforts at state-building that laid the foundation for reunification under the Song and ushered in the emergence of new social and political elites.[6]

---

[5] I expand on the nature of the Song-Yuan-Ming transition in "Introduction:
Problematizing the Song-Yuan-Ming Transition," Smith and von Glahn, *The Song-Yuan-
Ming Transition*, 1-34.

[6] This section draws heavily on my draft introduction to *The Cambridge History of China
Vol. 5: The Sung Dynasty and its Precursors, Part 1*, eds. Denis Twitchett and Paul Jakov
Smith (forthcoming), and is heavily indebted to the contributors to that volume.

In the north, territorial expansion constituted the first step in the process of rebuilding a stable state. From 907 to 960, the successive regimes of north China consolidated their control along a north-south axis encompassing all of north China and the Central Plains from the Yellow River south to the Huai and Han Rivers, and west along the Wei River valley. Sovereignty over north China was by no means complete during this period, for the Shatuo stronghold centered on Taiyuan (in modern Shansi) slipped the noose of central control in 951 and—most momentously for later events—the Sixteen Prefectures comprising the 300-mile barrier between the Central Plains and the steppe were ceded by the Shatuo state of Later Jin to the Khitan in 937. But the overall trend was towards the deepening of territorial control, culminating under the fifth, Later Zhou dynasty with the recapture of two of the Sixteen Prefectures in the north, and annexation of the plains between the Huai and Yangzi Rivers from the Southern Tang.[7]

The process of territorial consolidation in the north was propelled by the increasingly effective assertion of centralized political authority. During the latter half of the Tang, the court had been obliged to cede political power to the military governors (*jiedushi*) and increasingly autonomous generals (many of Shatuo descent) of north China.[8] It was these generals, military governors, and regional warlords who competed with one another for mastery over the north, and who sought to recreate their own image of the defunct Tang order that they themselves had helped to destroy. Thus the chief challenge facing the successive would-be dynasts was how to recentralize power from other members of their own kind—in particular the military governors—while rebuilding the apparatus of the centralized, bureaucratic state.

That process of recentralization began with the very first Five Dynasties ruler, when Zhu Wen, founder of the Liang Dynasty (907-923), began to systematically replace Tang-era military governors with personally-appointed prefects loyal to Zhu alone. Although Zhu Wen was never able to neutralize the animosity of major military governors deeply opposed to his imperial aspirations and ruthless approach to governance, the four succeeding regimes (three Shatuo and one Chinese) were able

---

[7] These issues are addressed by Naomi Standen in Chapter One of *The Cambridge History of China Vol. 5, Part 1*, "The Five Dynasties, 907-979".

[8] See especially Robert M. Somers, "The End of the T'ang," in *The Cambridge History of China, Vol 3: Sui and Tang China, 589-906, Part I*, ed. Denis Twitchett (Cambridge: Cambridge University Press, 1979), 682-789.

to build on his momentum to impose ever-greater centralizing pressure on the military governors. By mid-century the Later Zhou (951-960) rulers Guo Wei and his adopted son Chai Rong, assisted by an emerging civil bureaucracy, had begun to win the war of attrition against the once-autonomous military governors. Crucial to their victory was the recentralization of military authority through a series of reforms that transformed the two most potent armies—the Metropolitan and Palace Commands—from unpredictable power brokers to reliable agents of centralized imperial power, finally relieving the Later Zhou rulers from dependence on the allegiance of the military governors and moving power unequivocally from the provinces to the center.[9]

Meanwhile throughout this half-century of ostensible fragmentation a parallel process of state-building was taking place in the south. Whereas northern state-builders came out of the class of military governors with roots in the Tang political order, southern rulers emerged out of militarized outlaw elements unleashed by the massive social dislocation and demographic upheavals produced by the rebellions that helped topple the Tang.[10] As Tang political authority was seized by Zhu Wen and his Later Liang regime in the north, the most powerful of these military entrepreneurs carved out a total of nine initial and two successor states that coincided with the physiographic cores of south China. Moreover, despite their outcast origins, the rulers of south China underwent a process of political maturation that paralleled the evolution of their northern neighbors. Over time military prowess yielded to political effectiveness as the chief measure of prestige and governance, as once-itinerant bandit chieftains formed stable demilitarized regimes based on political acumen, alliances with local elites, and the support of refugee literati in search of security and employment. In fact, state-building in the regionalized south was even more robust than in the war-torn north. For the greater stability of the south enabled the new regimes to initiate agrarian projects—especially hydrology—that enhanced agricultural productivity, and to sponsor internal, inter-regional, and international trade over land and by sea. Thus while the successive northern regimes had to focus on the crucial political problem of wresting power from

---

[9] The most important overview of this process is Edmund Henry Worthy, Jr., "The founding of Song China, 950-1000: Integrative changes in military and political institutions" (Ph.D. thesis, Princeton University, 1975).

[10] This process is described by Hugh Clark in Chapter Two of *The Cambridge History of China Vol. 5, Part 1*, "The Southern Kingdoms, 907-979."

other military governors, fending off each other, and developing workable approaches to the increasingly powerful Khitan, the southern kingdoms were free to develop sophisticated ways of taxing and even facilitating the growth of the increasingly buoyant commercial economy. And just like their northern counterparts, the rulers of the southern kingdoms reintroduced bureaucratic governance into their regions, deploying a mix of local and refugee literatus lineages as local circumstances allowed.

The half-century process of state-building in north and south paved the way for dynastic reunification under the Song founder Zhao Kuangyin, by centralizing military power, reestablishing the structures of bureaucratic governance, and (by 950 or so) establishing momentum towards imperial reunification. Both Zhao Kuangyin (or Taizu, r. 960-76) and the dynastic consolidator, his brother and successor Kuangyi (or Taizong, r. 976-97), emerged from what Edmund Worthy calls the "militocracy" of the tenth century; for their father, who had served successively in the imperial armies of each northern dynasty but the first, helped the family make the transition from undistinguished civil officials in the late Tang to established members of the Five Dynasties military elite.[11] Zhao Kuangyin was not only a talented soldier who rapidly ascended to the position of Commander of the Palace Army under Chai Rong, he was also a keen observer of Zhou bureaucratic reforms and a direct participant in Zhou policies of military centralization and territorial expansion. By 959, when Chai Rong's death put a child on the throne, Zhao had earned the intense personal loyalty of a reinvigorated imperial army and its confident military commanders, who took advantage of a reported invasion by Khitan and Northern Han forces in 960 to proclaim their 34-year old commander as emperor. It is possible to imagine the new Song Dynasty becoming just another place-holder in the succession of short-lived northern dynasties. But the social turmoil and political fragmentation generated by the collapse of the Tang had gradually but inexorably given way to civic order and political stability in both north and south, and by mid-century the two most powerful states in north and south China had begun to look beyond immediate problems to contemplate the possibilities of reunification. By the time Zhao Kuangyin assumed the throne of the sixth northern dynasty since the fall of the

---

[11] For a discussion of militocracy and the transition from militocratic to bureaucratic absolutism under T'ai-tsung, see Worthy, pp. 295-316; John W. Chaffee traces the history of the Zhao lineage in *Branches of Heaven: a History of the Imperial Clan of Sung China* (Cambridge: Harvard University Asia Center, 1999), Chapter Two.

Tang, reunification had become a realistic ambition, and as a central player in the Later Zhou campaigns of centralization Zhao Kuangyin was in an ideal position to capture the great prize.

The Song founder's approach to state-building continued the measures practiced by his Five Dynasties predecessors, especially his own mentor Chai Rong. Although Taizu was very much a military man, he is best known for peacefully demobilizing his general staff, thereby severing the personalized links between commanders and their troops that had made "praetorian" coups—such as the one that brought Taizu to power—so common in the post-Tang era, and subordinating the military to bureaucratic control under the absolute authority of an unchallenged emperor.[12] Taizu built on his prestige as absolute military commander to extend bureaucratic control well beyond what his Zhou mentors could achieve. Not only was Taizu able to neutralize the power-brokering role of the great generals, but he and his successor Taizong finally eradicated the military governors as a ruling elite, dismantling their territorial jurisdictions and replacing them with civilian officials under direct control of the capital. Thus the era of the Tang military governors was finally terminated by its last incumbents, the Song founders it had brought to power, and the position of *jiedushi* turned into a purely titular office conferred primarily on aboriginal chieftains.[13]

In other areas of civil administration Taizu adapted Tang and Five Dynasties precedents to recreate a network of county, prefectural, and circuit officials that implanted imperial authority throughout the empire through a growing bureaucratic apparatus increasingly staffed by graduates of an expanded examination system. Very quickly, the examination system burgeoned to become a defining feature of Song (and indeed all of mid- and late-imperial) political, intellectual, and cultural life.[14] At the same time, it gave rise to a new, literocentric political elite that, however much it may have benefited by local prestige and the owner-

---

[12] The term "praetorian" coup is used by John Rich Labadie, "Rulers and soldiers: perception and management of the military in Northern Song China (960-ca. 1060)," Ph.D. thesis, University of Washington, 1981, p. 35.

[13] Worthy, "The founding of Song China," pp. 272-79.

[14] For complete studies of the Song examination system in English see John W. Chaffee, *The Thorny Gates of Learning in Sung China* (Cambridge: Cambridge University Press, 1985), and Thomas H. C. Lee, *Government Education and Examinations in Sung China, 960-1278* (Hong Kong: The Chinese University of Hong Kong, 1985). Benjamin Elman surveys the history of the examination system during the last millenium of the imperial era in *A Cultural History of Civil Examinations in Late Imperial China* (Berkeley: University of California Press, 2000).

ship of land, was nonetheless defined—by itself and others—through its mastery of learning and its prowess in the examination halls. Individually, the members of this new social class (known as the *shi*—literati—or *shidafu*—literatus-official) possessed little of the independent wealth or hereditary official status of their Tang aristocratic predecessors. In this sense, they posed less of a challenge to the absolutist inclinations of some Song emperors and (later in the dynasty) their chief councilors.[15] Yet while they never challenged the political prerogatives of the throne, the new exam-based literocracy came to dominate Chinese cultural institutions for the next nine-hundred years, as they "[captured] hauteur from aristocrats, . . . sustained it against merchants, and . . . grew as much as the monarchs in self-esteem and substance."[16]

Political consolidation paved the way for the founders to continue the process of territorial unification that had been initiated by the Later Zhou. By 978 all the kingdoms of South China had capitulated to the Song. But in the north, efforts to topple the last holdout against the Song—the Shatuo regime of Northern Han—were foiled by the regime's patron the Khitan Liao. In 979 Taizong launched a second invasion of Northern Han that Liao forces were unable to repel, bringing the breakaway Shansi region back under centralized control for the first time since 951. But this was as far as the Song would get towards restoring Chinese control over north China. Flush with victory over the Northern Han Taizong pressed his troops on towards the Sixteen Prefectures, where they were decimated by Liao forces near Youzhou (modern Beijing). Taizong launched a second massive invasion of the Sixteen Prefectures in 986, but once again Liao cavalry and their commanders overwhelmed Song forces. The Song were never to regain the Yan-Yun region, for Song state building came up against a second feature of the

---

[15] The issues of imperial and/or ministerial absolutism are recurring if still-unsettled motifs in the study of Song history. No later emperors (with the possible exception of Xiaozong, r. 1162-89) ruled with the personalized authority of the founders Taizu and Taizong. On the powers of the early Song emperors see Liu Jingzhen, *Bei-Song qianqi huangdi he tamen de quanli* (The early Song emperors and their authority, Taibei: Taoxiang chubanshe, 1996); on the increasing authority of the chief councilors over the course of the dynasty see Lin Tianwei, "Songdai xiangquan xingcheng zhi fenxi" (Analysis of the emerging authority of the chief councilors in the Song (1973), reprinted in *Songshi yan-jiu ji* Vol. 8 (Taibei, 1976), 141-170. Anthony Sariti captures the tension between monarchy and bureaucracy in "Monarch, Bureaucracy, and Absolutism in the Political Thought of Ssu-ma Kuang," *Journal of Asian Studies* 32.1 (1972), 53-76.

[16] Joseph R. Levenson, *Confucian China and its Modern Fate* (3 vols., Berkeley: University of California Press, 1964), Vol. 2, p. 64.

medieval transformation of Eurasia: a parallel process of state formation
on the steppe that was to shape events in China as well as the entire
Eurasian system for the next three centuries.

A cycle of state building on the steppe, tenth to thirteenth centuries

Overviews of Inner Asian state formation by Nicola Di Cosmo and
Frederick W. Mote suggest the magnitude of the challenge that confronted the Song from the steppe.[17] Over the long term, Inner Asian
state formation was often precipitated by economic, social, or political
crises that stimulated the militarization of pastoral societies. According
to Di Cosmo, crisis could create social dislocation within tribes that provided the opportunity for a charismatic leader to rise to a position of
supratribal ruler or khan. This disruption of traditional, semi-egalitar-
ian political relations was characterized by "a replacement of the clan
nobility with a much more powerful, hieratic, and autocratic form of
authority where collegial decisions were restricted to a small group of
people." Political authority was in turn supported by the increased militarization of society into permanent fighting units placed under the
direct control of the khan or royal clan.[18] But this conjoining of permanent militarization and political centralization within an aristocratic
class required far greater economic resources than pastoral society could
provide, stimulating the demand for invasions of wealthier sedentary
regions to secure predictable supplies of external resources. For Di
Cosmo, the development of forms of "state appropriation" of economic
resources evolved over time: "Cast in a historical perspective, inner
Asian state formations . . . display a gradual but sure tendency to form
more and more sophisticated means of access to external resources."
Moreover, this incremental growth in the ability of Inner Asian states
to secure revenues external to their productive bases "was coeval with
the emergence of the state apparatus and provided the basis for its survival, for foreign relations, for the projection of force beyond its polit-

---

[17] Nicola Di Cosmo models Inner Asian state building over the imperial era in "State
Formation and Periodization in Inner Asian History," *Journal of World History* 10.1 (1991),
1-40; Frederick W. Mote surveys the formation of individual frontier states and empires
in the mid-imperial era in *Imperial China 900-1800* (Cambridge, Mass.: Harvard University
Press, 1999), chapters 2-4, 8-12, and 16-20. See also the "Introduction" to *The Cambridge
History of China Vol. 6: Alien Regimes and Border States*, eds. Herbert Franke and Denis
Twitchett (Cambridge: Cambridge University Press, 1994).
[18] Di Cosmo, "State formation," pp. 21-3.

ical and territorial boundaries, and for the domination of different ethnic, linguistic, and economic communities."[19]

In Di Cosmo's formulation, then, the secular development of technologies of resource appropriation serves as a marker of Inner Asian state formation.[20] And the most intensive period of development and elaboration in the forms of Inner Asian resource appropriation occurred between the tenth and fourteenth centuries, when powerful steppes empires bordered and then eradicated the Song. During the first millennium of the imperial era, Inner Asian states slowly progressed from a dependence on tribute during Han times to a combination of tribute and the systematic control of intercontinental and border trade during the Sui and Tang. But the pace of change accelerated in the early tenth century, when the Khitan Liao (variously dated as 916 or 947 to 1125) pioneered a new form of governance that Mote describes as dual administration, and that Di Cosmo deems the beginning of the era of the "dual-administration empires" of the Liao, Jin, and early Mongol period (907-1259).[21]

The institution of dual administration grafted an alien system of civil governance over the conquered farming families along the Chinese and Korean borders to a native Khitan state that administered all military and tribal matters and collected tribute from subordinate peoples like the Jurchen.[22] Dual administration did not displace the collection of tribute from China, for the Khitan Liao used war or the threat of war to institutionalize tribute into a system of "indemnified peace" with the Song that later proved equally profitable for the Tangut Xi Xia (1038-1227) and the Jurchen Jin (1115-1234).[23] But by developing increasingly

---

[19] Di Cosmo, "State formation," p. 27. Because the process of Inner Asian state formation was fully reversible, with steppe states running the risk of dissolving and returning to a non-state condition, Di Cosmo eschews an explicitly evolutionary formulation. But this caveat notwithstanding, the developmental trajectory that he depicts, characterized by increasing sophistication based on explicit borrowing (what Mote, p. 226, likens to technology transfers) over the long duration from the Xiongnu to the Qing, approximates an evolutionary path.

[20] Di Cosmo, pp. 30-37, periodizes the stages of Inner Asian state formation as follows: tribute empires (209 B.C.-A.D. 551; trade-tribute empires (551-907); dual-administration empires (907-1259); and direct-taxation empires (1260-1796).

[21] Mote, *Imperial China*, 39-40, 72-5; Di Cosmo, "State formation," pp. 32-4. Although neither Mote nor Di Cosmo (both published in 1999) refer to one another, they depict the phenomenon of dual administration and the process of political evolution through adaptation and emulation in similar terms.

[22] Mote, *Imperial China*, pp. 39-40.

[23] Mote, *Imperial China*, p. 71. As Mote puts it, "The Inner Asian states learned to

effective techniques of dual administration, the Liao were able to supplement trade and tribute with an increasing proportion of revenues
from the direct taxation of sedentary peoples, which helped finance the
successful occupation and defense of the Manchu-Korean state of Bohai
and the "Sixteen Prefectures" of north China. These techniques of dual
administration were in turn adopted by the Jurchen at the very beginning of their ascent to statehood under Aguda (r. 1115-1123), and
employed in their governance of the sedentary domains conquered from
the Liao in 1125 and the Song in 1127.[24] The combination of Chinese
and steppe methods of governance pioneered by the Khitan evolved
into what Mote describes as a technology of statecraft that was augmented by the Jurchen and the Tanguts throughout the twelfth century, adding to the store of universal governing techniques that the
Mongols would draw on in their sweep through China and Eurasia in
the thirteenth century.[25] As Di Cosmo argues, the Mongol Yuan (1271-
1368) took the process of Inner Asian state formation one step further,
by circumventing tribute (though not trade) as a source of revenue and
extracting their resources from the conquered territories through a system of direct taxation. But Di Cosmo, like Mote, stresses the evolutionary trajectory by which the Yuan emerged as the first of the
direct-taxation empires: "The completion of the conquest of China under
Khubilai is the best example of the confidence achieved by the Mongols
to summon a wide array of political resources derived from the store-
houses of inner Asian, central Asian, northern Chinese (Liao and Jin),
and Chinese political traditions."[26]

The rapid evolution of Inner Asian statecraft in the tenth to thirteenth centuries allowed states on the northern frontier to support formidable armies that offset agrarian China's advantages in wealth and
numbers, thereby blocking Song from assuming a position of supremacy
at the center of a China-dominated world order and relegating it to a

---

threaten war, demand territory, or require other concessions, and the [Song] learned to
resist most of those demands by paying ever higher indemnities."

[24] Di Cosmo, "State formation," p. 33.

[25] Mote, *Imperial China*, p. 226.

[26] Di Cosmo, "State formation," p. 34. For Di Cosmo, the peak of the direct-taxation model was achieved by the Qing, which "achieved a level of social and political
integration between conquerors and conquered far higher than that of earlier inner Asian
polities" (p. 36). In her essay in this volume Michal Biran emphasizes that the Mongols
saw themselves as forging a completely new political path, and rejects the notion that
the Mongols represented the culmination of a long evolutionary phase of state-building
on the steppe.

position of equal participant in a multi-state East Asian system.[27] Even the Tangut Xi Xia, a tribute-trade empire (to follow Di Cosmo's formulation) occupying the largely unproductive lands of the Ordos bend and the Gansu Corridor, was able to match the Song in military power and confront it as a de facto diplomatic equal. Evolving Inner Asian states expanded ever further south of the Great Wall frontier that— even before the Ming creation of the Wall as we now know it—traditionally divided sedentary China from the steppe, seizing north China in 1127, encircling south China by the 1260s, and finally absorbing all of China into the vast Eurasian empire of the Mongol Yuan in 1279. This political evolution of Inner Asia, a crucial feature of the transformation of medieval Eurasia, imparted irresistible torque to the development of Song political culture and helped shape the course of Chinese history for centuries to come.

Irredentism and state activism in the late Northern Song

Song policy-makers formally acknowledged the irreversibility of a new multistate system regulated by treaties and the establishment of regular diplomatic intercourse when they approved the Treaty of Shanyuan in 1005. As a result of Taizong's failure to dislodge the Sixteen Yan-Yun Prefectures from Khitan control, advisors to his son and successor Zhenzong (r. 997-1022) instituted an extensive project of defensive construction centered on the fortification of frontier cities and the creation of a network of cavalry-blocking waterways that diminished Liao military superiority and dashed Khitan hopes of reestablishing a buffer zone between themselves and the Song. In response, the Liao launched a massive invasion of China's Central Plains in 1004 in the hopes of using war to achieve an advantageous peace that would bring Song irredentist attacks to an end. Although Khitan forces approached to within one-hundred miles of Kaifeng their own losses were considerable, and both sides soon came to appreciate the advantages of a negotiated and dependable settlement. The ensuing Shanyuan Treaty of 1005, in which the Song agreed to make annual payments to the Liao and repudiate claims to the Yan-Yun region, constituted a recognition by the Song court that the territorial, ritual, and financial costs of diplomatic parity

---

[27] This theme is recurs throughout the essays in *China Among Equals: The Middle Kingdom and its Neighbors, 10th-14th centuries*, ed. Morris Rossabi (Berkeley: University of California Press, 1983).

and a purchased peace were far less onerous than the social and political costs of mobilizing the country for protracted irredentist war.[28]

The diplomatic equilibrium that accompanied Song suspension of its
irredentist aspirations ushered in a concomitant period of political stability that lasted another half a century. The Shanyuan settlement coincided with the transition from battle-hardened dynastic founders to
court-nurtured successors, precipitating a shift in political power from
an absolutist throne to an increasingly complex and self-confident bureaucracy.[29] Of course the bureaucracy itself was by no means homogeneous: it was staffed by men from different parts of the empire, with
potentially conflicting political views, interests, and affiliations; and it
drew on a pool of examination graduates that grew faster than the number of available government posts, even as entry into government became
the most prized avenue of social mobility. Irreconcilable policy differences
and intense competition for office would eventually fracture the solidarity of the bureaucratic elite under the weight of factionalism and the
concentration of power in increasingly hegemonic ministerial regimes.
But in the decades following the Shanyuan settlement the *shidafu* bureaucratic elite was still relatively small and cohesive and the still-evolving
bureaucratic apparatus relatively robust.[30] As a result, the arbitrary exercise of state power was restrained by the constitutional division of authority over civil affairs (under the Secretariat-Chancellery), military matters
(under the Bureau of Military Affairs), and economic administration
(under the Finance Commission), while an institutionally embedded system of checks and balances prevented a single chief councilor from
dominating the Council of State and subjected all the state councilors
to independent oversight by a fully-developed system of policy critics

---

[28] See Nap-yin Lau, "Waging War for Peace? The Peace Accord Between the Song
and the Liao in AD 1005," in *Warfare in Chinese History*, Hans van de Ven, ed. (Leiden:
Brill, 2000), 180-221. These same events are analysed by Lau Nap-yin and Huang K'uan-
chung in Chapter Three of *The Cambridge History of China, Vol. 5, Part 1*, "Founding
and Consolidation of the Sung Dynasty under T'ai-tsu, T'ai-tsung, and Chen-tsung,
960-1022".

[29] The most important study in English of this post-Shanyuan evolution of the Northern
Song state is still Edward A. Kracke, Jr., *Civil Service in Early Sung China, 960-1067*
(Cambridge, Mass.: Harvard University, University Press, 1953). Winston Lo offers a
longer perspective, tracing the evolution of the Song civil (and military) service over the
course of the entire dynasty, in *An Introduction to the Civil Service of Sung China* (Honolulu:
University of Hawaii Press, 1987).

[30] For Robert M. Hartwell's influential analysis of this cohesive, state-centered "professional elite" see his "Demographic, Political, and Social Transformations of China,"
406-16.

and censors.[31] At the same time, governance was characterized by a relatively conciliar approach to decision-making, exemplified most graphically by the reliance on broadly staffed interagency ad hoc committees to advise the emperor on important policy issues.[32]

But the equilibrium sustained by the Shanyuan settlement was by no means unassailable, and could be shaken by any combination of internal or external shocks. Internally there was always the threat of a domestic challenge to frontier stability, for the consensus on accommodation was pragmatic rather than principled, offered grudgingly rather than with enthusiasm. Moreover the very "civilism" of the Song state marginalized some individuals and groups who might benefit more from war than peace, inclining them to acquiesce in if not agitate for frontier expansion. Externally, equilibrium could be jolted by the demise of a stabilizing ruler or state, or particularly by the entry of a vigorous new player on the steppe. Such was the case in 1038, when the Tangut ruler Li Yuanhao (1004-1048) proclaimed himself Emperor of the Great Xia empire, encompassing the Ordos and the Gansu Corridor and controlling the most important trade routes linking Inner Asia and the Song.[33] Song reluctance to extend appropriate diplomatic recognition to the new Xia emperor instigated a four-year war (1038-1042) that highlighted Song deficiencies in strategic planning, tactical execution, and troop battle-fitness, forcing the court to sign a treaty in 1044 that bought from Yuanhao the same kind of indemnified peace with which it placated the Liao.

Song incompetence in this first Sino-Tangut war exacerbated growing concerns about Song governance and bureaucratic morale, even as the problems of military impotence, bureaucratic demoralization, and growing Tangut power continued to fester. These potential threats to the post-Shanyuan equilibrium converged again in the mid-1060s, when the reigning emperor's premature death brought his young son Shenzong (r. 1067-1085) to the throne. Internationally, the Tangut court was

---

[31] Kracke, *Civil Service*, Chapter Three. On the structure and political role of Song remonstrance and censorial offices see Chia Yuying *Songdai jiancha zhidu* (The Song Censorial System, Kaifeng: Henan daxue chubanshe, 1996), especially pp. 155-212.

[32] On this important element of eleventh-century policy-making see Robert M. Hartwell, "Financial Expertise, Examinations, and the Formulation of Economic Policy in Northern Sung China," *Journal of Asian Studies* 30 (1971), 281-304 (293).

[33] The growth of the Xi Xia state is mapped in Ruth Dunnell, "The Hsi Hsia [Xi Xia]," in *The Cambridge History of China, Vol. 6,* 171. The first Sino-Tangut war is discussed in Michael McGrath's chapter for the *Cambridge History of China, Vol. 5, Part 1.*

inspired by the deterioration of Tibetan rule in the Gansu-Qinghai high-
lands to launch expeditionary forces against Tibetan political centers,
sinified frontier tribes, and even Song commanderies throughout the
northwestern borderlands.[34] Domestically, the very primacy of the exam-
ination-based civil service put indirect pressure on frontier stability by
producing a surfeit of potential officials. The numbers of men with
ranked civil service status almost doubled during the first sixty years of
the eleventh century, from some ten-thousand to around 24,000 men.
By the 1060s this glut of officials had begun to demoralize the entire
civil service, with far more candidates than the system could absorb
clamoring for posts, sponsors, and promotion from junior to senior status. In a socio-cultural environment dominated by the state, the career
aspirations of these supernumerary officials were best served by expansion in the scope of government activity in either the domestic or foreign arenas.

   Even more direct pressure came from a group increasingly marginalized by the mid-Song civil services, the hereditary military families
who comprised the core of the Song general command. In the half-
century following the Shanyuan Treaty the Song court had systematically excluded the military's contribution to strategic decision making,
replaced regular troops and effective generals with local militia, and
transferred military authority and even outright field command from
the generals to top-ranking civilian officials. Although the general staff
was not dismantled, it was transformed into a bureaucratized and subordinate appendage of the civilian-dominated state.[35]

   In mid-1067 Tangut incursions supplied the pretext for one military
man to take frontier matters into his own hands, when the frontier commander Chong E took it upon himself to kidnap a prominent Tangut
general and wall the Xia town of Suizhou (renamed Suide), just across
the hotly contested Sino-Tangut border. Civilian courtiers like the
influential Sima Guang (1019-1086), imbued with the worldview of the
Shanyuan settlement, demanded that Suide be returned to the Tanguts
and urged the newly-enthroned Shenzong to honor the policy of his
predecessors by treating their Tangut treaty-partner with respect and

---

[34] The following paragraphs draw on Paul Jakov Smith, "Irredentism as Political
Capital: The New Policies and the Annexation of Qingtang (Northeastern Tibet) under
Shenzong and his Sons," in Patricia Ebrey and Maggie Bickford, *Huizong and the Culture
of Northern Song China*, forthcoming.

[35] Labadie, "Rulers and Soldiers," p. 199 and Chapters Two and Four.

assuming a posture of compliance in order to reestablish diplomatic entente.

In the past, such sober-minded exhortations had sufficed to bring frontier adventurism to an end. But the flame of irredentist longing burned far more brightly in Shenzong's heart than it had for his predecessors, and he ascended the throne determined to "destroy the Xia Nation and then personally lead the campaign to subjugate the Great Liao."[36] Fanned as they were by imperial passion, irredentism and frontier adventure emerged during Shenzong's reign as a potent form of political capital that swept a new constellation of men—including generals, eunuchs, and hawkish bureaucrats—into power.

The blueprint for enacting Shenzong's vision was provided by Wang Anshi (1021-1086), a brilliant but temperamental proponent of activist statecraft who enacted a comprehensive program of reforms meant to revive the nation's moral fiber and mobilize its resources for the emperor's irredentist dream. These so-called New Policies (*xinfa*), which represent the epitome of state activism in the imperial era, dominated the political agenda for the last half-century of the Northern Song.[37]

From an institutional perspective, the New Policies reflected Wang Anshi's vision that bureaucracy could be expanded and fine-tuned to intervene in and reshape every aspect of the social, cultural, and (most especially for Wang) economic landscape. Under the banner of enriching the state without emisserating the people, Wang recruited ambitious "bureaucratic entrepreneurs"—young men with demonstrated expertise in finance and bureaucratic enterprises but low standing in the civil service—to staff a bevy of new, reform-specific agencies. This expanded apparatus was charged (in the reform parlance of the day) with commandeering surplus profits from private "engrossers" for the sake of the common good, by using state agents to displace rich landlords from their monopoly over rural credit markets (through the green sprouts or *qingmiao* policy) and great merchants in the capital and the provinces from their control of the wholesale and even retail commodities trades (through the state trade or *shiyi* policy). At the same time additional

---

[36] Shao Bowen (1057-1134), *Shaoshi wenjian lu* (Record of Things Heard and Seen by Mr. Shao, 1151: Beijing: Zhonghua shuju, 1983), 3.26.

[37] For analyses of the New Policies see Paul J. Smith, *Taxing Heaven's Storehouse: Horses, Bureaucrats, and the Destruction of the Sichuan Tea Industry, 1074-1224* (Cambridge, Mass.: Harvard University Council on East Asian Studies, 1991), and Chapter Five of *The Cambridge History of China, Vol. 5, Part 1*, "Shen-tsung's Reign and the New Policies of Wang An-shih, 1068-1085".

measures were enacted to professionalize local labor service obligations through the extension of a "service exemption fee" (*mianyi qian*) to all sectors of the population, and to enfold roughly half of all households in the realm into a vast mutual security (or *baojia*) apparatus that, in the capital and the northern frontier regions, required mandatory military drill.

Politically, the New Policies were abetted by the emperor's willingness to abandon the system of bureaucratic checks and balances brought to maturity in the post-Shanyuan decades, just as he was eager to repudiate the Shanyuan settlement itself. Persuaded by Wang that the only way to augment imperial authority was to unyieldingly support the reforms, Shenzong allowed Wang to dominate the Council of State, control remonstrance offices, circumvent existing administrative structures with his new reform agencies, and pack the government with his cadre of bureaucratic entrepreneurs, whom more established literati denounced as "mean and petty men." This newly mobilized cohort of reformers and their sons and brothers would, with the exception of an eight-year anti-reform Regency following Shenzong's death in 1085, come to control the government through the fall of the Northern Song.

Such drastic changes to the political landscape were certain to generate a significant backlash, and from the very start of Wang's tenure in 1069 a growing circle of officials inveighed against Wang Anshi's abuse of ministerial authority and the predatory intrusiveness of his New Policies. But driven by the potency of his irredentist dream, Shenzong acceded to Wang Anshi's insistence that dissent against the reforms be suppressed, by purging opponents of the activist agenda, punishing anti-reform censors, closing the "roads of remonstrance," and granting key reform cadre in the field immunity from censorial impeachment.

Except for brief interruptions, dissent against the New Policies remained silenced for the duration of Shenzong's reign. With the enthronement of Shenzong's eight-year-old son Zhezong, power passed to a coalition of men headed by Sima Guang and the Empress Dowager who were determined to abolish the hated New Policies and reverse the irredentist adventurism that spawned them. But despite the transfer of power to prudent, conservative men, political culture had been too thoroughly transformed by the heated partisanship of Shenzong's reign to permit a return to the relative collegiality of the post-Shanyuan decades. Thus while Wang Anshi's erstwhile foes moved to reverse his policies, they enthusiastically emulated Wang's political techniques of capturing the Council of State and monopolizing the censorate and remonstrance offices.

In particular, the Yuanyou partisans (so named for the Restoration reign period from 1086 to 1094) suppressed opponents with a counter-purge of New Policies adherents more sweeping than anything in the dynasty thus far, only to find themselves ousted from office in 1094, when the now mature Zhezong reinstated his father's reform measures and proponents. From this point on, Northern Song political culture was engulfed in a virulent factionalism that reached its peak around 1102, when Zhezong's brother and successor Huizong authorized his chief councilor Cai Jing (1047-1126) to proscribe all members of the "Yuanyou party"—whether dead or alive—and extirpate their political and literary legacies.[38] Indeed, as Huizong asserted in 1108, it was Cai Jing's suppression of policy opponents that enabled the emperor to fulfill his father's goal of annexing the Tibetan domains centered on Qingtang (modern Xining, Qinghai province), intended to be the first step in Shenzong's irredentist war with the Tanguts:

> Previously my Divine Ancestor began plans for military success by delineating the western frontier. Although at that time not even [Qingtang] had been recovered he established a unified circuit in order to bring all [the constituent regions] under a common name and to show that this great and sacred design must be brought to success. . . . In bringing this plan to fulfilment [We have] relied on my Chief Councilor [Cai Jing]. If he had not banished the doubting multitudes then how could [We] have fully realized [Our] forebear's ambition to spread Our majesty among the caitiffs beyond the borders?[39]

Through the reigns of Shenzong and his sons, then, irredentist ambition and imperial support for the chief councilors and statist policies that could help bring that ambition to pass had irreversibly undermined the constitutional division of authority that checked the arbitrary exercise of state power. The Song political system from the New Policies through the very end of the Southern Song saw a growing consolidation of executive authority in the inner court comprised above all of the sovereign and his long-reigning chief councilors.[40] At the same time purges, suppressions, and irreconcilable policy differences had fractured the tenuous and inherently unstable solidarity of the bureaucratic elite,

---

[38] Ari Levine analyses the politics and political language of factionalism in the late Northern Song in Chapters 6 and 7 of *The Cambridge History of China, Vol. 5, Part 1.*

[39] Smith, "Irredentism as Political Capital," citing Yang Zhongliang, *Zizhi tongjian changbian jishi benmo* (1253), chap. 140, p. 13b.

[40] The historian Lin Tianwei measures the growing power of the chief councilors over the course of the Song dynasty by the number of man/years the originally dual posi-

pitting insiders and outsiders against one another and eventually driving a wedge between the inner court and the ministerial political
machines that dominated it and the bureaucracy as a whole.

In the sphere of economic policy, despite the distinctly anti-New
Policies bias of the historical record it seems fair to conclude that Wang
Anshi's promise to "multiply the state's revenues without adding to the
people's taxes" went unfulfilled. For while the activist economic policies
of Wang and his successors generated huge cash reserves for the state,
the redistributive rationale that animated the reform economic measures
was quickly subverted by the court's inexhaustible hunger for revenues
to be stockpiled in preparation for its irredentist wars. In short order
the New Policies fiscal reforms were transformed from a collective effort
to liberate the productive resources of peasants, small merchants, mid-
dling landowners, and consumers into an interlinked set of new taxes
and fees, all collected by agents of the state energized by an action-ori-
ented incentive system that rewarded the most draconian fulfilment of
their tasks.[41] Wang Anshi's experiment in economic activism degenerated into confiscatory taxation, creating a legacy of levies and extrac-
tive mechanisms that turned the late-Northern and Southern Song states
into economic predators.

But what of the revanchist dream that underpinned the New Policies?
In order to mobilize the nation for war, Shenzong and Wang Anshi
promoted an intensive project of military strengthening that included
revitalization of the officer corps through reforms in the command structure, establishment of a national military institute, revival of the national
arsenal, creation of a reliable system of cavalry-horse procurement, and
the institution of mandatory military drill and review for virtually all
members of the new mutual security (baojia) system in north China. In
addition, both Shenzong and Wang Anshi chose to delegate autonomous

---

tions of "right" and "left" chief councilors were occupied by a single (and hence preëmi-
nent) incumbent. By that measure, 22 percent of the Northern Song's chief councilors
served alone, for a total of 63 of the era's 167 years or 33 percent of the time. During
the Southern Song, by contrast, 36 percent of the chief councilors served alone for 63
percent of the era's 149 years. See Lin Tianwei, "Songdai xiangquan xingcheng zhi
fenxi," 141-170. For discussions in English see James T. C. Liu, *China Turning Inward*,
81-104; and Gong Wei Ai, "Prevalence of Powerful Chief Ministers in Southern Sung
China, 1127-1279 A.D.," *Chinese Culture* 40.2 (June 1999), 103-114.

[41] On the galvanizing effect of the New Policies incentive systems see Smith, *Taxing
Heaven's Storehouse*, 177-90. On the degeneration of the reform economic measures into
confiscatory taxation see Smith, *The Cambridge History of China, Vol. 5, Part 1*, Chapter
Five.

authority to their generals in the field. With this they reversed a century-old policy of military centralization, setting off a counter-trend that reached its peak around 1115 when Huizong promoted the eunuch general Tong Guan (1054-1126) to the position of Generalissimo of Shaanxi, Hedong, and Hebei Circuits and concurrent head of the Bureau of Military Affairs, thereby granting one man supreme control over the entire Northern Song military apparatus.[42]

Song military reforms yielded their most impressive results in extended campaigns against the weak frontiers of north-eastern Tibet (the Qingtang region) and southwestern Sichuan, where Song forces showed that with adequate time and massive resources they could dislodge indigenous populations from their native settlements, fend off their guerilla defenders, and buy off their chieftains with emoluments and titles. But victory against scattered tribal forces meant little when it came to doing battle with the far more sophisticated armies of the Tangut Xi Xia, against whom Song forces under Shenzong and his sons never gained more than a stalemate when they weren't thoroughly humiliated. Yet by Huizong's reign so many men had ridden to power on the banner of Shenzong's irredentist mission that every victory, real or imagined, was an occasion for promotions and solemn celebrations. And so when in 1118 defectors from the north reported that Jurchen invaders had created havoc on the Khitan frontier, Huizong and his court defied anxious critics to make a pact with the Jurchen to help topple the Liao in return for recovery of the Sixteen Yan-Yun Prefectures. But in 1122, after four years of negotiating over Yan-Yun as Jurchen armies devoured the Liao domain, Tong Guan's expeditionary army was routed and humiliated by the putatively impotent remaining Khitan troops. After the Jurchen forces overthrew the last Liao remnants in 1125 they turned their sights on the Song, whose panic-stricken emperor abdicated to his son Qinzong. But with neither the trained corps needed to conduct effective diplomacy nor the military discipline and reserves of political capital required to mount an effective defense, the Song left itself open to a Jurchen blitz through north China "as if it were undefended," belying the half-century of war mobilization and military reform. In the first month of 1127 Kaifeng fell to the Jurchen, who marched both emperors and their royal entourage to exile in the alien north. Shenzong's revanchist dream had backfired, adding all of north China to the category of lost territory and placing the survival of the dynasty in doubt.

---

[42] For sources see Smith, "Irredentism as Political Capital".

*From the activist state to the semi-autonomous elite in the
Song-Yuan-Ming transition*

The loss of the north signalled for many the failure of state activism,
while simultaneously exacerbating the autocratic tendencies brought to
the fore under Shenzong and his sons. For Gaozong (r. 1127-1162),
first emperor of the truncated Southern Song, the overwhelming political objective was to recapture the equilibrium of the post-Shanyuan
decades. This not only entailed creating a safe haven for the regime in
the rebellious and war-torn south, but also meant suppressing widespread demands for a reconquest of the north in favor of gaining peace
through rapprochement with the Jin conquerors. Both objectives Gaozong
entrusted to his chief councilor Qin Gui (in power 1128-1155), whom
he authorized to use on behalf of accommodation the same political
tactics forged by Wang Anshi and Cai Jing on behalf of war: centralization of power, political intimidation, and suppression of debate.[43]
Under Gaozong's successor (Xiaozong, r. 1162-1189), political centralization assumed many of the classic attributes of autocratic rule by a
monarch unencumbered by other persons or institutions. For Xiaozong
not only by-passed the line bureaucracy but even circumvented his chief
ministers, personally assuming decision-making authority over so wide
an array of administrative affairs that outspoken representatives of bureaucratic professionalism like Zhu Xi (1130-1200) publicly decried the
emperor's arrogation of civil service powers and his enfeeblement of the
council of state.[44] Monarchical autocracy gave way once more to ministerial domination when Xiaozong's abdication in 1189 deprived the
Southern Song of its last effective sovereign. Yet the onset of a protracted era of weak emperors did nothing to reconstitute the relatively
conciliar, professionalized governance that had evolved under the passive rule of the post-Shanyuan rulers. Instead, the vacuum created by
imperial withdrawal was quickly filled by palace favorites and powerful
chief councilors, who either muzzled their civil service critics through

---

[43] Teraji Jun, *Nan-Sō shoki seijishi kenkyū* (1988), translated into Chinese as *Nan Song
chuqi zhengzhishi yanjiu* (Research on the Political History of the Early Southern Song) by
Liu Jingzhen and Li Jinyun (Taibei: Taohe chubanshe, 1995). See also Charles Hartman,
"The Making of a Villain: Ch'in Kuei and Tao-hsüeh," *Harvard Journal of Asiatic Studies*
58.1 (1998), 59-146.

[44] See, for example, Conrad Schirokauer, "Chu Hsi's Political Career: A Study in
Ambivalence," in *Confucian Personalities*, eds. Arthur F. Wright and Denis Twitchett,
(Stanford: Stanford University Press, 1962), 162-88.

heavy-handed purges or neutralized them through more cunning tactics of manipulation and cooptation.[45]

The centralization of executive authority in increasingly narrow circles at court in no way enhanced the administrative reach of the state, for the gap between the ruler and his proxies on the one hand and the bureaucratic establishment on the other hobbled the fiscal and defensive capacities of the state. In the realm of financial administration, for example, the centralization of executive authority in the hands of the emperor, chief councilors, and their minions was offset by the irreversible hemorrhaging of fiscal authority to regional agencies. According to Robert M. Hartwell, despite continued complaints by functionaries of the central government, regional fiscal agencies "supervised the accounts for nearly sixty percent of total government income and possibly more than seventy-three percent of expenditures" in the late twelfth century, giving them the power to retain the bulk of state fiscal receipts in the provinces. As a result, although total government revenues were approximately the same in the late eleventh and late twelfth centuries when North China is discounted, the Southern Sung court had weaker control over the empire's economic resources than its late Northern Sung predecessor, at a time of even greater national peril.[46]

With respect to national defence, the urgent frontier situation stimulated impressive advances in military technology during the twelfth and thirteenth centuries, including the development of a permanently stationed navy and the use of incendiary devices and projectiles employing gunpowder.[47] But the effective deployment of these sophisticated technologies was impeded by the baleful effects of arbitrary governance, which undermined the court's ability to reach broad-based, well-considered decisions about issues of war and peace and paralysed the Song policy-making apparatus at the very moment that the dynasty confronted its greatest threat. As Charles Peterson has shown, Song frontier policy from roughly 1200 on was timid and indecisive, with the court too

---

[45] The political atmosphere during the last century of the Southern Song is described by Richard Davis in Chapters 10-12 of *The Cambridge History of China, Vol. 5, Part 1*.

[46] Robert M. Hartwell, "The Imperial Treasuries: Finance and Power in Song China," *Bulletin of Sung-Yuan studies* 20 (1988):18-89, especially pp. 72-91.

[47] For the Song navy see, for example, Lo Jung-pang, "The Emergence of China as a Sea Power during the Late Sung and Early Yuan Periods," *Far Eastern Quarterly* 14 (1955), 484-503; for an overview of Chinese military technology see Joseph Needham and Robin D.S. Yates, *Science and Civilization in China, Vol. 5, Part 6: Military Technology: Missiles and Sieges* (Cambridge: Cambridge University Press, 1994).

fearful of provoking even a deteriorating Jin regime into war to give support to anti-Jurchen rebels in Shandong or even to undertake military preparations of its own, despite the urgent pleas of Zhen Dexiu (1178-1235) and like-minded *daoxue* (Neo-Confucian) revanchists.[48] From 1217 to 1224 Song forces fared well against a series of attacks launched by Jurchen armies made desperate by Mongol assaults further north; but the court's ambivalence towards the Shandong rebels eventually pushed the most powerful of them into the hands of the Mongols in 1226, quite possibly depriving the Song of "a golden opportunity to strengthen its position in the northeast and even to lay the basis for the occupation of parts of [Henan, Jiangsu, and Shandong]".[49] The Song had no direct contact with the Mongols until 1221, but even then fears about the disastrous Yan-Yün collaboration with the Jurchen a century earlier kept them shy of further entanglements.[50] These fears turned out to be prophetic, for when in 1234 the court did finally launch a preemptive campaign in Henan to wrest its old capitals of Luoyang and Kaifeng from the Mongols, the Song military lacked the information, leadership, training, and supplies to mount an offensive campaign. Two years later the Mongols responded to what they saw as unilateral provocation by unleashing a massive campaign against Sichuan that razed all but four of the region's fifty-eight prefectural capitals, initiating a long but inexorable process of conquest that for the first time in history made a steppe power sovereign over all of China.

At first glance there are few discernible continuities between the native but ineffective Southern Song state and the robust polyethnic regime of the Mongol Yuan (1271-1368). This is the position taken by John Dardess in his contribution to the volume on the Song-Yuan-Ming transition. There Dardess argues that both the Yuan and the early Ming states stand in sharp contrast to the Southern Song, by reversing the passivity and lack of political consensus that ensued following the Jurchen conquest. In Dardess's view, the dynamic Yuan agenda went beyond conquest to include the creation of a polyethnic regime with an international corps of civil and military servants, utilizing multiple languages and scripts and drawing on new institutions devised specially to regu-

---

[48] Charles A. Peterson, "First Sung Reactions to the Mongol Invasion of the North, 1211-17," in *Crisis and prosperity in Sung China*, John Winthrop Haeger, ed. (Tucson: The University of Arizona Press, 1975), 215-52.

[49] Charles A. Peterson, "Old Illusions and New Realities: Sung Foreign Policy, 1217-1234," in Morris Rossabi, ed., *China Among Equals*, 204-239 (231).

[50] Peterson, "Old illusions," pp. 218-31.

late intra-ethnic competition. Moreover according to Dardess the early Ming state continued this activist form of governance, as the Ming founder Zhu Yuanzhang (r. 1368-1398) used propaganda, coercion, and centrally-directed local organization to accomplish the ethical and behavioral transformation of the entire population of China, in accordance with ancient norms laid out in the Confucian canon.[51] But it is equally possible to see the activism of the Yuan and early Ming as transient phenomena, dependent more on command mobilization and ideological terror than on the creation of enduring structures of everyday governance. The Mongols were more effective conquerors than governors, and once they had subdued South China they undermined their own ability to establish long-term political control over their new domain by forfeiting public authority to local South Chinese magnates and other private agents in return for their accommodation to foreign rule. It was this passivity and devolution of power that Zhu Yuanzhang sought to reverse, through political terror, behavioral rectification, and autocratic control over matters of state. By the early fifteenth century however Zhu Yuanzhang's behavioral rectification was regarded by contemporaries as a dead letter. At the same time, the political vacuum created by his autocratic enfeeblement of bureaucratic institutions was filled by competing civilian and eunuch agencies, whose perpetual battles for control over policy, political spoils, and increasingly weak emperors reduced the Ming state to the same institutionalized passivity that resulted from autocracy and ministerial dominance during the Southern Song and the forfeiture of public authority to private agents in the Yuan.[52]

Of course the twelfth to the sixteenth centuries were a time of enormous cultural vitality and significant social and economic change, in spite of the wars, political turmoil, and autocratic but ineffective states that characterized the Song-Yuan-Ming transition. But in sharp contrast with the Northern Song, when the most important cultural and institutional innovations were generated by the activist state, during the Song-Yuan-Ming era the locus of cultural and institutional change shifted to the local, educated, landowning elite (variously referred to as the

---

[51] John Dardess, "Did the Mongols Matter? Territory, Power, and the Intelligentsia in China from the Northern Song to the Early Ming," in Smith and von Glahn, *The Song-Yuan-Ming Transition*, 111-134.

[52] I offer this argument in "Impressions of the Song-Yuan-Ming Transition: The Evidence from *Biji* Memoirs," in Smith and von Glahn, *The Song-Yuan-Ming Transition*, 71-110; and in "Fear of Gynarchy in an Age of Chaos: Kong Qi's Reflections on Life in South China under Mongol Rule," *Journal of the Economic and Social History of the Orient* 41.1 (1998), 1-95.

gentry, or *shidafu*). Although this emergent elite continued to depend on the examination system as a marker of social status, it no longer relied on the state as its principal source of income and power.

Elite separation from the state was in part a result of the growing surplus of qualified candidates for the civil service, which impelled the eleventh-century oligarchy of exam-based bureaucratic lineages to supplement office-holding with an alternative mobility strategy based on the accumulation of wealth and property and the strengthening of family, community, and employment ties at the local level. This emergent localism, which for Robert Hartwell and Robert Hymes constitutes the most salient transformation of Southern Sung society, "served to widen and to emphasize a gap between elite interests and state interests at the local level, and to confirm and strengthen the independence of elite status and social position from the efforts of the state to certify, to validate, and so to control it".[53]

This demographically-driven process of social differentiation was transformed into more pointed estrangement by the factional warfare of the late Northern Song, which raised the risks to individuals and their families of political service; and by the loss of North China to the Jurchen, which for many members of the political elite signalled the failure of state activism. The corrosive effects of factionalism and foreign conquest were exacerbated by the arbitrary governance of the Southern Song, which frustrated and alienated those officials who, in addition to their stress on local initiatives, continued to take the ideals of professional bureaucratic service to heart. The most impassioned heralds of that estrangement were the leaders of the movement known as the Learning of the Way (*daoxue*, conventionally termed Neo-Confucians), who— inflamed by their resentment over "barbarian" control of the North Chinese heartland—collectively articulated a critique of absolutist rule whether monarchical or ministerial and outlined the limits of literati

---

[53] Robert P. Hymes, *Statesmen and Gentlemen*, 212. See also Robert M. Hartwell, "Demographic, Political, and Social Transformations of China, 750-1550." For a useful review of the literature on the Song elite see Patricia Ebrey, "The Dynamics of Elite Domination in Sung China," *Harvard Journal of Asiatic Studies* 48.2 (1988), 493-519. It may be helpful to see the Song-Yuan elite as the evolutionary antecedent of the gentry class whose origins Shigeta Atsushi links to the mid-Ming: that is, an elite stratum that combined landownership with the prestige and access to office that flowed from learning and participation in the examination system. See Shigeta Atsushi, "The Origins and Structure of Gentry Rule," in *State and Society in China: Japanese Perspectives on Ming-Qing Social and Economic History*, eds. Linda Grove and Christian Daniels (Tokyo: University of Tokyo Press, 1984).

loyalty to an ethically compromised government.[54] As the breach between the state and the literati hardened, Neo-Confucian learning came to provide a sense of group identity that replaced national government service with moral transformation as the marker of elite status, and the centralized state with one's own locale as the proper focus of institutional reform. Thus just as the innovative capacity of the central state declined, elites from the Southern Song on transferred their energies onto local, often lineage-oriented reforms such as community granaries, charitable estates, and private academies.[55] Disenchantment with the state did not mean that local elites, even Neo-Confucians, cut themselves off from its potential largess. Because even a weak court could shape the outcomes of contests for power outside the domain of the central state, competitors at the local and national levels vied to influence its policies. And in these contests no single group enjoyed more notable success than the Neo-Confucian followers of the Learning of the Way, whose ascent constitutes one of the cardinal features of the Song-Yuan-Ming transition.

Although Neo-Confucianism gained traction as a critique of the absolutist state by high-minded but powerless political idealists, under the pressure of ever-greater national peril powerlessness gradually gave way to considerable (if at first only token) influence. After proscribing the Learning of the Way from 1194 to 1197, a panicked court reached out to its staunchly revanchist adherents for moral and political support in 1234, after the Mongols had conquered the Jin.[56] In 1241 Emperor Lizong (r. 1225-64) proclaimed the Neo-Confucian canon—especially the "Four Books" and Zhu Xi's commentaries to them—the orthodox standard for government schools and the civil service examinations. Although political disintegration in the face of relentless Mongol campaigns

---

[54] For an example of Wei Liaoweng's critique of ministerial absolutism and call for a return to constitutionally divided government see James T.C. Liu, "Wei Liao-weng's thwarted statecraft," in *Ordering the World: Approaches to State and Society in Sung Dynasty China*, eds. Robert P. Hymes and Conrad Schirokauer (Berkeley: University of California Press, 1993), esp. pp. 344-45; for *Zhu Xi's* refusal to serve in a government so politically degraded that it would constitute "an insult to my person" see Conrad Schirokauer, "Chu Hsi's Political Career," p. 170.

[55] The literature on local institutional initiatives is referred to by many of the essayists in Hymes and Schirokauer, *Ordering the World*. For one of the most influential contributions to the field see Denis Twitchett, "The Fan Clan's Charitable Estate, 1050-1760," in *Confucianism in Action*, ed. Arthur F. Wright (Stanford: Stanford University Press, 1959).

[56] James T. C. Liu, "How Did a Neo-Confucian School Become the State Orthodoxy?" *Philosophy East and West* 23 (1973), 483-505; Hoyt Cleveland Tillman, *Confucian Discourse and Chu Hsi's Ascendancy* (Honolulu: University of Hawaii Press, 1992), 232-34.

devalued the rewards of state support, the combination of augmented
jinshi quotas and official recognition produced a substantial crop of *daoxue*
followers in the waning years of the Southern Song.[57] When the Song
and its examination system collapsed these *daoxue* adherents—now more
committed to preserving the culture than to mourning the loss of their
dynasty—fanned out into their local communities, where they founded
private academies and staffed lineage schools that disseminated Neo-
Confucian learning throughout the local elites of South China. Indeed,
it was *daoxue*-inspired Confucian literati who sought to reform Yuan governance from the local level up in the crisis-ridden decades of the 1340s
and 1350s, a reformist zeal they later transferred to Zhu Yuanzhang's
fledgling dynasty. Reacting against the chaos of the Yuan era, the
Confucian intelligentsia preached to Zhu the need for total moral ren-
ovation of the Chinese people, joining with him to direct all efforts of
the new Ming regime "toward the truly revolutionary goal of national
psychobehavioral rectification" across all classes of Chinese society.[58]
Although Zhu Yuanzhang's rectification movement soon degenerated
into a campaign of political terror that numbered Neo-Confucian partisans among its tens of thousands of victims, Ming monarchs and Neo-
Confucian adherents came together again over a revived examination
curriculum that obliged candidates to master *daoxue* interpretations of
the Four Books and Five Classics. In the end, then, a cultural reaction
against monarchical autocracy and ministerial absolutism that had begun
in the twelfth and thirteenth centuries, when a vocal minority of literati
lost faith in imperial politics and increasingly turned to local social and
cultural institutions to reverse dynastic decline, culminated in the fourteenth to sixteenth centuries in the creation of a state-sponsored orthodoxy that fit the needs of both the literati and their rulers.

But even after their success in the national political arena, Neo-
Confucian partisans still focused their attention on local institutions,
above all the family and extended patrilineal lineage. To give just one
example, in her recent book and her essay for the Song-Yuan-Ming
volume, Bettine Birge shows how one response of the *daoxue* movement
to social and political crisis was to formulate new ideals of family structure and identity that undermined the legal status of women and their

---

[57] See Elman, *A Cultural History of Civil Examinations*, Chapter One.

[58] In addition to John Dardess' article in *The Song-Yuan-Ming Transition*, see his *Confucianism and Autocracy: Professional Elites in the Founding of the Ming Dynasty* (Berkeley: University of California Press, 1993).

control over property. The *daoxue* leadership envisioned a reconstitution of social order by redefining the position of individuals, both male and female, within the nuclear family, the lineage, and the wider community. Despite the success of the *daoxue* leaders in gaining a large elite following in the late Song, their views on women and property ran counter to established practices and attitudes, and Birge finds it questionable whether their agenda would have triumphed had Song trends continued without interruption. But in the same way that the Mongol conquest gave *daoxue* leaders an opportunity to refashion the examination curriculum to their own liking, Mongol rule and social practices provided the catalyst that *daoxue* legislators needed to bring marriage and property law into conformity with their own notions of patrilineal descent. The Mongols introduced new forms of property distribution and family formation drawn from their own heritage, such as levirate marriage, that were quickly picked up by individual Chinese of all classes, especially when economic advantage could be gained. The confusion that resulted from conflicting ideas of proper sexual, social, and economic relations precipitated endless lawsuits and a spate of contradictory rulings. Amid this ideological and legislative uncertainty, Neo-Confucian adherents seized the opportunity to promote laws conforming to the ideals of Zhu Xi and his followers that enabled an unprecedented institutionalization of patrilineal descent and inheritance.[59] The *daoxue* social agenda received a further boost during the Ming, which preserved Neo-Confucian legislation on women and family at the same time that it coopted for the Neo-Confucian banner such practices as widow fidelity that from the perspective of their female practitioners had earlier been framed in Buddhist and Daoist terms.[60] Thus even though the process took several centuries to evolve, the institutionalization of Neo-Confucian views on women and property can be seen as one element in the larger constellation of Song-Yuan-Ming trends that projected local gentry concerns onto the national political state, as succeeding regimes ceded ideology and local control to the gentry in return for their dynastic support.

---

[59] Bettine Birge, *Women, Property, and Confucian Reaction in Sung and Yüan China (960-1368)* (Cambridge: Cambridge University Press, 2002); and "Women and Confucianism from Song to Ming: The Institutionalization of Patrilineality," in Smith and von Glahn, *The Song-Yuan-Ming Transition*, 212-40.

[60] Katherine Carlitz, "Shrines, Governing Class Identity, and the Cult of Widow Fidelity in Mid-Ming Jiangnan," *The Journal of Asian Studies*, 56.3 (1997), 612-40.

Conclusion

The rising influence of Neo-Confucianism brings us back to the initial focus of this essay: the intersecting cycles of state-building in China and the steppe during the Eurasian transformation of the tenth through the thirteenth centuries. For it was precisely the intertwined anxieties caused by the rising steppe on the one hand and the increasingly unresponsive and autocratic state on the other that gave rise to the Neo-Confucian movement. Although Neo-Confucianism is associated above all with the Southern Song, we now know that however fervent its Southern Song adherents, Neo-Confucianism was a minority and much-maligned phenomenon during the twelfth and thirteenth centuries. It is really only after the fall of the Southern Song to the Mongols that Neo-Confucianism begins to emerge as the distinctive ideology of the educated local elite, growing numbers of whom explicitly subscribe to its cultural, behavioral, and institutional norms and to the status it confers on them as *ru* (Confucian) members of "our group" (*wubei*).

From a long-term perspective the rise of this semi-autonomous elite—attentive to the status rewards of the examination system but more focused on the local arena than on government service—emerged as the most important consequence for China of the Eurasian transformation of the tenth through the thirteenth centuries. From a Chinese perspective class-formation trumped state-building in the course of these four centuries. For following the fall of the Northern Song, the most important locus of innovation in statecraft passed from China to the steppe, providing the Mongols with a repertoire of organizational means to draw on as they finally conquered all of China and integrated it into a vast Eurasian empire. But conquering and governing are two different matters, and in less than a century the Yuan state had succumbed to chaos, violence, and civil wars brought on at least in part by Mongol misgovernance. But throughout the fall of first the Song and then the Yuan elite culture and institutions endured. For by the twelfth century the literocentric socio-political elite had gained autonomy from the Song state that had conceived it, facilitating its swift adaptation to life under steppe rule and ensuring its continued ability to flourish and to shape Chinese culture throughout the era of the Song-Yuan-Ming transition.

SOCIAL CHANGE AND CONTAINED TRANSFORMATIONS: WARRIORS AND MERCHANTS IN JAPAN, 1000-1300*

MIKAEL S. ADOLPHSON

ABSTRACT

Early eleventh century Japan was ruled by a group of aristocratic elites centered in and around Kyoto. Substantial social and economic changes took place during the subsequent three centuries as a result of the privatization of government that the Kyoto elites themselves had initiated. But these changes, which are most aptly represented by the rise of the warrior class and the mercantilization of the economy, were remarkably slow despite their internal forces. The elites' ability to coopt and contain these trends secured their survival for an extraordinarily long time, while delaying developments that in hindsight may seem inevitable. The warrior class only came to prominence in the mid-fourteenth century, and the merchant class was contained and controlled for even longer. In comparison to other cultures, the flexibility and the inclusiveness of the Japanese political system are particularly noteworthy.

In early eleventh century Japan, the prominent Fujiwara no Michinaga boldly proclaimed;

> This world, I think,
> Is indeed my world,
> Like the full moon
> I shine,
> Uncovered by any cloud![1]

To be sure, for the nobles of ancient Kyoto, there appears to have been few things troubling their way of life, for the early eleventh century is

---

* The diacritical mark for long vowels in Japanese is usually a long line over the vowel. Instead, a circumflex is used in this article (thus, û and ô).

[1] Entry for Kannin 2 (1018) 10/16 in Michinaga's diary *Shôyûki*, in *Dai Nihon kokiroku*, volumes 1-11 (Tokyo: Tokyo Daigaku Shiryôhensanjo, 1959-86); Ivan Morris, *The World of the Shining Prince*, 60-1. For a recent illuminating essay on Michinaga, see G. Cameron Hurst III, "*Kugyô* and *Zuryô*: Center and Periphery in the Era of Fujiwara no Michinaga," in Mikael Adolphson, Edward Kamens and Stacie Matsumoto, eds., *Centers and Peripheries in Heian Japan* (forthcoming).

characterized by grand court ceremonies and religious rituals, a vibrant capital where the luxurious lifestyles of the nobility was on display, and a tremendous literary production by both noble men and women. In fact, even though the Northern Fujiwara's domination of the imperial court and reigning emperors was not in accordance with the ideals of the bureaucratic state in the Tang-inspired law codes and the means by which the peripheries were controlled were becoming less dependent on political offices and edicts than private assets and ties, the capital elites had no reason to think that their dominance, based on their monopoly of social ranks and status, would change in the near future. However, before the century would end, this feeling of confidence began to dissipate over increasing instability and violence. For example, Buddhist monks, who spent their lives sanctifying the imperial state and supporting the leading nobles with religious services, had begun to stage protests in the capital against what they perceived to be unfair decisions contrary to their interests.[2] Retired Emperor Shirakawa (1053-1129), Kyoto's leading figure in in the early twelfth century, is believed to have lamented: "There are three things I cannot control—the flow of the Kamo River, the roll of the dice and the monks from Mt. Hiei."[3]

To contain such demonstrations, and to ensure their own positions within an increasingly competitive court, the noble elites began to employ mid-ranking aristocrats with warrior training. A trend of general militarization of society was in fact under way, and by the late twelfth century, the Kyoto elites could no longer effectively govern the provinces, or even settle disputes among themselves without the aid of the warrior class. As a result, a separate "warrior government" (bakufu) was founded in Kamakura in eastern Japan following the Genpei War (1180-85), and it came to co-exist with the imperial court with the explicit purpose of sustaining the status and privileges of the Kyoto elites by controlling the warrior class.[4] By the fourteenth century, it was the warrior aristocrats, not the old noble elites, who were the de facto rulers,

---

[2] For an analysis of the divine demonstrations, and the ideological and socio-political setting of tenth through fourteenth century Japan, see Adolphson, *The Gates of Power: Monks, Courtiers, and Warriors in Premodern Japan* (Honolulu: University of Hawaii Press, 2000).

[3] *Genpei Jōsuiki*, volume 1 (Tokyo: Miyai shoten, 1994), p. 124; *Heike Monogatari*, volume 1, in *Shinkō Nihon koten shūsei* (Tokyo: Shinkōsha, 1979), p. 93). Mt. Hiei housed the powerful monastic complex of Enryakuji, which became one of the most influential religious centers from Heian times. See also Adolphson, 27-28.

[4] See Jeffrey P. Mass, *Yoritomo and the Founding of the First Bakufu: The Origins of Dual Government in Japan* (Stanford: Stanford University Press, 1999), 253-255.

indicating that Japan had been ushered into a new age, an age ruled and dominated by military prowess and warriors.

The rise of the warrior class is undoubtedly a central theme in Japanese history, but it does not suffice to explain the changes that took place from the eleventh to the thirteenth centuries as one is lead to believe by many textbooks and monographs. In fact, one detects an overpowering tendency among both Japanese and Western scholars to exaggerate the extent of warrior power while all but ignoring other important developments. A more balanced understanding of this age requires a more critical scrutiny of the warrior class, as well as a broader approach to the social changes in general. For that purpose, I have chosen to focus on two themes; the protracted rise of the warrior class from retainers and servants of the capital elites to a position of rulership, and the growth of trade.

From Claws and Teeth to Rulers of the Realm

Together with the knights of Europe, Japan's samurai is arguably the best-known military figure in world history. Modern images of such figures as Ivanhoe, Robin Hood, Brother Tuck, Little John and the Knights of the Round Table are almost eerily similar to those of Miyamoto Musashi, Minamoto no Yoshitsune, Benkei and the Forty-Seven Rōnin in the popular imagination. This popularity is also reflected in many academic works, which tend to perpetuate many of the myths and exaggerate the martial valor and importance of the warrior class.[5] In particular, fanciful legends and myths of honor, loyalty, devotion, self-sacrifice and martial skills that were perpetuated from the Tokugawa age (1600-1868), not only put the class in the center of Japan's history but also made them appealing to Western audiences. The samurai's popularity is also related to the unusually long history of warrior rulership in Japan, by some accounts dating from the mid-tenth century until 1945, a full millennium. However, such images are in truth more the product of nineteenth and twentieth century culture than of records of the premodern age. In reality, the warfare preferences of mounted warriors of the late Heian (794-1185) and Kamakura (1185-1333) periods centered on arson, night and sneak attacks, ambushes, deception, and cowardly retreats in various humiliating guises (including women's

---

[5] For more critical treatments of these Japanese cult figures, see for example H. Paul Varley, *Warriors of Japan: As Portrayed in the War Tales* (Honolulu: University of Hawaii Press, 1994), Karl Friday, *Warfare and the State in Early Medieval Japan* (Routledge: New York and London, 2004).

garments).[6] Each and all of these acts are antithetical to the code of the Japanese samurai as it is understood today, which can only be described as shallow and a-historical, with little empirical evidence to support it.

A historically based interpretation of Japan's warrior class must first of all recognize two separate processes: the rise of the warrior class within the socio-political contexts of Heian and Kamakura Japan on the one hand, and the emergence of warrior-aristocrats as rulers on the other. The first process was prolonged and gradual, dating to the tenth through the thirteenth centuries, while the latter is mainly a story of the fourteenth century. What is remarkable is perhaps not that warriors played an important role in Japan, but rather the three-century lag between their rise and their emergence as rulers. It is this slow rise to power that falls within the parameters of this volume.

As noted at the beginning of this essay, the capital nobility confidently ruled Japan in the early eleventh century. This is not to say, however, that their grasp of the countryside was always unchallenged or that warriors did not perform important functions in provincial governments. Warrior leaders were crucial members of local administration from the ninth century, even as the ultimate authority still remained with the capital elites. They served as officials in the provincial headquarters with responsibilities related to tax collection, transportation and police duties, and their role only increased as the court came to rely increasingly on private ties in lieu of government posts in collecting taxes and dues. Abuse of these powers was not uncommon, and there were occasions both in the tenth and eleventh centuries when local warrior leaders even seemed to challenge the capital elites. For example, Taira no Tadatsune (967-1031), a regional administrator and warrior aristocrat, occupied three provincial headquarters in eastern Japan from 1028 to 1031 before a higher ranking warrior, to whom he had pledged allegiance earlier, could bring the provinces back under imperial control.[7] Tadatsune's insurgence was preceded by a more famous uprising by his

---

[6] Friday, 135-145.

[7] Karl Friday, "Lordship Interdicted: Taira no Tadatsune and the Limited Horizons of Warrior Ambition," in Adolphson, Kamens and Matsumoto, *Centers and Peripheries in Heian Japan*. See also Wayne Farris, *Heavenly Warriors: The Evolution of Japan's Military, 500-1300* (Cambridge: Harvard East Asian Monographs, 1992), 192-200, and Takeuchi Rizô, "The Rise of the Warriors," in *The Cambridge History of Japan*, Volume 2, *Heian Japan*, Donald Shively and William H. McCullough eds. (Cambridge: Cambridge University Press, 1999), 664-670.

maternal grandfather Taira no Masakado (?-940), who proclaimed himself the new emperor in eastern Japan in the 930s, and it was followed by other challenges in the north in the late eleventh century.[8] Traditional scholars concluded that these incidents were indisputable signs of a decline and a severe decentralization of the Heian court structure, indicating the disruptive forces of the warrior class at that time.

However, such interpretations have failed to take into account the circumstances surrounding the incidents, and to explain how the imperial court managed to subdue the disruptions, wielding authority throughout Japan for centuries after these crises. In short, the centripetal pull of offices and rewards in the capital far outweighed the potential benefits of disengaging oneself from it. For instance, Masakado only reluctantly rebelled against the court after failing at a career in Kyoto, and fallouts with his own kin and local competitors in the Kantô.[9] And Tadatsune's insurgence almost a century later was more than anything a local conflict, in which he opposed local officials and their tax policies. Even as he was labeled a rebel, his first inclination was to make peace with the court through his own allies in the capital. As Karl Friday has put it, "he was more like an unruly adolescent testing the limits of court patience, than a revolutionary seeking a new order."[10] These incidents were not, in other words, a challenge to the Heian style of aristocratic rule, nor were they necessarily a premonition of warrior rule as assumed by most historians. After all, warriors only came to wield even partial authority in the late twelfth century, and the nature of warrior hierarchies was by that time different from those of two centuries earlier.

What is important about these incidents, then, is not so much their occurrence, but rather how they were quelled and dealt with. Instead of relying exclusively on bureaucratic offices and appointments to administer and rule the realm, the members of the imperial court had come to favor more practical solutions, looking for leaders who could deal with local warrior problems regardless of their official posts. In many

---

[8] For Taira no Masakado, see Friday, *Hired Swords: The Rise of Private Warrior Power in Early Japan* (Stanford: Stanford University Press, 1992), 144-147; Farris, 131-142; Takeuchi, 653-656. For the wars in the north, see Takeuchi, 670-679.

[9] The main source for Masakado's rebellion is a problematic chronicle, known as the *Shômonki*. See Judith Rabinovitch's *Shômonki: The Story of Masakado's Rebellion* (Tokyo: Sophia University, 1986), and Giuliana Stramigioli's "Preliminary Notes on the Masakadoki" (*Monumenta Nipponica* 28, no. 3 [1973], 261-93).

[10] Karl Friday, "Lordship Interdicted".

cases, the court selected local competitors to or superiors of those who had disrupted the peace, a strategy that proved successful without exception until the mid-twelfth century. In fact, both Taira no Masakado and Taira no Tadatsune were subdued by warrior colleagues whom they knew quite well.[11] Despite the increased freedom local warriors enjoyed in the provinces, they were still quite heavily dependent on their ties with the capital elites; the result of the imperial court's successful move away from the rigid bureaucratic system of rule to one that relied primarily on private ties between the ruling elites in Kyoto and local strongmen.

The contexts of these disturbances, the way they were solved and authority exercised reflect above all a trend toward privatization of government. First, political power at the imperial court was monopolized by a few elite families. In particular, the chieftains of the Northern Fujiwara controlled much of the court, as indicated by the aforementioned Michinaga, not by virtue of their official appointments, but through their private connections with the emperor himself, most frequently as grandfathers or uncles. By marrying their daughters to future or reigning emperors, they developed a pattern of rule as regents on behalf of their grandsons, who were put on the throne at a very young age. Japanese scholars even refer to the era from 858, when the first child emperor at the age of eight ascended the throne and his Fujiwara father served as regent, to 1086, when the pendulum shifted back in favor of the imperial family, as the age of the regency (sekkan jidai).[12]

Second, religious ceremonies were performed for the state by temples and shrines attached to and sponsored by individual families and clans. Thus, whereas Buddhist lectures and rituals were sponsored through public funding in the eighth and ninth centuries, they were performed by temples and monks with direct ties to the leading nobles in the

---

[11] See Karl Friday, "Lordship Interdicted".

[12] The exact years for delimiting the age of the Fujiwara regency differ between scholars depending on their particular emphasis. The year 1086, for example, marks the voluntary retirement of Emperor Shirakawa, who proceeded to establish his own version of the Fujiwara regency by ruling behind the throne as retired emperor. However, it was not until after the (un)timely deaths of two Fujiwara leaders, in 1099 and 1101 respectively, that Shirakawa managed to assert his power at the expense of the Fujiwara (see G. Cameron Hurst III, *Insei: Abdicated Sovereigns in the Politics of Late Heian Japan (1086-1185)* [New York: Columbia University Press, 1976], 148, and Adolphson, *The Gates of Power*, 80-81). The question of a regental age is furthermore problematic, since there are few characteristics that clearly set such an age apart, except for unprecedented levels of influence by the Fujiwara, which in itself fluctuated.

eleventh. By that time, a handful of temples in the capital region—
Enryakuji, Miidera, Tôji, Tôdaiji and Kôfukuji—had emerged as the
leading Buddhist institutions, often competing to gather rewards and
positions while cooperating in the sanctifying of the state. And although
the major monasteries had an independent financial foundation and
judicial immunity within their own estates, they also claimed to protect
the state, never disassociating themselves from the court-centered polity.

Third, the financial foundation of rule gradually changed from taxation of public land to the usage of private resources even in government matters, as capital elites came to administer and tax land increasingly
as private estates. This was a slow and uneven process that began in
earnest in the late tenth century, when nobles and temples gained control of tax-exempt and immune estates known as *shôen*. By the late
twelfth century, much of the remaining public land was also treated as
proprietary provinces to exploit for powerful nobles and warriors.

Fourth, direct control of warfare was relinquished to warrior leaders,
who were appointed to suppress local uprisings and incidents based on
their perceived abilities to succeed, and on their private ties with members of the court. For example, Minamoto no Mitsunaka (912-997), a
personal retainer of the Fujiwara chieftain known in a later source as
the "claws and teeth of the Fujiwara," also performed official duties in
the name of the imperial court.[13] These leaders were important "bridging figures," to use Jeffrey P. Mass' words, serving as channels between
the central elites and local class of warriors. They were a blend of mid-
level aristocrats in the capital, who received appointments within the
provincial administration but retained residences and remained in close
contact intensive communication with the capital, and descendants of
long time provincial nobles.[14]

It is beyond doubt that these figures were of tremendous importance
in administering the provinces and delivering taxes to the capital. It
deserves to be reiterated, however, that they were working for the central elites and not against them. And those who chose to put themselves outside the unofficial hierarchies of authority in their drive for
local control and personal aggrandizement were doomed to fail as long
as a majority of the warrior class saw more advantages in advancing

---

[13] Varley, *Warriors of Japan*, 24.
[14] Jeffrey P. Mass, "The Kamakura Bakufu," in *Medieval Japan: Essays in Institutional
History*, edited by John W. Hall and Jeffery P. Mass (New Haven: Yale University Press,
1974), 49.

within the system instead of outside of it. To thus label Tadatsune's siege of three provincial headquarters an insurrection against the Heian court, or as part of a class struggle pitting warriors against nobles, as many historians have done, is misdirected. The courtiers were in fact in control even if the ways in which they maintained it differed from the principles of the Chinese imperial codes.[15]

Our focus in examining the warrior class in the mid- to late-Heian period should therefore be on its successful containment, not on the instances when individual members appeared to challenge the central elites. The rewards and advantages of serving the court were simply far more attractive than the potential benefits and independence that could be obtained through a separation from it. However, by the same token, the Heian elites could not disassociate themselves form their military retainers, who were crucial not only in provincial matters, but also useful in factional struggles in central Japan. By the mid-twelfth century, warrior retainers from the group of the bridging figures described above became increasingly involved in the pulling and tugging in Kyoto itself. Indeed, although caused by succession disputes within the imperial family and the Fujiwara, warrior leaders were the decisive players in both the Hôgen and Heiji Disturbances of 1156 and 1159-60 respectively. After having served Retired Emperor Go-Shirakawa (1127-1192) for two decades following these incidents, Taira no Kiyomori (1118-1181) finally became the first of the bridging figures to emerge as a force in his own right in the capital when he challenged the imperial court in the late 1170s. Soon thereafter, Minamoto no Yoritomo (1147-1199) took command of the warrior class by emerging victorious against Kiyomori and his clan in Japan's first national civil war, the Genpei War of 1180-85, establishing a political headquarters in Kamakura in the process. Yoritomo's headquarters, known as the *bakufu*, came to serve as the ultimate nexus of the warrior pyramid, with the *shogun* as its official head.[16]

To many historians, the end of the Genpei War has come to represent a watershed in Japanese history, marking, in their words, the beginning of warrior rule. However, as recent scholars have observed, the bakufu was established not to promote the expansive and aggres-

---

[15] This point has most convincingly been made in English by Friday, *Samurai, Warfare and the State in Early Medieval Japan*, 40-43.

[16] For a comprehensive treatment of Kiyomori and Yoritomo, see the works of Jeffrey P. Mass, especially "The Emergence of the Kamakura Bakufu," in Jeffery P. Mass and John W. Hall eds, *Medieval Japan: Essays in Institutional History* (Stanford: Stanford University Press, 1974), 127-156.

sive interests of the warrior class as much as to contain it in order to preserve a court-centered polity. In fact, once the enemy forces were subdued, Yoritomo voluntarily restricted his authority to the warrior class as its supreme commander, while leaving the realms of religion and courtly matters to the Kyoto elites.[17] And it is noteworthy that the first code issued by the warrior leaders was not proclaimed until 1232, almost fifty years after the establishment of the bakufu. Even then, it only contained practical principles and proclamations supplementing the existing codes of the imperial court and targeting solely members of the warrior class.[18]

Another persuasive example is the Jôkyû War of 1221, when an ambitious retired emperor decided to challenge the bakufu, only to suffer a devastating defeat after less than a month of warfare. Since the reigning emperor had also sided against Kamakura, the bakufu had little choice but to depose him, send three former sovereigns into exile, and to select a new ruler. But instead of using this opportunity to take control over civil matters and displace the imperial court, a task that would not have been difficult from a military standpoint, the bakufu's regental leaders—the Hôjô family—elected to yet again limit its authority to areas of warfare and the warrior class even as it increased its presence in Kyoto. As a result, the imperial court experienced a revival by mid-century, a period which might be considered the high point of court and bakufu cooperation.[19] The Kamakura Bakufu was, in effect, committed and tied to the old socio-political order, and it was only the decline of the bakufu itself that would spell the end to a polity that might best be described as shared rule by multiple elites.

The slow development of warrior rule bespeaks a rather unique system of sustained shared rulership between elites from different spheres of society. As argued by the Japanese historian Kuroda Toshio, these elites, known as *kenmon* ("gates of power" or "influential families"), emerged in the late eleventh and twelfth centuries to make up three larger power blocs, which performed specific duties (administrative, military and

---

[17] Mass, "The Emergence of the Kamakura Bakufu," 154-155.

[18] The Jôei Shikimoku is available in an outdated and error-prone English translation by John C. Hall, "Japanese Feudal Laws (go Seibai Shikimoku)," in *Transactions of the Asiatic Society of Japan*, First Series, volume 34 (1906), 1-44. For a more recent version in German, see Wilhelm Röhl, "Das Goseibaishikimoku: Eine Rechtsquelle der Kamakura-Zeit," *Oriens Extremus*, 5 (1956), 228-245.

[19] Jeffrey P. Mass, *The Development of Kamakura Rule, 1180-1250: A Study with Documents* (Stanford: Stanford University Press, 1979), 41; Adolphson, 193-194.

religious), thus sharing the responsibilities of rulership while receiving judicial and economic privileges in exchange.[20] The court nobility, consisting of the imperial family and the capital aristocracy, held the administrative and ceremonial responsibilities of the state. Supported by their private organizations and assets, the nobles maintained their privileges to government offices and remained the formal leaders of the state. All decisions concerning taxes, promotions, religious and courtly ceremonies were made within the confines of the imperial court, which also retained the right of appointing, under the leadership of the emperor, ranking members of the court as well as the *shogun*.

The second member of the ruling triumvirate—the religious establishment—supplied the state and its members with spiritual protection. It also supported a vertical differentiation among the rulers and the ruled through exclusive and expensive rituals that only the most prosperous and influential courtiers could afford. The elite temples moreover established and maintained a representation of the state through their many branch temples and extensive land possessions in the provinces. Buddhism's central role in supporting the courtly state was not without precedence in the sacred texts, but it was not until the mid-Heian age that a separate and fleshed out ideology of mutual dependence between the imperial and Buddhist laws became dominant among the elites. For example, a document from 1053 explicitly invokes this concept, comparing the laws of the state and Buddhism to the two wheels of a cart and the two wings of a bird.[21]

The warrior aristocracy (*buke*) served as the third leg in this tripod of rulership, responsible for keeping the peace and physically protecting the state. As already noted, these duties were entrusted to prominent warrior leaders of the Minamoto and Taira clans from the eleventh century, and the founding of the Kamakura Bakufu by Yoritomo served to institutionalize their participation in this division of responsibilities and rule.[22]

---

[20] For Kuroda's theory, see his *Jisha seiryoku: mô hitotsu chûsei no sekai*; *Nihon chûsei no kokka to shûkyô*; "Chûsei jisha seiryoku ron" in volume 6 of *Iwanami kôza, Nihon rekishi: Chûsei* 2, ed., Asao Naohiro et al. (Tokyo: Iwanami shoten, 1975), 245-95; "Chûsei kokka to tennô," in volume 6 of *Iwanami kôza, Nihon rekishi: chûsei* 2, ed., Ienaga Saburô et al. (Tokyo: Iwanami shoten, 1963), 261-301. For a summary in English, see Adolphson, 10-20.

[21] *Heian ibun*, volume 3, document 702, *Mino no kuni Senbu shôshi jûninra ge*, Tengi 1 (1053), seventh month (pp. 834-835); Adolphson, op. cit., 270-273.

[22] Kuroda, *Nihon chûsei kokka to shûkyô*, 17-18, 21; idem, "Chûsei kokka to tennô," 275-279.

This diffused and inclusive system of rulership worked through a heavy reliance on the private powers of each member of the elite, and appears to ultimately represent in the end a very pragmatic compromise between the Chinese bureaucratic system and a preference for informal means of exercising power. The elites used their own personnel to handle administrative and economic matters of both private and public nature, and their headquarters issued edicts to convey orders with the same kind of judicial efficacy as government edicts. Such orders did not completely supplant the function of government edicts, but they nevertheless became all but indistinguishable from those issued by official organs as they dealt with similar matters of land taxation, administration and adjudication. Finally, each elite had a number of retainers or followers, who were under the jurisdiction of the head. These retainers included both armed and civil personnel, and they were frequently employed in tasks of the state, as the elites increasingly used their private resources to perform government functions. In fact, warrior-administrators who were charged with executing orders by their noble masters saw no difference between matters of public (i.e. pertaining to the state) and private (concerning the family or the monastic master) nature. As such, warriors in the service of nobles in the capital or of one of the great monastic centers were no different from those in the service of the bakufu even if the latter were a privileged group within the warrior class.[23]

The increased reliance on private assets, caused by a realization that rule by bureaucratic offices alone would no longer work in the tenth and eleventh centuries, allowed both the warrior class and religious institutions to emerge as semi-independent powers of the state. The benefits of this pragmatic response to local socio-political conditions was undoubtedly a flexibility that was not possible in the Chinese-based imperial codes. Indeed, even though the wars of the twelfth century and the restructuring of the imperial court following the disastrous Jôkyû War resulted in adjustments among the elites, these changes took place within the system itself. Shifts among the factions and blocs were common, if not embedded in the system itself, but none of the elites was powerful enough to rule by itself, ensuring the exceptional survival of the Kyoto elites as rulers. Another distinguishing feature of this socio-political system was its inclusiveness. It was able to handle shifts and incorporate

---

[23] Kuroda, *Nihon chûsei kokka to shûkyô*, 7-11, 367; idem, "Chûsei kokka to tennô," 269-270; Friday, *Samurai, Warfare and the State in Early Medieval Japan*, 25-26.

newcomers and challengers, such as the warrior class and new religious sects as long as they worked within the system. It was this feature more than anything else that allowed the old elites to contain and control the rise of new classes, even if it came at the price of relinquishing some of their political authority. The drawback, of course, was that without a single authority at the top, the various elites depended on one another to control and contain their respective blocs. Therefore, when the Kamakura Bakufu began to lose control of the warrior class, it caused a severe crisis in the socio-political system of shared rulership, and its eventual decline.

The warrior class grew steadily throughout the thirteenth century to the extent that the land and managerial offices on which they made their living became insufficient to support all descendants of the families. Contrary to the customs of noble families, where one heir was designated the head of the family and thus the inheritor of the bulk of the assets, warriors held on to a more equal division among sons as well as daughters well into the thirteenth century.[24] Titles to both land and offices were consequently divided into smaller and smaller fractions, a development that appears strikingly similar to what happened to the warrior class in Europe two centuries earlier.[25] In an attempt to maintain the integrity of family assets, warrior parents began to assign the bulk of their titles to one heir, in large excluding other sons and above all daughters, who had previously held almost equal rights to property. It should come as no surprise that while this measure temporarily halted the division of warrior estates, it also caused increased social and economic tensions. The bakufu was unable to alleviate the pressure that resulted, and dissatisfaction with the bakufu leadership grew steadily from the late thirteenth century. Many warriors were in fact forced to borrow money from merchants just to survive and perform their duties as bakufu retainers, leading to prohibitive debts. Not even debt cancellations decrees from the bakufu issued from the late thirteenth century could improve the situation, since the basic question of diminished income was never addressed.[26]

These problems were compounded by the Mongol invasions of 1274

---

[24] For a detailed study of the emergence of unigeniture within the warrior class, see Mass, *Lordship and Inheritance in Early Medieval Japan: A Study of the Kamakura Sôryô System* (Stanford, Stanford University Press, 1989).

[25] See the essay by R. I. Moore eliminate in this volume.

[26] Ishii Susumu, "The Decline of the Kamakura Bakufu," in Kozo Yamamura, ed.,

and 1281. The defending Japanese warriors, aided by the fortunate occurrence of two timely typhoons, managed to prevent the Mongol forces from gaining a foothold on Japanese soil. But although Kublai Khan's attempts to incorporate Japan into his vast empire failed, the effects were in the end debilitating for the bakufu. With no land to confiscate following the war, the bakufu had few rewards to offer its armies, causing an even deeper rift between the bakufu and the warrior class. Worse, what few rewards it did hand out ended up benefiting religious centers, which claimed credit for the victories, while the Hōjō family took the opportunity to eliminate powerful warrior families it found threatening in the provinces. Still, it took an emperor to rally and channel and organize this dissatisfaction against the bakufu.

In the late thirteenth century, the imperial family had been split into two separate lines, and the bakufu had decided that succession to the throne should alternate between a senior and a junior branch. When Go-Daigo of the junior branch ascended the throne in 1318, he was determined to resolve the factional competition in his own line's favor. He saw the bakufu as the main obstacle to this goal and soon became a rallying point for anti-Kamakura sentiments. After first being exiled in 1331, he returned triumphantly two years later, while the bakufu's own retainers were busy dismantling the Kamakura headquarters. Go-Daigo subsequently took the first important steps toward unifying rulership in the hands of one authority, but he failed to satisfy the needs of the very same warriors that had supported his coup. His reign lasted a mere three years, and it was the second bakufu, established by the Ashikaga family in 1336, that accomplished what he had set out to do; unifying authority and ending the system of shared rule.[27] In contrast to previous warrior leaders, the Ashikaga located their headquarters in the capital itself and took command over the political responsibilities of the imperial court, while all but eliminating the privileges of the religious and noble elites.

Japan entered a new age in which the cooperative rule that had characterized Japan since around 1100 was replaced by a despotic warrior rule in the late fourteenth century. Kenneth Grossberg even argued that the Ashikaga Bakufu represented Japan's attempt at something comparable

---

The Cambridge History of Japan, Volume 3, *Medieval Japan* (Cambridge: Cambridge University Press, 1990), 128-131.

[27] For a thorough treatment of Go-Daigo, his policies and short-lived regime, see Andrew Goble, *Kenmu: Go-Daigo's Revolution* (Cambridge: Harvard University Press, 1996).

to a renaissance state, although it did not wield authority long enough
to actually carry out such a transformation.[28] In either case, the warrior class' rise in Japan from mere employment as retainers and servants of the capital elites in the tenth and eleventh to domination in
the mid- to late-fourteenth century was slow and gradual; a largely controlled process that involved not only checks and balance strategies but
also the active cooperation of the warrior class itself. It was a process
that was effectively contained and controlled for two hundred years,
conditioned by the structures of the late Heian system until a new warrior aristocracy had matured enough to promote a new order.

The Growth and New Currents of Trade

If the warrior class represents the most significant political challenge for
the capital elites of the Heian and Kamakura ages, then the growth of
trade and the emergence of new classes in commerce and commodity
production were its counterpart in the social sphere. Like the emergence of the warrior class, the commercial evolution of the twelfth and
thirteenth centuries was linked to and conditioned by the trend of privatization. Specifically, the intensification of the competition for control
at the imperial court and the increase in agricultural production must
be understood in this context, but the third important factor, the monetization of the economy, must additionally be associated with developments on the continent. In fact, it is no exaggeration to state that
Song China played a considerable role in Japan's mercantile developments in the late Heian and Kamakura eras. Each of these factors will
serve as the foundation for the discussion of trade in this section.

The creation of an imperial state in early Japan spanned some two
and a half centuries, culminating with the opening ceremonies of the
Great Buddha Statue at Tôdaiji in Nara in 752. This event both began
and represented a new kind of imperial state, characterized by a grand
scale capital with a population between 50,000 and 100,000, wide
avenues, elaborate palaces and celebratory rituals both in the palace
and in state-supported temples. In Kyoto, where the court moved in
794, the palaces alone came to house thousands of courtiers and even
more maids, guards and servants, and the city itself probably had a

---

[28] Kenneth Grossberg, *Japan's Renaissance: The Politics of the Muromachi Bakufu* (Cambridge:
Harvard University Press, 1981, reprinted by the Cornell University East Asia Program
in 2001).

population of 100,000 in an area covering up to 4.5 × 5 kilometers divided into some 1200 city blocks at its peak. To meet the demands of such a large population and the court's elaborate ceremonies, specific products were collected as taxes from certain provinces, whereas part-time artisan-merchants were employed directly by the imperial court to furnish a range of manufactured products. The day-to-day products included among other things fish, vegetables, charcoal, straw mats, timber and cypress bark, as well as both domestic and imported luxury items, such as writing instruments, ink, various art works and silk.[29]

The court prescribed and managed to maintain direct control of the production and transfer of specialty products in the Nara (710-784) and early Heian eras, but the trend toward privatization of government naturally came to affect the area of taxation and commodity production as well. In particular, the presence of several elites within the spheres of both religion and the imperial court fostered a new spirit of competition within each bloc. Displays of private wealth and refinement came to play a larger role than before, as the individual families and temples promoted their own ceremonial versions in the jostling for control and advantages in the capital area. Indeed, the rituals at the imperial palace as well as the religious ceremonies performed at various temples and shrines were supreme opportunities to maintain and enhance one's own status. The same can be said for poetry readings and various other noble parties, which, in addition to being entertainment and reflective of literary knowledge, also served to display the host's wealth and power. In fact, Michinaga's poem noted earlier was composed at such an occasion in celebration of his daughter's promotion at the court.

To obtain the products for such events, the capital elites encouraged local producers to engage in trade full-time by offering them tax-exempt status. From the late Heian age, proprietors began giving rice fields to artisans to maintain and support the handcraft production of ceramics, cloth, hemp, silk, cypress bark, iron works, oil, *sake*, fans, straw mats, metal works and leather products within their own estates.[30] To offer some concrete examples, artisans making leather products were granted

[29] Kozo Yamamura, "The Growth of Commerce in Medieval Japan," in *The Cambridge History of Japan*, volume 3, *Medieval Japan*, edited by Kozo Yamamura (Cambridge: Cambridge University Press, 1990), 349-350: W. Wayne Farris, *Sacred Texts and Buried Treasures: Issues in the Historical Archeology of Ancient Japan* (Honolulu: University of Hawai'i Press, 1998), 160; John W. Hall, "Kyoto as Historical Background," in Mass and Hall, eds, *Medieval Japan: Essays in Institutional History* (Stanford: Stanford University Press, 1974), 7-10.

[30] Nagahara Keiji, "Kodai shakai no tenkan to hôkenka," in Nagahara, ed., *Nihon*

tax-exempt fields in the Kanto in the late twelfth century; the Iriki'in, a temple in southern Kyushu, gave fields to Japanese paper and sandal makers; and metal workers, dyers and potter makers were granted exemptions in central Japan in the thirteenth.[31] The increase in trade from the twelfth century was thus to a considerable extent caused by the elites' need for displays of wealth and elaborate ceremonies, many performed at Buddhist temples. Indeed, despite a general assumption that Buddhism was in decline because of its increased involvement in secular matters, the unprecedented construction of temples, copying of sûtras and performance of religious ceremonies, all sponsored by the noble elites in the capital, seem to indicate exactly the opposite.[32]

The increase in commodity production and trade spurred an increase in the number of artisans not only in the provinces but also in Nara and Kyoto as well. Already in the eleventh century, temples and shrines used their tax immune status to organize and offer protection to artisans making products for festivals and religious ceremonies, in exchange for fixed fees. These groups, known as *za*, were similar to European guilds not only in their organization of traders, artisans and other professionals groups (including prostitutes), but also in their independence from government jurisdiction and the creation of their own stipulations and rules. For example, *sake* brewing guilds in Kyoto and Nara regulated the quality and characteristics of their rice wine by stipulating the exact ingredients to be used. On occasion, new breweries would attempt to enter the market using a different and cheaper malt, upon which the guild would invoke the protection of their temple-patron, who might send down monks to threaten and scare the newcomers into compliance.[33] The emergence of the *za* was one of the defining developments in the Late Heian and Kamakura ages, and may represent better than anything else the emergence of new classes and the new economy.

A second important factor promoting the growth of trade was an increase in agricultural production in the twelfth and thirteenth centuries. Behind this development lie technological improvements as iron

---

keizai shi (Tokyo: Yûzankaku, 1970), 70; idem, *Nihon chûsei shakai kôzô no kenkyû* (Tokyo: Iwanami shoten, 1973), 60.

[31] Nagahara, *Nihon chûsei shakai kôzô no kenkyû*, 86, 89-90. The original documents can be found in *Heian ibun* (Tokyo: Tokyo Daigaku shuppankai, 1963-1974), document 3590, Jôan 1 (1171); *Kamakura ibun* (Tokyo: Tôkyôdô shuppan, 1971-1992), document 7265, Kenchô 2 (1250), twelfth month; *Kamakura ibun*, document 19179, *Echizen* Einin 4 (1296) 11/1.

[32] Nagahara, "Kodai shakai no tenkan to hôkenka," 77.

[33] Adolphson, op. cit., 327-329.

implements became more widespread, the use of double cropping in some areas and the opening of new fields. Agricultural iron tools were not new to the Japanese, but they did not become commonplace until the twelfth and thirteenth centuries, in part as a response to the increased demand from the capital elites. Indeed, one of the biggest contrasts between the management of land as public land and as private estates lay in the involvement of the proprietors in the latter. Early attempts to stimulate an increase of production failed as local producers either lacked the means or the incentives to open new fields they were not allowed to possess. By contrast, as temples and nobles obtained *shôen*, it was in their own interest to promote the opening of new rice fields, which was most effectively accomplished by the presence of effective land-managers in the estates, whether monks or local strongmen. The increase was also spurred by local initiative, especially in the Kantô, where frequently local warriors or wealthy peasants spearheaded and came to benefit from reclamation projects.[34]

Monetization of the economy usually follows the growth of trade and demand for a more standardized means of exchange, but the case seems to be much less clear-cut in Japan. The presence of copper coins, imported from China, preceded the expansion of trade, and thus appears to have spurred the growth of the economy. The relationship with China was, however, also quite problematic. The imperial court terminated official missions to China in the late ninth century as the Tang Empire declined, but the need for luxury products in Kyoto seems to have outweighed such political decisions. Specifically, incense, fragrances, writing materials (brushes and ink), and various art objects were imported by individual nobles in exchange for gold, pearls, mercury, sulfur, scrolls, folding screens and fans. In 903, for instance, complaints were heard in Kyoto that Chinese traders were allowed to exchange goods in Kyushu despite restrictions against private trade, and lower ranking officials were punished in 1040 for having engaged in private trade.[35] In the end, the battle was a lost cause as the elites in Kyoto themselves, especially the likes of Fujiwara no Michinaga, sought such objects.

It was the import of Song coins, however, that made the most sub-

---

[34] Nagahara Keiji, "The Medieval Peasant," in Kozo Yamamura, ed., *The Cambridge History of Japan*, volume 3, *Medieval Japan* (Cambridge: Cambridge University Press, 1990), 310-315.

[35] *Ruijū sandai kyaku*, in *Kokushi taikei*, volume 12 (Tokyo: Keizai zasshisha, 1900), *Daijôkanpu* Engi 3 (903) 8/1; Delmer M. Brown, *Money Economy in Medieval Japan: A Study in the Use of Coins* (Yale, New Haven: Far Eastern Association, 1951), 9.

stantial impact on Japan's economy. Rice and silk was the main means
of exchange throughout most of the Heian age, in large because few
other options were available until the twelfth century. Trade was therefore rather limited, but as coins spread from Kyushu to the capital,
monetary exchanges gradually became more common. Then, following
the discovery of large deposits of gold in the mountains of Mutsu
Province in 1175, the volume of coins imported to Japan increased dramatically.[36] From that point on, the coin trade became large enough to
deplete Chinese coastal towns of their means of exchange after the
departure of a Japanese fleet of merchant ships. The Song court responded
by issuing decrees to restrict (1254) or even prohibit (1199) the export
of coins to Japan, but they had limited impact. Chinese traders were
all too happy to help load the Japanese ships with coins after the inspectors had left or to bribe the inspectors to look the other way. Not until
the Mongols ended the Song dynasty and threatened to further expand
their empire in East Asia did the coin import diminish.[37] Remarkably
enough, however, trade was only interrupted for a brief period, and
Japanese traders in the shape of Zen monks soon embarked upon new
trips to China in the fourteenth century, and the import of coins gained
momentum anew.

Song coins served as an important catalyst for fundamental changes
in the Japanese domestic economy at many levels. Rice fields were transferred and sold in the second half of the Heian age, but picked up considerably when Song coins spread into the countryside. For example,
between 1158 and 1185, 127 out of 156 sales of land that took place
were paid for in rice, 23 in silk or cloth and only 5 in cash. By contrast, between 1227 and 1229, 22 out of 42 sales were paid for in rice
and 19 in cash, representing an increase of cash payments from 3.2 to
45.2 percent.[38]

The convenience of coins was not lost on tax collectors and payers
alike, and many dues were now also delivered in Chinese cash. Given
the nature of taxes paid at toll stations and fees paid by guilds, it is
not surprising that they were paid in cash in the thirteenth century, but
even traditional land taxes increasingly became converted into and paid
in cash units. In fact, the preference for coins became so high that the
bakufu stipulated in 1226 that cash were to be accepted as payments

---

[36] Brown, op. cit., 10.
[37] Yamamura, 358-359, 366.
[38] Nagahara, *Nihon chūsei shakai kōzō no kenkyū*, 78.

for taxes, despite repeated ordinances to the contrary previously. And, Tôji, of one the largest temples in Kyoto, demanded payments in cash of all its rice dues and taxes from its estates in 1260.[39] With tax payments in cash, the capital elites were able to purchase commodities they desired as needed, instead of calculating their own needs and assigning specific products to be delivered to the proprietors. Kyoto and Nara merchants became intrinsic in this trend, and contributed to the further spread of cash in the countryside by purchasing products such as hemp, silk and rice, to peddle in the cities. It is in this context, naturally, that markets, both locally and in Nara and Kyoto, came to flourish.[40]

By the same token, the cash economy opened up new avenues for credit institutions, and bills of exchange, which emerged and spread in the late thirteenth century. The first bills of exchange were used in travel and transfers between Kyoto and Kamakura in the east, where the shogunate's headquarters was located. But it was above all money lending that affected central Japan's economy in the thirteenth century. Whereas temples sometimes functioned as lending institutions in the Heian age, it was *sake* shops that came to take over those duties from the twelfth and thirteenth centuries. Apparently, rice wine establishments accumulated enough cash to be able to offer loans, and they soon became one of the dominating businesses in Kyoto.[41] To evade taxation by the court and the bakufu, the pawnshops sought the protection of immune patrons such as temples and influential nobles. Enryakuji, for example, was the patron of 80 percent of all the moneylenders and *sake* brewers in Kyoto in the late thirteenth century.[42] In that way, the elites maintained their privileged position while sanctioning the activities of certain producers and merchant groups.

An important by-product of these developments was changes in city culture. The political system of the Heian age had been city-based before the expansion of trade, because both the noble and religious elites were located in and performed their displays of power, as well as factional struggles, within an urban setting. Nevertheless, the presence of guilds

---

[39] Brown, op. cit., 11; Nagahara, *Nihon chûsei shakai kôzô no kenkyû*, 24-25, 78-80.

[40] Nagahara Keiji, "Kodai shakai no tenkan to hôkenka," 71.

[41] Brown, op. cit., 12-13.

[42] Toyoda Takeshi and Sugiyama Hiroshi, "The Growth of Commerce and Trade," in Hall and Toyoda, eds., *Japan in the Muromachi Age* (Berkeley: University of California Press, 1977), 131-132; Toyoda Takeshi, *Za no kenkyû* (Tokyo: Yoshikawa kôbunkan, 1973), 447-451.

and markets, in particular in Nara, Kyoto, and later on in Osaka and Sakai, gradually transformed the city landscapes. Producers of *sake*, silk, clothing, umbrellas, sandals and other manufactured products clustered in areas protected by temples and shrines, while markets were established in the outskirts or in front of temples. As noted, temples were highly valued patrons of merchants because of their tax immunity, but they were also one of the largest consumers of goods, and markets in front of temples in fact grew into small cities in their own rights, known as *monzenmachi* ("city in front of the gate"). Thus, in contrast to the grid-planned city of the Chinese Tang style, we now find a more sporadic growth of urban areas, both close to monastic centers and in new high-traffic areas.[43]

By the late thirteenth century, Japan was well under way toward mercantilism and a money-oriented economy. All the traditional elites— nobles, the major temples as well as the leaders of the bakufu—were involved in trade and promoted the production of specialty products on unprecedented scales. The bakufu, under Hôjô leadership, controlled all major ports and thereby much of the international and domestic trade, but because it had few other income-producing enterprises in the area of trade, its finances were seriously hurt when the Mongols expanded in China. Noble families did comparatively well, despite a loss of political clout vis-à-vis the bakufu, by using their tax immune estates to create enclaves for markets and toll stations along the major roads leading to Kyoto. Markets were flourishing, and a number of smaller ports and intersections were emerging in strategic locations. Fan shops, umbrella makers, *sake* brewers and storage houses doubling as moneylenders became common sights in the capital. But it was temples and shrines that came to benefit the most. As already noted, they attracted groups of merchants and traders to markets held in front of the temple gates, in part as consumers of a wide variety of goods, but also as patrons who could offer protection against taxation and competition.

It was also this latter ability that made temples attractive as patrons of guilds. Although the guilds first and foremost appear to represent the interests of their members, they were in fact an effective means for those on top to contain what might otherwise have been an uncontrolled development of a more market-oriented economy. In other words, the guilds represented the elites' main tool to contain an uncontrolled growth

---

[43] Yamamura, 356-358, 364, 379-381.

of economic and social influence by powerful merchant groups. They came to dominate the production and sales of various commodities, especially in the capital area where almost all of the consumption took place.[44] Their rules prescribed not only the behavior and codes of the members themselves, but also the actual production, with specific rules for how the commodities should be produced. Thus, while these economic developments were accompanied by the emergence of new classes of cash croppers, merchants and artisans, we detect few matching changes in the social and political spheres. As the bakufu came to exist for the purpose of containing the warrior class, the guilds were primarily established to allow the elites both profit from and control the emerging class of merchants and artisans.

Comparative Perspectives

Scholars have tended to interpret Japan's medieval past separately from the East Asian continent, instead relating it to European patterns in an attempt to explain Japan's remarkable modernization. This raises the question of how exactly we should understand the first three centuries of the second millennium in a comparative and global perspective, in particular regarding the notion of Japan's feudal past. Asakawa Kan'ichi (1873-1948), a pioneering historian of premodern Japan at Yale University, described Japan's warrior rule from the twelfth to the nineteenth centuries as successive stages of feudalism, culminating with the Muromachi shogunate's almost "perfect feudal hierarchy" around 1400, and a "mature feudal authority" during the Warring States Era (1467-1573).[45] Basing his model on Weber's idea of contractual lord-vassal relationships and fiefs as the essential bond, Asakawa noted that the lord-vassal bond was less contractual and thus more autocratic in Japan, which explained, in his view, Japan's delayed modernization. Marc Bloch, who learned about Japan from Asakawa, similarly concluded that the Japanese "vassalage was much more an act of submission than was European vassalage and less contractual." Without being specific, he also claimed that the feudal era began in the late eleventh century when the bureaucratic state

---

[44] Yamamura, 350-356.

[45] Asakawa Kan'ichi, "Feudalism: Japan," written for *Encyclopedia of the Social Sciences,* printed in idem, *Land and Society in Medieval Japan* (Tokyo: Maruzen Book Co., 1965), 264-265. See also the chapter entitled "Japanese Feudal Institutions," in the same volume, pp. 193-218.

declined and "a certain slackening of commercial activity" took place.[46] It goes without saying that both Bloch and Asakawa ignored important evidence about the increasing consumption of commodities in the capital and the growth of trade. Moreover, the characterization of lord-vassal relationships as more authoritarian in Japan is based on idealized literary descriptions whereas historical sources indicate exactly the opposite. The switching of sides and fighting for one's own gain are in fact consistent themes of the warrior class throughout the pre-1600 age, and perpetual challenges for its military lords.[47]

John Whitney Hall (1916-1997), Asakawa's disciple and successor at Yale, successfully used the feudal paradigm to reach a broad audience by pointing out both similarities and contrasts between Japan and Europe, but at the same time one cannot help but feel a certain unease and awkwardness. For example, while he criticized the lack of methodological uniformity, his own solution appears as little more than an awkward compromise. His convoluted definition of the term itself indicates his dilemma, as he borrowed definitions from Max Weber, Karl Marx as well as Marc Bloch in incorporating lord-vassal relations, the dominance of social status in the holding of ranks and land, and an agrarian economy in which cultivators were tied to the land to define feudal societies. For Hall, these aspects came together in the Warring States period, when Japan was at its closest to the feudal model.[48]

Peter Duus, whose epic work *Feudalism in Japan* has been used for decades in colleges across America since its first publication in 1969, follows much the same pattern as Hall. He argues for the universality of feudalism as a model of political organization, including the familiar hodgepodge of characteristics. Looking at the institutional makeup of Europe, he relied, as did Hall and many scholars after him, on what they considered to be the fundamental tie between fief and vassalage. Thus, he characterized feudal government, based on interpretations of European history, as a decentralized state with political authority frag-

---

[46] Marc Bloch, *Feudal Society* (Chicago: University of Chicago Press, 1992, reprint), 446-447. It is worth noting that it was Bloch who encouraged Asakawa to write the entry for the *Encyclopedia of the Social Sciences*.

[47] See Friday, *Samurai, Warfare and the State in early medieval Japan*, and Conlan, "Largesse and the Limits of Loyalty," in Jeffrey P. Mass, ed., *The Origins of Japan's Medieval World* (Stanford: Stanford University Press, 1997).

[48] John Whitney Hall, "Feudalism in Japan: A Reassessment," *Comparative Studies in Society and History* 5:1 (1962), reprinted in John W. Hall and Marius Jansen, eds, *Studies in the Institutional History of Early Modern Japan* (Princeton: Princeton University Press, 1968), 15-51. The quote can be found on p. 44.

mented into small units, control of land as the foundation for wealth and political control in the hands of "an aristocracy of mounted warriors linked by ties of vassalage and the fief." Duus is certainly sensitive to deviations from the European model, but concludes in the end "that the political institutions of Japan between 1300-1600 closely resembled those of feudal Europe."[49]

Their contributions to Japanese history notwithstanding, these scholars' attempts to find definitions that made it possible for Japan to fit into a feudal paradigm have done more harm than good, reflecting an unsophisticated and modern-biased view of the more distant past. Yet, it has dominated descriptions of Japan from the 1100s to the 1800s, and it remains prominent among some scholars even today. Meanwhile, on the European side, Elizabeth Brown launched an all-out attack on feudalism in her 1974 article "The Tyranny of a Construct," exposing the dangers of overly strict commitments to a theory of evolutionary character. As Brown put it, historians tended to "disregard or dismiss documents not easily assimilable into [the feudal] frame of reference."[50] At the time, most European medievalists seem to have been too heavily invested in the feudal paradigm, thus few embraced her critique at the time. But her article did set in motion a new wave of skepticism that also became notable among Japanese historians, leading to a more critical usage based on empirical evidence. As a consequence, the third generation of American scholars of premodern Japan became more reluctant to cast Japan in European terms. For instance, Jeffrey P. Mass (1941-2001), Hall's student, addressed the issue of feudalism early in his career, but came to avoid it later. In his *Antiquity and Anachronism in Japanese History*, published in 1992, he reviewed earlier usages of the feudal model, noting that scholars such as Conrad Totman and Peter Arnesen tended to eschew the term altogether, in part because of the perceived incomplete nature of the tie between vassal and benefice, since, as Arnesen showed, even warlords during the sixteenth century used public powers to justify their local control of land. For Mass' own age of expertise, the twelfth and thirteenth century, he pointed out that Japan never experienced a "marriage of vassalage and benefice," which in his mind represented the European model of feudalism. Still, the very

---

[49] Peter Duus, *Feudalism in Japan* (Stanford: Stanford University, 1993, first published in 1969), 1-12. Quotes can be found on pp. 8 and 10.

[50] Elizabeth Brown, "The Tyranny of a Construct: Feudalism and Historians of Medieval Europe," *American Historical Review* 79:4 (1974), 1063.

fact that Mass felt compelled to characterize Japan in terms of feudalism, more specifically through a focus on vassalage and benefice, in
describing the first bakufu is a reflection of the power and persuasive-
ness of the feudal paradigm in Japanese studies.[51]

Amidst this rising criticism, a more narrow usage of the feudal model
became the lifeline for many scholars who came to focus on vassalage
and fief and their interconnectedness as the salient features. For this
reason, Susan Reynolds' 1994 analysis of these terms in medieval and
early modern Europe became a devastating blow to the feudal model.
In short, she showed that the tie between vassalage and fief was more
the construct of later scholars and lawyers looking back at Europe in
the preceding centuries than central terms in the world of the twelfth
and thirteenth centuries. She perceptively noted: "It is not just that all
the phenomena and notions of feudo-vassalistic institutions never existed
together anywhere, but that they are too incoherent, too loosely related,
and too imperfectly reflected in medieval evidence to be envisaged as
anything like an ideal type."[52]

Reflecting an increasing awareness of such skepticism among Japanese
premodern scholars, the debate as to whether Japan was feudal or not
quickly began to wane from the mid-1990s.[53] In my opinion, feudalism
as a concept serves no useful purpose as a synthetic theory, a descriptive tool or as an approach, and even as an ideal model it is foreign
to both Europe and Japan. It can therefore never accurately represent
any given society, and is doomed to mischaracterization because of its
emphasis on an invented historical model. For example, the notion of
an intimate relationship between vassalage and fief in "feudal" Europe
induced scholars to characterize Japan in different degrees of that relationship despite the awkward tweaking of the historical evidence. Moreover,

---

[51] Jeffrey P. Mass, *Antiquity and Anachronism in Japanese History* (Stanford: Stanford
University Press, 1992), 26-27, 85.

[52] Susan Reynolds, *Fiefs and Vassals: The Medieval Evidence Reinterpreted* (Oxford: Clarendon
Press, 1994), 1-14. For the quote, see p. 11.

[53] A panel entitled "Power and Society in Medieval Japan and Europe" at the
Conference for Medieval Studies in Kalamazoo in 1998, featuring unpublished papers
by Joan Piggott ("Feudal in the Medieval Pacific and Atlantic Worlds") and Paul Hyams
("The Atlantic Archipelago in a Japanese Perspective: What Is To replace the Model
Formerly Known as Feudalism") argued against the usefulness of the term "feudal" in
both Japan and Europe, and there is now a distinct trend among the present generation of Western scholars of premodern Japan to eschew the term altogether. Paul Hyams'
review of Susan Reynolds' book is also a useful contribution to this debate (Paul Hyams,
"The Death of Feudalism," *Journal of Interdisciplinary History* 27:4 [1997], 655-662).

the application of such Western concepts rests on the assumption of similar historical developments, in accordance with evolutionary theories, based on Japan's position in today's world economy. Thus, feudalism can only exist in and because of the paradigm of modernity: without the latter, the former loses its meaning. Indeed, the early proponents of the feudal paradigm acted under this impression. In addition to Asakawa and Hall, Edwin O. Reischauer (1910-1990), perhaps the best known historian of Japan in the West, consistently applied the feudal model in explaining Japan's modernization, noting that Japan's feudal past, "which so closely paralleled that of Europe, may have had something to do with the speed and ease with which the Japanese during the past century refashioned their society and government on European models."[54] In the case of Duus, whose stance is quite the opposite—namely that Japan modernized quickly owing to the erosion of its feudal heritage—we similarly find an inability to disengage from the idea that features in twentieth century Japan, such as militarism, were somehow inherited from the feudal institutions of the Tokugawa age (1600-1868).[55] In fact, however, Japan's imperialism has much less to do with a "feudal past" than with the lessons the country learned from other industrialist nations. No wonder then, that one often gets the sense from such claims that "feudal" simply represents little more than something that is either "anti-modern" or "ante-modern."

The application of the feudal model is certainly not the only challenge for comparative history. For example, it appears that the feudal label has been replaced by "medieval," whose usage is rarely, if ever, questioned among or explained by Japanologists. As Thomas Keirstead has pointed out, however, this concept has its own problems, associated, just like feudalism, with notions of modernity and evolution.[56] Suffice it to say that there is no more agreement about the beginning of Japan's medieval age than there was about its feudal past. Should we then avoid historical comparisons altogether? Certainly not, but it is important to base comparisons on observations of specific phenomena, and to ensure that they are firmly grounded in historical sources. In particular, I find at least two compelling reasons to borrow concepts and use comparative descriptive terms under those caveats.

---

[54] Edwin O. Reischauer, "Japanese Feudalism" in Rushton Coulborn, ed., *Feudalism in History*, (Princeton: Princeton University Press, 1956), 46.

[55] Duus, op. cit., 99-102.

[56] Thomas Keirstead, "Inventing Medieval Japan: The History and Politics of National Identity," *The Medieval History Journal* 1:1 (1998), 25-46.

First, an isolationist and historicist stance tends to assume the centrality and importance of the modern nation-state as the unit of analysis
of all periods. Ironically, the same is true for most comparative analyses,
where the very object of comparison is closely linked to the evolution-
ist paradigm. In both cases, however, cross-cultural exchanges and inter-
related developments have frequently been neglected in favor of simplistic
debates on indigenous developments versus external stimuli in developmental stages of Japan's history. For example, whereas the Nara period
(710-784) has been seen as one of intense import from and communication with China, the Heian age has been depicted as one of isolation and a reversal to more uniquely "Japanese" traditions. However,
as several Heian scholars have recently noted, this emphasis on
"Japaneseness" was more a product of nineteenth and twentieth century
nationalism than the reality of the Heian age, when traders and pilgrims
still traveled between the continent and Japan.[57] Even in early history,
no states or nations exist in a vacuum, and it would serve historians
well to consider the impact of nearby cultures more in explaining soci-
ety-wide transformations, a trend that is presently well under way.

Second, the value of history itself as a subject worth studying at institutions of higher learning depends on our ability to recognize influences
across borders, and to compare and point out significant patterns. But
it is important to keep the generalizations at a level that can be empirically verified or falsified. In short, all-encompassing terms such as feudal and medieval contain too many variables, whose inter-connectedness
is impossible to verify. A more productive way of comparing and using
cross-cultural approaches is to be cognizant of the level of generalization, making comparisons between specific characteristics and socio-political concepts, such as lordship or vassalage, as suggested by Reynolds,
that can be fruitfully gauged against the sources, instead of attempting
to fit complete models to a certain kind of society. For example, an
examination of lordship in late Heian and Kamakura Japan reveals an
emphasis on rule over men rather than land, as reflected not only in
its social organizations but also its warfare.[58] Comparative terms and

---

[57] See for example Thomas LaMarre, *Uncovering Heian Japan: An Archaeology of Sensation and Inscription* (Durham: Duke University Press, 2000), especially pp. 1-6.

[58] See Friday, *Samurai, Warfare and the State in Early Medieval Japan*, 165. Thomas Conlan has argued that the terms of lordship changed in the fourteenth century from one based on control of men ("hegemonic lordship") to direct control over land ("territorial lord-ship"). See Thomas Conlan, "Largesse and the Limits of Loyalty," 40-42. Paul Hyams

analyses need not be problematic as long as they are thoroughly defined, and meaningful discussions and conclusions can be generated through their usage.

In this spirit, I should like to conclude by offering a few observations from various perspectives that may serve as a foundation for further discussions and perhaps generate more inquiries into the nature of the transitions that took place in Japan. In the political arena, the most substantial changes occurred in the late eleventh century, when the trend toward privatization grew into a tripartite rule of aristocrats, religious institutions and warriors. This style of shared rulership enabled the noble elites to extend the rule of the imperial court by a full three hundred years, despite challenges of dramatic social developments. Although shifts occurred in the balance between the three blocs until the fourteenth century, in general in favor of the warrior leadership, no major changes to the way that power was exercised took place. Heian and Kamakura Japan remained a strictly hierarchical society, where social status and a diffusion of power among a broad spectrum of elites served as an effective shock-absorber of challenges from new classes.

From a religious and ideological standpoint, there were similarly few changes. The most powerful temples remained crucial as sanctifiers of the state throughout the period, and the supporting Buddhist ideology of a mutual dependence between secular and religious authority remained in effect the fourteenth century. In terms of culture, the noble pastimes and tastes continued to dominate the landscape of high arts. Even warriors who held high positions within the bakufu tended to support and patronize the rituals and the culture of the Kyoto elites. In short, Kyoto remained Japan's center in almost every aspect of society and the imperial court continued to function under the figurative leadership of the emperor as the ultimate legitimizer of political and social authority despite the emergence of a separate military headquarters.

By contrast, we see substantial changes in the economy and the social conditions during the very same period. Japan experienced unprecedented economic growth owing to an increase in agricultural production and the emergence of a professional class of merchants and artisans. Although the origins of these changes can be traced to periods even before 1100, they were gradual and only came to have an impact on

---

further points out the importance of recognizing various forms of lordship and "nonvertical loyalties," issues that tend to be ignored under all-encompassing theories (Hyams, "The Atlantic Archipelago in a Japanese Perspective," 3-5).

society beginning in the thirteenth century. This mercantilism unsur-
prisingly induced new social contexts, with more stratified and integrated
rural communities, new organizations, such as guilds, and even new
types of cities focused entirely on trade. Still, it is noteworthy that these
developments did not lead to a new social order. Despite their increasing importance, traders and artisans remained peripheral under warrior
rule for centuries to come.

Concerning Japan's position within a larger trend of global paradigm
shifts, a few points stand out as relevant to the theme of this volume.
It is clear that we find in Japan during this age the beginning of a new
kind of city culture spurred by the growth of trade. Kyoto had been,
and remained, an important political center since the ninth century, but
was now additionally a thriving commercial center, where markets and
entertainment districts came to cater to people from classes other than
the nobility. What is more significant, however, is the emergence of
smaller merchant cities. Nara came to prosper as a commercial and
religious center from the twelfth century, and port cities such as Hakata
on the coast of Kyushu and Sakai on the Inland Sea, grew in importance as well.[59] Although the growth of trade seems to be an unintended consequence of the privatization process under way since the
eleventh century, it must also be noted that the old elites were in fact
active participants in its promotion and development. For example, as
tax-exempt elite entities needing manufactured products, monks and
temples offered locations conducive to exchange of products. It must
also be reiterated that China's role in the growth of trade and the emergence of a mercantile economy in Japan from the twelfth century was
crucial. While the trend toward privatization provided the incentive for
commercialization, it was China and its copper coins that supplied the
conditions necessary for this growth. Unfortunately, the impact of the
continent on Japan's development has been consistently neglected by
most scholars, perhaps because it did not fit into the mold of how Japan
emerged into a warrior-dominated society.

These trends, the rise of the warrior class and the growth of trade,
were far from contradictory, and both in fact stand out as enduring
developments with origins in the twelfth and thirteenth centuries. The
biggest contrast lay in their political success. Whereas the warrior class
eventually came to the fore on the political scene in the fourteenth cen-

---

[59] By the fifteenth century, Nara's population was between 10,000 and 15,000, Sakai's
20,000 and Hakata's between 30,000 and 50,000 (Yamamura, 381).

tury, and would remain there until the late nineteenth, the merchant class was never allowed any political influence. Nevertheless, trade and merchants were central throughout the age of the Warring States era, and the first Westerners were welcomed in the midst of some of Japan's most bloody wars in the late sixteenth century for the sake of trade. Moreover, not even the repressive government of the Tokugawa Bakufu could keep trade developments under wrap. It seems then that what got under way in the age of shared rulership was a force too powerful to suppress altogether, even as warrior rulers managed to contain the merchant class politically. Perhaps it is this thread of mercantilism and social containment we should pay more attention to in the premodern and early modern eras, instead of insisting on making the samurai the central and only figure in our attempts to understand Japan's past.

THE MONGOL TRANSFORMATION:
FROM THE STEPPE TO EURASIAN EMPIRE[1]

MICHAL BIRAN

ABSTRACT

This paper discusses the rise of the Mongol Empire in its Inner Asian context, looking for evolutionary versus revolutionary features of the Mongol imperial enterprise.
It then assesses the Mongol impact on Eurasia from three angles: the Mongol contributions to Eurasian integration; their impact on the Eurasian geo-political balance; and the long-term impact of their statecraft on the different regions over
which they ruled.

What event or occurrence has been more notable than the beginning of the
government of Chinggis Khan, that it should be considered a new era?
(Rashīd al-Dīn)[2]

The Mongol conquests have been defined as the last chapter of the
Eurasian transformations of the tenth-thirteenth centuries. Yet with the
same, or even better, justification they can also be regarded as the first
chapter of a new era, perhaps the early-modern one.[3] Certainly the
impact of the Mongol period was strongly felt in the post-thirteenth
century world as well. Before addressing the issue of Mongol legacy on
Eurasia, however, I will analyze the Inner Asian background of the

---

[1] I would like to thank Thomas T. Allsen, Reuven Amitai and Peter Jackson for their
valuable comments on earlier drafts. This study was supported by grant 818/03 of the
Israel Academy of Sciences.

[2] Rashīd al-Dīn (d. 1317), *Jāmic al-tawārīkh*, 2 vols, ed. B. Karīmī (Tehran:Iqbāl,
1338/1959), 1:16. The translation follows D. O. Morgan, *Medieval Persia* (London:Longman,
1988), 51.

[3] Thomas T. Allsen, "Ever Closer Encounters: The Appropriation of Culture and the
Apportionment of Peoples in the Mongol Empire," *Journal of Early Modern History*, 1
(1997), 2-23; Sanjay Subrahmanyan, "Connected Histories: Early Modern Eurasia,"
Modern Asian Studies, 31 (1997), 737; see also, e.g., *Towards an Integrated History of Eurasian
Civilization, 1200-1700*, Reader for the NEH Summer 2002 Institute (Harvard University,
2002); David R. Ringrose, *Expansion and Global Interaction, 1200-1700* (New York: Longman,
2001); Robert Tignor et al. *Worlds Together Worlds Apart: A History of the Modern World from
the Mongol Empire to the Present* (New York: W. W. Norton and Co, 2002).

Mongol Empire during the tenth to twelfth centuries, looking for evolutionary versus revolutionary features of the Mongol imperial enterprise. Then, the Mongol impact on Eurasia will be reassessed from three
angles: the Mongol contribution to Eurasian integration, their impact
on the Eurasian geo-political balance, and the future impact of their
statecraft on the different regions under their realm.

The Mongols and the Inner Asian Tradition: Evolution versus Revolution

The Mongols did not arise from nothing, nor did they lack a cultural
legacy of their own. In terms of political culture, religion, and military
organization they continued a long tradition of steppe empires, while
in terms of their relations with the sedentary civilizations they were
influenced by the legacy of inter-regional nomadic states that arose in
Manchuria and Central Asia in the tenth to twelfth centuries. Combining
these two traditions, the unprecedented success of the Mongols resulted
in a situation which, despite many continuities, was more revolutionary
than evolutionary.

In terms of political-religious ideology, the Mongols followed the precedents established by earlier steppe empires that originated in Mongolia,
notably the Xiongnu (third century BCE to fourth century CE), the
Turks (sixth to eighth centuries CE), and their successors, the Uighurs
(744-840), among which the Turkic Empire was by far the most influential.
Those empires developed an ideology that legitimized the appearance
and endurance of a super-tribal unit, and employed a military organization as an important structural element in the consolidation of such
units.

The primary source of super-tribal unity in the steppe world was the
belief in Tengri (Heaven), the supreme sky god of the steppe, who was
able to confer the right to rule on earth to a single clan.[4] The heavenly charisma resided in the royal clan, individual members of which
could be elevated to the Khaqanate, the supreme office of the ruler, or
toppled; but non-members could not aspire to the throne. The Khaqan
was the political and military leader of the empire, whose possession of

---

[4] Whether this notion originated in the Chinese concept of the Mandate of Heaven,
in a similar Iranian concept or in an Indo-Aryan concept brought first to the steppe
and then into China is unimportant. For a recent discussion see Sanping Chen, "Son
of Heaven and Son of God: Interactions among Ancient Asiatic Cultures regarding Sacral
Kingship and Theophoric Names," *Journal of the Royal Asiatic Society*, 3rd series, 12 (2002),
289-325.

the Tengri mandate was confirmed by success in battle on the one hand, and by the shamanic apparatus on the other. As Tengri did not bestow a mandate on every generation, such confirmation was important for securing the Khaqan's power. Yet the Khaqan also had certain shamanic functions (apparent, for example, in the coronation ceremony), which enabled him to depose the shamans if they threatened his authority.[5] The center of the world ruled by the Khaqan was the area around the Ötükän mountains near the Orkhon river in Central Mongolia (where the Turks left their famous inscriptions and where the Mongol capital, Qaraqorum, was built more than four hundred years later), a territory that was considered the sacred land of the nomadic world already under the Xiongnu.[6]

The Turk ideology was also used by the imperial successors of the Turks, the Uighurs in Mongolia and the Khazars on the European steppes. Both ruled over smaller-scale empires and in both the elite adopted a universal religion, Manichaeism or Judaism, alongside its Turkic tradition. Even though after the collapse of those empires (840 in Mongolia, c. 965 in Khazaria), and until the rise of the Mongols, no nomadic force aspired to unite the steppe or to use its universal tradition, it still served as "an ideology in reserve"[7] among the former participants of the Turkic world, ready to be used in case the super-tribal empire should come into being.

Another important device for the endurance of a steppe empire was structural, namely, the decimal military organization, present already under the Xiongnu. Nomads are described as "natural soldiers," since their pastoral way of life enabled them to acquire individual military skills (such as riding, shooting, endurance) from an early age, but the effectiveness of this skilled army varied greatly over the years.[8] Since every nomad was a potential soldier, military organization was actually an important means for social organization. Although until the time of

---

[5] Peter B. Golden, "Imperial Ideology and the Sources of Political Unity amongst the Pre-Chinggisid Nomads of Western Eurasia," *Archivum Eurasiae Medii Aevi*, 2 (1982), 37-77; Joseph Fletcher, "The Mongols: Ecological and Social perspectives," *Harvard Journal of Asiatic Studies*, 46 (1986), 30-1.

[6] Golden, "Imperial Ideology," 48, 54; Thomas T. Allsen, "Spiritual Geography and Political Legitimacy in the Eastern Steppe," in *Ideology and the Early State*, eds. H. Claessen and J. Oosten (Leiden: Brill, 1996), 116-35.

[7] Nicola Di Cosmo, "State Formation and Periodization in Inner Asian History," *Journal of World History*, 10 (1999), 20.

[8] Nicola Di Cosmo, "Introduction: Inner Asian Ways of Warfare," in *Warfare in Inner Asian History (500-1800)*, ed. N. Di Cosmo (Leiden: Brill, 2002), 3-12.

Chinggis Khan the decimal units (of 10, 100, 1000 and 10,000) were roughly arranged according to tribal lines, their existence was an important device which enabled the Khaqan to bypass the tribal channels. The decimal organization was also a useful means of incorporating new nomads into the empire's army. The establishment of a royal guard, also present from the Xiongnu onwards, served the same functions and enabled the ruler to create a new elite, personally loyal to himself.[9]

While the Turkic Empire also created a political union across the vast area stretching from the borders of China to the Byzantine frontier, neither the Turks nor their predecessors or successors in Mongolia (until the rise of Chinggis Khan) ever tried to conquer the sedentary civilizations that bordered the steppe, implying that the universal rule of the Khaqan was limited to the nomadic world. Instead they consciously preferred to remain outside of the realm of their sedentary neighbors and use their mobility and superior military skills to secure their economic interests from the sedentary world through raids and alternating war and peace.[10] The resources needed for the sustenance of the empire were therefore acquired through tribute from the sedentary civilizations, and trade revenues, often derived through circulating a portion of the collected tributes throughout Eurasia. The Orkhon inscriptions attest that the Turks were fully aware of the connection between the need to remain outside of the realm of the sedentary world, with its seductive luxuries, and their ability to retain their distinct identity and the military superiority that enabled them to extract revenue from China.[11]

Yet the period that immediately preceded the Mongols, from the tenth century onward, saw the emergence of another kind of nomadic state. These new polities originated not in Mongolia, but either in Manchuria or Central Asia, i.e, in regions in which the coexistence of nomad and sedentary was far more common than on the Mongolian steppe. They rose to power in the absence of a strong force on the steppe after the fall of the Uighurs (840), and the decline of the bordering sedentary empires: i.e. the collapse of Tang China (906), the decline of the Abbasid Caliphate from the middle of the ninth century

---

[9] Fletcher, "The Mongols," 29-30; Di Cosmo, "Periodization," 17.

[10] Thomas J. Barfield, *The Perilous Frontier: Nomadic Empires and China* (Oxford:Blackwell, 1989), 49-51ff.

[11] T. Tekin, *A Grammar of Orkhon Turkic* (Bloomington: Indiana University Press, 1968), 261-7.

and the Samanids from the mid-tenth century. Unlike their Mongolian predecessors, these states did conquer parts of the sedentary civilizations that bordered the steppe, thereby creating empires in which a nomadic (or semi-nomadic) minority, backed by a strong military machine, ruled a multi-ethnic nomad and sedentary population. This required the acquisition of knowledge and administrative skills to manage the government of the sedentary areas as well as new forms of legitimization.[12] In establishing these states, the rulers became closely associated with the sedentary traditions of the peoples that they ruled; Chinese on the eastern steppe and Muslim on the western steppe (and, in the case of Hungary, even Christian). The sedentary influences played an important role in the shape of the royal institutions of these states and their administration, which included direct taxation of their sedentary population alongside tribute from China (on the eastern steppe) and a variety of indirect means of revenue collection (on the western steppe).[13] Yet those external influences did not supplant the steppe past, which remained an important part of the elite identity and government. Even when some of these rulers became sedentarized, the nomads and former nomads continued to share many common features. They shared social values, such as the central role of warfare in everyday life, the high position of women and merchants; certain aspects of political culture, such as alliances through marriage, hunting as royal sport, the policy of holding hostages, and certain aspects of military organization (although the states certainly diversified their military organization and tactics under

---

[12] Barfield, *The Perilous Frontier*, 164ff.; Di Cosmo, "Periodization," 32.

[13] Golden, "Ideology," 73-4; Di Cosmo, "Periodization," 32-3; Morgan, *Medieval Persia*, 34-40. While Hungary can be regarded as one of those mixed states that retained several Khazar influences, its limited connection with nomads after the collapse of the Khazars and the Christian ideology it adopted led to its rapid acculturation in the East-European world at the expense of its steppe roots, although it remained a frontier society. See P. B. Golden, "The Peoples of the Russian Forest Belt," in *The Cambridge History of Early Inner Asia*, ed. D. Sinor (Cambridge: Cambridge University Press, 1990), 242-8; N. Berend, *At the Gate of Christendom: Jews, Muslims and 'Pagans' in Medieval Hungary c. 1000-1300* (Cambridge: Cambridge University Press, 2001). In general, the European case is somewhat different than that of China or the Islamic World, mainly because after the period of the Huns (fourth-fifth centuries) and the Avars (sixth-ninth centuries) and certainly after the collapse of the Khazars in the tenth century, Europe was spared what China, Central Asia and the Middle East experienced time and again, namely invasion and domination by nomads. After the collapse of the Khazars, a modus vivendi between equals was arrived at between the nomads and "Russia," the part of Europe most closely connected to the steppe. For Europe, therefore, the Mongol invasion came without any preparatory stage. (M. Gammer, "Russia and the Nomads- An Overview," in *Mongols, Turks and Others: Eurasian Nomads and the Outside World*, eds. R. Amitai and M. Biran, forthcoming in Brill.)

the influence of their sedentary territories).[14] On the western steppes such states were established by splinter groups of the Turks, such as the Qarakhanids (c. 950-1213), Saljuqs (c. 1044-1194), and Khwarazm Shahs (c. 1127-1220) while in the east, and of more immediate relevance for the Mongols, the founders were Manchurian peoples: the Khitans, formerly part of the Turkic world who came under a significant Uighur influence, who established the Liao dynasty (907-1125) and later the Qara Khitai (Western Liao) dynasty in Central Asia (1124-1218); and the Khitans' former vassals, the Jurchens, who founded the Jin dynasty (1115-1234).[15]

In their pre-imperial history, the Mongols were closely associated with the Manchurian dynasties. They entered Mongolia after the Khitans conquered it in the early tenth century, driving most of its original Turkic population westwards.[16] Liao garrisons and the cities they established in Mongolia earned the Khitans great prestige among the Mongols. They also served as channels for transferring Chinese and Khitan institutions; some of the latter, such as the postal system (*yam*) or the *ordo* (camp of the ruler or a prince), were later adopted by the Chinggisids.[17] The Jurchens, who deposed the Khitans in 1125, did not rule Mongolia, but played an active role in its tribal politics. Chinggis Khan's forefathers had tribute relations with the Jin, and he himself probably spent several years in Jin captivity, thus becoming familiar with its institutions.[18] The pre-imperial Mongols also had less frequent connections

---

[14] Michal Biran, *The Empire of the Qara Khitai in Eurasian History: Between China and the Islamic World*, forthcoming in Cambridge University Press, Ch. 5.

[15] For the Qarakhanids see, e.g., P. B. Golden, "The Karakhanids and Early Islam," in *The Cambridge History of Early Inner Asia*, 343-70; For the Saljuqs and Khwarazm Shahs see, e.g., Morgan, *Medieval Persia*, 25-50; for the Liao, perhaps the most interesting example of using indigenous and sedentary components while retaining a distinct identity through the dual administration (one for the nomadic sector and one for the sedentary subjects) it developed, see, e.g., Wittfogel and Feng, *History of Chinese Society*: Liao 907-1125 (Philadelphia:The American Philosophical Society, 1949) and Zhongguo Lishi Bowuguan et al., *Qidan zhao wangchao: Nei Menggu Liaodai wenwu jinghua [The Liao Dynasty: Liao relics from Inner Mongolia[sic]]* (Beijing: Zhongguo cangxue chubanshe, 2002); D. Twitchett and K. P. Tietze, "The Liao," in *The Cambridge History of China, vol. 6: Alien states and Border Regimes 907-1368*, eds D. Twitchett and H. Franke (Cambridge: Cambridge University Press, 1994), 43-153; for the Jin, see, e.g., H. Franke, "The Chin Dynasty," in *The Cambridge History of China* vol. 6, 215-320. For the Western Liao see Biran, *Qara Khitai*.

[16] Owen Lattimore, "The Geography of Chingis Khan," *Geographical Journal*, 129 (1963), 1-7.

[17] Ibid.; David O. Morgan, *The Mongols* (Oxford: Blackwell, 1986), 44-51.

[18] Thomas T. Allsen, "The Rise of the Mongol Empire and Mongolian Rule in North China," in *The Cambridge History of China* vol. 6, 329-33.

with the Central Asian states, mainly through Muslim merchants. Of these states the Qara Khitai Empire was especially significant. Using Chinese trappings to rule a mostly Muslim population, the Qara Khitai narrowed the gap between the ways of ruling in Central Asia and China, thereby facilitating the Mongol's ability to borrow traditions and personnel from both directions.[19]

The Mongols owed much to their direct predecessors on the margins of the steppe, especially their ability to combine nomad and sedentary territories and populations under effective rule. These states provided the Mongols with ready-made pools of officials, experienced in mediating foreign rule, either from the indigenous bureaucrats and scribal classes of those states, or, more commonly, from ex- (or post)-nomads who were already active (mainly as bureaucrats, governors or merchants) under the Mongols' predecessors.[20] The important roles of the ex-nomads Uighurs, Khitans and, to a lesser extent, the Khwarazmians and Khurasanians in the ranks of the early Mongol Empire certainly support this notion.[21] Yet it would be misleading to describe the Mongols simply as the most successful of these states.[22] First, because they also continued the tradition of the Mongolian steppe empires and, more importantly, because the phenomenal success of the Mongols resulted not only in quantitative change (i.e. a vaster empire) but also qualitative change, thereby making the Mongol period the watershed of Inner Asian history.

Chinggis Khan died in 1227, ruling over the greatest territory any one man had ever conquered, from north China to the Caspian Sea.

---

[19] Biran, *Qara Khitai*, Conclusion.

[20] Thomas T. Allsen, "Technologies of Governance in the Mongolian Empire: A Geographical Survey," paper given in the MIASU Symposium on Inner Asian Statecrafts and Technologies of Governance, Cambridge UK, March 18-19, 2004. As Allsen claims, the absence of such personnel in Russia was at least partially responsible for the different—and indirect—government established by the Golden Horde.

[21] For Uighurs see Thomas T. Allsen, "The Yuan Dynasty and the Uighurs in Turfan in the 13th Century," in *China Among Equals*, ed. Morris Rossabi (Berkeley: University of California Press, 1983), 243-80; For Khitans, see Michal Biran, "Mongols, Turks and Chinese: The Khitans under Mongol Rule," paper presented at the International conference for Mongol-Yuan Studies, Nanjing, China, August 2002; For Khwārazm see Thomas T. Allsen, "Maĩmūd Yalawach," in *In the Service of the Khan*, ed. I. de Rachewiltz et al. (Wiesbaden: Harrassowitz, 1993), 121-31; for the importance of Khurasani officials to the Ilkhanate see Jean Aubin, *Emirs Mongols and visirs persans dans les ramous de l'acculturation* (Paris: Association pour l'advancement des etudes Iraniennes, 1995).

[22] Cf. Jerry Benteley, *Old World Encounters* (Oxford: Oxford University Press, 1993), 115.

His heirs continued to expand, creating an empire that at its height (1259) streched from Korea to Hungary, from Yunnan (in south China) to Iraq. Unlike their predecessors, the Mongols conquered not only the margins of the sedentary civilizations but their centers as well, and while doing so they broke down the boundaries between the eastern steppe, a Chinese sphere of influence, and the western steppes, influenced by Islam. Moreover, the conquest was conducted in a way that paved the way for the creation of a new reality.

One major factor for both the Mongol success and the revolution it created was the unprecedented amount of destruction that accompanied the Mongol conquests, which resulted (among other things) in the annihilation, transfer and downgrading of sizable segments of the established Eurasian elites.[23] A second factor was the new organization of the Mongol army: Chinggis Khan retained the classical decimal organization but abolished its linkage to the tribal system: the new Mongol units often comprised people from different tribes and were led primarily by Chinggis Khan's nökers (personal allies), who became the new elite of the empire. The soldiers' loyalty was thereby transferred from their tribe to their commander and beyond him to the Chinggisid family. The improved coordination of these newly created units certainly contributed to the success of their conquests.[24] Another significant reason for the Mongol success was their willingness to learn from their subjects and their skill in doing so. They borrowed and adapted institutions from different edges of their empire (again mainly from either the Muslim world or China), both for the conquest and for the consolidation of their empire. This brought new technologies and personnel to the edges of the empire, encouraged the Mongol tendency of ruling through foreigners, and created an imperial culture (also maintained in the separate khanates established after 1260) that comprised not only the Mongols social and cultural norms and the indigenous traditions of the conquered but also foreign traditions imported by the Mongols (more about this below).[25]

Thus, the background to the unprecedented success of the Mongols

---

[23] For different explanations to Mongol destruction see Fletcher, "The Mongols," 39-43, who sees the destruction mainly as a form of psychological warfare, and John Masson Smith Jr. "Demographic Considerations in Mongol Siege Warfare," *Archivum Ottomanicum*, 13 (1993-94), 329-34, who stresses the demographic and tactical concerns behind it.

[24] Morgan, *The Mongols*, 89-90. The military success of the Mongols owes much to this reorganization and to the efficient coordination between the units.

[25] Thomas T. Allsen, *Culture and Conquest of Mongol Eurasia* (Cambridge: Cambridge University Press, 2001), 203.

contributed to its revolutionary character. Moreover, this unprecedented success has its own implications, which in turn enhanced the new Eurasia created under the Mongols.

The phenomenal achievements of Chinggis Khan turned the Chinggisids into the new royal clan of the steppe. The Chinggisid principle, according to which only descendants of the Great Khan were eligible to bear the titles khan or khaqan, was sustained in Inner Asia for centuries, long after the dissolution of the Mongol empire.[26]

Moreover, already by the time of Chinggis Khan, the Mongols had revived the concept of universal nomadic rule sanctioned by Heaven. Unlike their predecessors, however, they broadened the concept, to include their right to rule over the whole world, in both its nomadic and sedentary realms. The center of the empire, however, remained in the steppe (at least till 1260), as suggested by the establishment of the Mongol capital, Qaraqorum, in the sacred place of the former nomadic empires in the reign of Ögödei, Chinggis Khan's successor (1229-1241).[27] Among the renowned expressions of this newly conceived ideology were the ultimatums the Mongol issued to different rulers of the world. Indeed, unlike their predecessors, the Mongols were unwilling to accept the coexistence of rival claimants to universal rule: they did not leave the Caliph intact, as the Saljuqs had done, nor were they prepared to accept the legitimacy of another Son of Heaven, as the Khitans and Jurchen had done vis-à-vis the Song emperor. The Pope, another significant claimant to universal authority, survived the Mongol onslaught, but the annihilation of the Song in China in 1276 and, more importantly, the Abbasid Caliphate in 1258, paved the way for major changes in these two realms.[28]

In terms of their relations with their sedentary subjects, after they had realized that it would be more profitable to tax their subjects than

---

[26] See below.

[27] Golden, "Imperial Ideology," 48; Allsen, "Spiritual Geography," 116-35.

[28] For the Mongol ideology of world dominion see e.g. R. Amitai-Preiss, "Mongol Imperial Ideology and the Ilkhanid War against the Mamluks," in *The Mongol Empire and its Legacy* (Leiden: Brill, 1998), eds. D. O. Morgan and R. Amitai-Preiss, 59-72, and the references on p. 62. This article shows that the ideology of world conquest was relevant even after the dissolution of the empire into four khanates in 1260 and into the fourteenth century; see also P. Jackson, "World-Conquest and Local Accomodation: Threat and Blandishment in Mongol Diplomacy," paper given in the MIASU symposium on Inner Asian Statecraft and Technologies of Governance, Cambridge UK, March 18-19, 2004.

to annihilate them, the Mongols used direct taxation as the principal
means of collecting revenues from their subjects, rather than the tribute
and most of the other indirect solutions employed by their predecessors.[29]

The vast empire and the eclectic state culture, combined with the
fact that the Mongols ruled over the two most economically productive
areas in Eurasia (China and the eastern Islamic world),[30] certainly contributed to their ability to integrate the Eurasian world more than their
steppe predecessors.

Integration on a Eurasian Scale

The Mongol period was a significant step towards closer integration
of the old world, both inside and outside the empire's realm. Certainly
the vast dimensions of the empire contributed to that, but the role of
the Mongols was not limited to the passive medium through which the
sophisticated sedentary subjects learnt from one another, as suggested
by the (problematic) term *Pax Mongolica*.[31] Instead they actively promoted
inter-cultural exchange.

The Mongols' active role originally derived from the fact that the
formation of the empire, its continued expansion, and the establishment
of its administration required a huge mobilization of people throughout the empire, and this mobilization was the first step towards cross-
cultural exchange and integration. The mobilization is to be explained
primarily by demographic considerations. In Chinggis Khan's times the
total population of Mongolia was about 700,000. Therefore, human capital was of primary importance to the nomads, and the political struggles that accompanied the formation of the Mongol state concentrated
more on the control of people and herds than on territorial gains. The
demographic balance also meant that in order to continue expanding,
the Mongols had to make use of the already conquered subjects. The
first and perhaps most wide-ranging means for Mongol mobilization was
therefore the army. Already Chinggis Khan appropriated defeated nomads
and subjugated tribes, organized in new decimal units among Mongol

---

[29] Di Cosmo, "Periodization," 34.

[30] Janet Abu-Lughod, *Before European Hegemony* (Oxford: Oxford University Press, 1989),
352ff.

[31] This passive view is held, for example, by Bentley, despite his stress on the role of
nomadic empires in the 1000-1500 period. See Jerry Bently, "Cross-Cultural Interaction
and Periodization in World History," *American Historical Review*, (1996), 766-7.

princes and commanders, and sent them to fight across Eurasia, a process continued in the even larger scale campaigns of his heirs.[32]

The mobilization was not limited to the military sphere. In fact as soon as the Mongols found themselves rulers of an empire with a significant sedentary sector, they realized that they were lacking not only numbers but also specialists. Nomadic culture creates generalists, as every nomad is versed in variety of skills that allow him to survive in the steppe; but these skills are not sufficient for ruling a world empire. The Mongols therefore looked for specialists "skillful in the laws and custom of cities,"[33] and redistributed them across Eurasia. This process involved both groups, like the 100,000 artisans taken in 1221 from Transoxiana to Mongolia and China, or the northern Chinese farmers sent to Merv and later transferred to Adharbaijan; and (many) individuals, specializing in various fields (such as military technology, administration, religion, trade, astronomy, medicine, cooking, wrestling, mechanical engineering). The collection of specialists was systematized already in the late 1230s by means of census, in which people were classified according to their skills (military, artisans, etc).[34]

Another factor that encouraged mobilization was the Mongol policy of ruling through strangers, a practice originating from the Mongol's numerical inferiority and their fear of potential local resistance. Chinggis Khan already sent the Khwarazmian Maḥmūd Yalawach to rule in North China and the Khitan brothers, Yelü Ahai and Yelü Tuhua, to rule in Bukhara. This policy was further systematized in Yuan China, where the Mongols created a special category of *semuren* (people of various kinds), second only to the Mongols and more privileged than the Chinese, for their foreign subjects.[35] The Mongols preferred foreigners who originated in the inter-regional nomadic empires, people who were not only skilled in the laws of the cities but also had connections to the steppe (e.g. Khitans, Uighurs, Khwarazmians), though other talented people (the famous example is Marco Polo) were also welcome. In order

---

[32] Allsen, "Ever Closer Encounters," 4; the best description of Mongol mobilization at its height, under Möngke Qa'an (1251-59) is to be found in Allsen's *Mongol Imperialism: The Policies of the Great Qan Möngke in China, Russia and the Islamic Lands* (Berkely: University of California Press, 1989), esp. 189-216.

[33] F. W. Cleaves (trans.), *The Secret History of the Mongols* (Cambridge Mass: Harvard University Press, 1982), par. 263, p. 203.

[34] Allsen, "Ever Closer Encounters," 4-6, 9; Allsen, *Mongol Imperialism*, 116-43; Allsen, *Culture and Conquest*, 83-176.

[35] Allsen, "Ever Closer Encounters," 6, and see n. 21 above; for the *semuren* see, e.g., Frederick W. Mote, "Chinese Society under Mongol Rule, 1215-1368," in *The Cambridge History of China* vol. 6, 644-8.

to secure the loyalty of this foreign strata, the Mongols aspired to give them "a taste of home," and therefore brought foreign (mostly Muslim or Central Asian) food, medicine and entertainment into Yuan China.[36]

As suggested by the examples above, the Chinggisids regarded human talent (from both inside and outside the empire) as a form of booty, to be shared out among the family like material goods. The different khanates competed for these specialists and exchanged them in order to get a better grip on the economic and cultural wealth of their sedentary lands and to enhance their kingly reputation.[37]

These Mongol attitudes created innumerable opportunities for cross-cultural contacts. Most of what was transmitted was not the Mongol's ethnic culture but elements of the cultures of their sedentary subjects, yet the Mongols initiated most of these exchanges; most of the carriers of culture were agents of the empire, while the Mongols served as the filter, directing which particular traits would be diffused across Eurasia. In short, the flow of people, ideas and goods across Asia was determined to a large extent by what the Mongols liked, needed and were interested in.[38] These interests also included mobilizing the spiritual forces in their realm, and therefore scholars and clergy also traveled between the Mongol courts. The Mongols showed great interest in fields that were compatible with their own norms, mostly with their shamanic beliefs, such as astronomy, divination, medicine (=healing) or geomancy. They therefore promoted scientific exchanges. In Allsen's eloquent argument, this meant that Muslim astronomers came to China not because they or their Chinese counterparts wanted scientific exchange, but because the Mongols wanted second opinions on the reading of portents.[39]

Trade was, obviously, another means of promoting integration, and the Mongols played an active role in promoting it too. The process of state formation among the nomads itself stimulated trade by increasing the demand for precious metals, gems, and especially fine cloth, all necessary to assert the new empire's authority.[40] Chinggis Khan was certainly aware of the benefits of commerce (which initiated the Khwārazm campaign), and Muslim merchants were among his earliest supporters,

---

[36] Allsen, *Culture and Conquest*, 195-6.

[37] Allsen, *Culture and Conquest*, 210.

[38] Allsen, *Culture and Conquest*, 189-211.

[39] Allsen, *Culture and Conquest*, 211.

[40] See in general Thomas T. Allsen, *Commodity and Exchange in the Mongol Empire: A Cultural History of Islamic Textiles* (Cambridge: Cambridge University Press, 1997).

even before he succeeded in uniting the Mongol tribes. Moreover, after
the early conquests, the Mongol elite, the principal benefactor of the
conquests' booty, became extremely wealthy. It recycled this wealth by
investing with their commercial agents (*ortogh*)—mostly Muslims and
Uighurs—in ways that were often similar to western *commenda* and Muslim
qirāḍ. The profits were spent on the lavish consumption characteristic
of the "nouveau riche." The establishment of Qaraqorum also promoted
trade, as the resources of Mongolia could hardly support such a big
city (in Mongolian terms) or its court. The Mongols were prepared to
pay generously to remain on the steppe while enjoying the best of the
agricultural world, and there were plenty of traders who seized the
opportunity, benefiting from the safe roads and access to the postal stations.[41] Even after the empire dissolved into the four khanates, Mongol
governments continued to promote both local and international trade,
which provided taxes, markets, profits and prestige. The khanates competed for commerce specialists, provided infrastructure for transconti-
nental travel, sometimes by building new cities, and were actively involved
in the manipulation of bullion flow.[42] Di Cosmo, who recently reviewed
Mongol relations with the Italian merchants on the Black Sea shores,
concluded that even in this arena of European expansion, the Mongol
khanate of Qipchaq (the Golden Horde) played a leading role in determining the development of the trade. Moreover, Italian trade with
Central Asia and China, places where the Italian city states refused to
interfere diplomatically to secure adequate agreements for their traders,
was made possible only by Mongols creating the infrastructure for such
contacts, and indeed came to an end with the collapse of the Yuan
dynasty in 1368.[43]

---

[41] Thomas T. Allsen, "Mongolian Princes and their Merchant Partners 1200-1260,"
Asia Major, n.s., 2 (1989), 83-126.

[42] Allsen, "Ever Closer Encounters," 20-23; A. Peter Martinez, "Regional Mint Output
and the Dynamics of Bullion Flows through the Il-Khanate," *Journal of Turkish Studies*, 8
(1984), 147-73; A. Peter Martinez, "Ducats and dinars (part I): currency manipulations,
paper money, arbitrage, the bullion trade, and monetary-commercial policy in the Il-
Xanate, 654-694 H. / 1256-1295 A.D.", *Archivum Eurasiae Medii Aevi*, 10 (1999), 118-206;
Michal Biran, *Qaidu and the Rise of the Independent Mongol State in Central Asia* (Richmond
Surrey: Curzon, 1997), 104-5; M. G. Kramarovsky, "The Culture of the Golden Horde
and the Problem of the "Mongol Legacy," in *Rulers from the Steppe*, eds. G. Seaman and
D. Marks (Los Angeles: Ethnographic Press, Center for Visual Anthropology, University
of Southern California, 1991), 255-73; Elizabeth Endicott-West, "Merchant Associations
in Yuan China: the Ortogh," *Asia Major*, n.s., 2 (1989), 127-53.

[43] Nicola Di Cosmo, "Mongols and Merchants on the Black Sea Frontier (13th and
14th Centuries): Convergences and Conflicts," forthcoming in *Mongols, Turks and Others.*

The wide-ranging mobilization and expanding trade led to frequent and continuous moves of people, goods, ideas, plants, and viruses throughout Eurasia. This in turn not only encouraged integration but also created means that facilitated further contacts, such as maps, which gave a visual dimension to the broadening horizons of the Eurasian people, multi-lingual dictionaries, and of course travel literature.[44] The effects of the integration are apparent, for example, in the diffusion of information and technologies (e.g., gunpowder and distilling alcohol);[45] in the adoption of "Tatar dress" in fourteenth century England, in Yuan and Ming China, in Ilkhanid and post-Ilkhanid Iran, in Chaghadaid and Timurid Central Asia and in Mamluk Egypt.[46] The famous pasta was imported from the Middle East by both China and Italy,[47] and the Bubonic plague travelled all the way from south China to Europe and the Middle East.[48]

---

[44] For cartography see Allsen, *Culture and Conquest*, 103-14; for travel literature see, e.g., John Larner, *Marco Polo and the Discovery of the World* (New Haven: Yale University Press, 1999). The development of lexicography is an especially good example of both the Mongol's role in scientific exchange and the radiance of cross-cultural effects to territories outside the empire. The Mongols used diverse languages and scripts in the management of their empire, and their multilingual empire was a major catalyst in the growth of language studies throughout Eurasia. They generously rewarded those with linguistic skills, i.e., mastery of both the Mongolian language, in its spoken, written or printed forms, and mastery of foreign languages often conferred status and power. Moreover, Mongolian words and usages penetrated into Chinese, Russian and Persian languages. The Mongols organized schools for language training, encouraged translation and sponsored or inspired the compilation of multi-lingual vocabularies. Multi-lingual lists of terms (i.e., dictionaries) appear in the thirteenth-fourteenth centuries not only in Iran and China but also in Armenia, Korea, North India, Egypt, Yemen and the Crimea. The two most famous compilations are the *Rasulid Hexaglot*, with entries in Mongolian, Turkic, Arabic, Persian, Tibetan and Greek, and the *Codex Cumanicus* with its Italo-Latin-Cuman-Persian vocabulary. The establishment of chairs of oriental languages in major European universities in the early fourteenth century is also ascribed to the Mongol's influence, as this kind of knowledge was considered essential for converting the Tatars. See Thomas T. Allsen, "The Rasulid Hexaglot in its Eurasian Cultural Context," in *The King's Dictionary*, ed. and tr. P. B. Golden (Leiden: Brill, 2000), 25-49.

[45] Allsen, "Ever Closer Encounters," 11-13.

[46] J. R. S. Phillips, "The Outer World of the European Middle Ages," in *Implicit Understandings: Observing, Reporting and Reflecting on the Encounters between European and Other People in the Early Modern Era*, ed. S. B. Schwartz (Cambridge: Cambridge University Press, 1994), 54; Henry Serruys, "Remains of Mongol Customs in China during the Early Ming Period," *Monumenta Serica*, 16 (1957), 148-65; Bernard Lewis, "The Mongols, the Turks and Mulsim Polity", in id., *Islam in History* (2nd ed. Chicago: University of Chicago Press, 1993), 198.

[47] Paul D. Buell, "Mongol Empire and Turkicization: The Evidence of Food and Foodways," in *The Mongol Empire and its Legacy*, 200-23.

[48] William H. McNeill, *Plagues and People* (New York: Anchor Books, 1977), 161-207.

Another significant mode of integration was in the field of religion. The Mongols provided a huge reservoir of potential converts for the different world religions, and missionaries were among those who roamed the open routes of the Mongol Empire. For reasons that cannot be discussed here (but had a lot to do with the Muslim ability to make their religion compatible with the Mongol's shamanic practices), Islam was the great winner in the struggle for converts.[49] By the mid-fourteenth century, after the Islamization of the Ilkhanate, the Golden Horde and the Chaghadaid Khanate, this resulted in the appearance of a new Turco-Mongolian elite in the region that lay between the Tian shan and the Volga as well as across most of the Middle East. This elite was Muslim, spoke Turkish and honored the traditions of the Mongol Empire.[50] While China and Europe remained outside of this phenomenon, it is certainly a good example of integration on a rather significant scale.

The Mongols and the Eurasian Geo-Political Balance

Despite the tendency of Russian and Muslim thinkers (as well as some Chinese nationalists in the early twentieth century) to ascribe everything that went wrong with their civilizations to the Mongols' influence,[51] or Archibald Lewis's assertion that the rise of Europe was made possible because it was spared the Mongol conquest,[52] the Mongols did not cause drastic changes in the geopolitical balance of Eurasia. True, the initial invasions were traumatic enough, but the destruction was limited, both in extent and duration. As soon as the Mongols understood that they could get more out of their territories by taxation than by ravaging them, which was apparent already in Möngke's reign (1251-59), they

---

[49] There is a growing literature on Mongol Islamization, the most comprehensive work being that of Devin DeWeese, *Islamization and Native Religion in the Golden Horde* (University Park, PA: The Pennsylvania State University Press, 1993); see also Peter Jackson, "The Mongols and the Faith of their Conquered," forthcoming in *Mongols, Turks and Others*; on Christian conversion attempts see, e.g., J. R. S. Phillips, *The Medieval Expansion of Europe* (2nd edn; Oxford: Oxford University Press, 1998), 83-102.

[50] Beatrice F. Manz, "Historical Introduction," in *Central Asia in Historical Perspective*, ed. B. F. Manz (Boulder, Colo: Westview Press, 1994), 6.

[51] Charles Halperin, "Russia in the Mongol Empire in Comparative Perspective," *Harvard Journal of Asiatic Studies*, 43 (1983), 239; B. Lewis, "The Mongols, the Turks and Muslim Polity," 189-90.

[52] Archibald Lewis, *Nomads and Crusades 1000-1368* (Bloomington: Indiana University Press, 1988), 166-93.

consciously tried to limit the damage.[53] This does not mean that there were no exceptions; the bloody conquest of Baghdad in 1258 is by far the most famous example. Furthermore, regions that became buffer zones between the Mongols and their enemies (e.g. Iraq) or between the different Khanates (Khurasan, Uighuria) certainly suffered multiple raids throughout the thirteenth and early fourteenth centuries. Yet alongside both calculated and accidental devastation, there were positive attempts by the Khans to restore the productivity of their lands, attempts that were facilitated by the multiple possibilities of regional and international trade.[54] The important productive regions, China and the Middle East, thus retained their status, both during and after the Mongol conquests.[55]

Mongol rule was, however, geo-politically important in two ways. First, it led to shifting the political center of most of the empire's regions, sometimes with enduring results. Second, the administrative divisions that after 1260 became four separate Mongol khanates were influential in shaping later political boundaries and ethnic identities.

Mongol rulers relocated the capitals of each of the established khanates, generally in a north-easterly direction. This may originally have reflected the location of Qaraqorum, the Mongol capital on the Orkhon river, or the nomads' need to reside closer to the steppe. In China the capital shifted from Kaifeng and Hangzhou to Beijing;[56] in the eastern Islamic world it moved from Baghdad to Tabriz in Adharbaijan, in Russia from Kiev to, first Saray (south-east of Kiev), and then Moscow (north-east again), and in Central Asia (the least defined case) from Balasaghun (modern north Kyrgyzstan) to the region of Almaliq, (in north Xinjiang). The central positions of Beijing and Moscow remain unchallenged; in Iran the area of Adharbaijan retained its importance until at least the end of the sixteenth century,[57] while in Central Asia,

---

[53] B. Lewis, "The Mongols, the Turks and Muslim Polity," 192; Allsen, *Mongol Imperialism*, 82; Morris Rossabi, *Khubilai Khan* (Berkeley: University of California Press, 1988), 77ff.

[54] Biran, *Qaidu*, 97-106; George Lane, *Early Mongol Rule in Thirteenth Century Iran: A Persian Renaissance* (London and New York: RoutledgeCurzon, 2003), 15-27; Donald Ostrowski, *Muscovy and the Mongols* (Cambridge: Cambridge University Press, 1998), 108-31.

[55] Abu Loghud, *Before European Hegemony*, 352ff.; Andre G. Frank, *ReOrient: Global Economy in the Asian Age* (Berkeley: University of California Press, 1998), 75-84; 108-16.

[56] Beijing was one of the capitals of the Liao and Jin dynasties before the Mongols, but only under the Yuan it was completely rebuilt to become the capital of the whole of China.

[57] Bert Fregner, "Iran under Ilkhanid Rule in a World History Perspective," in *L'Iran*

Samarqand and to a lesser extent Kashgar replaced Almaliq in the four-teenth century.

The Mongol conquests and the four khanates they later created also played important roles in defining later political and ethnic enti-ties. In China the Mongol legacy was unification, after 350 years of separation between north and south. The extended boundaries of Mongol and post-Mongol China included Yunnan in the south-west, Gansu in the north-west and, despite Ming attempts to avoid it, significant parts of Inner Asia, namely, Tibet, Xinjiang, Manchuria and (Inner) Mongolia.[58] Ethnically, on the one hand the first alien conquest of the entire country might have given a boost to a development of proto-ethnic or patriotic Chinese identity (opposed to the universalistic idea of *all-under-heaven*) or at least to a bitter anti-foreignism.[59] On the other hand, it also resulted in assimilation of large numbers of steppe peoples (Uighurs, Khitans, Jurchens, Tanguts and even Mongols) into Chinese society, especially from the fourteenth century onward. Today the People's Republic of China strongly emphasizes the multi-ethnic character of Yuan society as one of its major contributions to the "national char-acteristics of the contemporary Chinese people."[60]

The Mongols also contributed to Iran's emergence as a distinct polit-ical and ethnic entity within the Muslim world. Like the Sasanid Empire, the orientation of the Ilkhanate, the Mongol state based in Iran, was more towards China and Europe than the Muslim Middle East. Moreover, Mongol Iran had much the same borders as the Sasanid Empire (and the modern state). The use of the name Iran to denominate a political entity, a Sasanian concept not used during early Muslim rule in Iran, was revived by the Mongols; the Persian language finally replaced Arabic

---

face a la domination mongole, ed. D. Aigle (Tehran: Institut Français de Recherche en Iran, 1997), 128.

[58] H. Okada, "China as a Successor State to the Mongol Empire," in *The Mongol Empire and its Legacy*, 260-72; John W. Dardess, "Did the Mongols Matter? Territory, Power and the Intelligentsia in China from the Northern Song to the Early Ming," in *The Song-Yuan-Ming Transition*, eds. P. J. Smith and R. von Glahn (Cambridge MA: Harvard University Press, 2003), 111-34. Inner Mongolia remains part of the PRC, while Outer Mongolia, a dependent of China in Qing times, became the independent Republic of Mongolia in 1921.

[59] Allsen, "Ever Closer Encounters," 16.

[60] Qiu Shushen, "Lun Yuan dai Zhongguo shaoshu minzu xin tanju ji qi shehui yingx-iang," (On the New Pattern of National Minorities and its Impact on the Yuan Society [sic]), in *Abstracts of papers given in the international conference on Mongol-Yuan Studies* (Nanjing, August 2002), p. 143.

as the preferred vehicle for writing history and soon became the written lingua-franca of the Turco-Mongolic world; and the ethnic composition of the population became much as it has since remained, i.e. including many Turkic and Turco-Mongolian nomads.[61]

As for the rest of the Middle East, the Mongols' annihilation of the Abbasid Caliphate in Baghdad, reduced Iraq, once the center of the Islamic world, to a neglected frontier province, as it has remained almost ever since. Egypt, the only Muslim state to successfully defy the Mongols, improved its position as another center of the Muslim world; the establishment and consolidation of its Mamluk regime owes much to its successful struggle against the Ilkhanate.[62] Even the emirate of Othman, later to become the Ottoman Empire, rose within the Ilkhanid sphere of influence.[63] In general the Mongol period completed the process of Turco-Mongol (as opposed to Arab or Persian) dominance of the ruling elites of the Middle East, a process that had begun in the tenth century.[64]

In Russia, the Mongols contributed significantly to the rise of Moscow, though the exact nature of this contribution is still debated.[65] Moreover, Moscow used its claim as the successor to the Horde to justify its later expansion, and the emergence of Russia as a Eurasian power (as opposed to the few European city states in Kievan Rus times) can be traced to the legacy of the Horde.[66] From the sixteenth century, however, Russia also used the Mongols (or Tatars) as its significant other, developing the concept of the Tatar Yoke and defining Russian identity as its total opposite.[67]

In Central Asia the situation was more complex. While there is no modern continuation of the Chaghadaid khanate, in the late fourteenth

---

[61] Fregner, "Iran under Ilkhanid Rule," 120-130; cf. Elton L. Daniel, *The History of Iran* (Westport, CT: Greenwood Press, 2001), 75-81.

[62] B. Lewis, 206.

[63] R. P. Lindner, "How Mongol were the early Ottomans?" in *The Mongol Empire and its Legacy*, 282-9.

[64] B. Lewis, "The Mongols, the Turks and the Muslim Polity," 203.

[65] Ostrowski, Muscovy, 1-27; Charles Halperin, *Russia and the Golden Horde* (Bloomington: Indiana University Press,1985), 53-60 and passim; Janet Martin, *Medieval Russia* (Cambridge: Cambridge University Press, 1995), 382-5.

[66] J. Pelenski, "Moscovite Imperial Claims to the Kazan Khanate," *Slavic Review*, 26 (1967), 559-76; idem, *Russia and Kazan: Conquest and Imperial Ideology* (The Hague and Paris: Mouton, 1974), 65-173. For an extreme "Eurasianist" view see Nicolai S. Trubetzkoy, "The Legacy of Genghis Khan: A Perspective on Russian History not from the West but from the East (1925)," in his collected volume *The Legacy of Genghis Khan*, ed. A. Lieberman (Ann Arbor: Michigan Slavic Publications, 1991), 161-232.

[67] Ostrowski, Muscovy, 244-8.

century it gave rise to the empire of Tamerlane and his short-lived attempt (1370-1405) to revive the Mongol Empire. This in turn led to the Timurid cultural renaissance in Iran and Central Asia (1405-1501), and to the establishment of the Moghul dynasty (1526-1858), which brought Chinggisid and Timurid traditions into India.[68] In terms of ethnic change, however, the Mongol period was the most influential in this region. Mongol policies, especially military mobilization and the redistribution of the steppe peoples in their armies, led to the dispersion of many established peoples, who had long and celebrated pre-Mongol histories (such as the Uighurs, Khitans, Tanguts, Qipchaqs) and to the emergence of new collectivities, which formed the basis for many of the modern Central Asian peoples (e.g. Uzbeks and Qazaqs). From the fourteenth century onward, most of the pre-Mongol steppe peoples were either assimilated in the sedentary civilizations surrounding them, mainly in China or Iran, or reduced to clan or tribal units in the new collectivities established by the Mongols. After the disintegration of the empire these new collectivities had to refashion their identities. They often coalesced around the names of particular Mongol princes (e.g. Chaghadai, Özbeg, Nogai etc.) and eventually developed into the modern Central Asian peoples.[69]

As for Western Europe, its main benefit from the Mongol period was not geo-political or ethnic but intellectual. Indeed it avoided the initial demolition and (unlike India and Egypt), after 1260, was hardly bothered by Mongol raids or the threat of them; its own economic growth enabled it (principally the Italian city-states) to fully benefit from the new channels of trade and travel opened by the Mongols. Moreover, technologically inferior and more provincial than either China or the Muslim world, there was much to be gained from taking part in the

---

[68] Beatrice F. Manz, "Mongol History Rewritten and Relived," *Revue des mondes musulmans et de la méditerranée*, 89-90 (2000), 129-49; Beatrice F. Manz, "Tamerlane's Career and its Uses," *Journal of World History*, 13 (2002), 1-25. One of the main features of the Timurid renaissance was the emergence of Chaghatay (Eastern Turkic) as a written language. This is the only case in which the Mongols gave their name to a phenomenon of "high" culture.

[69] P. B. Golden, "'I will give the people unto thee,': The Chinggisid Conquests and their Aftermath in the Turkic World" *Journal of the Royal Asiatic Society* Series 3, 10 (2000), 21-41; Allsen, "Ever Closer Encounters", 16-18; Biran, "Mongols, Turks and Chinese," 1-3. Most of these people originated in the realm of the Golden Horde but especially after 1500 several of them (notably the Uzbeks) moved southward into the former Chaghadaid realm.

Mongol "information circuit."[70] However, it took several centuries (and overcoming the Black Death) to translate the broadening geographical and intellectual horizons and technological diffusion into geo-political advantage.[71]

The Legacy of Mongol Statecraft

The Mongol legacy had different institutional impacts on the various civilizations that were affected by it. The most profound effects were in the regions where Mongol rule was longer-lasting, and where there was no strong indigenous tradition of a centralized state; namely Central Asia and Russia. A certain institutional legacy, however, can also be discerned in China and Iran, but the Mongol influence also reached beyond the limits of the empire, most notably in the Muslim world. It is also worthwhile differentiating between the practical borrowing of Mongol institutions on the one hand, and adopting the Mongol political ideology on the other.

The basic component of Mongol statecraft was the Chinggisid principle, i.e., the notion that only descendants of Chinggis Khan were eligible to bear the title khan, which denotes the highest political office. Although attempts to manipulate this principle began rather early (e.g., under Tamerlane), in Central Asia it remained in effect until the late eighteenth century.[72] Moreover, in Uzbek Central Asia even the position of the non-Chinggisid military groups was determined according to the position of their forebears in Chinggis Khan's army during the military campaigns of the thirteenth century.[73] The Chinggisid principle was relevant in other parts of Eurasia as well: e.g. the Moghuls in India, although generally stressing their Timurid genealogy, also used their Chinggisid origins as a legitimating factor.[74] Even in the Ottoman Empire, where Chinggisid origins played no part in the (non Chinggisid) rulers' identities, the Uzbeks and Crimean Tatars enjoyed special prestige due

---

[70] Samuel A. M. Adshead, *Central Asia in World History* (New York: Macmillan, 1993), 70-3.

[71] As Adshead put it: "If Europe came to dominate the world, it was possibly because Europe first perceived there was a world to dominate" (Adshead, *Central Asia*, 77). For the connection between the Mongol period and European expansion in the modern period see, e.g., Larner, *Marco Polo*, passim; Phillips, *The Medieval Expansion*, passim.

[72] Robert D. McChesney, *Central Asia: Foundations of Change* (Princeton: Princeton University Press, 1996), 123-6.

[73] McChesney, *Central Asia*, 123-4.

[74] Richard C. Foltz, *Mughal India and Central Asia* (Oxford-Karachi: Oxford University Press, 1998), 12-51.

to their Chinggisid genealogy.[75] The Chinggisid principle also had a significant impact on Muscovy. The Russians were aware of it and in the Kulikovo era (around 1380) used it to justify their actions against the Golden Horde. Even after the overthrow of the Golden Horde in 1480, the grand princes of Moscow presented themselves as the successors of the Chinggisids, adopting the title *tsar*, which, aside from its Byzantine connotations, was also the title used exclusively to denote the Chinggisid Qipchaq khans. As late as 1575-6 Ivan the Terrible abdicated in favor of the Chinggisid Symon Bekbulatovitc. Chinggisid descent remained important in Russian politics until the westernization of Peter the Great in the seventeenth century, yet as late as the nineteenth century, Chinggisids living in the Russian Empire demanded a noble status on the basis of their genealogy.[76] The Chinggisid tradition was also relevant in Qing China (1644-1911), where the Manchus, after marring Chinggisid princesses and obtaining the Chinggisid seal from his heirs, used their position as successors of the Chinggisids as one facet in their complex legitimation.[77]

In Central Asia the adherence to the Chinggisid legacy was also expressed in the continued importance of the *Yasa*, the collection of laws ascribed to Chinggis Khan. Even after the Islamization of the Mongols in the fourteenth century the *Yasa* continued to be adhered to alongside Muslim law, the *Sharīʿa*, each having its own sphere of influence. The Yasa was authoritative in political and criminal matters as well as in determining court ceremonies and protocols, while the *Sharīʿa* prevailed in dealing with cult, personal status and contracts.[78] Our limited knowledge of the Chinggisid *Yasa* of the thirteenth century makes it difficult to establish how close the Timurid or Uzbek laws were to the original *Yasa* (certainly the Uzbek stress on seniority as the key principle for determining succession does not conform with the Mongol succession practices of the thirteenth century), but the mere fact that these laws were sanctioned by the name of Chinggis Khan is significant enough.[79] In Moghul India, the *Yasa* (or *Tūrāh*) continued to be followed.

[75] Cornell H. Fleischer, *Bureaucrat and Intellectual in the Ottoman Empire: The Historian Mustafa Ali (1541-1600)* (Princeton: Princeton University Press, 1986), 275-9.

[76] Halperin, *Russia and the Golden Horde*, 98-101.

[77] E.g., David M. Farquhar, "The Origins of the Manchu's Mongolian Policy," in *The Chinese World Order*, ed. J. K. Fairbank (Cambridge, Mass: Harvard University Press, 1968), 198-205; Pamela K. Crossley, *A Translucent Mirror* (Berkeley: University of California Press, 1999), 311-27.

[78] McChesney, *Central Asia*, 127-8.

[79] For the original Yasa see David O. Morgan, "Yasa," *Encyclopedia of Islam*, 2nd edn,

It was often invoked to highlight the rulers' links to Chinggis Khan and Tamerlane, yet its practical use seems to have been limited to the realm of court ceremonies and etiquette.[80] While not acknowledging any adherence to the *Yasa*, Russian diplomatic practices were borrowed from the Golden Horde, i.e., from the *Yasa*.[81] The *Yasa* might have also encouraged the promulgation of the Ottoman codex of "secular" law, the *qanun*.[82]

The borrowing of other elements of Mongol statecraft was typically more utilitarian in nature. The Mongols developed efficient means of ruling an empire, a fact that was not overlooked by their successors. The provincial division initiated in Yuan China remains the basis for Chinese provinces today, for example.[83] The Mongol's imperial postal system continues to be used in China, Iran and Muscovy.[84] Mongol military institutions have had enduring legacies, not only among the nomads of Central Asia and Iran but also in China and Russia: Ming China retained the decimal division of the army, the system of military households, the personal guard of the emperor, the Yuan garrison system (*weisuo*), as well as incorporating many Mongols into its army.[85] Muscovite Russia copied the Mongol's military organization, armaments, strategies, tactics and personnel,[86] although the development of firearms eventually marginalized the Mongols' military legacy.

Mongol financial institutions were also influential in Iran, Central Asia and Russia, all of which, for example, retained the *tamgha* (custom tax), despite (or because of) its un-Islamic character. In all three realms the names of the currency (*tümen* in Iran, *kepeks* in Central Asia [and Russia] and *den'ga* in Russia) come from the Mongol period, attesting to its role in shaping currency systems.[87] Loan words also suggest that

---

11 (2002), 293; David O. Morgan, "The Great Yasa of Chinggis Khan Revisited," forthcoming in *Mongols, Turks and Others*.

[80] Mansura Haidar, "The Yasai Chingizi (Tura) in the Medieval Indian Sources", in *Mongolia: Culture, Economy, Politics*, ed. R. C. Sharma *et al.* (New Delhi: Khama Publishers, 1992), 53-65.

[81] Halperin, *Russia and the Golden Horde*, 92.

[82] Fleischer, *Bureaucrat and Intellectual*, 284.

[83] John Langlois, "Introduction," in *China under Mongol Rule*, ed. J. Langlois (Princeton: Princeton University Press, 1981), 1-20.

[84] Serruys, "Remains of Mongol Customs in China," 147-8; Halperin, "Russia in the Mongol Empire in Comparative Perspective," 246.

[85] Serruys, "Remains of Mongol Customs in China," 144-5; Robert Taylor, "The Yuan Origin of the Wei-so System," in *Chinese Government in Ming Times: Seven Studies*, ed. C. Hucker (New York: Columbia University Press, 1979), 93-109.

[86] Halperin, "Russia in the Mongol Empire in Comparative Perspective," 250.

[87] Halperin, *Russia and the Golden Horde*, 92; Fragner, 128-30.

other Muscovite institutions originated in the Golden Horde (e.g., *kanza* for treasury; *tarkhan* for tax exempt privileges). Ostrowski's recent assertion that Muscovite central and provincial political institutions (such as the Boyar council) were directly borrowed from the Golden Horde is more questionable, but clearly the Mongol institutional legacy was stronger in the Russian realm, where the Mongol period was influential in turning a number of city states into the nucleus of a grand Eurasian empire.[88]

In sum, the role of the nomads in the Eurasian transformations of the tenth to thirteenth centuries should not be underestimated.[89] The period saw an intensification of nomad-sedentary relations, characterized by a growing nomadic political and military superiority, which reached its height under the Mongols. Although in the Mongol case there was no equation between political superiority and cultural dominance, the Mongols left a significant impact on Eurasian cultural and political development. They actively promoted contacts and exchange between different civilizations, both within and outside of their empire, and were the principal agents of cultural transfers, selecting which particular traits were diffused in either direction. The Mongols were also influential in shaping the future boundaries, centers, and ethnic definitions of their subject territories, as well as significantly contributed to their statecraft. The most enduring legacy of Mongol rule, in terms of both legitimation concepts and ethnic identities, was in Central Asia, which must be taken into account in any discussion of Eurasian transformations.

---

[88] Donald Ostrowski, "The Mongol Origins of Muscovite Political Institutions," *Slavic Review*, 49 (1990), 525-42; Ostrowski, *Muscovy and the Mongols*, 36-64; see also Halperin's criticism of Ostrowski in his "Muscovite Political Institutions in the 14th century," *Kritika*, 1 (2000), 237-57 and Ostrowski's answer in the same issue, 267-304.

[89] For recent minimalist evaluations of the Mongols see, e.g., Christopher Kaplonski, "The Mongolian Impact on Eurasia: A Reassessment," in *The Role of Migration in the History of the Eurasian Steppe: Sedentary Civilizations vs. "Barbarian" and Nomad*, ed. Andrew Bell-Fialkoff (New York: St. Martin's Press, 2000), 251-74; Michael Cook, *A Brief History of the Human Race* (New York: Norton, 2003), 271, 278.

INDEX